A Guide to Doing Statistics in Second Language Research Using SPSS

This valuable book shows second language researchers how to use the statistical program SPSS to conduct statistical tests frequently done in SLA research. Using data sets from real SLA studies, *A Guide to Doing Statistics in Second Language Research Using SPSS* shows newcomers to both statistics and SPSS how to generate descriptive statistics, how to choose a statistical test, and how to conduct and interpret a variety of basic statistical tests. The author covers the statistical tests that are most commonly used in second language research, including chi-square, t-tests, correlation, multiple regression, ANOVA, and non-parametric analogs to these tests. The text is abundantly illustrated with graphs and tables depicting actual data sets, and exercises throughout the book help readers understand concepts (such as the difference between independent and dependent variables) and work out statistical analyses. Answers to all exercises are provided on the book's companion website, along with sample data sets and other supplementary material.

Jenifer Larson-Hall is Assistant Professor in the Department of Linguistics and Technical Communication at the University of North Texas.

Second Language Acquisition Research Series
Theoretical and Methodological Issues
Susan M. Gass and Alison Mackey, Editors

Monographs on theoretical issues
Schachter/Gass *Second Language Classroom Research: Issues and Opportunities* (1996)
Birdsong *Second Language Acquisition and the Critical Period Hypotheses* (1999)
Ohta *Second Language Acquisition Processes in the Classroom: Learning Japanese* (2001)
Major *Foreign Accent: Ontogeny and Phylogeny of Second Language Phonology* (2001)
VanPatten *Processing Instruction: Theory, Research, and Commentary* (2003)
VanPatten/Williams/Rott/Overstreet *Form-Meaning Connections in Second Language Acquisition* (2004)
Bardovi-Harlig/Hartford *Interlanguage Pragmatics: Exploring Institutional Talk* (2005)
Dörnyei *The Psychology of the Language Learner: Individual Differences in Second Language Acquisition* (2005)
Long *Problems in SLA* (2007)
VanPatten/Williams *Theories in Second Language Acquisition* (2007)
Ortega/Byrnes *The Longitudinal Study of Advanced L2 Capacities* (2008)
Liceras/Zobl/Goodluck *The Role of Formal Features in Second Language Acquisition* (2008)

Monographs on Research Methodology
Tarone/Gass/Cohen *Research Methodology in Second Language Acquisition* (1994)
Yule *Referential Communication Tasks* (1997)
Gass/Mackey *Stimulated Recall Methodology in Second Language Research* (2000)
Markee *Conversation Analysis* (2000)
Dörnyei *Questionnaires in Second Language Research: Construction, Administration, and Processing* (2002)
Gass/Mackey *Data Elicitation for Second and Foreign Language Research* (2007)
Duff *Case Study Research in Applied Linguistics* (2007)
McDonough/Trofimovich *Using Priming Methods in Second Language Research* (2008)
Larson-Hall *A Guide to Doing Statistics in Second Language Research Using SPSS* (2009)

Of Related Interest
Gass *Input, Interaction, and the Second Language Learner* (1997)
Gass/Sorace/Selinker *Second Language Learning Data Analysis*, Second Edition (1998)
Mackey/Gass *Second Language Research: Methodology and Design* (2005)
Gass/Selinker *Second Language Acquisition: An Introductory Course*, Third Edition (2008)

A Guide to Doing Statistics in Second Language Research Using SPSS

Jenifer Larson-Hall
University of North Texas

Routledge
Taylor & Francis Group

NEW YORK AND LONDON

Please visit the companion website at
www.routledge.com/textbooks/9780805861853

First published 2010
by Routledge
711 Third Avenue, New York, NY 10017

Simultaneously published in the UK
by Routledge
2 Park Square, Milton Park, Abingdon, Oxon OX14 4RN

Routledge is an imprint of the Taylor & Francis Group, an informa business

© 2010 Taylor & Francis

Typeset in Goudy by Swales & Willis Ltd, Exeter, Devon
Printed and bound in the United States of America on acid-free paper by
Edwards Brothers, Inc.

Library of Congress Cataloging-in-Publication Data
   Larson-Hall, Jenifer.
   A guide to doing statistics in second language research using SPSS /
Jenifer Larson-Hall.
      p. cm. – (Second language acquisition research series. Theoretical and
   methodological issues)
   Includes bibliographical references and index.
   1. Second language acquisition–Research.   2. Second language
   acquisition–Statistical methods.   3. SPSS (Computer file)   I. Title.
   P118.2.L373 2009
   418.007′2–dc22

                                                                    2008054207

ISBN 10: 0–8058–6185–8 (hbk)
ISBN 10: 0–8058–6186–6 (pbk)
ISBN 10: 0–203–87596–6 (ebk)

ISBN 13: 978–0–8058–6185–3 (hbk)
ISBN 13: 978–0–8058–6186–0 (pbk)
ISBN 13: 978–0–203–87596–4 (ebk)

Contents

Introduction

I wrote this book for myself. I remember being a graduate student, working on my dissertation and struggling to make sense of the statistics I needed to analyze my dissertation. I wanted a book to help me understand SPSS that would use examples from my field, but none existed. This book was born of that longing. This book is written to help those new to the field of statistics feel they have some idea of what they are doing when they analyze their own data, and how to do it using a statistical program.

I originally wrote this book using two statistical programs side by side—SPSS and a statistical program called R. However, reviewers of the book and the editors felt that trying to include two different statistical packages was unwieldy, and that few people would take the time to learn R because it has a steeper learning curve than SPSS. In that case, the R information would just be an annoyance. Although it is true that it may take extra time to learn R because it does not have the same integrated graphical interface that SPSS does, some advantages of R are:

- It is free.
- It is supported by the statistical community and, as such, continues to be updated with new packages that can do different things all the time.
- R has more sophisticated analyses and is extremely strong in the area of graphics.
- Using command syntax for statistics helps users understand better what they are doing in the statistical analysis.

Because I will not be showing how to use R in this book, I have had to cut some points out of the book that I am very sorry to lose. One is access to a much more varied palette of graphics that can help both researchers and those reading research reports understand experimental data better. In some cases I have retained a graphic or two that was created with R, and this may inspire readers to find out more about it. So if you see a graphic in the book and you realize that it didn't come from SPSS, you'll know most likely I made it in R.

Without R I have also removed most information about robust statistics from the book. I am a strong advocate for using robust statistics, which basically rely on the techniques of parametric statistics but use computer-intensive techniques which eliminate the requirement that data be normally distributed (an assumption that is most often not true in our field; see Larson-Hall & Herrington, forthcoming). However, without access to R, performing robust statistics is not possible. It is true that one of the features of SPSS 16.0 is that it has a plug-in so that R command syntax can be used. However, I have taken a look at this plug-in and it is too complicated for me to figure out! Using R directly is much more feasible, and I would refer the interested reader to Wilcox (2005) for more information about performing robust statistics. In the tables that address assumptions of each statistical test, for the column that says "What if assumption is not met?" I have included instructions to use robust methods or boot-strapping methods. At the moment, these methods are not easily attainable for SPSS users. However, they may be in the future, so I have kept these instructions. I hope this will not be too frustrating for readers.

Almost all of the data sets analyzed in the book and the application activities are real data, gathered from recently published articles or theses. I'm deeply grateful to these authors for allowing me to use their data, and I feel strongly that those who publish work based on a statistical analysis of the data should make that data available to others. The statistical analysis one does can affect the types of hypotheses and theories that go forward in our field, but we can all recognize that most of us are not statistical experts and we may make some mistakes in our analyses. Providing the raw data will serve as a way to check that analyses are done properly, and, if provided at the submis-sion stage, errors can be caught early. I do want to note, however, that authors who have made their data sets available for this book have done so in order for readers to follow along with the analyses in the book and do application activities. If you wanted to do any other kind of analysis on your own that would be published using this data, you should contact the authors and ask for permission to either co-author or use their data (depending on your purposes).

This book was updated with the most recent version of SPSS available at the time of writing, and I was working on a PC. As of this writing, the most recent version of SPSS was 16.0.1 (November 15, 2007). SPSS 16 is quite different in some ways from previous versions, and for those who may be working with an older version I have tried to provide some guidance about possible differences. I have used small capitals in order to distinguish commands in SPSS and make them stand out on the page. For example, if you need to first open the File menu and then choose the Print option, I would write File > Print.

I have written this book mainly as a way for those totally new to statistics to under-stand some of the most basic statistical tests that are widely used in the field of second language acquisition and applied linguistics. I suggest that the best way to read most chapters is to open the data sets that are included with the book and work along with me in SPSS. You can learn a lot just by recreating what you see me do in the text. The application activities will then help you move on to trying the analysis by yourself, but I have included detailed answers to all activities so you can check what you are doing. My ultimate goal, of course, is that eventually you will be able to apply the techniques to your own data. I assume that readers of this book will be familiar with how to use Microsoft Windows and pull-down menus, and how to open and close files. These data files will be available on the website that accompanies this book. SPSS files have the .sav extension.

Some parts in the chapters are labeled "Advanced Topic." These parts can be skipped by novices who are already feeling overwhelmed by the regular statistics, but they provide additional information or justifications for choices I've made to more statistically knowledgeable readers.

For the novice to statistics, the book is meant to be read in chronological order for both parts of the book. Part I introduces fundamental concepts in statistics that are necessary to beginning a statistical analysis. Part II then provides information in individual chapters about basic statistical procedures that are commonly used in second language research. In some cases these chapters also build upon one another, although users who are familiar with statistics and just looking up information on one specific technique can skip directly to the relevant chapter.

Part I consists of four chapters. Chapter 1 starts things off by telling readers how to set themselves up with SPSS and how to start entering data and manipulating it. Throughout the book important terms are highlighted in bold, and summaries of their meanings are found in the glossary. Chapter 2 discusses some essential ideas that are necessary to understanding further chapters, such as identifying whether variables are independent or dependent and what null hypothesis testing is. Chapter 3 shows how to produce numerical summaries of data, such as means, medians, and standard deviations, and how to check for measures that might indicate problems with standard statistical assumptions such as a normal distribution and equal variances for all groups. Graphic ways of evaluating the same types of information have been intentionally placed in the same chapter, for I feel that graphic summaries are just as informative as, if not more informative than, the numerical summaries, and I argue strongly for more use of graphic summaries in our research. Chapter 4 is a result of my reading many papers which argue that we are often on the wrong track with our statistical analyses when we rely on a single dichotomous measure such as a p-value (less than or greater than .05) to tell us whether our results are important. In this chapter I follow many statistical experts who have argued that we need to bring other types of measures such as effect sizes and confidence intervals into our analyses. I then try throughout the book to do this myself and to show readers how to do it too, because I think many times we haven't done it because we just haven't known how. I also explain why I eschew the use of the term "statistically significant" and instead just talk about results as being "statistical." As linguists, if we understand the types of reformed thinking that are likely to help us better understand our data from a statistical viewpoint, we should be committed to using language that reflects the fact that just because an analysis has a p-value below 0.05 does not mean that the result is important or "significant." It is just statistical, and that has very much to do with sample size and less so with effect size.

Chapter 5 lays out the different statistical tests that will be covered in Part II. It gives information about how to choose a test, depending on the questions that you have and the types of data you have. This chapter illustrates how these statistical tests are used in actual studies in second language research. I hope this will help you understand the differences between the tests, although you should know that figuring out statistics does take some time and you shouldn't expect to be an expert after reading Chapter 5! But maybe you'll have a small inkling of how the various tests are used. The remaining nine chapters of Part II go over various types of statistical analyses that are common in the field of second language research. Chapter 6 covers correlation, Chapter 7 introduces the reader to multiple regression, and Chapter 8 deals with chi-square. Chapter 9 concerns t-tests, Chapter 10 looks at the one-way analysis of variance (ANOVA), and Chapter 11 extends ANOVA to the case where there is more than one independent variable (factorial ANOVA). Chapter 12 extends ANOVA even further to the case where there are repeated measures, Chapter 13 explains ANCOVA, an ANOVA analysis with covariates, and Chapter 14 covers non-parametric tests available in SPSS. In general, the chapters go from conceptually easier tests to more difficult ones, although this is not true for regression.

Writing this book has given me a great appreciation for the vast world of statistics, which I do not pretend to be a master of. Like our own field of second language research, the field of statistics is always evolving and progressing, and there are controversies throughout it as well. If I have advocated an approach which is not embraced by the statistical community wholeheartedly, I have tried to provide reasons for my choice for readers and additional reading that can be done on the topic. Although I have tried my hardest to make this book accessible and helpful for readers, I would appreciate being informed of any typos or errors in this book or answers to application activities, or any areas where my explanations have not been clear enough.

Last of all, I would like to express my gratitude to the many individuals who have helped me to write this book. First of all is Richard Herrington, who has slowly guided me along in my statistical thinking. He provided many articles, many answers, and just fun philosophizing along the way. Susan Gass and Alison Mackey were instrumental in helping me get my book accepted into the Second Language Acquisition Research Series and providing encouragement. Many thanks to the students in my Research Methods courses who provided feedback on the book in its various stages. I thank the reviewers of the book as well for their careful work in reading the manuscript and providing useful feedback. I again want to profusely thank the authors who have given permission for the reproduction of their data in the numerical examples presented. They are cited individually in their respective places, but I feel this book is much more relevant and interesting to readers because of the data that they provided me, so I want to thank them together all in one place. Last I want to thank my husband, Andrew Hall, who took care of everything else so I could actually write this book, and let me share his office to escape from everyone else.

Part I

Statistical Ideas

Chapter 1

Getting Started with SPSS and Using the Computer for Experimental Details

In this chapter I will provide instructions for getting started with SPSS. SPSS is probably the most commonly used statistical program in the field of social sciences in general (it was originally developed for the social sciences) and is used by a majority of researchers working in the field of second language research. It uses a graphical user interface (GUI) with drop-down menus that should be familiar to those who use programs such as Microsoft Word or Excel. In this chapter I will first explain how to physically get started by opening SPSS and either importing or entering your own **data** into the SPSS spreadsheet (data is the information you have). Another important part of getting started is being able to save data. Once you have some data to work with, this chapter then goes on to explain ways you might like to manipulate your data, such as combining columns or calculating percentages, filtering out some cases of participants that you don't want to include in the analysis, or creating new groups from existing columns of data. The instructions throughout have been tested only with a PC (not Mac), but the SPSS interface should be similar on a Mac.

1.1 Getting Started with SPSS

First open SPSS by either clicking on the SPSS icon or going through the Programs menu from Windows. When you open SPSS you will see an "SPSS Data Editor" as in Figure 1.1, which looks like a spreadsheet for entering data. In SPSS version 10.0 and later, before you get to the **Data Editor** you will have a pop-up window which tries to help you get started. Usually you will choose either to type in new data or to open up an existing data set, like the ones provided for this book. Data files saved using SPSS have the extension .sav.

Note that there are two tabs in the Data Editor at the bottom of the spreadsheet. One is the "**Data View**," which is the default view. The other is the "**Variable View**." If you click on this tab, you'll see a different spreadsheet which is used to enter specific information about your variables, such as their names, type, and number of decimal points you want to see, among other things.

SPSS has two different types of windows that appear. One is the Data Editor, which we have already talked about. The other type of window is where any output appears. This window is called the "**SPSS Viewer**". In SPSS, any calls to perform data analysis, such as creating a graph, doing a statistical test, or creating a table will result in objects automatically appearing in the SPSS Viewer (see Figure 1.2). If you save data from the SPSS Viewer, these files have a .spv extension (versions of SPSS older than 16.0

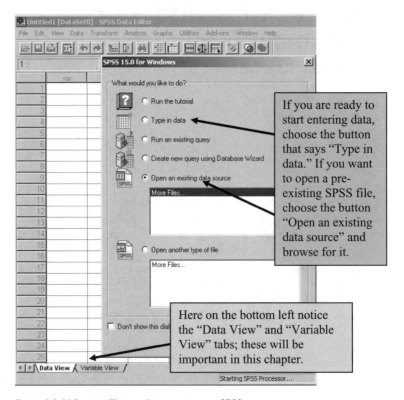

Figure 1.1 What you'll see when starting up SPSS.

created .spo files from output, and these cannot be opened in SPSS 16 unless you install the SPSS 15.0 Smart Viewer, available on the installation CD, according to the SPSS help files).

One new thing I have noticed about SPSS Version 16.0 is that the output will not run (be calculated) until you actually scroll down over it. In other words, you may call for an analysis and in previous versions of SPSS you might have had to wait a minute for it to finish running and show the output in the Viewer. However, in Version 16.0, if you go to your output after several minutes it will still not be available until you scroll down over the areas where it says *Processing. . . .* I have shown this situation in Figure 1.3.

1.1.1 Opening a Data File

Once you have SPSS open I'm sure you'll want to get started trying to do things! If you have not used the initial pop-up menu in Figure 1.1 to open a file that has already been created, you can also do this through the menus using the sequence FILE > OPEN > DATA and then navigating to the .sav file you want. If you do this, you'll see that the spreadsheet in the SPSS Data Editor becomes filled with data, as in Figure 1.4.

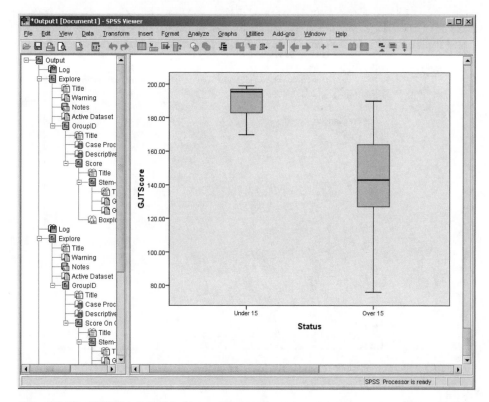

Figure 1.2 The SPSS Viewer, which shows output.

1.1.2 Entering Your Own Data

If you are going to create your own data file and would like to open a new spreadsheet through the menu system then you would go to FILE > NEW > DATA, which opens a blank spreadsheet. New to SPSS Version 16.0 is the insertion of SPSS syntax for every command you carry out through the menus. For example, Figure 1.5 shows the Viewer after opening up a new file.

There are a few things you need to know about data entry before you start inputting your numbers:

* Rows in SPSS are cases. This means that each participant should occupy one row.
* Columns in SPSS will be separate variables, such as ID number, score on a test, or category in a certain group.
* You can name each case (participant) by making your first column the ID number of each participant.

Your first step in entering data is to define the columns, which are your variables. To do this, go to the "Variable View" tab in the lower left-hand corner of the spreadsheet, shown in Figure 1.6 (the format of the spreadsheet will change, and the tab that says

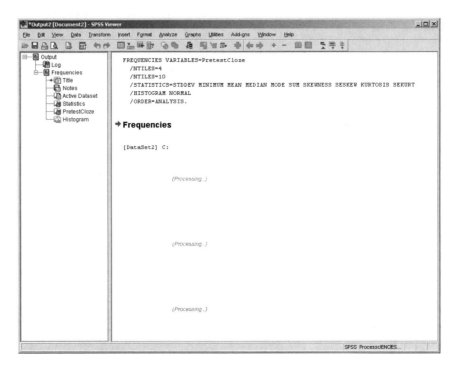

Figure 1.3 Output that is processing in the Viewer window.

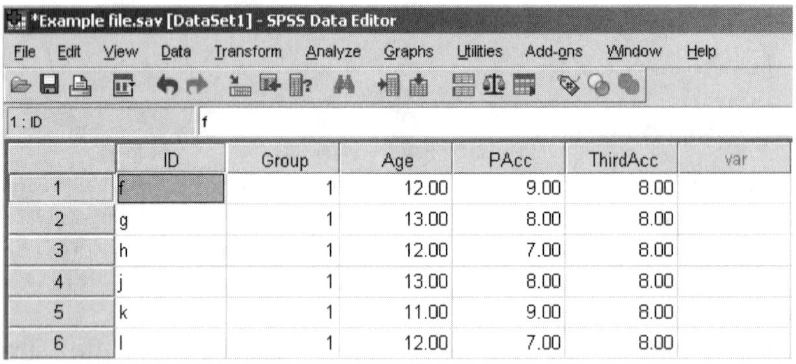

Figure 1.4 Data entered on a spreadsheet in the SPSS Data Editor.

"Variable View" will turn yellow). By the way, since I will be talking about variables a lot, let me define them here. A **variable** is a collection of data that all belong to the same sort (it can also be called a **factor**). For example, the ID numbers of all of your participants are one variable. Their scores on a certain test will be another variable. If the participants belonged to a certain experimental group, that group will be another variable. You can see that a variable, then, can consist of a collection of numbers, non-numeric labels (such as "control" or "group 1"), or just a string of information (such as MQ433 in a participant label).

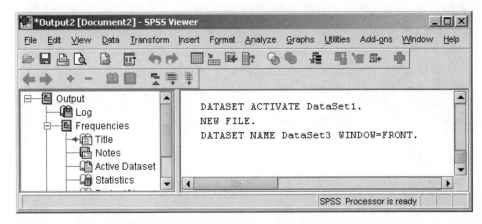

Figure 1.5 SPSS Version 16.0 includes SPSS syntax for every command.

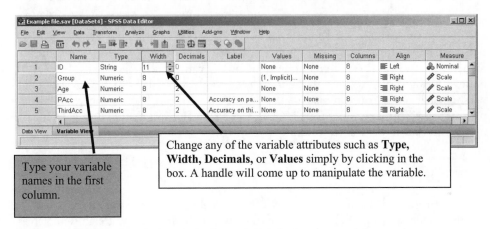

Figure 1.6 Variable view in SPSS (click the "Variable View" tab at bottom left corner).

In the Data Editor, when you are looking at the Variable View you will see the following columns:

When you are naming your variables, you want to give them informative names to make it easier to remember what information is contained in each column. Here are a few things to remember about naming your variables:

*   Names can be up to 64 bytes long, resulting in 64 characters for most languages or 32 characters for languages like Japanese, Chinese, or Korean (previous versions of SPSS, up to Version 12.0, allowed only eight characters).
*   Names cannot start with a number.

- Names cannot contain certain characters that are used in SPSS syntax (such as a slash "/", question mark "?", exclamation point "!", or quantity sign ">" or "<").
- Names cannot contain blanks (such as My Data File).

When trying to give your variables informative names it is probably a good idea to use the "first word capitalized" convention, for example "EnglishSpeakingTest." This convention makes it easy to read the words. Current versions of SPSS are case-sensitive and will preserve capitalization.

Type

The Type column will define your type of variable. The default choice is Numeric, which means your variable will be a number and can be used in statistical calculations. If you want to make your variable a different type, click on the right side of the cell and a small grey box will appear, like this: Numeric … . If you click on the box you'll see a choice of many different types of variables, as shown in Figure 1.7.

I have never actually used any other types besides Numeric and String. In SPSS **string variables** are used for non-quantitative information you want to enter, such as names or comments. Your alphanumeric ID number might also be a string. Be careful, because string variables can only be used as categorical variables such as group membership or gender. You can also make categorical variables by labeling your participants' groups with a number (say, 1=male and 2=female) and then defining what each number means in the Values column.

Width

The Width column specifies how many characters should be displayed in the column. For most *numbers* you will not need anything wider than the default eight characters.

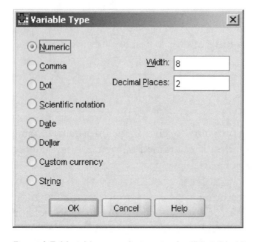

Figure 1.7 Variable type choices in the "Variable View" tab of the Data Editor.

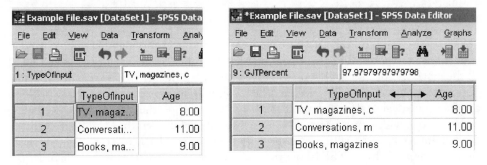

Figure 1.8 How the width of the column limits the number of characters.

However, if you have a string (treated as just words, not numbers, by SPSS) you might want to increase the width of the column. For example, Figure 1.8 shows a column, "TypeOfInput," which has a width of 16. In the default size of the column on the left you cannot actually see all 16 characters, but the ". . ." indicates that more data is included than you can see. To see all of the characters which are entered, just put the mouse on the line between columns—an arrow will appear (as shown in Figure 1.8) and you can pull the column over to be wider. Thus the Width specification limits how many characters you can actually enter into a column but says nothing about how many you can *see*.

Decimals

The Decimals column specifies how many decimal points to show for Numeric variables. The default is 2. If you have whole integers, you may want to change the decimals to 0. You can change the default to 0 by going to EDIT > OPTIONS and then the DATA tab. Under "Display Format for New Variables" change the decimal place to 0. You can change the default width here as well. One potential problem with 0 as a default, however, is that, if you enter in data that has decimal places, SPSS cannot show that, and will round numbers up or down, so that 1.5 becomes a 2 and 1.1 becomes a 1. Don't worry! The actual number you entered is still there; you just need to see it by telling SPSS to show you more decimal places.

Label

The fifth column in the Variable View is for giving a variable a more detailed name. This column is pretty much a holdover from the days when SPSS only let variable names be eight characters long, and you might have wanted to type in something more descriptive so when you came back to your data set after a long absence you would know what the variable was. At this point, labels are not really necessary and can actually be distracting. This is because in current versions of SPSS the label, and not the variable name, will appear on print-outs and may prove cumbersome for interpreting data if you type a name that is too long (although this default can be changed by going to the EDIT > OPTIONS menu choice).

Values

I have already told you that, if you have a category like group membership or gender, you will need to enter this as numbers, so that all of the females might be labeled 1 and all the males 2. But how will you remember which is which? If you enter this information as a string, say by using "M" and "F," you will not be able to use the variable to conduct statistical analyses, so you definitely want to enter the information by labeling each category with a number as a Numeric variable. However, these numbers will not be very informative to you later, especially if you come back to your data file years later. The thing to do in SPSS is to give your variable Values. Click on the cell under the Values column that you want to define, and a grey handle will appear on the right-hand

side of the box like this: None [...] . Click the grey handle once to open it, and

you will see a box as in Figure 1.9. Enter the value and the label, and then click ADD. Go back to the "Value" and "Label" boxes to add more definitions as needed. The CHANGE and REMOVE buttons below ADD can be useful if at a later time you want to edit your definitions or remove some categories.

> Tip: If you are going to be setting up the same values for more than one row of data in the Variable View it is easy to copy the values from one variable to another. In Variable View, first set up the values for one variable. Right-click on
>
> that box with the values (like this box: {1.00, Under...) and a menu will come
>
> up (don't right-click on the grey handle; instead, click anywhere else in the white cell). The menu has the choice of COPY or PASTE. Copy the variable values you want, then go to the cell under the Values column where you want to apply the same values, right-click on the white cell, and choose PASTE.

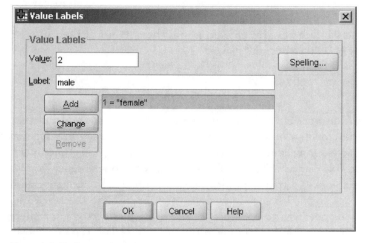

Figure 1.9 Defining values for variables in SPSS.

This column lets you specify what value you want to give to data which is missing. For example, some people like to label all missing data as "999" instead of just having an empty space.

Use this column to define how wide a column you'll see (not how many characters you can put in it, which is what the confusingly named Width column does). You can also manipulate the width of columns manually with a mouse by dragging.

Align

This specifies whether data in the Data Editor are aligned to the left or right of the column.

Measure

In this column you can label your variables as Nominal, Ordinal, or Scale (Interval). I have never found a reason to do this, however!

Tip: There is a way to customize many aspects of SPSS. For example, say that you do not expect most of your variables to need any decimal points, but the default for SPSS is two decimal places. Use the EDIT > OPTIONS menu choice. In the Options box you'll see lots of places where you can customize the way SPSS looks, including:

- whether names or labels are displayed in output (GENERAL tab)
- the language used (GENERAL tab)
- the fonts used in titles and output (VIEWER tab)
- display format for new variables—width and number of decimals (DATA tab)
- what columns are displayed in the "Variable View" tab (the "Customize Variable View" button in the DATA tab)
- the look of output in tables (in the PIVOT TABLES tab)

. . . and many more. Check it out for yourself!

1.1.3 Application Activity for Getting Started with SPSS

1   Open up an existing SPSS file. If you have downloaded the data for this book, open up the DeKeyser2000.sav file. What are the names of the variables? What do the numbers "1" and "2" refer to in the group membership variable "Status"?

2   Open a new file in SPSS and name it "Trial." Create three variables entitled "Group," "Results," and "Gender." Fill the columns with data for three groups of ten participants each. Define each group however you want and give the groups variable labels. Give the Gender column variable labels as well.
3   Change the default setting in SPSS for which columns to display in the Variable View. You'll have to decide for yourself which columns you'd like to keep and which you'll get rid of.

1.1.4 Importing Data into SPSS

You may want to use SPSS with files that have previously been saved in another format. SPSS can convert data that is saved in Microsoft Excel, Notepad, or Wordpad (.txt files), SAS, Lotus, dBase or Microsoft Access.

To import Excel files, dBase, or Microsoft Access files, open the "Database Wizard." You can choose this as an option when you first start up SPSS (see Figure 1.1, fourth choice down on the list of options) or start it manually by going to FILE > OPEN DATABASE > NEW QUERY. The wizard will pop up and guide you through the process of importing dBase, Excel, or MS Access files, giving a preview of the data along the way so you can see how the data will be arranged when it is imported into SPSS.

To import Notepad or Wordpad (.txt) files, go to OPEN > FILE > READ TEXT DATA. You can open other types of files that SPSS can read, such as SAS or Lotus files, using this way as well; just click on the "Files of type" drop-down menu and you will be able to choose the type of file you want (see Figure 1.10).

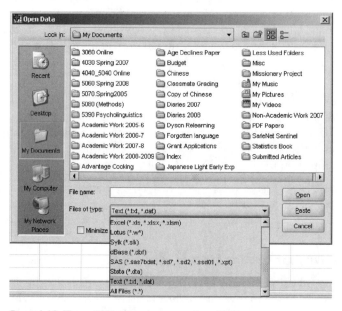

Figure 1.10 Type of files you can import into SPSS.

1.1.5 Saving Your Work in SPSS

Once you have created your data set or imported it into SPSS, you will want to save it as an SPSS file so you can easily open it again. Do this by going to FILE > SAVE. It is also possible to save SPSS files in other formats by using the FILE > SAVE AS choice. In previous versions of SPSS the program would not allow you to have more than one Data Editor open, but SPSS 16 allows this (and adds the Viewer for each one as well). You can also click on the icon that looks like a floppy disk to save your data. SPSS does not automatically back up your files, so if you are entering data you should save often, probably every five minutes or so.

In older versions of SPSS, it was not possible to have more than one Data Editor spreadsheet file open at a time. Now you can have multiple Data Editors open, but be aware that, if you have only one Data Editor open and then you close it, you will leave SPSS. To open another file SPSS will need to start up all over again (this principle holds true for Microsoft Word and plenty of other Windows software as well). If you want to close one file and open another, open your next file before closing the previous one and you will not have to open the SPSS program again.

In older versions of SPSS if you tried to open another file before closing the previous one, a dialogue box would come up to ask if you wanted to save the file before closing. If you said no, all of your data was lost. Ouch! If you are working with an older version of SPSS (such as 12.0), be careful of this point and always save your data before opening a new file.

Another type of object that you might want to save is your output. This is what appears in the SPSS Viewer window (see Figure 1.11). If you want to save only parts of the output, you can just click on certain parts and delete them before saving the file. This file is saved as a .spv file (this extension is new to SPSS 16.0; older versions had .spo) and can be opened later as "Output" (FILE > OPEN > OUTPUT). As you can see in Figure 1.11, there are two parts to this window. On the left side of this window there is an outline view of all of the parts of the output, while on the right is the actual output.

New to Version 16.0, any time you make a choice from a menu, the SPSS syntax for

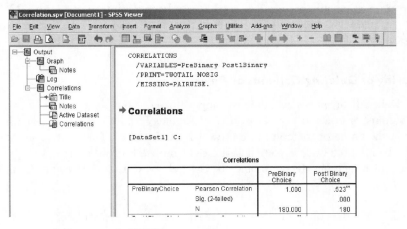

Figure 1.11 Output in the SPSS Viewer window.

that choice is recorded into the output file (if you don't like this, you can change it in the EDIT > OPTIONS box, VIEWER tab, click off the "Display commands in the log" box). If you save the output associated with your file, save your entire session and you can recreate your choices by running the syntax.

> Tip: To run syntax from your output, click on the syntax commands you want, and copy them using the Ctrl + C button sequence (or EDIT > COPY). To open up a syntax window, choose FILE > NEW > SYNTAX. Paste in the commands; then in the Syntax Editor choose RUN > CURRENT. Also, using syntax in SPSS can be helpful if you have to run the same analysis many times and just need to modify one part of it (say, the variable name).

1.1.6 Application Activity for Importing and Saving Files

1   Either find the file for this book called read.txt or find/create your own text file (using Windows Notepad). The read.txt file has data separated by a space. Import this data into SPSS. You may have to try to experiment with the Text Import Wizard to get the SPSS file to come out looking good.
2   Create a simple output by going to ANALYZE > DESCRIPTIVE STATISTICS > FREQUENCIES and moving one variable to the "Variable(s)" box. Press OK to continue. Now you have both a Data Editor and an SPSS Viewer open. Save both of them.

1.2 Manipulating Variables

It is likely that you will want to manipulate your variables at some point after entering them. For example, you may have entered the scores from three subtests of one test and then want to combine these scores for a total score. You might want to calculate a new variable by changing the range of numbers you group into one set. A concrete example is that in one analysis you might want a very broad grouping of participants into only two age groups: below 50 and above 50. However, in another case you might want to group participants by decades, so that you have a number of groups: 20–29, 30–39, 40–49, 50–59, 60–69, and so on. This section will explain how to perform such manipulations.

1.2.1 Moving or Deleting Columns or Rows

The SPSS Data Editor makes changing the appearance of your data almost as easy as moving columns or rows in a Microsoft Word table. To move a column or a row, just click on the name of the column or row, which is in grey. The entire column or row will be highlighted and, if you click the right mouse button, a menu of options will appear, which includes the commands to CUT, COPY, CLEAR and INSERT VARIABLE (see Figure 1.12):

*   CUT will delete the column or row and let you paste it in a new place.
*   COPY will leave the original column or row but let you paste a copy in a new place.

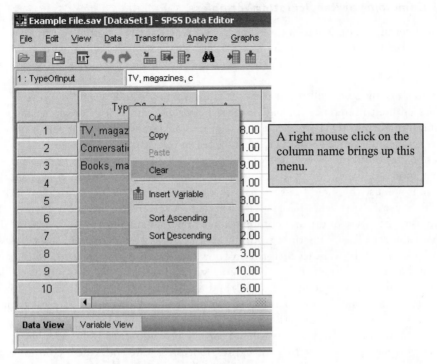

Figure 1.12 Manipulating columns in the Data Editor.

- CLEAR will delete the column or row entirely.
- INSERT VARIABLE puts in a new blank row or column.

Tip: There is one thing to be very careful about when moving variables in SPSS. If you PASTE a copied column into an existing column, the new data will be pasted in but the column name will be the same. This could be highly confusing! I suggest using INSERT VARIABLE first; then PASTE in the copied column and give it a name different from that of the original column.

Tip: If you want to create a whole bunch of variables with the same values (type, decimal point, values), create one example. Then, in the Variable View, COPY the row and then paste it using EDIT > PASTE VARIABLES. You will be able to specify how many copies of the variable you want and what name they'll have. SPSS will automatically append a different number to the end of each name to differentiate the variables.

1.2.2 Combining or Recalculating Variables

You will certainly come across times when you will want to combine some of your original variables, or perform some type of mathematical operation on your variables such as calculating percentages. In those cases, you will use the COMPUTE VARIABLE command in SPSS.

For this example we will use a data set from Torres (2004). Torres surveyed ESL learners on their preference for native-speaking teachers in various areas of language teaching (see Torres.sav). This file contains data from 34 questions about perception of native- versus non-native-speaking teachers. For example purposes, let's say that we are interested in combining the data from the first five questions into one measure of student motivation. We want to combine these five variables, but then average the score so it will use the same 1–5 scale as the other questions.

In SPSS, use TRANSFORM > COMPUTE VARIABLE. A screen like the one in Figure 1.13 will appear, and you can use any combination of mathematical formulas to derive the new variable set. The "Function group" area provides a listing of various types of operations you might want to perform on your data, but the only ones I have personally found useful are those in the "Arithmetic" group (useful for transforming variables so their distribution will be more normal) and the "Statistical" group (basic functions such as mean and standard deviation). If you click on any of these functions (which appear in a box below the "Function group" box, and are not shown in Figure 1.13), an explanation of what the function is will appear in a box underneath the calculator.

Once you have finished with your expression, press OK and a new column with whatever name you gave in the "Target Variable" box will be appended to the end of your spreadsheet in the Data Editor. In the case of the Torres (2004) data, it is a column with the average score of the first five questions.

To calculate a percentage score instead of a raw score, divide by the total number of possible points and then multiply by 100. For example, if we had the variable Test-Score with a possible maximum score of 37 points, this expression would result in a percentage:

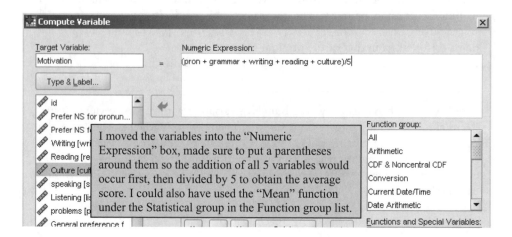

Figure 1.13 Computing variables in SPSS.

(TestScore/37)*100

If you had a questionnaire with some questions reverse-coded, it would likewise be quite easy to reverse the coding before adding several variables together using the COMPUTE VARIABLE command. For the Torres data, the **Likert scale** items were scored on a 5-point scale, with 1=strongly disagree, 2=disagree, 3=neither agree nor disagree, 4=agree, and 5=strongly agree. Assume that the Writing item was reverse-coded, meaning that, whereas for the other questions a 5 would indicate a preference for a native speaker, in the Writing item a 1 would indicate a preference for a native speaker. Here is how I could obtain the average of the first five items on the questionnaire while reversing the Writing item:

(pron + grammar + (6 − writing) + reading + culture)/5

By subtracting from 6, what was originally a 5 will become a 1, and what was originally a 1 will become a 5. Because the output just gets added to the end of your data file, it will never hurt you if you make a mistake in computing variables. You can just delete the column if you calculated something you didn't really want.

Combining Variables or Performing a Calculation on a Variable

1   From the menu bar, choose TRANSFORM > COMPUTE VARIABLE.
2   Move the variable(s) to the "Numeric Expression" box and add the appropriate mathematical operators.

1.2.3 Application Activities with Calculations

1   Open the BeautifulRose.sav file. This is a made-up file containing responses of 19 participants to a pre- and post-treatment cloze test, and an adjective test. Calculate the gain score between the pre- and post-treatment cloze tests (call this variable GAINCLOZE). Are there any negative gains? What is the largest gain score?
2   Open the LarsonHall.Forgotten.sav file. The researcher (me!) decides that the Sentence Accent variable would work better for her report if it were a percentage instead of a raw score. The highest possible score was 8, and this score represents a composite from several judges. Create a new variable that gives scores as a percentage of 100 (call this variable ACCENTPERCENT). What is the highest percentage in the group?

1.2.4 Recoding Group Boundaries

Another way you might want to manipulate your data is to make groups different from the groups that are already entered. To illustrate recoding group parameters, let's look at data from DeKeyser (2000), found in the DeKeyser2000.sav file. DeKeyser administered a grammaticality judgment test to Hungarian L1 learners of English who immigrated to the US. DeKeyser divided the participants into two groups on the basis of whether they immigrated to the US before age 15 or after (this is his STATUS variable).

But let's suppose we have a theoretical reason to change the age groupings to create four different groups.

To do the recoding in SPSS, choose TRANSFORM > RECODE. . . . At this point you will notice you have some choices. You can choose to RECODE INTO SAME VARIABLES, RECODE INTO DIFFERENT VARIABLES, or AUTOMATIC RECODE. Generally you will not want the AUTOMATIC RECODE. However, for the other two choices, if you choose RECODE INTO SAME VARIABLES, you will rewrite your previous variable and it will be gone, whereas if you choose RECODE INTO DIFFERENT VARIABLES then your original categories will still be visible. This latter choice is probably the safest one to make when you are new to SPSS. If you create your new group and are then sure you do not need the old category, you can always delete it (right-click and then choose CLEAR). When you choose TRANSFORM > RECODE INTO DIFFERENT VARIABLES then a dialogue box as in Figure 1.14 will come up. The STATUS variable is really a division of the AGE variable into two groups. Therefore, to make four groups, move the AGE variable into the "Numeric Variable → Output Variable" box as shown in Figure 1.14.

In order to tell SPSS how to break up the groups, push the OLD AND NEW VALUES button. A dialogue box like the one in Figure 1.15 will appear.

I decided to break up the range of ages into four categories: 0–7, 8–15, 16–22, and 23–oldest. To do this, I used several parts of the "Old Value" side of the dialogue box in Figure 1.15. For the 0–7 category, I used the fifth choice, "Range, LOWEST through value" and typed in "7." Then, on the "New Value" side of the box, I entered a "1" and pressed the "Add" button. This labeled all cases of immigrants between the ages of 0 and 7 as belonging to group 1. For the categories 8–15 and 16–22, I used the fourth choice on the left side, called "Range." Finally, for the 23–oldest category I used the sixth choice, as shown in Figure 1.15. I used numbers to label my groups instead of strings because if the labels are strings this category is not seen as a variable, which means it cannot be used in statistical calculations.

In this example I took a continuous variable (AGE), one that was not a group already, and collapsed the numbers into groups. It would also be possible to collapse a number

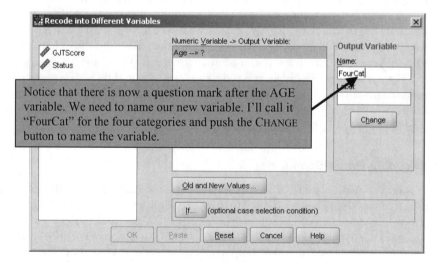

Figure 1.14 Recoding a variable into different groups.

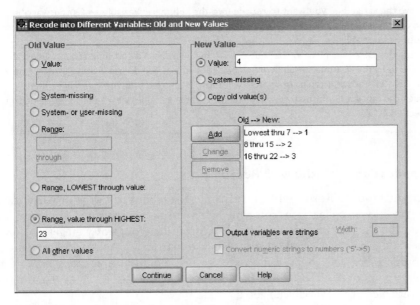

Figure 1.15 Specifying old and new values for recoding.

of groups into smaller groups. For example, suppose you had conducted a test of vocabulary learning with four levels of learners, which might be 1=intermediate low, 2=intermediate high, 3=advanced low, and 4=advanced high. Then for some reason after looking at the data you decided you wanted to combine the intermediate learners into one group and the advanced learners into another group so that you had only two groups. In this case, in the dialogue box in Figure 1.15 you would simply put in the actual values of the groups as the old values ("1" first and then "2" in the example I gave) and give them both the new value "1," adding each group separately. The recode directives seen in the box would reflect that the old group "1" would be labeled "1" and the old group "2" would now also be labeled group "1."

One problem I found with recode in SPSS is that, if you want to recode more than one variable in the same file, SPSS will use the same recoding for *both* variables. Let's say for some reason I wanted to recode DeKeyser's GJTSCORE variable into two groups, and I tried to use RECODE INTO DIFFERENT VARIABLES to do it. I try to erase the recoding instructions for the AGE variable and enter new ones for the GJTSCORE variable, but when I try to record this choice I get an error message and cannot complete the command. I do not know of any way for SPSS to let you use two different directives for recoding within the same file. If you want to do this, you should copy over the relevant columns to a new file and then you will be able to start with a new recoding directive.

Recoding Groups of Variables

1   From the menu bar, choose TRANSFORM > RECODE INTO DIFFERENT VARIABLES (there are several choices, but this one will be the basic choice).

2   Move the variable(s) you want to recode into the "Numeric Variable → Output Variable" box and give the new variable a name in the "Output Variable" area. Press CHANGE to name your new variable.

3   Press the OLD AND NEW VALUES button and define your old and new groups. Generally avoid using the "Output variables are strings" box unless you do not want to use your new variable in statistical calculations. You will most likely give your new variables numbers, but you can later informatively label them in the "Variable View" tab as explained in Section 1.1.2.

1.2.5 Application Activities with Recoding

1   Open the BeautifulRose.sav file. It turns out that about half of your participants were traditional college students and half were older, returning students. You decide you want to investigate scores by comparing groups of younger and older students. Create a new variable called AGEGROUP from the AGE variable and divide the participants into younger and older groups. Find out how many are in each group by going to ANALYZE > DESCRIPTIVE STATISTICS > FREQUENCIES and putting the new variable in the "Variable(s)" box.

2   Open the LarsonHall.Forgotten.sav file. The STATUS variable here groups participants by the age at which they started learning English intensively. Let's pretend I want to make another group that puts people into groups pertaining to their English usage. Half of the participants scored 10 or below, and half scored 11 or above, so I decide to make a cutpoint at this level. Create a new group called USEGROUP that categorizes participants as either LowUse or HiUse (be sure to create value labels as well for this variable). Find out how many are in each group by going to ANALYZE > DESCRIPTIVE STATISTICS > FREQUENCIES and putting the new variable in the "Variable(s)" box.

1.2.6 Using Visual Binning to Make Cutpoints for Groups (Advanced Topic)

SPSS has a special function that can helps you decide how to make groups. In this case you would be taking a variable that has a large range of values and collapsing those values into groups. One word of warning about this type of procedure is that you are actually losing data if you do this. For example, in the DeKeyser data discussed in Section 1.2.4, making groups from the variable of AGE puts people into only one of two groups, whereas leaving them with their original age of immigration creates a variable that can show finer gradations. In DeKeyser's analysis, however, he did use the data from the AGE variable, thus exploiting the fact that he had a wide variety of ages of arrival. However, in another part of his analysis he wanted to divide the participants into groups, and there may be cases where this is a good idea.

If you use the menu option TRANSFORM > VISUAL BINNING, SPSS can help you decide how to collapse your large range of values into a much smaller choice of categories if you do not already have any theoretical reason for making cuts. When you open this menu choice you will be able to choose which variable you want to collapse into groups. Just for illustration, I chose DeKeyser's GJTSCORE variable. After pressing OK,

I get the dialogue box seen in Figure 1.16 (click on the variable in the "Scanned Variable List" too).

A box displays a histogram of scores on the test. The **histogram** shows separate bins which are taller when there are more cases of scores in that bin. The histogram here shows that the most people received scores around 199 (because that is the tallest bin). In the area called "Binned Variable" you can enter your own name for this new variable you will create. To make cutpoints, open the button that says MAKE CUTPOINTS and you will have three choices. If you want to divide the data into equal groups, use the "Equal percentiles based on scanned cases" box. Let's say you want three groups. Then in the box labeled "Number of cutpoints," enter the number 2, because with two cuts that will make three groups. On the other hand, let's say you wanted to use cutpoints that didn't divide the data equally but instead divided it at the mean and then at the standard deviations (the first standard deviation would cover the middle 68% of the data, the second standard deviation would cover the middle 97.5% of the data, and the third standard deviation would cover 99.5% of the data). For this, use the "Cutpoints at mean and selected standard deviations based on scanned cases" choice. Press "Apply" when you are ready with your choice. In Figure 1.16 I have made cutpoints based on equal percentiles.

In the grid in the middle of the dialogue box you see that all of the values of the test up to a score of 141 are in the first group, those between 142 and 175 are in the second group, and those 176 or higher are in the third group. If you click on the MAKE LABELS button, labels will be created automatically, or you can type your own in next to the given value. When you press OK you will see a warning that "Binning specifications

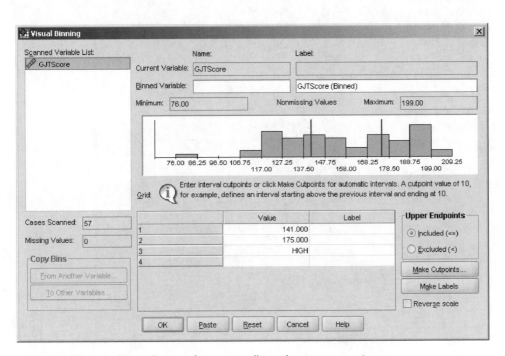

Figure 1.16 Using the VISUAL BINNING feature to collapse data into categories.

will create 1 variables." This is what you want, so go ahead and press OK! You'll see a new column in your spreadsheet now.

1.2.7 Excluding Cases from Your Data (Select Cases)

Sometimes you may have a principled reason for excluding some part of the dataset you have gathered. For example, Obarow (2004) tested children on how much vocabulary they learned in different conditions (see Obarow.sav). Some children who participated in the vocabulary test achieved very high scores on the pre-test. Children with such high scores would not be able to achieve many gains on a post-test, and one might then have a principled reason for cutting them out of the analysis (although you should tell your readers that you did this).

To cut out some of the rows of the data set in SPSS, go to the DATA > SELECT CASES line. You will see the dialogue box in Figure 1.17. First choose the variable that will be used to specify which cases to delete. For the Obarow data we want to exclude children whose pre-test scores were too high, so I'll choose the PRETEST1 variable. We will select the cases we want to *keep* (I often get confused and work the opposite way, selecting the cases I want to get rid of!). We need a conditional argument, so I select the second choice under the "Select" area, which is the IF button (in Figure 1.17 I have already

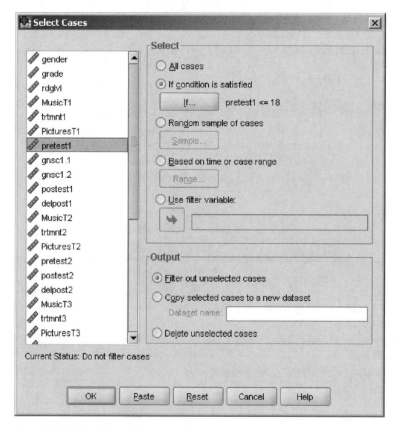

Figure 1.17 Deleting cases from the data set.

completed the choice done in the box in Figure 1.18, which is why there is a condition listed after the IF button). If you press this button, you will see the dialog box in Figure 1.17.

I want to keep all of the cases where the pre-test score is 18 or less. Therefore, in the "Select Cases: If" dialogue box, I move the PRETEST1 variable to the right and then push the calculator button for "<=", meaning less than or equal to.

After I finish specifying the condition I want to keep data in, I have a choice in the "Output" section of Figure 1.17 as to what to do with my unwanted data. The safest choice is the default one and the first under the "Output" area, called "Filter out unselected cases." If you choose this, a slash will appear over the rows that you do not want, and these will not be entered into calculations. If you choose the "Delete unselected cases" option, you won't be able to recover this data, even with the UNDO button.

1.2.8 Application Activity for Selecting Cases

1 Open the DeKeyser2000.sav file. Select only the participants under 15 (Group 1).
2 Open LarsonHall.Forgotten.sav. Pretend I want to exclude all participants who have spent more than four weeks overseas. How many participants are excluded?

1.2.9 Sorting Variables

You might like to order the data in a column from smallest to largest or vice versa. To do this, choose the menu options DATA > SORT CASES (the DATA > SORT VARIABLES choice will move your columns around). You can choose to sort by just one variable or by several. If you sort by several variables, the one you insert first will take priority. If there are then ties, the second variable will decide the order.

Figure 1.19 shows the results of sorting the column PRETEST1 from the Obarow data set and then copying it to the beginning of the file. Notice that, when it is copied, it loses its name. Notice also that, by ordering, it is easy to see that two cases are missing data. Last of all, I want to point out that the numbers that define the rows stayed the same, even though the data was moved around. Do not depend on the SPSS row numbers to define your participants—put in your own column with some kind of ID

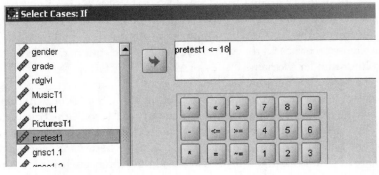

Figure 1.18 Using the "If" button for selecting cases and specifying a score of 18 or under on the PRETEST1 variable.

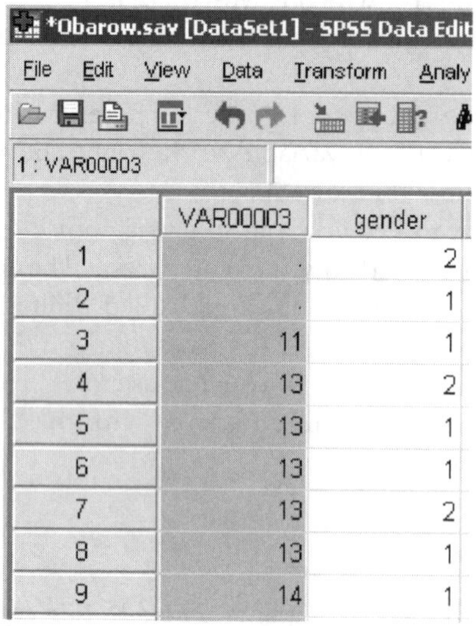

Figure 1.19 Sorting a column in ascending order (from smallest to largest).

number for your participants. If you do this, that ID number will move with each case (row) when the data file is sorted and you will be able to remember which row of data belongs to which participant!

1.2.10 Application Activities for Manipulating Variables

In this section you will bring together many of the skills you learned about for manipulating variables in SPSS to accomplish these tasks:

1   Add a new column to the DeKeyser2000.sav file entitled AGEGROUP. Split the participants into groups depending on their age of arrival (AGE) to the US by decades. So, for example, you will have one group for those who were 10 or under, another group for those 11–20, and so on. How many groups do you have? Label your new groups in the "Variable View" tab. Delete the old column STATUS. Do a simple report to see if your values are appearing: Go to ANALYZE > DESCRIPTIVES > FREQUENCIES and put the AGEGROUP column in the box on the right. Press OK. You should see a report that has your new variable names. Save your new SPSS file with the four columns under the name DeKeyserAltered.

2   Open the LarsonHall.Forgotten.sav file. The data come from an unpublished study on Japanese learners of English who lived in the US as either children or adults. Move the RLWTEST variable from the end of the file to be the first variable after ID. This variable is a variable with 96 points. Reduce it to two groups by dividing at the halfway point to separate those who are better and worse at distinguishing R/L/W in English, or, if you have read the Advanced Topic section on using Visual Binning, do that to find a suitable cutpoint. Save the file as LarsonHallAltered.

3   Open the LarsonHallAltered.sav file (you should have created it in step 2). Create a new variable, TALKTIME, with four categories that distinguish between participants' use of English (you'll use the ENGUSE variable and reduce it to four groups). Create the groups so that ENGUSE has the following cuts: lowest-8, 9–11, 12–13, 14–highest. Prepare the file so that only participants with data in the RETURNAGE column will be evaluated. Sort the file by ascending order of AGE. How many participants were 18 when tested?

4   Open the BEQ.Swear.sav file. The data come from a very large-scale study on bilinguals conducted by Jean-Marc Dewaele and Aneta Pavlenko (2001–2003). The column AGESEC refers to the age of acquisition of a second language. First, move the column so it is the first column in the Data Editor. Filter out any participants who learned their second language at age zero. Count how many participants are left by going to ANALYZE > DESCRIPTIVE STATISTICS > DESCRIPTIVES. Move the AGESEC variable to the right and press OK.

5   Open the BeautifulRose.sav file. For the adjective test, not all of the participants answered the questions in the way the researcher wanted, so the total possible number of adjectives varies by participant. The researcher would like to change these scores into percentages so the scores of all participants are comparable. Calculate a new variable called ADJPERCENT that gives the percentage correct of each participant. What is the highest percentage correct?

1.3 Random Number Generation

When you are starting to do an experiment, you may want to **randomize** participants, sentences, test items, and so on. This means that you do not select them deliberately but that you use some sort of way of selection that involves chance. You can use your computer to help you generate random numbers that you will apply to your participants, your sentences, your test items, or whatever you need.

1.3.1 Generating Random Numbers in Excel

First, when you open Microsoft Excel, if you are using Microsoft Office 2007, you will see the formula bar below the tool bar. The formula bar is marked by the character "f_x" as shown in Figure 1.20. To create random numbers, simply type the following syntax into the formula bar, exactly as shown:

=RANDBETWEEN(1,100)

After you type this, press the ENTER button.

The RANDBETWEEN command shown here will generate random numbers between 1 and 100. Of course, if you want random numbers between, say, 1 and 10 you just alter the syntax in the command. At first, only one number in the top cell will appear, but just use the handle to pull the random numbers down as many rows and over as many cells as are necessary.

If you are using an older version of Excel, you will need to make sure the Analysis ToolPak has been installed. Do this by pulling down the TOOLS menu. If you see DATA ANALYSIS on the list, the ToolPak is installed. If it is not, find ADD-INS (still in the TOOLS

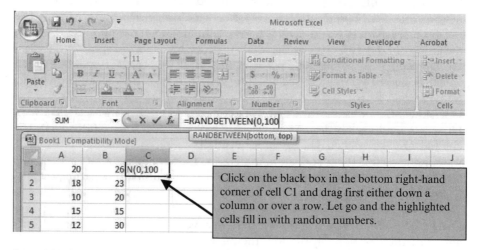

Figure 1.20 Generating random numbers in Excel.

menu) and click on it. A box will open; click on ANALYSIS TOOLPAK and then OK. It is not necessary to actually open the Data Analysis box. You will then be able to use the RANDBETWEEN function as explained above.

1.4 Summary

In this chapter you have become familiar with the SPSS environment. When we open up SPSS, there are two basic windows that will open. One is the Data Editor, where we enter data in the "Data View" tab and define variables in the "Variable View" tab. The other window is the SPSS Viewer, where we can see the output we request. Both windows contain all of the menu options available in SPSS.

You've tried your hand at both importing data into SPSS and creating new data files. Once you have data in SPSS, you can start working with it and manipulating it. Some useful techniques we went over in this chapter are calculating new variables, recoding old variables into new variables, excluding cases from a data set, and sorting variables. You also know how to save both your data files and your output files once you're finished.

Chapter 2
Some Preliminaries to Understanding Statistics

> . . . to steal a line from Winer (1971, p. 442), "Statistical elegance does not necessarily imply scientifically meaningful inferences." Common sense is at least as important as statistical manipulations.
>
> David Howell (2002, p. 463)

Since becoming interested in statistics, I have had my colleagues occasionally send me their students who are working on an experiment for their thesis. "Help them with their statistics!" my colleagues plead. These novice researchers know conceptually what they want to test, but empirically are not sure how to go about designing an experiment that involves statistical analysis. For example, the student may know they want to test whether listeners will rate some accents as more desirable than others, but they do not know where to go from there. This chapter contains information that is essential in understanding how to do an experimental project. This chapter does not explain what test you will want to use to evaluate your data statistically (that will come later), but it covers the basic concepts that are necessary to understanding what test you will need. This will give those who are new to experimental design and statistics a brief overview of some of the basic issues that must be understood in order to carry out a statistical analysis. These concepts may not seem like "common sense" (a reference to the quotation at the beginning of the chapter) yet, but doing statistics should not be mysterious hand-waving that results in a "**statistically significant**" finding. You need to understand your numbers and understand what you are testing when you use statistics. This chapter is a start to that understanding.

In the first chapter I defined a variable as a collection of data that are all of the same sort. We saw in Chapter 1 that variables are shown as columns in a spreadsheet collection of data in SPSS's Data Editor. The first part of this chapter will help you to understand more about the characteristics of your variables, because these characteristics will to a large part determine what types of statistical tests you can use. If you can, you should try to understand *before* you start your data collection what types of variables you are going to be collecting and recording. The second part of the chapter will describe some rather abstract ideas that you will nevertheless need to be aware of as you undertake to do statistical tests. I have set this up as a discussion of the hidden assumptions underlying statistical testing because most of the time you will not openly read of these ideas in a journal article or a report on research, but they are ideas that are understood by those who do statistics (or, at least, they *should* be understood!).

These include understanding the difference between the sample of people that you collect data from and the wider population of people you hope to generalize your results to. Statistics which can be generalized to a population wider than your sample are called inferential statistics. In this section I will also introduce (but will revisit in Chapter 4) the concept of hypothesis testing in statistics, which rather perversely is set up to test hypotheses that you hardly ever believe in! In the latter part of the hidden assumptions section I will explain some of the parts of the statistical result that are common to every test and that you will often see reported in research articles, including p-values, confidence intervals, and degrees of freedom. I will also try to demystify how statistical testing works. Having a basic understanding of these concepts will help you start with your own research project or just help you understand more when you read statistical results in a journal article. The last section of the chapter deals with an emerging type of statistics called robust statistics and recommends their use in the future (this section is optional; those who are more statistically advanced might like to read it).

2.1 Variables

My first question to the novice researcher will be "What is your **research question**?" I cannot help you formulate this—you will have to do this on your own! Your research question can be informal at first, but it will contain the seeds to beginning a formal statistical investigation. Here are some of the questions my recent graduate students have had:

1   Would playing an online role-playing game in another language help students learn Spanish better?
2   Will providing different types of targeted feedback on written work help students improve in their ability to use grammar accurately?
3   Are people who are good at music better at detecting Chinese tone than people who are not?
4   Will students learn vocabulary better if they are able to associate them through multiword expressions rather than just singly?
5   What kinds of phonological problems will Koreans and Japanese learners of English have?

Once I know what your research question is, my next question will be "What are your variables?" In other words, before we can proceed with any kind of statistical analysis we need to know what kinds of measurements will be done. For this question we need to think about how we can **operationalize** the research question or, in other words, take an abstract idea and make it measurable. For example, in the first question above, my student wanted to know if students would get better at Spanish. How will we measure their Spanish? Are we interested in their speaking ability, their listening ability, their reading ability, or all of these? Say we are interested in their speaking ability. Then how will we measure it? Will we give them a standardized Spanish oral proficiency interview test (OPI)? Will we just have an informal interview? Will we use grades from their last Spanish class? All of these are ways to operationalize the variable of "speaking proficiency in Spanish."

Think about what needs to be measured in order to operationalize the research question in each of the questions listed above. Here are the ideas I can see that need to be measured:

1 How will we measure Spanish proficiency? What group will participants be in (we'll need at least two groups in order to show that it is the game playing that helps participants improve)?
2 What types of feedback will be provided and to how many groups? How will we measure grammatical accuracy and on what forms? How will we measure improvement in accuracy?
3 How do we measure how good people are at music? How do we measure how well they perceive Chinese tones?
4 How will we measure vocabulary knowledge? What group will participants be in (will there be a control group that does not try to learn any vocabulary at all)?
5 How will we measure phonological problems (will we target contrasts or specific sounds), and how many will we test?

2.1.1 Levels of Measurement of Variables

Answering these questions and thus operationalizing your research question will result in measuring variables. These variables may differ substantially from each other. For example, measuring Spanish speaking proficiency will probably be done through some kind of test where participants will receive a variety of scores. This type of variable is called a **continuous variable**. The values of a continuous variable consist of numbers that represent a measurement and involve a large range of possible answers. A continuous variable contrasts with a **categorical variable**, where the values of the variable basically do not have any inherent numerical value and consist of categories where one category is not rated any higher than any other. Categorical variables often have a very restricted range of possible values.

In the examples above, the number of groups that will be tested is a categorical variable, while scores on tests or measurements such as grammatical accuracy or perception of Chinese tones are continuous variables. Below I have listed the variables that will be needed for each of the operationalized variables in the five research questions my students asked, and a possible way of operationalizing the variable. Decide if each one is a continuous or categorical variable (I'll give the answers following the list):

1	Spanish proficiency will be measured by an OPI.	continuous or categorical
	There will be three groups: those who play games, those who speak with a conversation partner, and those who do not do anything special.	continuous or categorical
2	There will be three types of feedback given to students on article usage: direct correction, indirect correction by circling, and no feedback.	continuous or categorical
	Grammatical accuracy will be measured by the number of accurate article usages out of all obligatory contexts. This will be measured on four different essays.	continuous or categorical

(Continued)

3 Facility with music will be measured through a perfect pitch test, with a maximum possible score of 20 points.	continuous or categorical
Chinese tone perception will be measured through an identification test of four tones, with 30 items in total.	continuous or categorical
4 Vocabulary knowledge will be measured by having students put a check by the words they know and then totaling this number out of ten words.	continuous or categorical
There will be three groups: those who learn multiword expressions, those who focus on single words, and those who are not specifically asked to memorize any words at all.	continuous or categorical
5 Five contrasts in English with ten items each will be played for the listeners, resulting in a test with a maximum possible score of 50 points.	continuous or categorical
There are two groups of people with different first language (L1) backgrounds: Korean and Japanese.	continuous or categorical

Here are the answers: 1) continuous, categorical; 2) categorical, continuous; 3) continuous, continuous; 4) continuous, categorical; 5) continuous, categorical. It should be clear now that any type of grouping of participants will result in a categorical variable. In addition, whenever you give someone a test with a large number of items, this will result in a continuous variable.

I have started out with this broad division of measurements into continuous and categorical variables. The skill of identifying whether your variables are continuous or categorical is absolutely essential for deciding what statistical test to use, and in general the division between continuous and categorical is the most important division to know when it comes to performing statistical tests, as some tests can be used only when all variables are continuous, while other tests can be used only when there is at least one categorical and one continuous variable. However, many authors make a more detailed division of variable measurement into three or even four different types of measurement. For example, Mackey and Gass (2005) discuss three levels of measurement: nominal, ordinal, and interval scales. **Nominal scales** (which measure **categorical variables**) do not have any inherent numerical value. They are used to group people or data, and include measurements like gender, group membership in an experiment, first or second language background, or presence/absence of a linguistic feature. **Ordinal scales** are rank-ordered and do have some inherent numerical value. For example, we might have first-, second-, and third-year students of French. If we assigned the students a number based on their number of years of study, we would expect this to be reflected in their knowledge of French, with students with a higher number having more knowledge of French. We might not expect, however, that the difference between third-year students and second-year students would be the same as between second-year and first-year students. In other words, there is no guarantee that there are equal intervals of measurement between the participants. In an **interval scale** (which measures **continuous variables**), however, we would like to say that the difference between getting a 9 and a 10 on a 10-point test is the same as the difference between getting a 3 and a 4 on the test. In other words, the intervals are assumed to be equal. Some authors will also distinguish a **ratio scale** (Howell, 2002), which has all the properties of an interval scale plus the scale has a true zero point. I can't think of any of these that exist in the applied linguistics field, but an example Howell (2002) gives is of weight. A 40-lb rock is twice as heavy as a 20-lb rock, and something that weighed 0 lb means that the thing that is being measured is absent, so the scale truly has a zero point.[1]

Why do you need to know about nominal, ordinal, and interval scales? The truth is, you probably don't, but it is good to be familiar with the terms (Howell, 2002, agrees with me on this!). As I noted above, the division between categorical and continuous variables (which is the same as the division between nominal and interval scales) is in practice the division which is important in deciding which statistical test to choose. Researchers who use a measurement which is ordinal end up classifying it as either categorical or continuous, often depending on how many points there are in the scale. For example, if you have recorded the years of study of college learners of French and you have three levels, you will most likely call this a categorical variable with no inherent numerical value, even though you do realize that most learners in their third year of French study will perform better than learners in their first year. On the other hand, if you have a seven-point Likert scale measuring amount of language anxiety, you will be likely to call this a continuous measurement, even though you may acknowledge that a score of 4 on the scale (moderate anxiety) may not be exactly twice of what the score of 2 is (little anxiety).

In truth, it is not the measurement itself but how the researcher chooses to look at it that is the deciding factor in whether you will call a measurement continuous or categorical. For example, you may ask people their age, which is certainly an interval scale (in fact, it is a ratio scale, because it has a true zero point), but then classify them as young versus old, making your measurement into a nominal scale. This example shows what Howell (2002) states, which is that the researcher must remember that the event itself and the numbers that we measure are different things, and that "the validity of statements about the objects or events that we think we are measuring hinges primarily on our knowledge of those objects or events, not on the measurement scale" (p. 9).

2.1.2 Application Activity: Practice in Identifying Levels of Measurement

Look at the following studies. The variables measured in the study to answer the research question are listed in the tables. Look at each variable and decide whether it is categorical or continuous.

---

[1] The more advanced reader may want to be aware of several other types of measurements. Within the category of interval scale that I have outlined here, Crawley (2007) distinguishes several more levels that can affect the choice of statistical test. Thus, for a dependent variable which a beginner might treat as an interval scale, we can distinguish between those measurements which are proportions or counts. If the measurement is a proportion (such as the number of mistakes out of every 100 words) then a logistic model would provide a better fit than a normal regression or ANOVA model. If the measurement is a count (such as the number of mistakes on a writing assignment) then a log linear model provides a better fit. And if a dependent variable which is nominal has only two choices and is thus a binary scale, a binary logistic model provides a better fit. These types of statistical tests are not treated in this book, however, and the interested reader is advised to consult Crawley (2007) or Tabachnick & Fidell (2001).

Kondo-Brown (2006): Does accuracy in guessing the meaning of unfamiliar Japanese words differ depending on proficiency level?

1	Proficiency level (divided participants into high and low proficiency on the basis of reading comprehension tests, with maximum possible score of 20 points).	continuous or categorical
	Accuracy level measured on a series of different tests, but generally most of the tests had about 16 points or more.	continuous or categorical

Boers, Eyckmans, Kappel, Stengers, and Demecheleer (2006): Will explicit instruction in noticing formulaic sequences help one group speak more fluently than another group that does not get this instruction?

2	Two experimental groups, one that was led to notice formulaic sequences and another that wasn't.	continuous or categorical
	Fluency ratings done by judges who listened to taped conversations and rated them for fluency on a 20-point scale.	continuous or categorical

Paavola, Kunnari, and Moilanen (2005): Does the number of times a mother changed her behavior because of a child's action affect the number of phrases an infant understands?

3	Number of times mother modifies behavior contingent on child's action counted in two separate sessions of 20 minutes each (these are all added up together).	continuous or categorical
	Number of phrases the child knows based on the MacArthur Inventory parental report.	continuous or categorical

Erdener and Burnham (2005): Does first language orthography affect how well participants can produce nonwords in a language that has an orthography similar or different to their L1?

4	Two groups of participants with different orthographies (L1=Australian English or L1=Turkish).	continuous or categorical
	Two groups of target languages with different orthographies (L2=Irish English or L2=Spanish).	continuous or categorical
	Number of phoneme errors on 96 nonwords.	continuous or categorical

Bialystok, Craik, Klein, and Viswanathan (2004): Do age and being bilingual affect the accuracy with which participants perform on the Simon test (a test that measures whether participants can ignore irrelevant information)?

5	Score on the 28-item Simon test.	continuous or categorical
	Age, divided into two groups (young, 30–54, and older, 60–88).	continuous or categorical
	Status as bilingual or monolingual.	continuous or categorical

2.1.3 Dependent and Independent Variables

Another important dichotomy between variables is whether they are considered independent or dependent. Both independent and dependent variables can be measured as nominal, ordinal, or interval, so this division is independent of the measurement scale. This dichotomy relates to *the way the variables function in the experiment.*

Independent variables are those that we think may have an effect on the dependent variable. Often the researcher controls these variables. For example, an independent variable would be membership in one of three experimental conditions for learning vocabulary: mnemonic memorization, rote memorization, and exposure to context-laden sentences. The researcher randomly assigns participants to the groups, and suspects that the group the participant is in will affect their scores on a later vocabulary test. Independent variables are not always variables that the researcher manipulates, however. If you think that amount of motivation and presence at a weekly French conversation chat group influence fluency in French, you will simply try to measure motivation and chat group attendance. In this case your measure of motivation and a count of number of French club meetings attended are your independent variables. You have not fixed them in the way you might assign students to a certain group, but you are still interested in how these variables influence fluency.

Here are some common independent variables in second language research studies:

- experimental group membership
- L1 background
- proficiency level
- age
- status as monolingual or bilingual
- type of phonemic contrast
- amount of motivation or language anxiety
- amount of language use

The variable that you are interested in seeing affected is the **dependent variable**. For our French example, the dependent variable is a "fluency in French" measure. If the independent variables have been fixed, then the dependent variable is beyond the experimenter's control. For example, the researcher may fix which experimental group the participants belong to, and then measure their scores after the treatment on a vocabulary test. Assignment to a group has been fixed, but then scores on the vocabulary test are out of the control of the researcher. Of course, the researcher is hoping (betting? guessing?) that the scores *will* be affected by the experimental group. In this sense, the dependent variable "depends" on the independent variable.

Here are some common dependent variables in second language research studies:

- fluency ratings
- score on discrete-point tests
- number of accurate grammatical forms out of all instances of that grammatical form used
- EKG or MRI brain response patterns
- pronunciation rating
- reaction time
- holistic writing score
- number and length of t-units

As Howell (2002, p. 4) says, "Basically, the study is about the independent variables, and the results of the study (the data) are the dependent variables." I remember first encountering the idea of dependent and independent variables, and it took a little while before I got them straight, but maybe it will help if you look at a variable and think, "Do I think this data will be influenced by some other variables?" If so, it is a dependent variable. If you think the data will be an explanatory factor for some other results, then it is an independent variable. While dependent variables may be categorical or continuous, independent variables are generally categorical. It is extremely important to understand the difference between independent and dependent variables correctly because this classification will affect what test you will choose to analyze your data with.

Now I hate to tell you this, but actually the difference between independent and dependent variables is not always clear cut, and in some cases this traditional dichotomy may not really be applicable. In this discussion I have been assuming that you will have a variable that depends for its outcome on some other variables (the independent variables). In such a case the researcher is clearly trying to establish some kind of causal relationship. In other words, I cause outcomes to differ because I put the participants in different experimental groups, or I cause reaction times to differ because some participants had to answer questions with syntactical violations.

However, sometimes you will not find a cause-and-effect relationship. You will only be looking at the relationship between two variables and you would not be able to say which one depends on the other. For example, if you want to know how time spent in the classroom per day and time spent speaking to native speakers are related, you would be interested in the relationship between these two variables, but you could not say that time spent in the classroom necessarily affected the time students spent speaking to native speakers of the language, or vice versa. In this case, correlation is the type of test you would look at to examine whether there are important relationships between the variables. Robinson (2005) has a research question where he was not looking for a cause-and-effect relationship between the variables. His question was whether there was a relationship between measured intelligence scores and the ability to abstract rules of language implicitly (without conscious awareness). He thus used a correlation to examine the possible relationship between intelligence and implicit induction ability.

The next section gives some practice in identifying dependent and independent variables in experimental studies. All of the research questions given here are from real studies, but for the sake of simplicity sometimes they have been modified so that they focus on one specific aspect of the entire study. But be careful—there may be some questions here where the answer is that there *is* no dependent or independent variable!

2.1.4 Application Activity: Practice in Identifying Variables

Write the independent and dependent variables in the tables. In some cases, there may be more than one independent variable, but there is never more than one dependent variable.

1 Wharton (2000): Do high-proficiency learners use more language learning strategies than low-proficiency learners?

Independent:	Dependent:

2 Munro, Derwing, and Morton (2006): Does L1 background influence the way that English learners rate the speech of other English learners for comprehensibility?

Independent:	Dependent:

3 Hirata (2004): Does pronunciation training with visual feedback help learners improve their perception of phonemically contrastive pairs of words more than training without visual feedback?

Independent:	Dependent:

4 Proctor, August, Carlo, and Snow (2006): What kind of relationship exists among an oral language measure and a reading comprehension measure in English for fourth-grade bilinguals?

Independent:	Dependent:

5 Bialystok, Craik, Klein, and Viswanathan (2004): Do age and being bilingual affect the accuracy with which participants perform on the Simon test (a test that measures whether participants can ignore irrelevant information)?

Independent:	Dependent:

6 Wartenburger et al. (2003): Do age of acquisition (AOA) and proficiency level affect what neural substrates are activated in the brain among different types of Italian–German bilinguals?

Independent:	Dependent:

7 Mizuno (1998) hypothesized that there would be a relationship between the amount of cultural exposure students had before they went overseas and the amount of cultural exposure they would obtain once they were living in the country.

Independent:	Dependent:

8 Larson-Hall (2004): Do learners perform differently in their ability to perceive phonemic contrasts in nonwords in the second language depending on their proficiency level and on the sounds that are contrasted?

Independent:	Dependent:

2.1.5 Summary of Variables

You should now be able to take a research question and decide what the variables are, whether they are categorical or continuous variables, and whether they are dependent or independent variables. Once you can take this step, you will be very far along on the path toward deciding what type of statistical test you'll need to analyze your data. For example, if you know that you have two continuous variables and that you are examining a relationship between the variables (and there is thus no independent or dependent variable) then you'll want to use the statistical technique of correlation. On the other hand, if you have a research question that has a dependent and an independent variable, and the dependent variable is continuous while the independent variable is categorical with only two groups, then you know you'll want to choose a t-test. We'll leave more of this type of fun until later (won't it make you feel *smart* to know what type of test you want?) and now delve into some abstract ideas about statistics that are also necessary for understanding how statistical testing works.

2.1.6 Fixed versus Random Effects (Advanced Topic)

In this book I will not generally distinguish between fixed and random effects. We will essentially treat all independent variables as fixed effects in regression and ANOVA models. A research model that contains both fixed and random effects is called a mixed-effects model, and this is not treated in this book. However, there may be times when it is important to understand the difference between fixed and random effects, so I will include that discussion here.

Fixed effects are those whose parameters are fixed and are the only ones we want to consider. **Random effects** are those effects where we want to generalize beyond the parameters that make up the variable. A "subject" term is clearly a random effect, because we want to generalize the results of our study beyond those particular individuals who took the test. If "subject" were a fixed effect, that would mean we were truly only interested in the behavior of those particular people in our study, and no one else. Note that the difference between fixed and random factors is *not* the same as between-subject and within-subject factors.

Table 2.1 contains a list of attributes of fixed and random effects, and gives possible examples of each for second language research studies (although classification always depends upon the intent of the researcher). This table draws upon information from Crawley (2007), Galwey (2006), and Pinheiro and Bates (2000).

2.2 Understanding Hidden Assumptions about How Statistical Testing Works

If you are a beginner to statistics and have done some reading in the literature that contains statistical results, here is how you might think statistical testing works:

- The researcher lays out a research **hypothesis** that seems plausible given previous research and logical reasoning.
- The researcher presents basic information about participants such as their age, gender, first language, and proficiency level in a second language, and then gives mean scores on whatever test was used.
- The researcher then reports something called a "*p*-value" and proclaims whether the results are statistically significant or not.
- If the results are **statistically significant**, the researcher assumes the hypothesis was correct and goes on to list implications from this finding. If the results are not statistically significant, the researcher tries to explain what other factors might need to be investigated next time.

This impression of how statistical testing works is often not mistaken on the surface (this is indeed what you often read in the research paper), but there is a variety of issues

Table 2.1 Characteristics of Fixed and Random Effects

Fixed effects
Fixed effects have informative labels for factor levels.
If one of the levels of a variable were replaced by another level, the study would be radically altered.
Fixed effects have factor levels that exhaust the possibilities.
We are only interested in the levels that are in our study, and we don't want to generalize further.
Fixed effects are associated with an entire population or certain repeatable levels of experimental factors.

Examples of fixed effects: treatment type
male or female
native speaker or not
child versus adult
first language (L1)
target language

Random effects
Random effects have uninformative factor levels.
If one of the levels of a variable were replaced by another level, the study would be essentially unchanged.
Random effects have factor levels that do not exhaust the possibilities.
We want to generalize beyond the levels that we currently have.
Random effects are associated with individual experimental units drawn at random from a population.

Examples of random effects:
subjects
words or sentences used
classroom
school

that lie beneath the surface that the researcher understands but does not communicate directly to you. It is to these hidden assumptions that we will turn our attention in this section.

2.2.1 Hypothesis Testing

In a research paper, the author usually provides a research question, either directly or indirectly. As a novice reader, you will think that this hypothesis, based on previous research and logical reasoning, is what is tested statistically. You are wrong.

It turns out that a statistical test will not test the logical, intuitively understandable hypothesis that you see in the paper but, instead, it will test a **null hypothesis**, which is rarely one the researcher believes is true. This topic will be treated in more detail in Chapter 4, but it is very confusing to new researchers, so I will introduce it briefly in this chapter.

To conduct null hypothesis testing, we will set up a **null hypothesis** (H_0) that says that there is no difference between groups or that there is no relationship between variables. It may seem strange to set up a hypothesis that we may not really believe, but the idea is that "we can never prove something to be true, but we can prove something to be false" (Howell, 2002, p. 98). Actually, this is a good point to remember for the whole enterprise of scientific hypothesis testing in a **quantitative approach** (one that deals with numbers, thinks that truth can be ascertained objectively, and seeks to have replicable and verifiable results). You should be careful when you make claims that a study has "proved" a point, because we can't prove something to be true! Instead, say that a study *supports* a certain hypothesis or *provides more evidence* that an idea is plausible. The old chestnut says that you cannot prove that unicorns don't exist; you can only gather data that show it is likely that they don't. On the other hand, it will only take one unicorn to prove the hypothesis false.[2]

So the statistically savvy researcher does indeed list the plausible, logical hypothesis in the research paper, but also knows that, when they perform a statistical test, they are testing the null hypothesis. Let's walk through the steps of this with our researcher. Let's say our researcher believes that pre-class massages will decrease language learning anxiety (a unique idea that I have not seen in the literature, but I'm sure I'd like to be a participant in the study!). In the research report, the researcher lays out the logical hypothesis:

$H_{logical}$: Pre-class massages will decrease language learning anxiety, so that a group that gets pre-class massages will have less anxiety than a class that does not.

However, the researcher has also somewhere, perhaps only in their head, laid out a null hypothesis:

H_0: There is no difference in language learning anxiety between the class that gets pre-class massages and the class that does not.

---

2 For advanced readers, it turns out that there *are* ways to prove the null hypothesis, although they are statistically more complicated. See Streiner (2003) for more information.

Now suppose that we indeed find that the amount of language learning anxiety is lower, on average, in the group that gets massages. This is our one unicorn we needed to prove the hypothesis false! Now just because we have proved the hypothesis false does not mean that we have proved the opposite (or the logical) hypothesis is true. But what we saw is that we can **reject the null hypothesis**. Now, if we reject the null hypothesis, this means we reject the idea that there is no difference between groups or no relationship among variables. Once we reject the null hypothesis we will be able to accept the **alternative hypothesis**, which in this case would be:

H_a: There is a difference in language learning anxiety between the class that gets pre-class massages and the class that does not.

If we consider an extremely simplified example relating to groups we can see that mathematically it is easier to prove the null hypothesis false than to prove it true:

H_0: The difference between the groups is 0 (no difference between groups).
H_a: The difference between the groups is not 0 (a difference between groups).

Let's say that we then calculated the average score for each group and found that the difference between groups was only 0.0003. Although this seems like a very small difference, it would refute the null hypothesis that the difference was zero (it would be our unicorn). On the other hand, to prove the alternative hypothesis, we could gather lots of examples of times when the difference between groups was not zero, but this would not *prove* that the difference was zero (in the same way that collecting lots of evidence that horses but not unicorns exist would not prove that unicorns do not exist).

Although hopefully I've convinced you here that a null hypothesis is much easier to prove than the logical reasoned hypothesis you might really set out to investigate, there are problems with using this system of null hypothesis testing. We'll examine the problems with this approach and how to best remedy them in more detail in Chapter 4.

2.2.2 Application Activity: Creating Null Hypotheses

Look at the research questions given below and create a null hypothesis:

1   Boers, Eyckmans, Kappel, Stengers, and Demecheleer (2006): Will explicit instruction in noticing formulaic sequences help one group speak more fluently than another group that does not get this instruction?
2   Proctor, August, Carlo, and Snow (2006): What kind of relationship exists among an oral language measure and a reading comprehension measure in English for fourth-grade bilinguals?
3   Wartenburger et al. (2003): Do age of acquisition (AOA) and proficiency level affect what neural substrates are activated in the brain among different types of Italian–German bilinguals?

2.2.3 Who Gets Tested? Populations versus Samples and Inferential Statistics

The next assumption you may have about how statistics works is that a researcher tests a group of people and these are the people that the researcher wants to comment about. You may think this because the researcher presents summary information about the participants such as their mean age, the number of males and females tested, their L1 backgrounds, and so on. In most cases, you are wrong.

The researcher must indeed test a certain selection of people, called a **sample**. But the researcher in fact does not want to comment just about these people, but instead wants to make a generalization to a wider group of people. If the researcher were really going to comment only on whether brain activation patterns from an fMRI differentiated eight bilingual participants from eight monolingual participants in Dresden, Germany, you probably wouldn't care much. Usually you will care because of what you think the research study says about differences between bilinguals and monolinguals in general and in a variety of languages. What you care about is the wider **population** of people that the sample was drawn from. The population is the group of people (or collection of texts or test scores) in which you are interested.

Many second language research studies test a sample of only 10 or 15 participants in each group, but they are of interest to the wider research community because of the population that readers suppose the findings apply to. The population may be assumed to be all English as a second language learners in the United States, or all French as a foreign language learners in England, or all immigrants of all language backgrounds to any country. Put this way, it may sound a little grandiose to think that our studies, done with a very small sample, apply to such large populations!

The reason that we may be able to make the leap from conclusions drawn on a sample to conclusions drawn to the wider population is because of **inferential statistics**. Inferential statistics are those that can be used to make inferences to the population that the sample is assumed to come from. Inferential statistics can be contrasted with **descriptive statistics**, which are measures that are derived from the sample. So when you read a research report and see the number of males and females who participated, and their mean ages and their mean scores on a test, these numbers are all descriptive statistics. Descriptive statistics may include counts of how many times some feature is found in a piece of writing, or graphs such as histograms which graphically show such counts. Descriptive statistics are very appropriate in situations where you want to numerically describe some kind of phenomenon. More information about how to calculate descriptive statistics is found in the following chapter. You will definitely want to include descriptive statistics in your research report; conversely, if you are reading a research report you should understand what an average score means.

But usually a research report will not stop with descriptive statistics. If a statistical test is conducted, then the researcher assumes that the results of that test can be applied to the wider population from which the sample was selected (unless they explicitly note some reservations). One of the problems with making this kind of inference, however, is that, for inferential statistics to be applicable, the sample should be a **random sample**. This means that each person (or every thing) in the population is equally likely to be picked. When a second language research study is conducted with intact classrooms, although this is convenient for the researcher, the sampling is not random. Maybe students have heard about the teachers and some have deliberately chosen a teacher they think they will like; maybe most of the students who are taking the 8 a.m. Spanish class are business majors who all have required classes at the other times that Spanish is offered. There are any number of factors that may make the intact classroom less than a random sampling of students. An experiment that uses volunteers is also not a random sampling because those who volunteer to do something are often different from those who would never voluntarily include themselves in a study. Hatch and Lazaraton (1991) note that a pool of volunteers is a group from which a random sample might be drawn, although the volunteers still may not be representative of the population.

To imagine a truly random sample, think of a political survey you might hear about on the news that says how many people will vote for the Republican candidate this election year and how many are voting for the Democratic candidate. Such surveys do not sample every registered voter in the country; however, they do identify registered voters in a certain area as their population and then contact a random sampling of those voters until they reach a certain number of participants that has been decided on beforehand (they test about 1,000, I heard John Zogby, a pollster, say on the Diane Rehm show on September 3, 2008). With such a random sampling, pollsters can then perform **inferential statistics** on the data and say that they would expect the same kinds of results even with different samples of people (within certain boundaries of error). They thus try to generalize the results from a particular sample of people to a wider population. Inferential statistics try to say something about the overall population of people or data that they describe, without sampling every piece of data or every person in that set.

As you read this, you may be getting worried. You have never heard of a study in second language research that collected data from a truly random sampling of people! Does that mean that we cannot make any inferences from these studies to a wider population? Come to think of it, you may have noticed that most researchers do not identify the wider population that their sample comes from. If they tested English as a second language (ESL) learners at a certain university, is their sample representative of all ESL learners at that university, or all ESL learners in the entire country, or maybe the entire world? It seems to me that most people who write reports and most people who read them are content to let this issue be fairly vague. Although not having random samples may compromise the external validity of a study, probably the best we can hope for in our field is that both readers and researchers will try to be careful in the limits of the generalizations they make and only draw those that are truly justified. Generalizing to wider populations would also be supported by replication studies, which are not widely seen but have been called for in the field (Polio & Gass, 1997). If you are creating your own research project, you should consult a book such as Mackey and Gass (2005), which gives more detail on research methodology as you decide how to sample your population.

2.2.4 What Does a P-Value Mean?

When you read a research report, you will have noticed lots of mind-numbing mathematical symbols in the Results section. If you are like most novices to statistics, you probably just skip over this entire section and go to the Discussion section, where the author interprets all that gobbledygook for you. That can be OK in some cases but in other cases the author may not be completely accurate in interpreting the results or may overstate their case. If you think the only thing you need to glean from the results section is the *p*-value, then you are wrong.

You won't be able to be a savvy consumer of research (let alone carry out your own analyses) unless you can understand more about all those symbols in the Results section of a paper. So in this section I will try to introduce you to the reasoning behind a statistical test and what things get reported.

At this point we have seen that the descriptive statistics about the sample which was tested should be reported, things like which first language background the participants have, and their mean scores on a test. The next step the researcher will take is to perform a statistical test with the data, which means using inferential statistics. The main results that the researcher will report are the statistic, the degrees of freedom, and the *p*-value. Here is an example from Munro and Derwing (2006, p. 526):

> To compare the accentedness scores across the seven error conditions, we first submitted the listeners' ratings to a one-way repeated measures analysis of variance, with seven levels of the repeated measure. A significant effect of error condition was observed, $F(6, 72) = 76.22$, $p < .001$, h_{2p} (partial eta-squared) = .864.

Munro and Derwing reported an F statistic of 76.22, the degrees of freedom (the total degrees of freedom split into two numbers which reflect the allocation to variability between groups first and variability within groups second), which were 6 and 72, and a *p*-value of <.001. They additionally reported an **effect size** (partial eta-squared) of .864 (an effect size measures how much effect can be attributed to the influence of an independent variable on a dependent variable, or to the relationship between variables; effect sizes will be discussed further in Chapter 4). I will give a brief explanation here of what these numbers mean.

First of all, even if the researcher does not explicitly state what kind of statistical test was used, you can tell what kind of test was used by the **statistic** that is reported. Each statistical test has a certain mathematical symbol associated with it. For example:

- a chi-square test has a chi (χ)
- correlation has a Pearson's *r*
- a *t*-test has a *t*
- an ANOVA has an *F*

This statistic is calculated and its result is a number. In general, the higher this number is and the greater it is than the number 1, the more likely the *p*-value is to be very small. Munro and Derwing (2006) report a very large *F*-value of 76.22, and you can notice that their *p*-value is very small. I will return to the question of what this statistic is presently. At this point, you can think of it as the result of a calculation involving mostly mean scores and standard deviations. I assume that you are familiar with what means or averages are, but I will elaborate on standard deviations in Chapter 3. For now, think of **standard deviations** as measuring how much people vary from the mean.

The next number you should see is something that represents the degrees of free-dom. The **degrees of freedom** basically counts how many free components you have in your data set. To understand what that means, let's imagine we have four contestants on a game show, and each gets to pick one of four doors, behind which there is either a great prize, such as a car or a boat, or a booby prize. How many of the contestants have any freedom to choose a door? Figure 2.1 will show visually what I will describe in words here.

Contestant 1, Alice, can choose door 1, 2, 3, or 4. She chooses door 2. Contestant 2, Gary, can choose door 1, 3, or 4. He chooses door 4. Now Contestant 3, K'Lynne, can choose either door 1 or door 3. It's not as much choice as Alice had, but it's still a choice. She chooses door 3. Now the last contestant, Contestant 4, Eric, has no choice. He is left with door 1. In this case, we would say there were 3 degrees of freedom, because three of the four people have a choice, but the last person's choice is fixed. We have only three choices that include some variation, and this means we have 3 degrees of freedom.

When you perform a test that has group variation as well as individual variation, as shown in the quote by Munro and Derwing (2006) above, you will need to report two numbers for the degrees of freedom. The first one deals with the amount of variation due to groups. Thus, even if Munro and Derwing had not told you, you would know that there were seven groups in the ANOVA test because the first number, for group degrees of freedom, is 6, and that means there were seven groups.

The second number is reported as the "error" degrees of freedom in an ANOVA

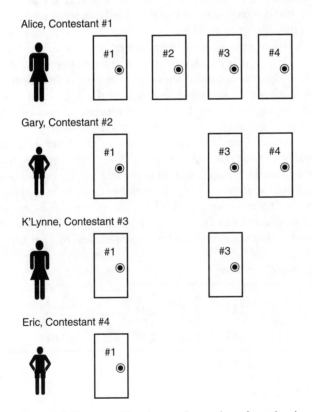

Figure 2.1 Degrees of freedom as the number of people who can make a choice (=3 here).

table, and this is the total degrees of freedom (which is always N–1, where N is the **sample size** or number of participants in the study) minus the variation for number of groups (k, or the between-group variation).[3] The second degree of freedom (df) reported is equal to $k(n-1)$, where n=the number of observations per group. We can therefore figure out how many observations are in each group in the Munro and Derwing report: $72=k(n-1)=7(n-1)$, therefore $7n=72 + 7 = 79$, so $n=79/7 = 11.3$ (this is not quite equal to the 13 listeners in each group reported in Munro and Derwing but possibly they used a correction, which can affect the df).

You may wonder why you need to know what degrees of freedom are anyway. When researchers had to look up information for their statistical tests in tables, the degrees of freedom was a piece of information that was necessary to determine the **critical value** for finding statistical significance or not (the number above which the statistical test would be considered "significant"). Nowadays, if you use a computer to calculate your statistics (which is what I am assuming you will do!), you will not personally need to take note of your degrees of freedom. However, you should still report it. Table 2.2 gives you an idea of how this worked. For example, if you had a t-test, you would look up the alpha level you were interested in (Table 2.2 includes only a=0.05, but a real table would include many choices) and find the degrees of freedom; that would tell you the critical value for a one-tailed test (but I have doubled it so that the critical value given here is for a two-tailed test). As an example, if you calculated a t-value of 2.05 when you had 14 degrees of freedom, and your a=0.05, then you would find that your critical value was 2.14, and you would thus be able to reject the null hypothesis because your calculated t-value was less than the critical value.

Another reason to understand what degrees of freedom are is that, in studies where authors may neglect to tell you the number of participants or groups they used, you can calculate this yourself by knowing the degrees of freedom. And last of all, degrees of freedom can be a check on someone else's statistical work. If the degrees of freedom are impossible (given what the author has told you about numbers of groups and sample size), you will know something strange has happened with the statistics.

Finally in this section we want to understand what a p-value is. The **p-value** is the probability that we would find a statistic as large as the one we found if the null hypothesis were true. In other words, the p-value represents the probability of the data given the hypothesis, which we could write as $p(D|H_o)$. Remember that our hypothesis is the null hypothesis, which says there is no relationship between variables or no difference between groups. So, in Munro and Derwing's results above, the p-value of less than .001 says that the chance that we would find an F statistic of 76.22 if there

Table 2.2 Selected Critical Values of the *T*-Distribution

df =	1	2	3	4	5	6	7	8	9	10
p=0.05	12.71	4.30	3.18	2.78	2.57	2.45	2.36	2.31	2.26	2.23
df =	11	12	13	14	15	16	17	18	19	20
p=0.05	2.20	2.18	2.16	2.14	2.13	2.12	2.11	2.10	2.09	2.09

---

3 This does not hold true if the test has repeated measures, however.

were really no difference between groups is less than 1 in 1,000. This is a pretty small chance, and we decide we are safe in rejecting the null hypothesis and in assuming there are some differences among the groups. In general, in the field of second language research we use a cut-off point of 0.05 when we decide whether to reject null hypotheses (although I will argue in Chapter 4 that it would be a good idea to set this higher to 0.10).

In Chapter 4 I will also talk more about understanding *p*-values. But, for now, just memorize this phrase in order to understand *p*-values the correct way:

> Meaning of the *p*-value: The probability of finding a [insert statistic name here] this large or larger if the null hypothesis were true is [insert *p*-value].

In sum, the researcher will not just proclaim the *p*-value and declare their hypothesis to be statistically significant or not. They will in fact tell you, overtly or not, what kind of statistical test they used and report the value of that statistic, they will report the degrees of freedom associated with the test (which can tell you something about the number of participants or groups if this was not mentioned), and they will report a *p*-value. I will argue in Chapter 4 that we can improve our statistics by not just reporting these three data points but also adding information about effect sizes, power, and using confidence intervals instead of *p*-values.

2.2.5 Understanding Statistical Reporting

The previous section explained briefly how to interpret three numbers you will often see reported in experimental results—the test statistic, the degrees of freedom, and the *p*-value. Let's practice using results from real journal articles and see if you can begin to understand what those mysterious statistical reports mean. In this section I'll walk you through the answers; then I'll ask you in the next section to do it on your own.

1   Larson-Hall (2008, p. 49):

> In fact, the correlation [with amount of input] is not statistical for the phonemic discrimination task among the earlier starters ($r=-.07$, $n=61$, $p=.57$, power $=.08$), but it is statistical for the GJT ($r=.27$, $n=61$, $p=.035$, power $=.56$).

a.   What does the *r* reported here refer to?
The statistic r *is used to give the results for a correlation.*

b.   This report does not give the degrees of freedom. Why not?
The total number of participants is given instead of the degrees of freedom (n=61). Correlations don't report degrees of freedom; they report total sample size.

c.   What does $p=.57$ mean (spell out the meaning of a *p*-value in words; also make the inference as to what it means for the null hypothesis that there is no relationship between the variables)?
p=.57 means "the probability of finding an r *this large or larger if the null hypothesis were true is 57%." This is quite likely, so we cannot reject the null hypothesis and*

we conclude that there is no relationship between amount of input and scores on the phonemic discrimination task.

d.   The second reported correlation has a p-value less than 0.05, making it a statistical correlation. What do you notice about the relative sizes of the r-values of the non-statistical versus the statistical results?

The r of the first correlation is negative, but this doesn't make any difference. However, the second r-value is 0.27, which is much larger than the first r-value of 0.07. The larger a statistic is, the more likely it will have a small p-value. A correlation can only range from 0 to 1, so you can see that relatively the 0.27 is not huge but it is not so small either.

2   Baker and Trofimovich (2006, p. 239):

The perception and production scores . . . were submitted to two separate one-way analyses of variance (ANOVAs). These analyses yielded a significant group effect (defined as a combination of AOA and LOR variables) in perception, $F(4,45) = 31.30$, $p < .0001$, and in production, $F(4,45) = 46.03$, $p < .0001$.

a.   What does the F reported here refer to?

The F-value reports the results of an ANOVA test.

b.   Using the degrees of freedom, calculate how many groups were tested. How many participants were in each group?

The first degree of freedom (4) refers to the number of groups. The number of groups equals df +1, so there were 5 groups tested. The second degree of freedom refers to the number of participants (45), and the formula is df=k(n−1) where n=number in each group. We know there were 5 groups, so 45 = 5(n−1). Solving the equation, n=10. There were 10 participants in each of the 5 groups.

c.   What does $p < .0001$ mean (spell out the meaning of a p-value in words; also make the inference as to what it means for the null hypothesis that the groups do not differ)?

p < .0001 means "the probability of finding an F this large or larger if the null hypothesis were true is less than 1 in 10,000." This is a very low probability so we can reject the null hypothesis and accept the alternative hypothesis that the group categorization affected scores in perception and production.

3   Inagaki and Long (1999, p. 22):

Gain scores of subjects receiving models were not statistically different from those of subjects receiving recasts, however, $t(14) = .23$, $p>.05$, again disconfirming Hypothesis 3.

a.   What does the t reported here refer to?

The t-value reports the results of a t-test.

b.   Knowing that the degrees of freedom associated with a t-statistic equal the number of participants minus 2 (1 for each of the groups), how many total participants were there?

There were 16 participants (14 + 2).

c.   What does $p>.05$ mean (spell out the meaning of a p-value in words; also make the inference as to what it means for the null hypothesis that the groups do not differ)?

p>.05 means "the probability of finding a t this large or larger if the null hypothesis were true is greater than 5%." By the way, it would be nice to know how much larger this number is than 0.05, because if it were, say, .057 that would be very different from 0.75. Anyway, the inference is that we cannot reject the null hypothesis and conclude that the groups do not differ.

d. What do you notice about the size of the t-statistic in this study compared to, say, the F statistic in question 2?

The t-statistic is 0.23 while the F-statistics were 31 and 46. The t-statistic is a lot smaller. In fact, as a rule of thumb, if a t or F or χ^2 is larger than 2 the p-value will probably be lower than 0.05.

4   Mackey (2006, p. 421):

... learners who noticed questions being significantly more likely to develop in terms of higher-level questions (83% of those who noticed questions developed): $\chi^2(1, 23) = 7.326$, $p = 0.007$.

a. What does the χ^2 reported here refer to?

The χ^2 reports the results of a chi-square test.

b. Normally only one df is reported for this test, and that is the first number in parentheses given here after the statistic. The df is equal to the number of rows in the table (R) minus 1 multiplied by the number of columns in the table (C) minus 1. Knowing that df=(R−1)(C−1), how many rows and columns were involved in this test?

There are two rows and two columns.

c. What does $p=.007$ mean (spell out the meaning of a p-value in words; also make the inference as to what it means for the null hypothesis that there is no relationship between the variables)?

p=.007 means "the probability of finding a χ^2 this large or larger if the null hypothesis were true is 7 in 1,000." This is a very small probability and we can reject the null hypothesis and conclude that there is a relationship between noticing questions and progressing to higher-level questions.

d. What do you notice about the size of the statistic?

It is 7, which is quite a bit larger than 2 (and thus the p-value is quite low).

2.2.6 Application Activity: Understanding Statistical Reporting

Now that you've worked through the examples in the previous section, try a few more on your own:

5   French and O'Brien (2008, p. 9):

... tests, conducted to test whether participants differed on the measures between Time 1 and Time 2, showed that, overall, the participants did improve on ENWR, $t(103)=14.292$, $p<.001$.

a. What does the t reported here refer to?

    b. How many people participated in this test?

    c. What does $p < .001$ mean (spell out the meaning of a p-value in words; also make the inference as to what it means for the null hypothesis that there is no difference between Time 1 and Time 2)?

    d. What do you notice about the size of the t-statistic?

6   Polio, Fleck, and Leder (1998, p. 54):

Table 6 Results of ANOVA for EFT/TT

Source of variance	SS	DF	MS	F	sig
Between subject					
E/C	.00	1	.00	.01	.935
within group	3.51	63	.06		

This one is a little different! Polio, Fleck, and Leder did not report statistical results in words; they reported them in a table and then interpreted the inferences for their hypotheses. This part of the statistics tested whether there were differences in groups which received error correction or not.

    a. What does the F reported here refer to?

    b. What do you notice about the size of the F?

    c. How many people in total participated in this test (if I tell you that there were two groups and remind you that n=number in each group)?

    d. What does sig=.935 mean (sig refers to the p-value; spell out the meaning of a p-value in words; also make the inference as to what it means for the null hypothesis that there is no difference between groups)?

7   Rosa and O'Neill (1999):
Rosa and O'Neill also reported their results in a table, but I am going to interweave those results with their prose:

> Frequency counts of the number of individuals that produced each type of verbal report were performed. . . . Results revealed a significant relationship between formal instruction and type of verbal report [p. 536]. . . . df=4, $\chi^2=16.454$, $p<.05$ [p. 537].

    a. What does the χ^2 reported here refer to?

    b. How many rows and columns were involved in this test, if I tell you the number of rows=the number of columns?

    c. What does $p<.05$ mean (spell out the meaning of a p-value in words; also make the inference as to what it means for the null hypothesis that there is no relationship between the variables)?

8   Williams (2005, p. 287):

> Next, correlations between mean phase 1 generalization performance and the following factors were calculated: performance on the PSTM test, $r=.01$, the number of L2s spoken to an intermediate level or better, $r=.263$, and the

number of gender languages spoken to an intermediate level or better, including L1, $r=0.357$, $p<.05$.

a. What do the rs reported here refer to?
b. How many people's results were tested in this statistical test?
c. What does $p<.05$ mean (spell out the meaning of a p-value in words; also make the inference as to what it means for the null hypothesis that there is no relationship between the variables; lastly remark on the fact that there are three tests but only one p-value)?

2.2.7 The Inner Workings of Statistical Testing

As a novice to statistics, when you read a research report it may seem that finding "statistically significant" results is the holy grail of research. If a p-value of less than 0.05 is found, the author seems to assume that their (logical and plausible) hypothesis was correct and moves ahead assuming that the hypothesis is now established. It is much rarer to find in the published literature results that do not establish the hypothesis that the author was hoping for. Russell and Spada (2006) state that a publication bias against studies which do not find "significant" results for treatments is an established fact. When a study gets published where a treatment did not result in a positive result, the author will often try to explain the problem by referring to another explanation that could be plausible (instead of just thinking that, especially in the case of studies with small sample sizes, the lack of an effect may be due to too little power; I argue this case in the last section of Chapter 4). In this section I want to explain how hypothesis testing works so that it will seem less mysterious and you will be able to be more critical of the process.

You already know from previous sections that the result of a statistical test is a statistic such as t or F, and there is an associated probability for that statistic. But how is that probability calculated? Let's start from the beginning thinking about what a statistical test tests. To illustrate this process, let's take the question proposed by one of my students and listed earlier in the chapter. We want to know whether students of Spanish who play an online role-playing game will learn Spanish faster than students who meet with a conversation partner for the same amount of time every day. So let's say we set it up so both groups do this extra work in Spanish for 30 minutes a day, three times a week. After a semester, we test our students using a 50-item cloze test. We tested both groups at the beginning of the semester too, and we find that the game group on average gained 10 points on the test over the semester while the conversation group gained 7 points. There is thus a mean difference between the groups of 3 points.

Now there is always variability in measurement. For example, if the same Spanish student took the cloze test one day and then again a day later, that student might receive different test scores (you might rightly argue that the increase was because the student had learned from the test, but let's suppose we had two different but equal versions and the student took a different one each time). The same kind of variability happens on a group level as well. The group who played online games might have had a gain score of 12 if they were tested on another day (with a different but equivalent version of the test). Since fluctuation is normal, we want to know what amount of fluctuation is not just due to chance alone. That is, if the groups differ by 3 points only, this amount of variation may just be due to random fluctuations in scores. However, if the groups differ by 10 points, it will become unlikely that this much variation is due to simply chance. As Crawley (2005, p. 2) says, "We need a way of discriminating between variation that is scientifically interesting, and variation that just reflects background heterogeneity. That is why we need statistics."

This part is where common sense can come in too. Statistically it may be possible to find a difference between our groups when there are only 3 points difference in gain scores, but you yourself should realize that a gain of 3 points on a 50-point test is not very much. Now this may be good news—if students could use the role-playing game and get the benefits of talking to native speakers without having to actually seek out native speakers to talk to, then even if online game playing isn't spectacularly better than talking to native speakers it may be a much easier choice with pretty much the same results. Do you see in this case that it really doesn't matter whether your statistics say the difference between the groups is "significant" or not? Even if the statistics say that the game-playing group is statistically better than the conversation group, the size of the difference is not huge (this can be measured formally by something called an effect size, which I discuss in detail in Chapter 4). And if the statistics say there is no difference between the groups, that doesn't matter, because playing an online game may logistically be easier than finding native speakers, but has good results.

Now we return to how statistical testing works. In this case we would use a t-test to find out whether the difference between two mean scores is statistically significant. The t-test is not mysterious—it calculates a number based on subtracting the mean score of one group from that of the other group and then dividing this by a measure of the variation in scores that involves the standard deviation and the sample size. This calculation results in a number. This number is a point on the x-axis of a **t-distribution**. The t-distribution looks a lot like a **normal distribution** (what you might think of as a bell-shaped curve) but is slightly different, and its shape has been calculated by previous statisticians depending on the degrees of freedom it has. For example, the left panel of Figure 2.2 compares the t-distribution for 2 degrees of freedom to a normal distribution. The two distributions are similar, but you can see that the normal distribution (in black) is more concentrated around the mean than the t-distribution (in grey). The right panel of Figure 2.2 shows how the shape of the t-distribution changes as more degrees of freedom are used (the more degrees of freedom, the more the center peaks and gets sharper, the more the tails get lower, and the more it looks like a normal curve!).

Let's say the value of the t-statistic is somewhere around 3.5 with a df=2. The probability that we would find a number this large or larger will be the area under the curve from the point of that t-statistic number to the end of the curve. Actually, the area calculated will be from both sides of the curve, the extreme right and extreme left, if you are testing the hypothesis that the difference between groups could go either way; this is called **two-tailed testing**, and I will explain it further in Chapter 4. So Figure 2.3 shows that, if you run a line up from +3.5 on the x-axis to the density probability curve, all of the area to the right under the curve is 0.0364. Add to that the area under the curve on the left tail, and the p-value is 0.0364 + 0.0364=0.0728. This area is the p-value that the computer will calculate for you!

Now you already know what the p-value means. It is the probability of finding a statistic that large or larger (but now you know *why* we say "or larger," since the probability is counting the area under the curve for larger numbers as well) if the null

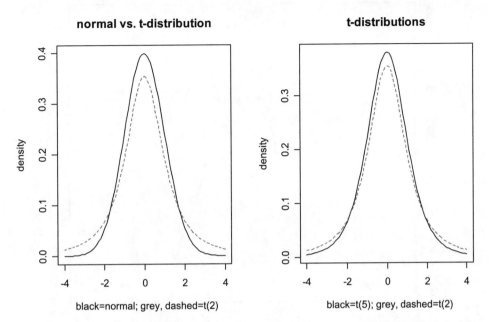

Figure 2.2 Probability density functions. On the left, the normal distribution (the black line) has less data in the tails (the extreme ends) than the *t*-distribution with 2 df. On the right, the *t*-distribution at df=2 (grey line) and df=5 (black line) are compared.

hypothesis is true. If the probability of finding such a number is large, that means that it is quite likely we would find a variation this large in the sample just from random chance, and thus we could not **reject the null hypothesis**. Just because we cannot reject the null does not mean, however, that we must accept the null hypothesis (in other words, we do not have to conclude that our treatment had no effect).[4] One reason for not accepting the null hypothesis might be because we did not have enough **power** to find differences when there actually were differences—perhaps sample sizes were too small or the measurement error was too large to find real differences (power is the probability of detecting a statistical result when there are in fact differences between groups or relationships between variables. You might think of the analogy of a microscope, which needs sufficient power in order to see sufficient detail). In this case we might conclude that no conclusion could be made! Further testing with more participants would be necessary.

Now in this example I demonstrated how the *p*-value would be calculated for a *t*-test using a *t*-distribution, but the other types of statistical tests also use their own distributions. For example, there is a chi-square distribution and an *F*-distribution. Just like the

---

4 Some authors, including Wilkinson and the Task Force on Statistical Inference (1999), believe that the phrase "accept the null hypothesis" is unfortunate and should never be used. Instead, we should say "fail to reject the null hypothesis." Howell (2002) states that there is still much debate in this area and that some traditions encourage the idea of either rejecting or accepting the null hypothesis. In order not to confuse novice readers further in this confusing area, I will use the term "accept the null hypothesis" instead of "fail to reject."

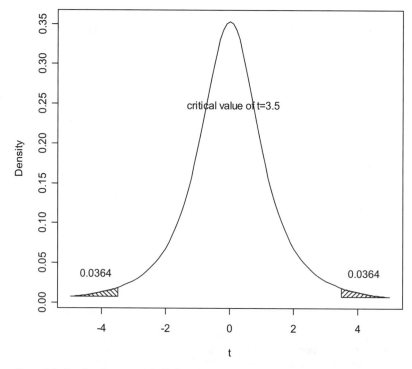

Figure 2.3 A *t*-distribution with df=2 evaluated at a critical value of 3.5. The area shaded under the curve is the probability that we will find a critical value this large or larger.

t-distribution, these tests change shape depending on the number of degrees of freedom. The details of this don't matter to you, but what I do want you to understand is that there is no mystery to the entire process.

2.2.8 Application Activity: The Inner Workings of Statistical Testing

1   In your own words, explain what a statistic such as a *t*-value is.
2   In your own words, explain how a *p*-value is associated with a statistic such as a *t*-value.

2.2.9 One More Thing I Wish Researchers Would Report— Confidence Intervals

If you are an astute reader, you may have detected some bit of skepticism from me about the whole enterprise of using *p*-values to make decisions as to whether your findings are important or not. Although what you normally read in a research report does, on the surface, all seem to hinge on whether that *p*-value is below 0.05 or not, hopefully you have seen throughout the discussion here that 0.05 is a rather arbitrary number. There is nothing magic about it, and if you have a *p*-value of 0.051 this of course will not mean that what you have found is unimportant. Most authors will label a *p*-value of 0.051 as "approaching significance," but Kline (2004) points out that they would never label a p-value of 0.049 as "approaching insignificance"! In any case, as I will argue further in Chapter 4, too great a reliance on p-values obscures the more important issue of how important your results are, and how reliable they are in the sense of whether they could be replicated.

I will suggest that a better result to report is the **95% confidence interval**. A **confidence interval** can provide the same information that a p-value does and more. A 95% confidence interval will give a range of values for some statistic such as the mean difference between scores. In the example in Section 2.2.7 I said the mean difference between the online game group and the conversation group was 3 points. A 95% confidence interval for the mean difference for the groups might be (−1, 4.28). This would mean that the difference between groups could be as high as 4.28 (with, say, the online game group doing better than the conversation group) or as low as 1 point in the opposite direction (with the conversation group now doing better than the online game group). The 95% confidence interval gives the range of values that the mean difference would take if the study were replicated 100 times. By looking at the confidence interval, we can see that there is no statistical difference between groups. That is, because the mean difference may be zero (since the confidence interval passes through zero), we know that the difference of 3 points between groups is not surprising. It most likely happened just because of chance variation in scores. But additionally we know something about how reliable and precise our statistic of 3 points difference is too. If the difference could be as large as 4.28 points or as small as −1 point, we get a sense of how different the groups would be in future replications of the study.

How can we say anything about future replications of the study? Well, here is where I need to clean up the precision of what I said in the previous paragraph. I said there that the 95% confidence interval will give a range of values for some *statistic* such as the mean difference between scores. Actually, that is not quite right. The confidence interval (CI) will give a range of values for a **parameter** such as a mean difference. What is the difference between a statistic and a parameter? When we perform a statistical test, whether descriptive or inferential, we label the number that we have calculated as a **statistic**. Statistics are designated by letters such as X for the mean (a **sampling statistic**) or r for the measure of correlation between two variables (a **test statistic**). Statistics are the measurements we take from our particular sample, but these statistics are really just guesses for the actual parameter that applied to the population. What we really want to measure is the parameter of our population, and by basing statistical inferences on certain distributions (such as the normal distribution or the t-distribution seen earlier in the chapter) we can infer properties of our population parameters. Statisticians distinguish between statistics and parameters by writing a statistic with a hat above the letter like this $\hat{\chi}$ or by writing a bar above it, like this $\overline{X}$ (but in this book I will just use the symbols for samples mainly). So the 95% confidence interval uses the sampled data but, by basing calculations on parametric distributions like the normal distribution, it returns a "range of plausible values for the corresponding parameter" (Kline, 2004, p. 27) of whatever statistic we are interested in.

To summarize, confidence intervals provide the same information as p-values in the sense that they provide information about whether to accept or reject the null hypothesis, but they also provide additional data. If the confidence interval is very small we know that we have a precise estimate of the parameter, while if the interval is quite large we know that we are not very sure about the value of the parameter and that the statistic we found may not be a very good estimate. SPSS does not always provide confidence intervals for every statistic, but I will report them when possible throughout the book.

2.2.10 Summary of Hidden Assumptions

Hopefully, after going through this section of the book you have realized that there is more to the results section to think about than just a p-value. First, you need to realize that the researcher has had to set up a null hypothesis in order to test their real and plausible hypothesis. Second, you should realize that, if the researcher uses inferential statistics such as a correlation or an ANOVA, they are hoping that the results of their research will apply to a wider population than just those sampled in the study. Third, you have learned how to interpret what a statistic means, what degrees of freedom are, and how a p-value is calculated. Last, I have provided a little bit of information to show that p-values should not be the main way of deciding if research findings are important or interesting. Other types of statistics, such as confidence intervals or effect sizes (discussed further in Chapter 4), provide more information about such questions.

2.3 Parametric and Non-Parametric Statistics

I said earlier that statistics that make inferences about the population are called inferential statistics. Another name for this kind of statistics is **parametric statistics**, and the reason for this should be clear to you now. Parametric statistics try to determine, from the statistics calculated from an actual sample, what the parameters of the population are. In other words, it uses what can actually be measured (the statistics) to estimate what the thing of interest that we can't actually measure is (the parameter). Parametric statistics are based on assuming a certain type of distribution of the data, which is why there are many assumptions about data distribution that need to be met in order to legitimately use parametric statistics.

Parametric statistics are not the only kind of statistics available, however. Many people have heard about **non-parametric statistics** as well. Non-parametric statistics do not rely on the data having a normal distribution. Almost all of the parametric tests which are discussed in this book have non-parametric counterparts, and these tests will be addressed in Chapter 14. Some non-parametric tests you may have seen performed in the literature include Mann–Whitney U tests for two independent samples, or the Kruskal–Wallis one-way ANOVA.

Many researchers are reluctant to use non-parametric statistics because they have heard that they have less power than parametric statistics. If we understand that the term "power" means the probability of finding a statistical difference when one exists, using either a parametric test or a non-parametric test when the data do not follow the assumptions can result in the loss of power to find statistical differences when they do in fact exist. Thus it is not accurate to say that non-parametric tests always have less power than parametric ones.

Non-parametric tests do not require that data be normally distributed, but they still impose assumptions on data distribution, such as the requirement that **variances** be equal across groups or across the data set (the variance is a measure of how tightly or loosely bunched up scores are around the mean). Maxwell and Delaney (2004, p. 113) note that a non-parametric Kruskal–Wallis test requires variances to be equal and, if they are not, this non-parametric test will perform just as badly as the parametric one-way ANOVA when variances are not equal. Rank-based methods such as Kruskal–Wallis can provide some protection against the effects of **outliers** (data which is markedly different from the rest of the data), which parametric methods cannot. However, one cannot make a blanket statement about which kind of test is more powerful—it all depends on the circumstances. Maxwell and Delaney state that Kruskal–Wallis will be more powerful than an ANOVA F-test when the population distribution is symmetric but has heavy tails (what Wilcox, 2001, calls a "mixed normal" distribution), and can also be more powerful when distributions are identical but skewed (Maxwell & Delaney, 2004, p. 142). A "mixed normal" distribution or "contaminated normal" distribution looks much like a normal distribution in the middle part of the distribution, but has slightly heavier tails than a normal distribution.

Another kind of non-parametric statistics that has gained favor recently among statisticians is called **robust statistics** (see Larson-Hall & Herrington, forthcoming, for more information about why robust statistics are desirable in applied linguistics). Wilcox (2001) laments that, although modern statistics has made great strides in improving methodology and practical applications for quantitative methods, the average researcher in an applied field generally has no knowledge of these modern advances. Introductory statistics textbooks cover the classic statistics methods which were formulated prior to 1960 and, most tellingly, before modern computing power was available. Robust methods were developed in response to the realization that even small deviations from a normal distribution could cause the "classical" parametric statistics to fail (Jurečková & Picek, 2006; Wilcox, 2001). In other words, "classical" procedures were not robust (did not perform well) in the face of some kinds of violations of assumptions.

2.3.1 More about Robust Statistics (Advanced Topic)

Many textbooks will claim that parametric statistics are robust to violations of assumptions. For example, you may have heard that the Student's t distribution (the t-test) is rather robust to violations of assumptions. According to Wilcox (2003), the Student's t distribution upon which the t-test is based can perform accurately if both groups have identical distributions, equal variances, and equal sample sizes. Student's t is not very robust to even slight departures from a normal distribution. Even just one outlier in a group can change our conclusion from rejecting the null hypothesis to one where we would have to accept it. This is because an outlier will inflate the group variance, and having a larger variance in the denominator will decrease the t-statistic. The smaller the t-statistic is, the more likely we will reject.

Wilcox (2003, p. 242) gives a striking example of the influence of just one outlier. Suppose that we had two groups who received the scores shown in Table 2.3 on a vocabulary test.

Table 2.3 Scores on an Imaginary Vocabulary Test

Group 1:	4	5	6	7	8	9	10	11	12	13
Group 2:	1	2	3	4	5	6	7	8	9	10

In Table 2.3, the sample mean for Group 1 is $X_1 = 8.5$, the mean for Group 2 is $X_2 = 5.5$, and the value of a t-test comparing the two groups is $t=2.22$. The critical value for t is 2.1, so, since the t is higher than the critical value, the probability that the two groups come from the same population, given the results we found, is less than 5%, and so we would reject the null hypothesis that the groups have equal means. We would say that Group 1 performed better than Group 2, because their mean score is higher, and the t-test tells us it is statistically different from that of Group 1. Now consider what would happen if we increased the largest score in Group 1 from 13 to 23. Clearly 23 would be an **outlier** to the data point in this distribution. This would make the sample mean $X_1 = 9.5$. It would seem then that we would have even more reason to find the groups to be different from one another. However, the increase in this one score means that the sample variance (s^2) has also increased, from $s_1^2 = 9.17$ to 29.17. As a result, t now decreases to $t=2.04$ and we can no longer reject the null hypothesis! This example illustrates how even one outlier can have a large effect on the conclusions we draw when we use theoretical assumptions about our distributions.

It is true that most second language researchers, when faced with an obvious outlier like this, would probably just remove it, apparently removing the problem. However, taking away outliers in this fashion is not objective and not replicable. Sometimes, in a large data set, when one outlier is removed, other points that previously did not seem like outliers then become so. Robust statistics provides objective and replicable ways to remove outliers, such as using a trimmed mean.

The problem with the mean is that it is unduly influenced by outliers and is not robust to small deviations from normality in the sample distribution. The median is useful when the distribution is skewed or non-normal, but it discards all of the information in the sample except for one or two numbers. Modern statistical estimators of location such as the trimmed mean have been formulated to be more robust to violations in normality and to outliers than the mean, but include more information than the median. Although it may seem counterintuitive to "throw away" information from the sample by using trimmed means or M-estimators, Wilcox (2001) asserts that, when there are outliers in the data (which results in a distribution with heavy tails), the 20% trimmed mean gives higher power, shorter confidence intervals, and a variance that is smaller, and thus closer to the population means. Even when the distribution does not have heavy tails, Wilcox says that for skewed curves the trimmed mean will be a more accurate measure than the untrimmed mean, again providing an advantage when hypothesis testing or computing confidence intervals. And when distributions are completely normal (as I suspect they almost never are in our field), trimmed means are only slightly less accurate than the sample mean, so almost all the evidence is in favor of consistently using robust measures of location.

According to Herrington (2001), robust estimation "involves calculating estimators that are relatively insensitive to the tails of a data distribution, but which conform to a normal theory approximation at the center of the data distribution" (p. 2). Robust estimators thus use principled ways of eliminating data points that can be considered outliers. Robust statistics will be nearly as powerful as parametric statistics if data is completely normally distributed, but they will be more powerful (meaning they will be more likely to find differences if they exist) and more accurate (meaning they will estimate more precise confidence intervals) than parametric statistics if the data is not normally distributed. There are thus very good reasons for preferring robust statistics over parametric or classical non-parametric statistics. Robust statistics are different from both parametric and non-parametric statistics, not just a way of cleaning up the data before using parametric statistics. However, in kind robust statistics are more similar to parametric statistics than non-parametric statistics.

Unfortunately, at this time SPSS does not incorporate robust statistics into its menu of statistical procedures. However, look for such procedures to be implemented in the future as this type of analysis replaces the classical methods that will be covered in this book. Such robust procedures are available already in statistical programs like S-PLUS or R, which have incorporated advances in statistical methods more rapidly than SPSS.

Chapter 3

Describing Data Numerically and Graphically and Assessing Assumptions for Parametric Tests

The business of the statistician is to catalyze the scientific learning process.

George E. P. Box

Science often consists of taking objects and putting them in some kind of arrangement in order to see a pattern which we could not previously see. This chapter will describe different ways to order your data in order to find patterns. Although numerical summaries can be helpful in finding patterns, human beings often find that graphics are even more helpful in achieving this goal. In general I will provide information and examples of graphics that are most suited to the statistical tests treated at the beginning of each chapter. However, this chapter provides information that is common and necessary for every statistical test treated in this book.

First of all, I will talk about measures of location which try to give a sense of the typical score of a data set. The number we will be most interested in is the mean, but I will also discuss the median and the mode. Next I will talk about measures of variability in the data, such as the standard deviation and the variance. These measures give a sense of how far scores deviate from the average. SPSS has tests that can call for a variety of measures of location and variability at the same time.

A second focus of the chapter is to look at both numerical and graphical summaries of data that help explore whether data fit the assumptions that are necessary to perform parametric statistics. It may seem strange to talk about satisfying assumptions for statistical tests before we have even begun to talk about the statistical tests themselves, but the assumption that your sampled data come from a **normal distribution** of data holds for every test in parametric statistics. I will demonstrate a variety of graphic and numerical ways to test this assumption. The assumption of equal variances (called the **homogeneity of variance** assumption) if there are different groups of data is one that applies in every case where groups are found. The main ways to test this assumption are to look at the standard deviation and graphically at **boxplots**.

3.1 Numerical Summaries of Data

The more data that is given in a research paper the better. I personally think it would be very valuable if the data sets which research studies are based on were widely available, either as online appendices to journals or published in their entirety along with submitted articles (and I do again thank those researchers who have allowed me to use their data in this book). At the very least, researchers can mention that data sets are available upon request. Anyone who has done a statistical analysis on their data realizes that not every question that could be asked has been asked. Not every piece of information about the data has been inserted into the article (I know, I've tried to, and reviewers have found it very tedious!). Having this information available could help future researchers who want to ask different questions than the ones the author did. It also provides a check against errors. I personally have had reviewers find some errors in my data set by noticing some anomalous entries in the data tables I submitted along with my articles. When I have gone back to check, I have found mistakes in data entry. I am getting personal here because I want to show that everyone can make mistakes with statistics and it is perhaps to be expected. When authors do not provide a way for others to check on their numbers and calculations, we are left to trust that an expert in *linguistics* has done all of their *statistics* in a reasonable way, and this may not be a good assumption.

Every original research paper should include both a numeric and a graphic summary of the data set. A numeric summary should include at a minimum the mean, standard deviation, and number of observations. It could also include the range or the actual minimum and maximum points. The following sections will show how to calculate means, standard deviations, and number of observations.

One of the goals when doing a numerical summary is for you to become familiar with trends in your data, such as the "typical" score (which you will often measure with the mean), how spread-out your data is (which you can measure with the standard deviation and the range), and, if you have groups, how they differ from one another. Another goal should be to screen your data. Sometimes errors will enter your data set during data entry, and numerical summaries can help you look for anomalies in your data. For example, if you look at the minimum and maximum scores on a 200-point test, a maximum score of 300 would alert you to a problem. If you found that the mean and standard deviation of one group were wildly divergent from those of another group, you may also have reason to suspect there is some problem with your data entry. In these cases, using graphic summaries (described in all of Section 3.4) can also help you quickly pinpoint points in your data set that may be implausible. If you have entered data correctly but think you have found outliers, then you will have to decide what to do with these. Section 3.6.2 deals with this issue.

3.1.1 The Mean, Median, and Mode

The **mean** of a variable is what most people think of as the average. Let's take for an example made-up scores on a hearing test from a group of 10 elderly people:

Table 3.1 Fictional Hearing Test Data

Hearing test:	354,	289,	580,	446,	268,	575,	425,	739,	518,	483

There are 10 scores in Table 3.1, and the mean involves adding all of them together and dividing by 10 to get $\overline{X} = 467.7$ ($\overline{X}$, pronounced "x bar," is the way statisticians represent the mean, but when it is difficult to find this symbol on your computer you can use the symbol M instead to designate the mean; the bar on top symbolizes the fact that this is data from the sample, not the population). The mean is represented mathematically as $\overline{X} = \dfrac{\sum X}{n}$ where $\sum X$ = the sum of all of the numbers in the set and n = the number of items in the set. The idea is then that we could ask what score would be typical of the 10 participants. Of course, some participants scored higher than this number and some scored lower. In fact, no one actually scored 467.7. However, this is the number that results in the smallest amount of distance between the mean score and the amount that each actual score differs from the mean.

The following example shows that the mean is the line that minimizes the distance to all the data points in the set. If we want to know how far it is from the mean to each point, we might think we should just subtract each point from the mean, and add up all those distances, like this: $(467.7 - 351) + (467.7 - 289) + \ldots + (467.7 - 483)$. The problem is that because the distances are both positive and negative (see Figure 3.1) the distances will cancel each other out and become zero. So one way to get around this is to do the exact same thing, except just square each distance and then take the square root

of the whole thing, like this: $\sqrt{((467.7 - 351)^2 + (467.7 - 289)^2 + \ldots + (467.7 - 483)^2)}$

This procedure is called the **sum of squares** because it squares all of the differences and then sums them. It turns out that the sum of squares always minimizes the distance to all the data points in the set, and this is called the **least squares principle**. The sum of squares for the mean in this case is 187,528.1.

If we picked a different number that was *not* the mean, for example 483, the sum of squares would be 189,869. If we picked 466, the sum of squares would be 187,557. We could continue to test this out with other numbers, and find that the smallest number

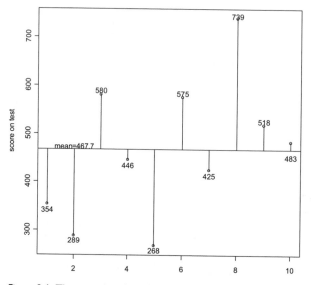

Figure 3.1 The mean line (at 467.7) is the one that minimizes the distance from all 10 points to the line. Any other line would result in larger absolute distances from the points to the line.

is the one calculated when we use the mean. The mean thus uses all of the numbers in a data set and is the number that, in the sense of minimizing the distance from itself to all other points, best represents a typical score.

The mean is foundational in statistics and is used in almost every kind of statistical test discussed in this book. There is one large problem with the mean, though, as a summary of data. This problem is that extreme values, called outliers, can have a disproportional influence on the mean score. Because the mean takes every point into account, if an extreme score is included in the data set the mean can change drastically. For example, if the person recording the data made a mistake in data entry and changed the last value from 483 to 4833, the mean score would become 902.7. Although this number still minimizes the sum of squares, you can see that it now does not seem very representative of the group, since 9 out of the 10 participants scored much lower than this point.

The median and mode are not nearly as important to statistical calculations as the mean. The **median** is the point at which 50% of the scores are higher and 50% of the scores are lower. In our hearing test example, there are 10 scores, so no single one can be the median. If we order the numbers from lowest to highest as in Table 3.2, we see that the point where half of the numbers are below and half are above lies between 446 and 483. In fact, the median is calculated as half of the distance between these two points, which would be 464.5.

Table 3.2 Ordered Hearing Test Data

Hearing test:	268,	289,	354,	425,	446,	↕ 483,	518,	575,	580,	739

When a distribution of data is **symmetric**, meaning that both halves of the distribution curve around the midpoint are mirror images of each other, the mean and the median will be at approximately the same point. Here we see the median of 464.5 is quite close to the mean of 467.7. In the case where we mistakenly typed 4833 instead of 483, however, the median would be 464.5 while the mean became 902.7. These two numbers are *not* very close together, and illustrate how one advantage of the median is that it is resistant to extreme values. One drawback of the median is that it essentially throws away all information about the data set except for the middle score. Another problem that Howell (2002) points out is that the median cannot readily enter into calculations, and this is the major advantage that the mean has over both the median and the mode.

The **mode** is the most frequently occurring score in the data set. In the hearing test data set, no score occurs more than once, so there are multiple modes. Although the mode may be an appropriate estimator of location for some data sets, I have never seen it used in second language research data. However, in graphic representations we sometimes see reference to more than one "mode" in the distribution. This means there is more than one peak of data in the distribution.

3.1.2 Standard Deviation, Variance, and Standard Error

It is not just enough to have a measurement of the typical score or the middle of the distribution. We also want to know something more about the spread or dispersion of the data. We might find all of the observations tightly clustered around the typical score, or we may find them extremely spread out from that typical score.

The standard deviation, variance, and standard error are measurements of the spread of the data. They are very important concepts in statistics but may be less familiar and less intuitive initially to the beginner than mean and median.

The **variance** is the average squared distance from the mean to any point. This is not an intuitive idea, but the idea of the sum of squares explained above showed that the sum of squares seeks to minimize the distance from the mean to any point. We want an average of this number, so we divide by $N - 1$ (the reason why we divide by $N - 1$ instead of just N is that $N - 1$ is a better estimate of the sample variance, while dividing by N is a better estimate of the population variance). Thus we can say that the variance is the expected squared distance of a point from the mean value of the data set (Wilcox, 2003, p. 96). As an intuitive idea, if the mean is the horizontal line that minimizes the distance to all of the points (as in Figure 3.1), the variance is the average of those distances or, from Figure 3.1, the average of the length of those lines from the mean to every point. Mathematically, this looks like: $s_x^2 = \dfrac{\sum (X - \overline{X})^2}{N - 1}$ For the hearing test data $s^2 = \dfrac{187,528.1}{(10 - 1)} = 20,836.5$. You will also see the Greek symbol sigma squared (σ^2) used to represent the variance. This is the population variance, which we want to estimate and which in real life we rarely ever know.

The **standard deviation** (written as s, sd or SD if calculated from the actual data set, σ if it is an estimator of the population) is just the positive square root of the variance. For the hearing test data, the square root of s^2 is 144.3. Basically what we are doing is taking an average of the amount each observation varies from the mean score, although we have to square and then take the square root of it in order not to end up with zero.

It is clear that, if the scores are more tightly clustered around the mean, the standard deviation will be smaller, while, if they are spread out further from the mean, the standard deviation will be larger. Figure 3.2 tries to graphically illustrate this difference. The two sets of data have the same mean (5.6), but the data on the left are much more spread out from the mean and thus have a much larger standard deviation (3.6). In

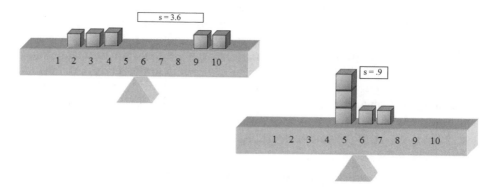

Figure 3.2 Smaller standard deviations are closer to the mean and larger ones are more spread out.

contrast, the data on the right are tightly bunched near the mean and thus the standard deviation is much smaller (.9).

Figure 3.3 graphically shows what different normal distributions look like when their standard deviations differ. A standard normal distribution has a mean of 0 and a standard deviation of 1 (there's an interactive graph at http://www-stat.stanford.edu/~naras/jsm/NormalDensity/NormalDensity.html where you can change the standard deviation of a normal distribution and see how it affects the shape of the curve).

Whatever the size of the standard deviation, if the data come from a normal distribution there is a rule for determining what percentage of the data falls within each standard deviation. Approximately 68% of the data will fall within ±1 sd of the mean (34% on each side of the mean; this is illustrated graphically in Figure 3.4). Two standard deviations from the mean will encompass 95% of the data (34 + 34 + 13.5 + 13.5), and three standard deviations will cover 99.7% of all data. Flege, Yeni-Komshian, and Liu (1999) used this fact to label any data from non-native speakers which fell within 2 standard deviations of the mean of native speakers as "native-like." For example, if native speakers got a mean of 9.3 on a 10-point test, with a standard deviation of .4, then if a non-native speaker scored 8.5 or higher on the test they would be considered to be within the "native speaker range" of scores. This seems a legitimate and objective way to classify a native speaker range of performance.

In summary, both the standard deviation and the variance measure the same thing, which is the average amount of distance from the mean to any point. The variance is just the square of the standard deviation. Sometimes you will hear the term "standard error" used as well, and you may wonder how that relates to the variance and the standard deviation. The **standard error of the mean** (SEM) is the standard deviation of

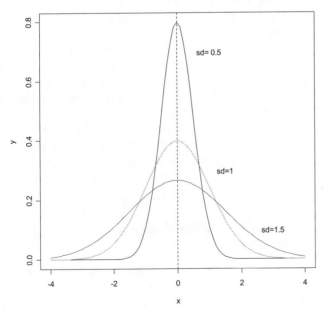

Figure 3.3 Varying standard deviations for a normal distribution with mean zero. Notice that the distribution spreads out further from the center as the standard deviation gets larger.

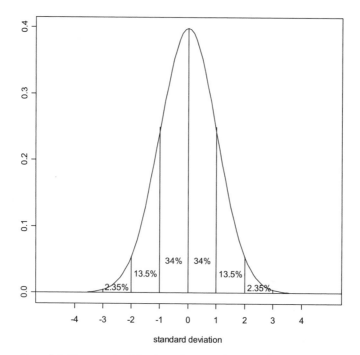

Figure 3.4 How much of the data of a normal curve is found in each standard deviation away from the mean.

the distribution of the mean. It is calculated by dividing the standard deviation of the population distribution (σ, but usually estimated by the sample standard deviation, s) by the square root of the number of observations (N). Dalgaard (2002) explains the SEM as an estimate of the variation in the mean that you would get if you repeated the same experiment several times over, and looked at the distribution of the mean. This distribution would be narrower than the amount of dispersion found in the original distribution. Thus the standard error is used in estimating confidence intervals because we can calculate an interval of 2 SEMs above and below the sample mean where we know the true mean should fall with 95% probability. Another important point to note is that larger sample sizes, with correspondingly larger Ns in the denominator, will make the standard error of the mean smaller. Because smaller SEMs make confidence intervals smaller, which means that we have a more precise estimate of the population parameter, a smaller SEM is desirable.

3.1.3 The Number of Observations and Other Numerical Summaries You Might Want to Report

Besides reporting the mean and standard deviation, you'll want to be sure to report the number of participants in your study. Since not all studies consist of those done with participants, we can say that you also want to report the number of observations in the study. Two other numerical summaries of data that you might want to include or that are good to understand are the **range** and the **interquartile range**.

The range is simply a single number that is the maximum data point minus the minimum data point. The range can be used to get a sense of how far apart the ends of the data points are spread. You might decide instead to just report the minimum and maximum points of a data set as well.

It is possible to divide the data into four parts, or quartiles. The part of the data from the 25th to the 75th percentile is also the area from the 1st to 3rd quartile (often called Q_1 and Q_3), and is called the **interquartile range**. This is another way of looking at the central part of the distribution. It is probably wiser to report the interquartile range (IQR) by visually displaying a boxplot than by giving the actual numbers. The hinges of the boxplot are not exactly the same as the interquartile range, but according to Howell (2002, p. 58) they are "closely related to the first and third quartiles."

3.2 Using SPSS to Get Numerical Summaries

It is a simple matter to obtain numerical summaries with SPSS. What may be more perplexing is deciding how to report them. I have had reviewers of my articles object to including both a numerical summary and a graphic summary. However, I argue in this book that both are necessary, so I would urge readers to include numerical summaries, either through including summary tables or through inserting means, standard deviations, and counts when statistical tests are reported. As an example of reporting summaries along with statistical test results, I give the follow-ing report of the *t*-test conducted with the fictional hearing test group data shown in Section 3.1:

> An independent samples *t*-test was conducted with a group of elderly participants ($\overline{X} = 467.7$, $s = 144.3$, $N = 10$) and young participants in their 30s ($\overline{X} = 322.9$, $s = 138.4$, $N = 10$) and found to be statistical ($t_{18} = 2.298$, $p = .034$, PV = .23). The effect size (the percentage of the variance) was large, accounting for 23% of the variance in scores between the groups.

In order to illustrate how the software performs numerical summaries, I will use data I gathered in an experiment on how age affects the phonological abilities of Japanese learners of English (Larson-Hall & Connell, 2005). In this experiment three groups were tested with various phonological measures. The groups were: 1) Japanese who had lived in the US as children for one to five years but returned to Japan by the age of 7 and subsequently had very little contact with English (labeled "early immersionists"); 2) Japanese who were living abroad at the time of testing and had lived in the US for one to four years ("late immersionists"); and 3) Japanese who were majoring in English at college and had never lived abroad ("non-immersionists"). I will report on their scores on a phonemic contrast test. The test contained 96 items that started with either [r], [l], or [w]. The participants had to listen to the words and choose the sound that the word started with.

The following sections will show how to obtain the mean scores for each group, the standard deviation, the range and the minimum and maximum points, and a count of how many participants are in each group. In addition, we will look at skewness and kurtosis numbers. **Skewness** and **kurtosis** are terms that refer to the shape of the curve, whether it is symmetric around the mean (skewness) or pointy versus flat (kurtosis). I will discuss these concepts in more detail in Section 3.4.2, where we will see that the concepts may be more easily comprehended visually, but you also might want to obtain numerical results for skewness and kurtosis at times, and they are easy to ask for in a numerical summary with SPSS.

3.2.1 Obtaining Numerical Summaries with SPSS and Splitting Groups

There are several ways to get numerical summaries with SPSS. One of the easiest is when you actually run your statistical test. However, even without running the test there is a variety of ways of obtaining numerical summaries. One is ANALYZE > DESCRIPTIVE STATISTICS > DESCRIPTIVES. If you choose this way and you have groups whose descriptive statistics you'd like to see separately, you'll need to tell SPSS to split up the data based on these groups. If you do not have separate groups, there would be no need to perform this step. To split data into groups, choose DATA > SPLIT FILE (I'm using the LarsonHall.Forgotten.sav file to demonstrate this, and it's shown in Figure 3.5).

Tip: When splitting the data, both the "Compare groups" choice and the "Organize output by groups" will provide separate group analyses. The former will provide the output in one table while the latter will provide separate tables. I find the "Compare groups" side-by-side option visually more useful.

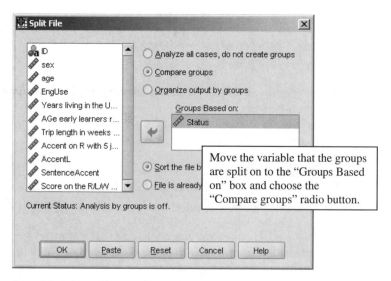

Figure 3.5 Splitting files into groups for data analysis.

Tip: You may enter up to eight variables to split your groups by. Each one is nested within the previous variable. Therefore, if I entered **Status** first and then **Sex** I would receive summaries where each group was also separately summarized for males and females.

Now that the data are ready to be analyzed, we can proceed to obtain various descriptive statistics for the data using ANALYZE > DESCRIPTIVE STATISTICS > DESCRIPTIVES (Figure 3.6).

To pick which statistical measures you want, open the "Options" button from the DESCRIPTIVES box (the "Options" button is shown in Figure 3.7).

As a default, you will find the descriptive statistics for mean, standard deviation, and minimum and maximum scores already ticked. I also asked for the range and the kurtosis and skewness numbers.

The box that says "Save standardized values as variables" on the DESCRIPTIVES box will create a column of **z-scores**, which are the scores adjusted so that they reflect how many standard deviations the score is away from the mean. I've never had to use this function myself so I don't recommend doing this, but I just wanted to point out what this box meant. Table 3.3 shows the output from this call.

Table 3.3 shows that the data have been split into the three groups that exist for the STATUS variable. The first column shows how many participants there are in each group. The second column shows the range of scores, and we note that the Late group has the largest range. The actual minimum and maximum scores on the test are shown in the next two columns. The data in the mean column show that the Early group has the highest mean score on the test, while all groups have similar sizes of standard deviations. For skewness, the Non group has the least, but it has the most kurtosis.

At this point, if you have split your data you might want to go back to DATA > SPLIT

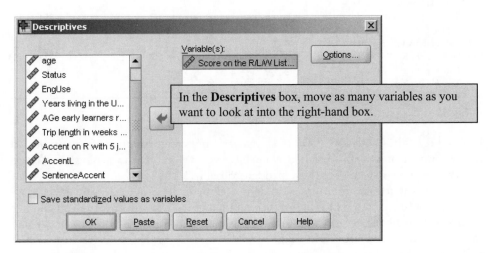

Figure 3.6 Using the ANALYZE > DESCRIPTIVE STATISTICS > DESCRIPTIVES option to get numerical summaries.

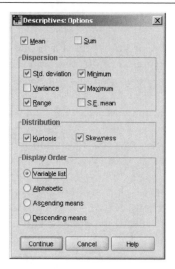

Figure 3.7 Choosing options for numerical summaries in the DESCRIPTIVES box.

Table 3.3 Descriptive Statistics for the LarsonHall.Forgotten Data Set, with the Set Split by the STATUS Variable

Descriptive Statistics

Status		N	Range	Minimum	Maximum	Mean	Std. Deviation	Skewness		Kurtosis	
		Statistic	Statistic	Statistic	Statistic	Statistic	Statistic	Statistic	Std. Error	Statistic	Std. Error
Non	Score on the R/L/W Listening test	15	44	47	91	67.73	13.761	.077	.580	−1.089	1.121
	Valid N (listwise)	15									
Late	Score on the R/L/W Listening test	15	54	36	90	69.20	15.377	−.383	.580	−.054	1.121
	Valid N (listwise)	15									
Early	Score on the R/L/W Listening test	14	48	47	95	80.86	14.277	−1.128	.597	.773	1.154
	Valid N (listwise)	14									

FILE and reset the choice to "Analyze all cases, do not create groups." If you do not do this, when you later perform statistical analyses you will receive a warning like "There are fewer than two groups for the dependent variable."

Another way to obtain a numerical summary with SPSS is to use the ANALYZE > DESCRIPTIVE STATISTICS > EXPLORE choice on the menu. With this choice, you will not need to split your file because you can put the splitting variable (if you have groups) in the "Factor List" box (see Figure 3.8).

If you open the "Statistics" button on the EXPLORE box you will not find the same detailed options for descriptive statistics as was available in the DESCRIPTIVES option, but the statistics that will appear are the mean, the 95% confidence interval for the mean, the 5% trimmed mean, the median, the variance, the standard deviation, the minimum and maximum points, the range, the interquartile range, skewness, and kurtosis. Also, by default the EXPLORE option will give you a boxplot and a stem and leaf plot. I will not show this output, as we will look at graphs later in the chapter, but this choice certainly provides lots of information. I prefer the DESCRIPTIVES option because the data are more compactly provided and I don't find any need for some of the statistics provided in the EXPLORE option (such as the 95% CI for the mean, the trimmed mean, or the interquartile range), but you should experiment to see which ones you like the best.

Obtaining a Numerical Summary with SPSS

There are two major ways to do this if you are not also running a statistical test:

1   Use the ANALYZE > DESCRIPTIVE STATISTICS > DESCRIPTIVES option. If you have groups, first separate them by going to DATA > SPLIT FILE, choosing the "Compare groups" option, and moving the group variable into the right-hand box.
2   Use the ANALYZE > DESCRIPTIVE STATISTICS > EXPLORE option. If you have groups, put the splitting variable into the "Factor List" box. Choose whether to receive just numerical statistics, plots, or both.

3.2.2 Application Activities for Numerical Summaries

1   Use the DeKeyser2000.sav file. Split the data by the STATUS variable and examine the GJT scores. Make sure you have data for the number of participants, the minimum and maximum scores, the mean, and the standard deviation. By just eyeballing the statistics, does it look as though the groups have similar mean scores (maximum possible score was 200)? What about the standard deviation?
2   Use the Obarow.sav file. Look at the numerical summaries for the gain score in

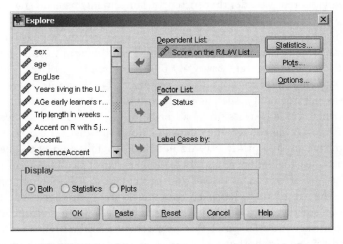

Figure 3.8 Using the ANALYZE > DESCRIPTIVE STATISTICS > EXPLORE option to get numerical summaries.

the immediate post-test (gnsc1.1) split according to the four experimental groups (trtmnt1). Each group was tested on 20 vocabulary words, but most knew at least 15 of the words in the pre-test. Obtain summaries for number of participants, mean scores and standard deviations, and minimum and maximum score. Do the groups appear to have similar mean scores and standard deviations?

3.3 Satisfying Assumptions for Parametric Tests

In the field of second language research, very few researchers actually say anything about whether they have satisfied the **assumptions** underlying parametric statistical tests when they report the results of their experiments. It always seemed to me upon reading books of the kind that you are now holding that the authors made statements about how important satisfying the assumptions were, but then in practice either used made-up data sets which were constructed to satisfy the requirements, or paid little attention to deciding whether the data did indeed satisfy requirements. One of my goals when I approached writing this book was to pay more attention to these assumptions and help readers understand how to do this too.

I soon found that answers in this area are not easy. Take, for example, the assumption of a **normal distribution** of the data. Probably most people have heard of a normal curve and a normal distribution of data, and understand that with respect to grades, for example, a normal distribution would mean that most people in a class would receive Cs, a lesser number Bs and Ds, and then the smallest number would receive As and Fs. An assumption underlying every kind of "classic" statistical procedure that will be reviewed in this book, from correlation to multiple regression, is that the data are normally distributed. Yet how do we know if our own data are normally distributed? As we will see in the next section, there are no clear rules about a cut-off level for "normal" and "non-normal" distributions. Sometimes writers in this area like to make pronouncements, such as "A non-normal distribution is one in which the skewness level is over 1." However, such pronouncements are essentially arbitrary. I understand that, for those who do not know statistics well, absolute rules and pronouncements are quite attractive. Yet I will assure my reader that such pronouncements have no standing in the statistical field.

As we shall see in this chapter, unless a data set is quite large it can be impossible to tell whether the data is normally distributed or not. Visually looking for normality by examining graphics such as the histogram or a **Q-Q plot** (both explained later in this chapter) can help, but such methods are not always conclusive. Furthermore, there are numerical ways of assessing normality, such as the **Kolmogorov–Smirnov** goodness-of-fit test, but these formal kinds of tests often suffer from low power, which means they cannot always accurately detect whether data are normally distributed or not (Wilcox, 2003). It seems we are in a pickle—we do not have any failsafe way to determine whether our data are normally distributed, but our tests require it. If we continue to use the "classical" types of statistical tests that I present in this book, our only solution appears to be the same one as has been used for so long—soldier on pretty much just assuming that our data are normally distributed unless we find strong and clear evidence to the contrary. I do advocate that researchers examine their data the best they can, looking for normality both visually and numerically, but you should also understand that such methods are not always accurate.

One common problem for the assumption of a normal distribution in real data sets is finding **outliers** in the data, points that stand out as not fitting with the rest of the data set. The presence of outliers means there is more data in the extreme ends (the tails) of a distribution curve than there should be. Maronna, Martin, and Yohai (2006) note that these tails are the crucial point in determining whether one has an exactly normal distribution, but these are also the places where you have less data. The way you deal with outliers is very important and I will discuss possible treatments later in this chapter.

Another common problem with real data sets in second language research is that they often do not satisfy the other foundational assumption of classic statistics, which is that group variances should be equal (the **homogeneity of variance** assumption). This assumption says that the mean scores of the groups may differ but their variances should be the same. If groups that we assume are going to differ, such as native versus non-native speakers of a language, are paired in an experiment, it is likely that the variances will be quite different, usually with non-native speakers having a much larger variance than native speakers. For some tests (like the t-test) there are ways to adjust for violations of this assumption, but for others (such as ANOVA) there are no handy corrections. The problem is not that the violation of these assumptions offends a "god of statistics" who exists in the ether, but rather that with violations of the assumptions one might not be able to find differences that do exist between groups of participants (or relationships that do exist between variables). Again, I reiterate that better ways of doing statistics, namely robust statistics, will be routine in the near future, and the reason for their success will be because we will then be able to ignore many of the assumptions of parametric statistics but will get more accurate results anyway. For the time being, however, soldier on with me to look at ways of examining the assumptions I've outlined in this section.

3.4 Graphic Summaries of Data: Examining the Shape of Distributions for Normality

Applied researchers should always look at the shape of their data before conducting statistical tests. Looking at data can give you some idea about whether your data are normally distributed. Although there are authors, such as Weinberg and Abramowitz (2002, p. 276), who say that sample sizes larger than 30 eliminate the need to check data for normality, researchers using simulation studies have found that, depending on the kinds of deviations from normality, even sample sizes of 160 may not be robust enough to overcome problems when distributions are skewed (Wilcox, 1998). What this means is that, even though you may be comparing two groups with 150 participants each, if your data are highly skewed, even with no outliers, you may not be able to find group differences which really do exist.

Another reason to look at your data visually is that it will give you a means of verifying what is happening. For example, if you have examined histograms of your two groups and found their distributions are quite similar and centered at the same basic mean, you would then be surprised to numerically find a large difference between groups. Graphics give you a way to look at your data that can replicate and even go beyond what you see in the numbers when you are doing your statistics. A recent report by the APA statistical task force strongly urges all researchers to look at their data before undertaking any statistical analysis (Wilkinson & Task Force on Statistical Inference, 1999). This is not a "fishing expedition" to look for statistical relationships, but rather a sound practice that can save grief later by catching anomalies in the data.

Statisticians have long been emphasizing the need to see graphical summaries of data as just as essential as numerical summaries. Anscombe (1973) noted that there is a feeling that numerical summaries are precise while graphs are rough, and that looking at the data is cheating. However, he produced an example which showed the absolute necessity of looking at graphs. The data he used were those in Table 3.4. In each case, the X variable will be matched with the corresponding Y variable, so X1 will be correlated with Y1, X2 with Y2, and so on.

Numerically, all of these data sets look the same; they share the same mean of the xs ($\overline{X} = 9$) and ys ($\overline{Y} = 7.5$), the straight line that can be drawn through the data is the same ($y = 3 + 0.5x$), their R^2 effect sizes are the same ($R^2 = .667$), and so on. However, when we take a look at the graphs that are generated by **scatterplots** of the data (the X column crossed with the Y column and each point plotted on the graph), we see that not all of the data sets are appropriate for running correlations (regressions) because they are not all linear.

For Graph 1 in Figure 3.9 the assumption of linearity is met, and this is what we think the data is like when we are doing a correlation. Graph 2 has a curvature to the data set (Anscombe says possibly it would fit a quadratic distribution). Graph 3 has one outlier, which means the line is not the best fit for the rest of the points, and Graph 4 seems to be described very unsatisfactorily by assuming a linear fit! The point of this illustration is to help you realize that graphs are just as necessary and useful as numerical summaries.

3.4.1 Histograms

One way to look at the distribution of data is to look at a graph called a **histogram**. A histogram divides data up into partitions and, in the usual case, gives a frequency distribution of the number of scores contained in each partition (called a bin). If, instead of a frequency count, we use proportions, the overall area of the graph will equal 1, and we can overlay the histogram with a normal curve in order to judge whether our

Table 3.4 Anscombe's (1973) Data Showing a Need for Visual Examination

X (1–3)	Y1	Y2	Y3	X4	Y4
10	8.04	9.14	7.46	8	6.58
8	6.95	8.14	6.77	8	5.76
13	7.58	8.74	12.74	8	7.71
9	8.81	8.77	7.11	8	8.84
11	8.33	9.26	7.81	8	8.47
14	9.96	8.10	8.84	8	7.04
6	7.24	6.13	6.08	8	5.25
4	4.26	3.10	5.39	19	12.50
12	10.84	9.13	8.15	8	5.56
7	4.82	7.26	6.42	8	7.91
5	5.68	4.74	5.73	8	6.89

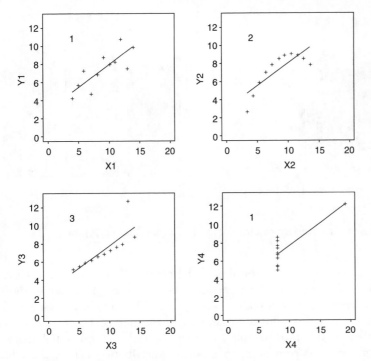

Figure 3.9 Anscombe's (1973) data examined visually.

data seems to follow a normal distribution. Notice that a histogram is *not* a **barplot**. A barplot is a common plot in the field, but this kind of graph usually shows the mean score of some group rather than a frequency or proportion count of the score divided up into various breaks. The left panel of Figure 3.10 shows a histogram of a variable from Ellis and Yuan (2004) that measured the number of words participants produced in a written essay. The histogram divides the result up into bins that measure the frequency of certain numbers of words, so that we see that the most frequent number of words produced in the essays was about 185 words (the bin just below the 200) and 230 words (both happened nine times). In contrast, the right panel of Figure 3.10 shows a barplot of the average score of the number of words produced by each of the three groups. The PTP group produced the most words, at somewhere over 200 on average. Although in both cases the graphics produce bars, they answer very different questions and only the histogram is appropriate for looking at the distribution of scores.

Histograms can give information about whether distributions are symmetrically distributed or skewed, and whether they have one mode (peak) or several, and a histogram with an overlaid normal curve can be evaluated to see whether the data should be considered normally distributed. I should note here, though, that the shape of a histogram does depend on how the data is binned, or split into groups. There are different algorithms for doing this (although you cannot change this algorithm in SPSS), and histograms can only be a general, not exact, measure of the normality of a distribution. They should be used in conjunction with other graphics and with numerical measures of normality.

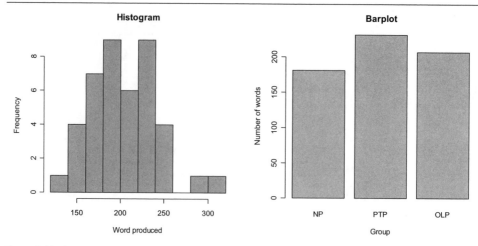

Figure 3.10 A comparison of a histogram to a barplot for the Ellis and Yuan (2004) data.

In Figure 3.11 I show normal distributions that I generated, all with zero as their mean and a standard deviation of 1. The histograms in Figure 3.11 differ in the N (number of sampled points) they contain, starting with 20 points, then going to 50 and then 500. There are two reasons for examining these graphs. The first is to see visually how a larger number of samples, even though all are generated from a normal distribution, will conform more to a normal distribution. The second reason is to show that, because of inherent variability, even samples taken from a *known* normal distribution will not follow the density curve of a normal distribution exactly. In other words, I want to show a range of what could be considered "normally distributed" samples.

3.4.2 Skewness and Kurtosis

Skewness and **kurtosis** are two ways to describe deviations in the shape of distributions. If a **sampling distribution** (in other words, the actual distribution we obtain through our experimentation) is skewed, that means it is not symmetric around the mean. A distribution can be **positively skewed**, which means that scores are bunched up toward the left side of the graph, or **negatively skewed**, which means that scores are bunched up toward the right side of the graph. Both of these situations are shown in Figure 3.12. This nomenclature has always seemed non-intuitive to me, but I remember it by thinking of the position of the tail (the end of the distribution where there are fewer data points). If the tail of the distribution goes to the right and toward larger numbers, it is positive, while if the tail of the distribution goes to the left and toward smaller numbers and negative numbers, it is negative.

As was seen in the SPSS output previously, there are numerical measurements of skewness that can be obtained. Howell (2002) states that these are not used in the social sciences, and they do not seem to be used in second language research either. We can find some statements giving us some rules of thumb for using the skewness number to evaluate the normality of the data. Weinberg and Abramowitz (2002, p. 278) says that, if the skewness ratio is less than 2, normality is not violated (the skewness ratio is the

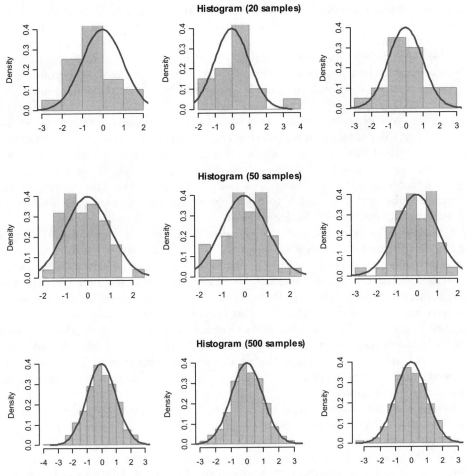

Figure 3.11 Distribution of various sample sizes generated from a normal distribution.

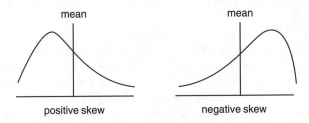

Figure 3.12 Non-normal distributions (skewed and bimodal).

skewness level divided by the standard error of the skewness). The SPSS help files say a skewness level over 1 indicates a significant departure from normality. Porte (2002) says that if the skewness level is under 1 there is no cause for concern.

However, these statements seem to be some of those rules which we would like to have but which we should be cautious about trusting. In fact, Westfall and Young (1993) performed a simulation study that found that, even with N = 160, a skewed distribution could change the conclusions that should have been drawn from the data. This means that, if our data are skewed, group differences (or relationships among variables) that do exist may not be found. What can be done if your data are skewed? Transformations (treated later in this chapter) can help reduce the skewness of data.

As Figure 3.11 with multiple samples from a normal distribution should have hinted, with smaller sample sizes there will be an immense amount of variation in the distribution of data, even if we know it is taken from a normal distribution. At the level of 10 or 15 samples per group, it is extremely unlikely that even samples generated from a normal distribution will follow the smooth line of a normal distribution. However, none of these small samples showed the amount of skewness that is seen in Figure 3.12. So while it may be impossible to say that one's data comes from an exactly normal distribution, it is possible to visually note whether there is extreme skewness by looking at a histogram of the distribution.

If skewness describes the shape of the distribution as far as symmetry along a vertical line through the mean goes, **kurtosis** describes the shape of the distribution as far as the concentration of scores around the mean goes. Howell (2002, p. 30) gives the clearest explanation I have encountered: "basically [kurtosis] refers to the relative concentration of scores in the center, the upper and lower ends (tails), and the shoulders (between the center and the tails) of a distribution." A distribution that is too flat at the peak of the normal curve is called **platykurtic** (it is like a plateau), and a curve that has too many scores collected in the center of the distribution is called **leptokurtic**. Figure 3.13 (taken from Wikipedia) demonstrates distributions with kurtosis. The graph on the left shows leptokurtic distributions and the graph on the right shows platykurtic distributions.

As with skewness, kurtosis is, in my experience, never remarked upon in the literature in our field. Nevertheless, it is important to understand that there are many ways distributions could differ from a normal distribution.

As an example of visually looking at histograms to check for skewness, let's look at histograms of the r/l/w listening test variable from the Larson-Hall and Connell (2005) data in Figure 3.14. The data are separated into groups of non-immersionists (those who never lived abroad), late immersionists (those who went to live in the US as adults), and early immersionists (those who lived in the US as children).

Figure 3.14 shows a range of distributions. In each group there were about 15 participants. Although the non-immersionists' distribution looks fairly symmetrical, the distribution of the early immersionists seems markedly negatively skewed. For the late immersionists the distribution seems to be **bimodal**, meaning there are two prominent peaks of data. In the case of the late immersionists, these peaks are of the same height (but that is not necessary to call a distribution a bimodal or multimodal one). This means that both "late" and "early" groups received higher scores on the measure than one would expect if the data were normally distributed. A bimodal distribution might be a sign that there your data should be divided into two different groups.

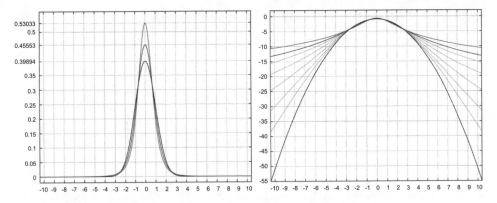

Figure 3.13 Leptokurtic (left panel) and platykurtic (right panel) distributions.

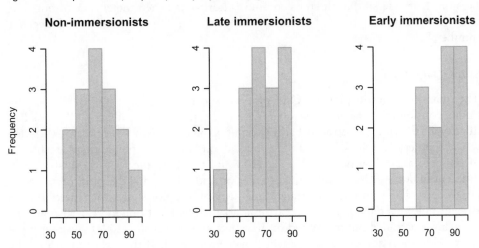

Figure 3.14 Histograms of the Larson-Hall and Connell (2005) data.

3.4.3 *Stem and Leaf Plots*

Histograms display data using somewhat arbitrarily defined slices of the data to create the bins of the plot. Individual data points cannot clearly be seen. **Stem and leaf plots** basically display the same kind of information as a histogram that uses frequency counts, but use the data itself to show the distribution, and thus retain all of the data points. An example of a stem and leaf plot using the Larson-Hall and Connell (2005) data from the r/l/w listening test is shown in Table 3.5, divided up by the three Japanese groups.

The results are for a test that had a maximum of 96 points. Looking at the data from the non-immersionist group (those who had never lived abroad), the scores are divided into their tens values to the left of the bar, and their ones value to the right of the bar. Thus the lowest score was 47. There were four scores in the 50s, all of them different. However, two people in this group score 67, so the 7 is repeated twice after the 6. Thus, every individual point is clearly represented.

Table 3.5 A Stem and Leaf Plot of the Larson-Hall and Connell (2005) Data

Non-immersionists (N=15)	Late immersionists (N=15)	Early immersionists (N=14)
4 | 7	2 | 6	4 | 7
5 | 0167	4 | 278	5 |
6 | 377	6 | 3456357	6 | 48
7 | 018	8 | 4990	7 | 068
8 | 026		8 | 799
9 | 1		9 | 01355

However, we can also look at the shape of the distribution. Although there is some clustering of scores in the middle for the non- and late immersionists, the early immersionists' scores are clearly skewed negatively (think of turning the numbers on their side so that the tens column is horizontal; then the cluster of numbers is on the right, and the tail extends to the left, or toward smaller and negative numbers).

3.4.4 Q-Q Plots

The **quantile-quantile plot** (or **Q-Q plot** for short) plots the quantiles of the data under consideration against the quantiles of the normal distribution. If a median divides the distribution up at its halfway point, a quantile divides the data up the same way at a variety of points. For example, the 25th quantile notes the point at which 25% of the data are below it and 75% are above it. The Q-Q plot uses points at many different quantiles. If the sampling distribution and the normal distribution are similar, the points should fall in a straight line. If the Q-Q plot shows that there is not a straight line, this tells us it departs from a normal distribution, and can also give us some information about what kind of distribution it is. Verzani (2004) says that if the right tail is short the quantile line will curve down, while if the right tail is long the quantile line will curve up.

Figure 3.15 provides a series of Q-Q plots where samples were drawn from a normal distribution. The reference line passes through the first (25th) and third (75th) quantiles. It can be seen that as sample size increases the points conform more closely to the reference line, but the figure is meant to show the type of variation that may occur even with samples from normal distributions.

Figure 3.16 shows Q-Q plots for the Larson-Hall and Connell (2005) data we have been examining. The Q-Q plot for the early immersionists shows a clear departure from a straight line, with the top of the line bending down because the right tail is short. The late immersionist Q-Q plot shows more departure from the reference line than that of the non-immersionists.

3.4.5 Generating Histograms, Stem and Leaf Plots, and Q-Q Plots

One easy way to obtain many exploratory graphs in one fell swoop is to "Explore" the data (this was noted earlier in the chapter as one way to obtain numerical summaries as well). Choose ANALYZE > DESCRIPTIVE STATS > EXPLORE from the menu. I put the RLW test in the "Dependent List" and the categorical variable "Status" in the "Factor List" box

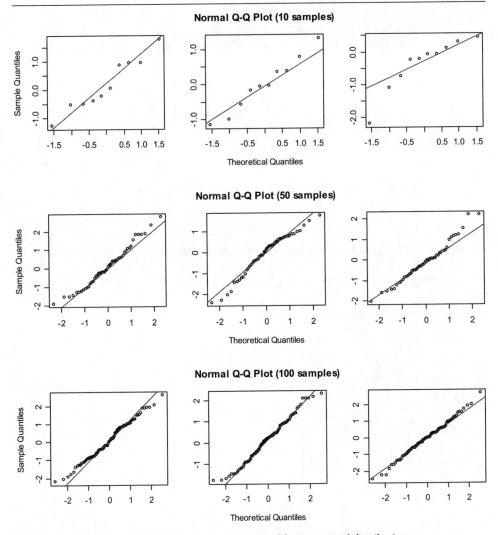

Figure 3.15 Q-Q plots of various sample sizes generated from a normal distribution.

(see Figure 3.8 for the dialogue box). To see what graphics are available, open the "Plots" button.

Figure 3.17 shows what plots are available. I have asked for stem and leaf plots, histograms, and normality plots with tests. The boxplots provided by this option are not very informative (Chapter 9 gives information on how to obtain better boxplots).

If you continue with the Explore option and leave the default for both statistics and plots, the output produces a large amount of descriptive statistics. After these numerical summaries you'll see the results of tests for normality (but note—if you have left your data in a split-group format, the output will be considerably less compact than what I show here). These tests give formal tests of the hypothesis that the distribution of the variable (or group) follows a normal distribution. Because the null hypothesis is

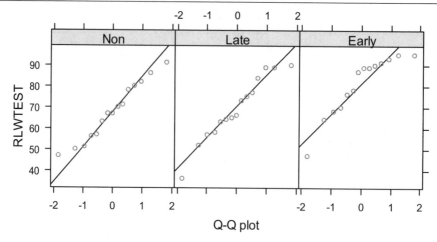

Figure 3.16 Q-Q plots for the Larson-Hall and Connell (2005) data.

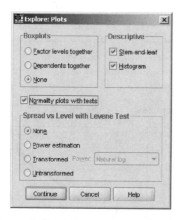

Figure 3.17 Plots available in the ANALYZE > DESCRIPTIVES > EXPLORE (then "Plots" button) option.

that the sampling distribution comes from the same distribution as the normal distribution, if the p-value (Sig. column) is less than .05 you would reject the null hypothesis and accept the alternative hypothesis that the data are *not* normally distributed.

The output shown in Table 3.6 gives the results of both the Kolmogorov–Smirnov (with the Lilliefors correction) goodness-of-fit as well as the Shapiro–Wilk goodness-of-fit test. Ricci (2005) states that the Shapiro–Wilk test is the most powerful test for small sample sizes (under 50). Notice that both goodness-of-fit tests indicate that the early immersionist data set differs statistically from a normal distribution. That is what we have also deduced from looking at histograms, stem and leaf plots, and Q-Q plots.

If the p-value is greater than .05, we do not reject the null hypothesis, but we also cannot conclusively say that our distribution is normal. This is because these kinds of formal tests of assumptions often suffer from low power, which means they do not have enough power to detect violations of the null hypothesis (Wilcox, 2003). Thus, we cannot be any surer that a distribution is exactly normal by looking at the numer-

Table 3.6 Output from ANALYZE > DESCRIPTIVES > EXPLORE Concerning Tests of Normality

Tests of Normality

	Status	Kolmogorov-Smirnov[a]			Shapiro-Wilk		
		Statistic	df	Siq.	Statistic	df	Siq.
Score on the R/L/W	Non	.116	15	.200*	.961	15	.714
Listening test	Late	.116	15	.200*	.951	15	.545
	Early	.238	14	.031	.870	14	.042

[a] Lilliefors Significance Correction
* This is a lower bound of the true significance

ical results of these tests than we can of looking at a histogram. For this reason, it is important not just to rely on a formal test of normality but to examine graphics as well (Wilkinson & Task Force on Statistical Inference, 1999).

The next part of the output provides a wealth of graphs. There are histograms, stem and leaf plots, normal Q-Q plots and detrended normal Q-Q plots.[1] All of these graphs provide slightly different ways of visualizing your data. Most of these graphs can be called for separately by going to the GRAPHS drop-down menu as well.

Tip: Another way to explore your data is through ANALYZE > DESCRIPTIVE STATISTICS > FREQUENCIES. Although it provides the same kind of information as the Explore option does, it can be a better format when you are looking at variables for correlation or multiple regression because it puts the variables side by side in columns instead of on top of each other, like this:

Statistics

		SK.NR.raw	SK.L1.WR. loggged	SK.L2. WM.raw	SK.L2.NS. logged	SK.L2.PA. logged
N	Valid	40	40	40	37	40
	Missing	0	0	0	3	0
Mean		48.6000	.6015	2.5750	2.2414	1.4854

In addition, you can call for histograms with normal curves imposed in the "Charts" button, like those seen in Figure 3.11. This can be a useful feature.

1 A detrended Q-Q plot plots the deviation of the points away from the diagonal in a Q-Q plot. There should be no specific pattern of points, and points should be found both above and below the line.

Obtaining Graphics to Assess Normality in SPSS

There are two major ways to do this through the Descriptive Statistics menu (individual graphs can be called through the Graphs menu):

1   Use the Analyze > Descriptive Statistics > Explore option and pick graphs in the "Plots" button.
2   Use Analyze > Descriptive Statistics > Frequencies. This can call up histograms with overlaid normal distribution curves. If you use this option you will need to use Data > Split Files to split up groups first.

3.4.6 Application Activity: Looking at Normality Assumptions

Note: Keep your output from these activities open, as you will use some of the same output for the following application activity:

1   Chapter 6 on correlation will feature data from Flege, Yeni-Komshian, and Liu (1999). Use the FlegeYKLiu.sav file and use one or both of the two options from the Descriptive Statistics menu to examine the data for pronunciation divided according to groups. From the available evidence, does the data appear to be normally distributed?
2   Create a histogram with the GJT variable for each of the two groups in the DeKeyser2000.sav file. What is the shape of the histograms?
3   Chapter 12 on repeated measures ANOVA will feature data from Lyster (2004). Use the Lyster.written.sav file and use one or both of the two options from the Descriptive Statistics menu to examine the gain scores for the comprehension task (CompGain1, CompGain2) divided according to groups (called Cond for condition). From the available evidence, does the data appear to be normally distributed?

3.5 Examining the Shape of Distributions: The Assumption of Homogeneity

Another important assumption when parametric statistics are applied to group data is that the variances of the groups are equal (the **homogeneity of variances** assumption). Remember that the variance is a number that measures the average squared distance from the mean to any point, so it measures dispersion around the mean, and the standard deviation is just the square root of this number. The idea of a statistical test of two groups is that, if we look at two groups whose distributions are equal and whose variances are equal, all we then need to do is to check whether their mean scores differ enough to consider the groups part of the same distribution or in fact as two separate distributions.

Some graphics that illustrate this idea will be helpful. The left panel of Figure 3.18 shows density plots of non-overlapping distributions that have equal standard deviations ($s = .25$), but whose means are at different points (means are −3, 0, and 3). The second graph shows density plots of distributions which do overlap. They have the same means as the first figure. Their standard deviations are all equal at 1.

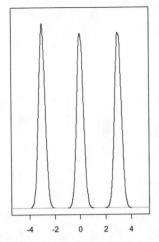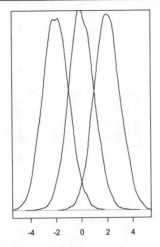

Figure 3.18 Density plots of three groups whose means differ.

The distributions of the left panel of Figure 3.18 would certainly be considered as statistically different, while for those of the right panel this is not a certainty. This figure shows the importance of variance (or standard deviation) as well as mean for determining whether distributions from different groups are the same or different. One can also infer from these figures that, if the standard deviations (and thus the variances) of all the groups were of different sizes, then a test that assumed they were the same and was only looking for differences in the means might easily run into problems.

Just as with the assumption of normality, there are different ways of examining the homogeneity of variances in one's own data. First and most simple is just to look at the numerical output for the standard deviation. One can eyeball these numbers in relation to the scale that they were measured on and get a sense of whether variances are in fact equal. A second way of checking variances is to look at side-by-side box-plots of groups (see Chapter 7 for more information about making and interpreting boxplots). Although the box in the boxplot is not the standard deviation (it is the area from the 25th to 75th quantile), it is showing the amount of variability in the central part of the distribution and thus can be examined for a rough sense of variance. The boxplots in the first graph (a) of Figure 3.19 for the r/l/w test variable show that variances are not substantially different among the three Japanese groups, as the lengths of their boxes are not markedly different (although the early immersionists' distribution is skewed, as shown by the fact that the median line is not in the middle of the shaded box).

However, in a different test of accentedness where native speakers of English were also tested (graph b in Figure 3.19), there are clear differences in variances. The native speaker group has a shorter box (and less variance) than any of the non-native groups, and the "non" group has a much longer box than any of the three other groups as well.

A third way to test for homogeneity of variances is to use **Levene's test** of homo-geneity of variances. Tabachnick and Fidell (2001) state that, while most formal tests of homogeneity of variances also measure normality, Levene's test does not. This test can

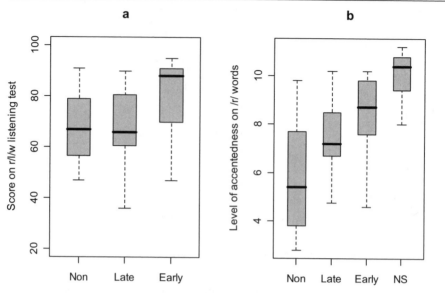

Figure 3.19 Boxplots can be examined for homogeneity of variances; in graph (a) the lengths of the boxes are all roughly equal, meaning variances are approximately equal, while in graph (b) the boxes have markedly different lengths, violating the homogeneity of variance assumption.

be called for when doing statistical tests with SPSS (such as a t-test, ANOVA, etc.) and will be seen in the separate chapters that follow in this book. As with the formal tests of normality seen in previous sections of this chapter, if the probability is *over* .05 for Levene's test, variances are considered to be homogeneous. This is because Levene's test checks the null hypothesis that variances are equal, so, if the probability is less than p = .05, we will reject the null hypothesis. As with many other formal tests of assumptions, however, with small sample sizes this test may not have enough power to detect violations of assumptions (Dalgaard, 2002; Wilcox, 2003).

What recourse do we have if our groups do not have homogeneous variances? If we use a t-test, there is a correction that is performed for groups whose variances are not the same. If we use an ANOVA there is no such correction, but we could choose not to compare groups which have non-homogeneous variances or combine certain groups to achieve a better effect. Again, the main effect of not having homogeneous variances is that, although group differences may actually exist, we might not be able to find them. Thus, if you perform a statistical test and find that the group differences you thought would be there are not found, you might consider that this result is due to non-homogeneous variances. In the future, using robust statistics with SPSS will be a way to avoid problems with this assumption.

3.5.1 Application Activities for Checking Homogeneity of Variance

1   Check the homogeneity of variance assumption for pronunciation for the groups in the Flege, Yeni-Komshian, and Liu (1999) study (use the FlegeYKLiu.sav file) by

looking at standard deviations for each group. The maximum number of points on this test was 9. What do you conclude about the equality of variances?

2   Check the homogeneity of variance assumption for the GJTSCORE variable for the two groups in the DeKeyser (2000) study (use the DeKeyser2000.sav file) by looking at standard deviations for each group. The maximum number of points on this test was 200. What do you conclude about the equality of variances?

3   Check the homogeneity of variance assumption for the CompGain2 variable for the four groups in the Lyster (2004) study (use the Lyster.Written.sav file) by looking at standard deviations for each group. The maximum number of points any person gained was 21. What do you conclude about the equality of variances?

3.6 Dealing with Departures from Expectations

3.6.1 Imputing Missing Data

It is a very common occurrence, especially in research designs where data is collected at different time periods, to be missing data for some participants. The question of what to do with missing data is a rich one and cannot be fully explored here, but see Tabachnick and Fidell (2001) and Little and Rubin (1987) for more detailed information. I will merely give a short summary of what can be done when the missing data points do not follow any kind of pattern and make up less than 5% of the data, a situation that Tabachnick and Fidell (2001) assert can be handled equally well with almost any method for handling missing data. An example of a pattern of missing data would be that in administering a questionnaire you found that all respondents from a particular first language background would not answer a certain question. If this whole group is left out of a summary of the data, this distorts the findings. In this case, it may be best to delete the entire question or variable.

In SPSS the default way for handling missing data is to delete the entire case from the calculation (called "listwise deletion"). You also have options to delete the case only when the value is missing (called "pairwise deletion"). I would like to point out, however, that Wilkinson and the Task Force on Statistical Inference (1999) assert that the worst way to deal with missing data is listwise and pairwise deletion. If you delete an entire case because a value in one variable is missing, this of course means that all the work you went to in obtaining data from that participant is wasted, and of course with a smaller sample size your power to find results is reduced.

Two methods that Howell (n.d.) recommends are maximum likelihood and multiple imputation. The details of how these methods work are beyond the scope of this book, but Howell provides a comprehensible summary at http://www.uvm.edu/~dhowell/StatPages/More_Stuff/Missing_Data/Missing.html#Return1. A free program called NORM, available at www.stat.psu.edu/~jls/misoftwa.html, will perform both maximum likelihood and multiple imputation. There is a stand-alone package for Windows that you should look for on this page—it is NORM Version 2.03 for Windows. Multiple imputation is also available in SPSS with a program called AMOS, which may or may not be included with the version of SPSS that you are working with at your institution (it is an add-on to SPSS, but I don't have it through my institution).

If you choose to download and run the NORM 2.03 version, when you save it I recommend you save it in the Program Files folder under a folder called Norm because you will have to later go and find the .exe file and open it (on my computer it was saved under the C drive in a folder called winimp automatically, but I didn't pay close attention and thus wasn't sure where it was).

To prepare your data to be imputed, you will need to save it in Notepad with each individual's information on one line with each piece of data separated by a blank space or a tab. To show you how this can be done, I will illustrate with the Lafrance and Gottardo (2005) data, which has some missing values. First, I open up the file in SPSS (LafranceGottardo2005.sav). All missing data must have a numeric code for NORM, so I will sort the data in SPSS (DATA > SORT, then use "Ascending order" for each variable serially) so that if there are any blank cells they will be visible at the top of the column. I will then enter −9 into these cells (it turns out there are only missing values in the NS (naming speed) variable. I then choose FILE > SAVE AS and choose the "Tab delimited" choice so that the data in each column for each individual is separated by a tab). This will be saved as a .dat file, which is what NORM needs. NORM will not accept non-numeric (string) variables, so these will have to be removed or converted to numbers before saving as a .dat file. One more problem is that when you save your .dat file it will have the variable names in the first row, and NORM needs these to be removed. So open your file with Notepad and delete this line; then resave the file.

Now open NORM (by clicking on the .exe file, wherever you have saved it). Use the FILE > NEW SESSION menu choice. This will let you find the .dat file you created from your SPSS file. The first thing to do is make sure the code for missing variables is set to the code you used. Figure 3.20 shows that it is set to "−9," which is the code I used for missing variables.

The NORM help topic suggests you run the EM algorithm before imputing missing data (the EM algorithm is a method for obtaining maximum-likelihood estimates). To

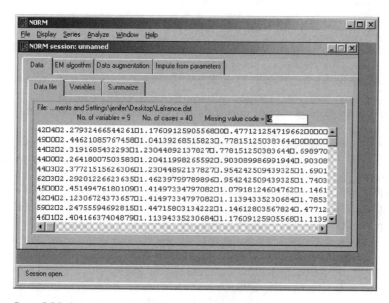

Figure 3.20 A session of NORM for imputing data (make sure "Missing value code" is set properly).

run this, just click on the tab that says "EM algorithm" and hit the "Run" button. When you run this an output file will come up on top, but just click on the area in blue that says "NORM session" to go back to the tabs. Once you have run the EM algorithm, NORM suggests running the data augmentation algorithm to simulate the values of the missing data. To do this, click on the "Data augmentation" tab and click the "Run" button. Last of all you'll use the "Impute from parameters" sheet, which will create an output file with the imputed missing data. Click "Run" again and the imputed data set will be saved to wherever you saved the original .dat file. I named my original file Lafrance.dat, and the imputed file was saved as Lafrance_0.imp.

To get the data back into SPSS, rename the file with the extension ".dat." Then, in SPSS, go to FILE > READ TEXT DATA. With the .dat extension you should be able to see your data in the browser window, so click on it and tell SPSS to "Open" it. You'll then be taken to the "Text Import Wizard." Basically you can just click "Next" through all of the steps. When SPSS opens up the file, it will not have variable names, but you can rename those with the "Variable View" tab. You will also be able to see that your missing data (labeled with "−9" before) is now replaced by imputed values.

3.6.2 Outliers

Sometimes in your data you will find points which stand out as being different from the bulk of the data. We saw in earlier sections that, if we are using the mean, one outlier can have a large effect on describing the typical value of a data set. Outliers are very problematic for "classic" statistics (and by this I mean parametric statistical methods which do not use robust methods of estimation) because data are assumed to follow a normal distribution *exactly*. If you have a distribution that is *approximately* normal, this unfortunately does not result in *approximately* the correct conclusions, as Maronna, Martin, and Yohai (2006) point out. If you are doing a complex math problem and you forget to carry a one to the tens position when adding numbers together, this will result in a *completely* wrong conclusion, not an *approximately* wrong conclusion. The presence of an outlier means that the distribution is not exactly a normal distribution.

Many texts which talk only about classic statistics advise you to use graphic summaries to identify outliers, and then remove them or run the analysis both with and without them. This chapter has explored many graphic approaches which can identify univariate outliers (outliers in a single variable), such as histograms, Q-Q plots, or stem and leaf plots. Tabachnick and Fidell (2001) argue that deletion is a good solution if the point is "highly correlated with others or is not critical to the analysis" (p. 71).

There are, however, several problems with simply manually deleting outliers. The first is that it is not objective, and completely up to the discretion of the individual researcher (Huber, 1981; Maronna, Martin, & Yohai, 2006). In addition, sometimes one outlier may mask another, so that when you throw away one data point you then find another that stands out, and where do you stop? Another objection is that the data may have come from a genuinely non-normal distribution, but you are ignoring that by cleaning up the data (Huber, 1981). A third problem is that, after removing an outlier, the data are not independent anymore, which is one of the assumptions of all statistical tests (Huber, 1981; Wilcox, 1998).

The problem becomes even more complex when you have more than one variable, such as in a regression analysis, and you need to examine whether there are multivariate outliers. This is again one of those difficult areas where "classic" statistics does really not have a better answer than that of manually deleting outliers and reporting the results both with and without what you consider to be outliers. In the future, SPSS should provide ways of dealing objectively with outliers through robust procedures. Robust methods will result in the objective elimination of outliers and will perform better than if data had been simply cleaned up. Robust methods are a more principled and powerful way to both identify and eliminate outliers.

3.6.3 Transforming Data

Another procedure that is commonly advised in books that treat "classic" statistics is to **transform** your data when you find it does not fit the parameters of a normal distribution, such as being skewed or having outliers. Transforming your variables can also result in more homogeneous variances. Most authors also caution, however, that interpreting the transformed values may be difficult. Tabachnick and Fidell (2001) note that if you are using a scale that has little intrinsic meaning, however, transformation does not seriously hinder later interpretation.

I have very rarely seen researchers in second language research report transforming variables. I suspect that many feel as I did, which is that this is a complicated area that I didn't understand well enough to actually use in my work. In fact, it is not very difficult to transform variables, and it is a perfectly legitimate thing to do to improve distributions to be more normal. Tabachnick and Fidell (2001) note that they have had success with improving distributional assumptions using transformations when variables are skewed in different directions, or some variables are skewed while others are not. However, when all the variables are skewed to about the same level, the authors say that in such a case transformations do not seem to make much difference.

Tabachnick and Fidell (2001) have a very useful table which gives recommendations for what kinds of transformations to use when data appear in various shapes. These transformations are simple to do. If you do decide to transform your data, you should check all of the indicators of normality and homogeneity of variances (as well as other assumptions that apply only in certain tests, such as the linearity assumption in correlation) with the transformed data to see whether any improvement has been achieved. Tabachnick and Fidell's recommendations are gathered into Table 3.7.

Table 3.7 Recommended Transformations for Data Problems

Distributional shape	Recommended transformation (X=column you want to transform)	Transformation if any zeros found in data
Moderate positive skewness	sqrt(X)	
Substantial positive skewness	log10(X)	log10(X + C*)
Severe positive skewness	1/X	1/(X + C)
Moderate negative skewness	sqrt(Z**–X)	
Substantial negative skewness	log10(Z**–X)	
Severe negative skewness	log10(Z((–X)	

 * C is a constant that is added so that the smallest value will equal 1
** Z is a constant that is added such that (Z–X) does not equal 0

To perform transformations of the data in SPSS, go to TRANSFORM > COMPUTE. Choose the appropriate function that you want to use. In SPSS 12.0 you could choose these directly from the list under the "Function" box, but in SPSS 15.0 and higher there is a box of "Function groups." Most of the functions you will want can be found in the "Arithmetic" group, such as the log function or the square root. Double-click on the function you want and it will appear in the "Numeric Expression" box with a question mark. Put the column you want to transform into that question mark area (see Figure 3.21). A new column appears and you can use this to perform statistical calculations (after checking to see if your transformed variable is better than the original one!).

Throughout the exercises in this chapter we have seen that the "GJTScore" variable in DeKeyser (2000) is negatively skewed. I will walk the reader through an example of transforming this data using SPSS. Tabachnick and Fidell recommend using a reflect and square root transformation for moderately negatively skewed data. To determine the Z constant, we first find that the largest value in the data set is 199. We will add 1, so that Z = 200. The expression I write in the box is SQRT(200-GJTSCORE). After obtaining this new column, I need to check on the distribution of this new variable, which I will do by looking at a histogram. Although the histogram in Figure 3.22 seems to show less skewness in the transformed variable, the skewness value of the non-transformed variable is −.3, while the skewness of the transformed variable is −.4, a little worse but really not much of a difference. It's probably not worthwhile to transform this variable, given there is little improvement. A check of the more extreme transformation using the LG10 function does not reveal a more normal distribution either.

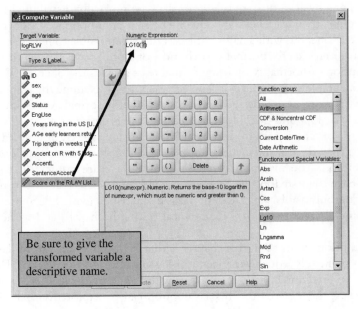

Figure 3.21 Performing a log transformation in SPSS.

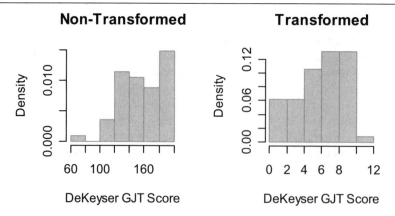

Figure 3.22 Checking the "GJTScore" variable with and without transformation for skewness.

3.6.4 Application Activities for Transforming Data

1   In previous exercises we have seen that the distribution of data for group 11 in the Flege, Yeni-Komshian, and Liu (1999) data is positively skewed. Perform the appropriate transformation on the data and look at the histograms for all groups. What is your conclusion about using a transformation for this variable?

3.7 Summary

There are many ways your data may not fit the standard assumptions for parametric statistical tests. Two of the assumptions about your data that can be examined through both numerical and graphical means are that your data are normally distributed and that, if there are groups, their variances are equal. The first assumption of a normal distribution is an exact one, but with small sample sizes it is impossible to tell whether your data comes from an exactly normal distribution or not. You can numerically examine the assumption of normality by using formal tests such as the Shapiro–Wilk test (the best one for sample sizes under 50). You can graphically examine the assumption of normality by looking at graphs such as histograms (with normal curves superimposed), stem and leaf plots, and Q-Q plots. With sample sizes under 30, the best you can hope for in these examinations is to see whether the data are skewed or not. If the data are skewed, you may try transformations to make the data conform more closely to a normal distribution. You may also be able to tell if there are outliers in your distribution, and I have suggested in this chapter that, although such treatment is not optimal, basically the only tools you have in "classic" statistics (with SPSS) are to remove outliers manually and to report on statistical testing both with and without outliers.

   The second assumption explored in this chapter is that, if you have groups of data, they will have approximately equal variances (this assumption is not exact). This assumption can be explored numerically by comparing the standard deviations of your groups and considering the scale used. This assumption can be explored visually by looking at boxplots and examining the length of the boxes. If this assumption is not met, a t-test can correct for the problem. For other tests, you might want to consider not including a group with a highly different variance.

Last of all, if your data set is missing data this can also be problematic for running the best statistical analysis possible. I have gone through some steps that you can use for imputing missing data values using the free NORM program that uses multiple imputation. This is a good way to continue to use all of the data that you have collected in your analyses.

Chapter 4

Changing the Way We Do Statistics: Hypothesis Testing, Power, Effect Size, and Other Misunderstood Issues

> To the [researcher] who practices this religion, Statistics refers to the seeking out and interpretation of p values. Like any good religion, it involves vague mysteries capable of contradictory and irrational interpretation. . . . And it provides Salvation: Proper invocation of the religious dogmas of Statistics will result in publication in prestigious journals. This form of Salvation yields fruit in this world (increases in salary, prestige, invitations to speak at meetings) and beyond this life (continual reference in the citation indexes).
>
> (Salsburg, 1985, p. 220)

As I have gotten immersed in statistics literature while writing this book, I have discovered that many people who are knowledgeable about statistics are dismayed by the almost fetishistic and uncomprehending use of significance tests by most applied researchers. Their dismay is easy to understand when applied researchers understand two things:

1 The question of whether a researcher can reject the null hypothesis (H_0) depends mostly upon the size of the sample being tested.
2 The information gleaned from **null hypothesis significance testing (NHST)** is quite impoverished. If the null hypothesis states that there is no difference between two groups ($\mu_1 - \mu_2 = 0$), then with large enough group sizes a difference of $\mu_1 - \mu_2 = 0.003$ could be a "statistically significant" result! The difference is really insignificant, but NHST is statistical.

Some statisticians have argued that, because of the way applied researchers misunderstand hypothesis testing, NHST should be abolished (see Kline, 2004, for a summary of the arguments). The weight of statistical history means that even with all these problems null hypothesis significance testing will probably not disappear, but there are a few important steps that researchers can take to make the statistical results from their studies meaningful and useful. They are:

1 Perform a **power analysis** *before* undertaking a study in order to determine the number of participants that should be included in a study to ensure an adequate level of power (power should be higher than .50 and ideally .80). Briefly put, power is the probability that you will find differences between groups or relationships among variables if they actually do exist.

2   Never set an **alpha level** lower than .05 and try to set it higher, to .10 if at all acceptable to the research community one is working in.
3   Report **effect sizes** and their interpretation.
4   Report **confidence intervals**.

The rationale for these steps and the practical tools to carry them out will be explained in this chapter and incorporated throughout the analyses in the following chapters.

4.1 Null Hypothesis Significance Tests

In Chapter 2 you received a preliminary introduction to null hypothesis significance testing. My impression is that the whole process of significance testing is fairly murky to the novice researcher. In this chapter I want to propose some corrections to this process, but I think you have to understand the process well in order to understand why corrections are necessary. Thus, in this section I will revisit the question of what null hypothesis significance testing involves.

First, let's say a researcher has a question in their mind—will adults who practice meaningful grammar drills for 15 minutes every day learn and retain the grammar better than adults who tell a story that causes them to use the grammar for 15 minutes every day? We will call this the research hypothesis (H_R):

H_R: Will 15 minutes of practice of meaningful drills result in more accurate grammar scores than 15 minutes of telling a story where the grammar in question must be used?

A researcher with this question in mind might then examine two groups: one group will do the explicit but meaningful grammar drills while in the other group students will use the grammar implicitly by telling stories to each other. The groups can then be tested and mean scores for their grammatical accuracy computed. Clearly, the two groups will not have exactly the same mean scores. There are two possibilities to explain the differences in mean scores between groups:

1   The difference in scores between the groups is due to the fact that there were differential effects for the way that grammar was practiced, and this effect was large enough that it cannot simply be attributed to sampling error.
2   The differences in scores between groups is small and can reasonably be attributed to the normal variation in scores we would expect to find between groups of people (the **sampling error**).

As was discussed briefly in Chapter 2, the way to test which of these possibilities is correct is to transform our original question into a statement that there is no difference between groups, or no effect for treatment (the **null hypothesis**, H_0):

H_0: There is no [statistical] difference between a group which practices grammar using explicit meaningful drills for 15 minutes each day and a group which uses grammar implicitly by telling stories where the grammar is needed for 15 minutes each day.

Now we need to have an **alternative hypothesis** as well, something that we can use if we are able to reject the null hypothesis:

H$_a$: There is a [statistical] difference between the explicit and implicit group.

Note that neither the null nor the alternative hypothesis is the same as the research hypothesis. However, if we are able to reject the null hypothesis and accept the alternative hypothesis, looking at the mean scores will tell us which group performed statistically better than the other, and we can thus address the research hypothesis.

Now that the hypothesis has been formulated, a test statistic is used to assess the correctness of the hypothesis. Since only two groups are being compared, a t-test can be used. The t-test statistic is calculated based on three pieces of information: the mean scores of the groups, their variances, and the size of each group (the sample sizes). The distribution of the *t*-statistic is known and has been calculated already by statisticians. However, the value of the t-test statistic depends on the **degrees of freedom**, because the distribution changes shape as the degrees of freedom change. As Baayen (2008, p. 68) says, "What we want to know is whether the test statistic has a value that is extreme, so extreme that it is unlikely to be attributable to chance. . . . Whether a test statistic has an extreme value is evaluated by calculating how far out it is in one of the tails of the distribution."

In the NHST process, we should have already decided on a cut-off level that we will use to consider the results of the statistical test extreme. This is usually called the **alpha (a) level** or **significance level**. Before the advent of computers, after one calculated the *t*-statistic by hand, one then looked up the critical value for the statistic at a certain level of degrees of freedom in a table. For example, for a t-test with df = 18 (that would mean there were 10 people in each group, minus 1 degree of freedom for each of the two groups), the critical values of *t* are 1.33 for $a = 0.10$ and 1.73 for $a = .05$. This means we would expect to find a value of *t* that was 1.33 or larger only 10% of the time, and a value of *t* that was 1.73 or larger 5% of the time, if the null hypothesis were true.

With computers and SPSS, then, the actual *p*-value that is returned when doing a statistical test is the probability that we would get a value of the *t*-statistic as extreme as we have found assuming that the null hypothesis is true (in other words, there is no need to look up critical values anymore). This *p*-value is the proportion of the distribution that has a value as extreme as the *t*-statistic or larger (it tells us how far out in the tails of the distribution we are). I like how Baayen (2008, p. 68) phrases it: "The smaller this proportion is, the more reason we have for surprise that our test statistic is as extreme as it actually is." If the *p*-value is lower than the alpha level we set, we reject the null hypothesis and accept the alternative hypothesis that there is a difference between the two groups. If the *p*-value is larger than the alpha level, we "fail to reject" the null hypothesis (this doesn't necessarily mean the alternative hypothesis is correct, but most of the time that is what authors will assume).

Now in Chapter 2 I drilled the following interpretation of *p*-values into your head:

> Meaning of the *p*-value: The probability of finding a [insert statistic name here] this large or larger if the null hypothesis were true is [insert *p*-value].

I did this because *p*-values are often misinterpreted. One common misinterpretation is that the *p*-value is the probability that the null hypothesis is true. Not so. The *p*-value is the conditional probability of the *data* (the test statistic value that we found) given the hypothesis. In other words, if we were to repeat the experiment a large number of times, and if it were true that there was no difference between groups (or no relationship among variables), what is the probability that we would find this particular data outcome? For a *p*-value of 0.05, that probability is 5%. Notice that this is the probability of the data given the hypothesis or, written using logical notation, p(Data | H$_0$), *not* the probability of the hypothesis given the data. Think it doesn't matter? Young (1993) says a favorite example from statistical philosophers to illustrate this difference in perspectives is that the probability of being dead, if hung, P(Dead | Hung) is quite different from the probability of having been hung, if dead, P(Hung | Dead). You can see these are not the same thing at all! What you know from a *p*-value is the probability of the *data* given the hypothesis, so you cannot say anything at all about the probability that the hypothesis is true or not.

Notice that the *p*-value is also *not* the probability that the results are due to chance. Since we have *assumed* that the null hypothesis is true, we are looking at a conditional probability, not at the probability of chance. This is a subtle difference and one that many textbook writers get wrong as well, so I have spent some time here going through the logic of null hypothesis significance testing to try to help you understand it correctly. It is true that I will argue against a heavy reliance on *p*-values throughout the book because I think that, for example, confidence intervals are more informative, but NHST is the type of logic that you will see in studies in the second language research literature, and it is necessary to understand how NHST works before you can comprehend how other measures might be better.

4.1.1 One-Tailed versus Two-Tailed Tests of Hypotheses

In the type of hypothesis testing I have just described, the default method of testing the hypothesis is to use a **two-tailed test**. Thus, if we have an alpha level of $a = .05$, this means that we would reject results that fell in the highest 2.5% of the distribution *or* the lowest 2.5% of the distribution, making up a total 5% probability that the data would be as extreme as or more extreme than what we found. In other words, in our null hypothesis, we would be examining both the possibility that the explicit group was better than the implicit group and the possibility that the explicit group was worse than the implicit group. The hypothesis could go in either direction.

However, if the only thing we care about is just *one* of the possibilities, then we can use a one-tailed test. For example, let's say at the current moment we are already using the explicit way of practicing grammar in our classes. So we don't really care to know if the explicit way is better than the implicit way; we only want to know if the implicit way is better than the explicit one, because if it is we'll then implement that into our curriculum (in reality, I think I would want to know if the implicit method was worse, but, for purposes of illustrating what a one-tailed test is, let's just pretend we only care about one outcome). A **one-tailed** or **directional** test of a hypothesis looks only at one end of the distribution. A one-tailed test will have more power to find differences, because it can allocate the entire alpha level to one side of the distribution and not have to split it up between both ends. Figure 4.1 tries to illustrate this idea. The figure shows

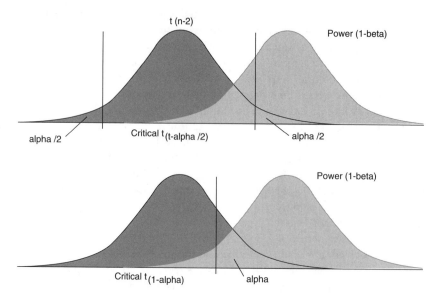

Figure 4.1 The top diagram shows the area under the curve used for testing a two-tailed hypothesis, while the bottom diagram shows a one-tailed hypothesis (*Source:* http://www.psycho.uni-duesseldorf.de/aap/projects/gpower/reference/ reference_ manual_02.html. With permission).

a *t*-distribution where the curve on the left represents the *t*-distribution, and the curve on the right is the amount of power. In the top diagram, a two-tailed test, both the left and right sides of the *t*-distribution are tested for difference, resulting in an area of alpha/2. This means that the possibility of one group being better than the other and the possibility of that group being worse than the other are both tested. In the bottom diagram, a one-tailed test, all of the alpha is tested on the right side of the distribution, which could represent the possibility of one group being better than the other only (the possibility that that group is worse than the other is not tested). With all of the alpha concentrated on one tail, the critical value can be lower (in terms of its value on the *x*-axis), and it can be seen that there is more power to find differences because the area under the curve for alpha overlaps more with the power distribution than it did for the top diagram.

If you do decide to conduct a one-tailed test, however, you will want to make sure that you can live with the result if no differences are found. It would be considered cheating to first examine which way the differences lay and then, after the fact, decide to change from a two-tailed to a one-tailed test in order to be able to reject the null hypothesis.

4.1.2 Outcomes of Statistical Testing

Table 4.1 shows the four possible outcomes for testing hypotheses when using inferential statistics. Two of the boxes in the table correspond to correct situations. In other words, this is when the actual situation that exists is correctly matched to the outcome

Table 4.1 Four Situations that a Researcher may Encounter

		True situation in the population	
		No effect exists	Effects exist
Outcome observed in study	No effect exists	Correct situation (probability=$1-a$)	Type II error (probability=β)
	Effects exist	Type I error (probability=a)	Correct situation (probability=$1-\beta$)

↑
Power

of the statistical test. However, there are two boxes in the table that correspond to incorrect situations. These are outcomes that are mismatched to the real situation in the population.

The first is called a **Type I error**, and this is when a researcher concludes that there was an effect for some treatment, but the truth is that there is actually no effect. Traditionally researchers have been most concerned with avoiding Type I errors. In this way, we avoid making mistakes and thinking there are statistical differences between groups when in fact there are none. A Type I error has been called being gullible or overeager (Rosnow & Rosenthal, 1989).

A **Type II error** is directly connected to the power of the study. This kind of error is made when a researcher concludes that there is no effect of a treatment when in fact there is an effect. A conclusion like this would result in researchers losing information because they were not able to detect the effect in their sample when it actually does exist in the population. Type II errors have been called errors of being overly cautious or blind (Rosnow & Rosenthal, 1989). Table 4.1 tries to set out the conditions in which Type I and Type II errors occur (and the times when the correct inferences are made).

Avoiding Type I error is desirable, but it comes at the price of increasing the chance of Type II error. That is, the steps one takes to decrease the chance of a Type I error (such as setting the alpha level lower) directly affect the amount of power in the study, which will increase the chances of a Type II error. In fact, some have argued that if researchers do not actually believe the null hypothesis is true (or, in other words, they think that the treatment they are implementing does have some effect) then a Type I error cannot actually be made! Some researchers have argued that this means the results from such a patently false hypothesis are meaningless (Murphy, 1990) or that the *p*-value of an implausible null hypothesis will be low to begin with, so it is little accomplishment to find that you can reject it (Kline, 2004). Murphy and Myors (2004) argue that, if the null hypothesis is wrong, which researchers almost always believe it to be, then there is no way a Type I error can be made (rejecting the null hypothesis when it is true). The implication is that researchers' concern with protecting against a Type I error is misguided, so avoiding Type II errors by making sure power is adequate is the critical issue for researchers (Maxwell & Delaney, 2004; Murphy & Myors, 2004). If power is high enough, treatment effects will be able to be found. Murphy and Myors (2004, p. vii) state that if we "fail to detect the real effects of treatments or interventions [this] might substantially impede the progress of scientific research."

4.1.3 Avoiding Type II Errors

Type I error (being overeager): Concluding there is a relationship when there is none.
- Set Type I error level by setting alpha (a) level
  - Commonly set at $a = .05$
  - Possibility of a Type I error is thus 5%.

Type II error (being overly cautious): Concluding there is no relationship when there is one.
- Set Type II error level (β) and then calculate power (power = $1 - \beta$)
  - Commonly set at $\beta = .20$, resulting in power = .80
  - Possibility of Type II error is thus 20%.
- Avoid low power by:
  - having adequate sample sizes
  - using reliable dependent variable
  - controlling for individual differences
  - including a pre-test
  - using a longer post-test
  - making sure not to violate statistical assumptions.

(Maxwell & Delaney, 2004, p. 26)

Note: Power is not the same thing as effect size.

Readers may wonder how best to avoid both types of errors. A list of possibilities is given in the box above. As can be seen from the box, the only way to change the probability of a Type I error is to change the alpha level one sets as a cut-off for their experiment. If you want to decrease the probability of a Type I error, you would need to set the alpha level lower than $a = 0.05$. However, if the probability of a Type I error is already low to begin with (just 5%), it might make sense to actually increase the alpha level to allow more possibilities of Type I errors. Although it may sound strange to advocate higher possibilities of error, the reader must remember that the probabilities of Type I and Type II errors are a tradeoff, and if the probability of a Type I error is lowered then the probability of a Type II error is increased. An increase in the alpha level to $a = .10$ would then decrease the probability of Type II errors, which, as we will see, are probably at least 20% or higher in most studies. It doesn't make a lot of sense to keep Type I errors at 5% while Type II errors are 20% or more! I don't know if this type of change would have to be instituted by journal editors in order to be adopted, or if individual authors could just quote people who advocate such an increase in the alpha level, but . . . why don't you try it? Quote me, and quote also Kline (2004) and Murphy and Myors (2004), who have argued that the alpha level should be set to $a = .10$ in the social sciences.

Beyond changing the alpha level, the next easiest way to avoid Type II errors is to increase power through increasing sample sizes. Although some researchers may argue that it is difficult to increase sample sizes, fewer studies with more power to find results would be preferable to more studies which do not really have enough power to make any clear conclusions about treatment effects. These kinds of studies with low power lead to inconsistent results across similar studies and instability in the field. If a study does not reject the null hypothesis, the first place a researcher should look is at power. It is likely that power was not high enough in the study to make any conclusions. However, because researchers do not understand power, they most often try to explain their lack of results through some kind of alteration to their theory. Murphy and Myors (2004, p. 107) state, "If power analyses were routinely included in the process of designing and planning studies, large samples would be the norm and sampling error would not loom so large as a barrier to cumulative progress in research."

I know this type of admonition can be hard to hear. Students in my language acquisition classes are routinely scornful of the small sample sizes (10–15 participants) they see in the published literature, but, when the time comes to run an experiment, obtaining 15 participants per group may seem like a great accomplishment! The fact of the matter is that it can be hard to find enough people who fit in certain categories to obtain more participants, and I myself have published studies with only 15 participants or fewer in a group. Furthermore, the field of second language research is not so different from other disciplines in the social sciences or even the medical field which may make broad recommendations based on not that many participants in a study. Therefore, I urge researchers to do the power analyses and then try to collect large sample sizes, but not to give up if they cannot reach the intended number for the sample size. We should strive to improve, but if large samples cannot be gathered we can at least be cognizant of the fact that our small sample sizes may be responsible for inconsistent results when addressing theoretical questions.

4.1.4 Problems with NHST

I have mentioned several times that there are problems with using the NHST method of making conclusions about experiments. Several recent books (Kline, 2004; Murphy & Myors, 2004) and the report by Wilkinson and the Task Force on Statistical Inference (1999) have sounded the alarm about the problems that NHST presents in the social sciences. Although there are many problems, I will lay out just one or two that I can do something to remedy right away. One is that some authors interpret a low p-value as indicative of a very strong result. On the one hand, you have probably read that a lower p-value does not make a study more significant, in the generally accepted sense of being important. On the other hand, the p-value of a study is an index of group size and the power of the study, and this is why a p-value of .049 and a p-value of .001 are not equivalent, although both are lower than $a = .05$. If the p-value is going to be reported, it is worth knowing the exact value of it, so I (and many others, including Kline, 2004; Maxwell & Delaney, 2004; Murphy & Myors, 2004; Wilkinson & Task Force on Statistical Inference, 1999) advocate reporting exact p-values, instead of reporting only that they are above or below critical levels. One thing a low p-value may indicate is that the same results would be found in a replication of the study, but the fact that a "statistically significant" result has already been found may stop others in the field from in fact trying to replicate studies.

Going along with this problem of interpreting p-values as indicating the importance of a study is the tradition of talking about "statistically significant" results. As linguists who care about the meaning of words we may want to follow Kline's (2004, p. 20) recommendation that we "drop the word 'significant' from our data analysis vocabulary" and instead reserve it for its usual connotation, which is as something important.

Just because a result has a *p*-value below 0.05 does not mean it is an important result. An effect size will have more to say about the importance of results than a *p*-value. And reporting confidence intervals when possible is something that statistical researchers believe would have a great effect on how others view the results of statistical studies. If we see a confidence interval that does not go through zero but is quite wide, this would indicate that there is low precision in any estimates (mean differences, statistics, etc.) given from the study. Kline (2004, p. 76) says that "relatively wide confidence intervals indicate that the study contains only limited information, a fact that is concealed when only results of statistical tests are reported."

In summary, I will change the way I do statistics in this book by making the following changes:

- reporting exact *p*-values (unless they are so small it would take too much room to report them)
- talking about "statistical" results instead of "significant" or "statistically significant" results
- providing confidence intervals and effect sizes whenever possible

4.2 Power Analysis

Many readers may have heard that it is important to consider statistical power, but have little idea of what power is or how to calculate it. Researchers' ignorance of what power is most likely causes valuable data to be lost. Tversky and Kahneman say that the "prevalence of studies deficient in statistical power is not only wasteful but actually pernicious: it results in a large proportion of invalid rejections of the null hypothesis among published results" (1971, p. 107).

What is power? **Power** is the probability of detecting a statistical result when there are in fact differences between groups or relationships between variables. Sufficient power will ensure that real differences are found and discoveries are not lost. Because most researchers are testing a treatment that they believe has some effect, "power often translates into the probability that the test will lead to a correct conclusion about the null hypothesis" (Murphy & Myors, 2004, p. vii).

4.2.1 What Are the Theoretical Implications if Power is Not High?

If the power of a test is .50, this means that there is only a 50% chance that a true effect will be detected. In other words, even though there is in fact an effect for some treatment, the researcher has only a 50/50 chance of finding that effect. A survey of power in articles published in experimental psychology showed that the median power for medium effects at the alpha = .05 level was only .37 (Sedlmeier & Gigerenzer, 1989), a dismally small level of power that means that, in many cases when significant differences or correlations are not found, it is not because they do not exist but because there is not enough power in the study to discover them (Cohen, 1988). A lack of power leads to instability in results from similar studies, and researchers may look for theoretical explanations for the failure to distinguish between groups when their first question should be whether the study actually had enough power to adequately detect a difference in the first place. The truth of the matter is that researchers should not be conducting studies that do not have enough power to detect possible effects (Murphy & Myors, 2004). The only reliable way to avoid doing this is to calculate a priori power levels and use these to guide the choice of sample size.

4.2.2 What Is the Optimal Level of Power?

Murphy and Myors (2004) state that there is a consensus that power should be above .50 and would be judged adequate at .80. A power level of .80 would mean that four out of five times a real effect in the population will be found. A power level of .50 would mean that you as a researcher would "accept a .50 risk of failing to confirm a valid research hypothesis" (Tversky & Kahneman, 1971, p. 110).

If studies in the field of second language research currently follow the trend in psychological studies (and there is no reason to think they would fare any better), power levels are so low as to set researchers up for failure to find statistical results. Clearly, we need to take the issue of power seriously. Power levels ought to be calculated before a study is done, and not after. As Kline (2004) says, "a post hoc analysis that shows low power is more like an autopsy than a diagnostic procedure" (p. 43).

I will use the free internet program R in order to show you how to calculate power. I like the R program for calculating power because one can calculate post-hoc power and also use Cohen's guide to effect sizes for estimating how large the effect will be. Previously when I have read about calculating power, I was always put off by the fact that I had to estimate how large my effect size would be before I performed my experiment. I didn't understand how I would do that. Of course, it would be wonderful if every time you planned an experiment you had pilot data or effect sizes from previous research, but I don't think that is a realistic expectation in our field right now. I have investigated another free internet program for calculating power devised by Russ Lenth and found at http://www.cs.uiowa.edu/~rlenth/Power/. There are several reasons I prefer R to Lenth's program, even though Lenth's program may be more sophisticated. One is that Lenth does not let you calculate post-hoc power, just sample size or effect size (so I could not demonstrate what kind of power studies in the field have had). The second problem is that, instead of using effect sizes (which could be estimated with Cohen's guidelines), Lenth uses means and standard deviations. This works well if you have already performed the test but I think it leaves the average researcher feeling lost if they try to plan what the standard deviations of the groups, or the mean difference between groups, will be *before* they are tested. If you do have such information, then I can recommend Length's program. If you are like I was and are not sure how to get started with power, then please download R from http://cran.r-project.org/ (click on the first highlighted link you come to that is appropriate for your system—Linux, Mac, or Windows; for Windows you'll then choose "base" and look for the .exe file; for Mac look for a .dmg file).

Once you have installed R and opened it, you will see some menus across the top of the R graphical interface (RGui). Pull down menu choice PACKAGES > INSTALL PACKAGES. This should first take you to a CRAN mirror site, where you will have to choose a geographically close download site. Once you choose that, you will see a very long list of packages. Choose the one called "pwr." Click on it, and it will be downloaded into R. You are now ready to follow the directions in the next section for obtaining power estimates. Just one word about R though—it is an environment where precision must be used in the commands. Therefore, when you open the library, you'll need to type "library(pwr)" (without the quotation marks), but if you typed "Library(pwr)" with a capital "L" it would not work. The commands seen in Section 4.2.3 will be given after a prompt (>), which is what you will see in the R window.

4.2.3 Examples of Power Analyses

A number of examples using my own data (which I consider by no means out of the ordinary from others published in the field) will demonstrate that the levels of power that are currently found in our studies are often wanting. A study I did with Japanese learners of English (Larson-Hall & Connell, 2005) asked the question of whether length of residence correlated to accuracy in producing words beginning with R and L. There were two groups of Japanese learners who performed quite differently in the study: experienced Japanese ($n = 15$) and inexperienced Japanese ($n = 15$). Therefore, I calculated the correlation separately among these groups, and I will calculate the power of each correlation separately.

The power test for correlations requires four out of these five arguments:

1   number of participants
2   effect size (linear correlation coefficient=r)
3   significance level
4   power
5   specification as one-sided (**one-tailed**) or two-sided (**two-tailed**) test

By the way, to find out more about the arguments that you will need in the power test for correlation, type "help(pwr.r.test)" at the R prompt. A help window will appear and you will be able to see what arguments must be included in the test. Some of these arguments have a default which you can see under the "Usage" area (such as a significance level of $a = .05$), so, if you don't type them, R will just use the default value.

Also, I know that you may not know much about effect sizes yet. I will explain effect sizes in Section 4.3, and this section shows that one of the reasons for understanding effect sizes is to understand power. But for now just think of **effect size** as a number which shows how big the difference is between groups or how much of a relationship is explained by the variables you've used. For correlation, the effect size can range between 0 to 1, with larger numbers showing more of a relationship between your variables.

To implement the correlation test with my data, first I will look just at the experienced group. Since I know the effect size for my correlation ($r = -.58$, but only the size, not the sign, matters), the number of participants (15), the cut-off level for alpha that I was setting (.05), and the fact that it was a two-tailed test, I can easily calculate my power:

```
>library(pwr)
>pwr.r.test(n = 15, r = .58, sig.level = .05, alternative=c("two.sided"))

approximate    correlation    power    calculation    (arctangh
transformation)
```

```
            n = 15
            r = 0.58
    sig.level = 0.05
        power = 0.6311853
  alternative = two.sided
```

The R results show that my power was 63%. Although at this level my power is better than 50%, it is not great. A power level of 0.63 means there was a 37% chance I would not find the real result. According to Cohen (1988), the effect size (r = .58) I found for this correlation was large, but the number of participants was small, which is why the power was not large. However, among the inexperienced Japanese, I found a smaller effect size (r = .37). Although this is a medium to large effect size according to Cohen (1992), my power was only .27, which means I had only about a one in four chance of finding a statistical correlation if it in fact existed.

This discussion is of course an a posteriori power analysis, which does not do me much good if I want to find statistical results! Ideally, I would have performed a power analysis *before* I conducted my experiment. Let's say I decided I wanted to perform this analysis, and I anticipated a medium effect size. Cohen (1992) says for correlation that a medium effect size would be r = .3. Not knowing any other literature on the topic that would give me a better sense of the magnitude of effect sizes in this area, I decide to start with Cohen's suggestion. I know I'd like a power level of .80, so I get the following power analysis:

```
> pwr.r.test(r = .3, sig.level = .05, power = .8)
```

```
            n = 84.74891
            r = 0.3
    sig.level = 0.05
        power = 0.8
  alternative = two.sided
```

Notice that I didn't specify the type of test but R used the two-sided test as a default.

According to this analysis, I would need 85 people to be able to have a power level of 80%. This seems like a lot, and I'm not sure I'll be able to gather that many people. I decide to think about using a one-tailed test, to test the hypothesis that a longer length of residence is positively correlated to more accuracy on the pronunciation test.

```
> pwr.r.test(r = .3, sig.level = .05, power = .8, alternative=c("greater"))
```

```
            n = 67.19195
            r = 0.3
    sig.level = 0.05
        power = 0.8
  alternative = greater
```

If I am only looking for a positive correlation I would need 67 participants in order to find a medium effect size, if the relationship exists. If I decide to do a one-tailed hypothesis test, however, I will have to be sure I can live with the results if I do not find a positive correlation.

It is usually better to plan your power analysis by expecting small or small to medium effects, because if the effects are larger you will also find them (Murphy & Myors, 2004). However, if you plan for a large effect but the effects are small, you will have little useful information.

Another study I did with Japanese learners of Russian (Larson-Hall, 2004) used a repeated measures ANOVA statistical analysis. Calculating the power found in this test is somewhat more complicated than for the correlation, as this was a repeated measures ANOVA, not a one-way ANOVA. However, Cohen (1988) states that multiple ANOVAs can have their power analyzed simply by looking separately at the power of each variable or **interaction** (an interaction is when two variables must be considered together to explain their effects—they are not just the addition of one effect plus the other). My variables were proficiency level and contrast. I had four levels in my proficiency level variable, but there were unequal numbers of participants in each of the levels ($n = 11,12,10,8$). Cohen (1988) says that in cases of unequal groups one should use the harmonic mean of the group sizes,[1] which in my case would be $4 / \frac{1}{11} + \frac{1}{12} + \frac{1}{10} + \frac{1}{8} = \frac{4}{.399} = 10.025$ or 10, rounding to the nearest integer.

I will look only at the power for the proficiency level variable. The **pwr.anova.test** command for the **pwr** library requires four out of the following five parameters:

1   number of groups
2   number of participants in each group
3   effect size (Cohen's f^2, but just f is used; note that this is NOT Cohen's d)
4   significance level
5   power

There are four groups ($k = 4$), with 10 in each group (using the harmonic mean calculation). The effect size called for in this test is **Cohen's f^2** (although actually this test uses the f, not the f^2). This effect size is most often used with multiple regression and ANOVA, and can range larger than 1. The larger the number, the bigger the difference. Cohen's f can easily be converted from an eta-squared (η^2) effect size (see one-way ANOVA entry in Table 4.7), which can be calculated from the ANOVA printout which gives the sums of squares. I did not report an ANOVA-style table in this article (for information about figuring out sums of squares with only F-values, p-values and group sizes, see Young (1993)). Of course, I have access to my own data and, to demonstrate how to calculate eta-squared using information from an ANOVA computer analysis, I will insert my data here.

I used a repeated-measures ANOVA with one between-group factor (proficiency level) and one within-group factor (contrast). The proficiency level factor whose effect size I want to examine is fixed, so according to Olejnik and Algina (2000) I can calculate eta-squared using this formula: $\eta^2 = \dfrac{SS_{between-groups}}{SS_{total}}$.

---

[1] The harmonic mean is $H = n/(1/a_1 + 1/a_2 + \ldots + 1/a_n)$ where a_n is each number and n is the number of numbers; this number is usually not very different from the arithmetic average.

Table 4.2 ANOVA Table for Larson-Hall (2004) Data

Source	SS (sum of squares)	DF (degrees of freedom)	MS (mean squares)	F
Between subjects**	30.22	40		
Level	16.05	3	5.35	13.97
SS w/in groups (labeled Error (level) from SPSS print-out)	14.17	37	.38	
Within subjects**	161.34	615		
Contrast	39.22	15	2.62	14.0
Contrast*level	18.38	45	.41	2.19
Contrast*SS w/in groups (labeled Error (contrast) from SPSS print-out)	103.74	555	.19	
Total**	191.56	655		

* Multiplied by
** I calculated these numbers by adding together the relevant rows; for example, the "Between subjects" SS value was obtained by adding together the SS for level (16.05) and the SS of the error for level (14.17)

Using the data in Table 4.2, the calculation of eta-squared for the overall effect size of this repeated-measures ANOVA is: $\eta^2 = \dfrac{30.22}{191.56} = .157$. Then $f^2 = \dfrac{\eta^2}{1-\eta^2} = \dfrac{.157}{.843} = .186$, so $f = .432$.

```
> pwr.anova.test(k = 4,n = 10,f = .432)

Balanced one-way analysis of variance power calculation

          k = 4
          n = 10
          f = 0.432
  sig.level = 0.05
      power = 0.568864

NOTE: n is number in each group
```

The analysis shows that my power was only 57%, which means I essentially had a 50/50 chance of finding the actual result. I put my own work forward so as not to point fingers at this stage of our statistical sophistication (or lack of it) in the field, but more to say that we should take advantage of the relative ease of computing power to help us get a better understanding of the size of groups we should be aiming for, since it is the size of the group which is the most easily manipulable part of the power equation (if done a priori!).

Let's say that I used this study as pilot data in order to see how many participants I would need in each group to get increased power. I decide I will try to increase my power to .80, keeping the same number of groups and assuming the same effect size.

```
> pwr.anova.test(k = 4,f = .432,power = .8)
```

The results tell me I need about 16 in each group. This is not so much, and I hope it shows that a priori power testing can be very helpful for determining group sizes and need not result in ridiculous or unattainable numbers of participants.

Last of all, I will show an example of calculating power when only two groups are involved. I will use the **pwr.t.test** command, which requires five out of the six parameters:

1   number of participants per sample (n)
2   effect size (**Cohen's d**)
3   significance level
4   power
5   specification as one-, two-, or paired-samples
6   specification as two-tailed test or one-tailed hypothesis

I will continue to look at the data from Larson-Hall (2004). In this study, I looked at specific sound contrasts. I found that Japanese learners of Russian especially had trouble with two contrasts, one of which was /l/ versus /r/. There were three groups of learners, but I looked at **post-hoc tests** which just compared two groups at a time. So let's say I wanted to see how much power I had in doing these post-hoc comparisons. For number of participants, as seen above this was not equal, but I will use the harmonic mean of 10. To calculate the **Cohen's d**, an effect size used with t-tests which has no range limits and measures differences in terms of standard deviations, I need to know the mean scores, the standard deviations, and the group sizes. I list these in Table 4.3 for the /l/ to /r/ contrast only.

In my paper I reported that the contrast between the beginner group and native speakers (NS) of Russian and the intermediate group and NS was statistical at the $p < .05$ level. However, I did not report the effect size of these differences. Using the data given, I can calculate effect sizes for the three comparisons I was interested in, those of each of the learner groups against the native speakers. The formula for Cohen's d is $d = \dfrac{\overline{X}_1 - \overline{X}_2}{\sigma}$, where the denominator is the correct standardizer. If the variances are equal, the standard deviations can be pooled. Here, it seems the variances are not equal, so I should pick a standard deviation from one of the groups, usually the control group, to be the standardizer. In this case, I will choose the standard deviation from the learner group to be the standardizer, because that will make the effect size smaller than if the NS group SD were used. Thus, for the comparison of the beginners and the NS $d = \dfrac{.98 - .71}{.14} = 1.93$, for the intermediates and NS $d = 1.0$, and for the

Table 4.3 Data for Larson-Hall (2004) Study

	Beginners	Intermediates	Advanced	Native speakers
n size	11	12	10	8
Mean	.71	.78	.82	.98
Standard deviation	.14	.20	.11	.07

advanced and NS $d = 1.45$. These are all considered fairly large effect sizes, and indicate that the difference between groups is at least one standard deviation apart. This is interesting, because the effect size of the difference between the advanced group and the NS is large even though the post-hoc comparison was not statistical.

Now to find out how much power I had to find real results:

> pwr.t.test(n = 10, d = 1.93, type=c("two.sample")) #for Beginners

The power in the beginner versus NS comparison was very high, at 98%. For the intermediates, with their lower effect size, the power was 56%, and for the advanced group the power was 87%. To have reached a power level of 80% for the intermediate group, with their effect size of $d = 1$, I would have needed 17 participants in each group.

4.2.4 Help with Calculating Power Using R

The previous section demonstrated how the "pwr" library in the R program could be used with real data. Table 4.4 provides you with a guide to the necessary elements for each test that is available. This section brings together information about how to use the arguments for the "pwr" library, how to calculate effect sizes, and Cohen's guidelines as to the magnitude of effect sizes. Cohen meant for these guidelines to be a help to those who may not know how to start doing power analyses, but once you have a better idea of effect sizes you may be able to make your own guidelines about what constitutes a small, medium, or large effect size for the particular question you are studying. Remember that obtaining a small effect size means that you think the difference between groups is going to be quite small. If you think the difference between groups is going to be quite large and obvious, you will not need as many participants.

If you are planning a study before you run it, the most useful way to use the power analysis is to decide how many participants you will need. You can try substituting in different levels of power, such as .6 or .8 to see how they will affect the number of participants you need.

You can run the power analysis after you have conducted your study to see how much power you had. If you find your power was low, you might surmise that non-statistical results were due to low power and should not be used to justify accepting the null hypothesis. Although many of the authors cited in this section urge researchers to conduct power analyses, it is likely that power analysis will not become truly popular (and thus useful) until, as Sedlmeier and Gigerenzer (1989) postulate, journal editors begin to require power analyses as well as p-values and effect sizes.

4.2.5 Application Activity with Power Calculation

1   Suppose you wanted to do a study to find out whether pronunciation training could help improve the comprehensibility of call center workers in Mexico. You have three treatment groups: 1) one-on-one tutoring for individual pronunciation problems; 2) computer-adaptive training; 3) a video course for pronunciation problems for L1 Spanish speakers. You want to see if there are any differences between the comprehensibility ratings for each of these groups of speakers, but

Table 4.4 Using R Commands to Calculate Power

Power test: One-way analysis of variance

Note: This test specifies a one-way ANOVA with the same number of participants in each group. If you have different numbers of participants in your groups, Cohen (1988) recommends calculating the harmonic mean. If you have a factorial or repeated measures ANOVA, you can use power analysis on each factor (or the most important factor) in order to estimate the power you need.

R Command	pwr.anova.test(k=NULL, n=NULL, f=NULL, sig.level=.05.power=NULL)
Required Elements (4 out of 5)	1) number of groups (k) 2) number of observations per group (n) 3) effect size (Cohen's f) 4) significance level (sig.level=.05) This is a default setting and does not need to be specified unless you want to change the default 5) power (power=)
Effect size for *f*	$f^2 = \dfrac{(df_{hyp} \times F)}{df_{err}}$ $f^2 = \dfrac{\eta^2}{1 - \eta^2}$	Cohen (1992) effect size magnitude guidelines for *f*: small=.10 medium=.25 large=.40

Power test: Correlation

R Command	pwr.r.test(n=NULL, r=NULL, sig.level=.05, power=NULL, alternative=c("two.sided", "less","greater"))
Required Elements (4 out of 5)	1) number of observations (n) 2) linear correlation coefficient (r) 3) significance level (sig.level=.05) This is a default setting and does not need to be specified unless you want to change the default 4) power (power=) 5) specification as two-sided test or one-sided (either "less" or "greater") (alternative=c("two.sided")) OR (alternative=c("less")) OR (alternative=c("greater")) Note that "two-sided" is default and does not need to be specified
Effect size for *r*	*r* is obtained directly from reported statistics of correlation	Cohen (1992) effect size magnitude guidelines for r: small=.10 medium=.30 large=.50

Power test: t-test

R Command	pwr.t.test(n=NULL, d=NULL, sig.level=.05, power=NULL, type=c("two.sample", "one.sample", "paired"), alternative=c("two.sided", "less", "greater"))
Required Elements (5 out of 6)	1) number of participants per sample (n) 2) effect size (Cohen's d)

3) significance level (sig.level=.05)
This is a default setting and does not need to be specified unless you want to change the default
4) power (power=)
5) specification as one-, two-, or paired-samples (type=c("one.sample"))
OR (type=c("two.sample")) OR (type=c("paired"))
6) specification as two-sided test or one-sided (either "less" or "greater")
(alternative=c("two.sided")) OR (alternative=c("less")) OR
(alternative=c("greater"))
Note that "two-sided" is default and does not need to be specified

Effect size for d	$d = \dfrac{Mean_1 - Mean_2}{\dfrac{(s_1^2 + s_2^2)}{2}}$ where s=standard deviation	Cohen (1992) effect size magnitude guidelines for d: small=.20 medium=.50 large=.80

Power test: Chi-square

R Command	pwr.chisq.test(w=NULL, N=NULL, df=NULL, sig.level=.05, power=NULL)
Required Elements (5 out of 6)	1) effect size (w) 2) total number of observations (N) 3) Degrees of freedom (a chi-square has two variables; calculate df by taking the number of categories or levels for each of the variables, subtract one from each, and multiply those two numbers together) 4) significance level (sig.level =.05) This is a default setting and does not need to be specified unless you want to change the default 5) power (power=)
Effect size for w	$w = \sqrt{\dfrac{\chi^2}{N}}$ Cohen (1992) effect size magnitude guidelines for w: small=.10 medium=.30 large=.50

you don't know how many participants to include from each group. Assuming you will see an effect size of Cohen's $f = .30$, and using a desired power level of 80% with the alpha level set at 0.05, calculate how many participants you will need in each group (this is a one-way ANOVA design).

2   Pretend you have just read about a study which tried to look at the relationship between scores on the Words in Sentences aptitude test and scores for the personality trait of neuroticism. The study had 10 participants, and found that the Pearson's correlation coefficient was $r = .04$. The authors conclude that there is no relationship between these two variables. Check to see how much power the test had, and calculate how many participants would be necessary to test the hypothesis given that the effect size was $r = .04$ in order to conduct the test with 80% power (this is a correlation test design). What do you conclude about the results of this correlation?

3   You are planning to do a study which will use a chi-square test. You will test

first-year French students to see if their speaking ability in French is low, medium or high (three levels) and then see whether that affects whether they carry on to take second-year French (yes/no). You hypothesize that there will be a medium effect size and you want to know how many participants you need at 80% power. Calculate df by taking the number of levels in each of the two variables, subtracting 1 from each and then multiplying the two together.

4   You have just read an article which examined the difference between two groups of ESL students, those with higher socio-economic status (SES) and those with lower SES. The study examined whether scores on a test of reading comprehension in their first language depended on SES, but found no statistical effect of group, contradicting previous studies. For the high-SES group the average score was 55 (with a standard deviation of 3.5), and for the low-SES group the average score on the reading comprehension test was 45 (with a standard deviation of 4). There were 15 participants in each group. Check to see how much power the t-test between the groups had, and calculate how many participants would be necessary to reach 80% power. Do you think that, based on this study, it is time to re-examine previous assumptions?

4.3 Effect Size

A power analysis directs researchers to pay attention to what Murphy and Myors (2004, p. 106) call "the most important parameter of all"—effect size. In general an **effect size** is "the magnitude of the impact of the independent variable on the dependent variable" (Kline, 2004, p. 97). Effect size gives researchers the information that they may have thought they were getting from a null hypothesis significance test (NHST), which is whether the difference between groups is important or negligible. An NHST merely tells the researcher and research consumer whether the study had sufficient power to find a difference that was greater, even if by a very small amount, than zero. An effect size gives the researcher insight into the size of this difference. If the effect size is quite small, then it may make sense to simply discount the findings as unimportant, even if they are statistical. If the effect size is large, then the researcher has found something that it is important to understand.

Whereas p-values and significance testing depend on the power of a test and thus, to a large measure, on group sizes, effect sizes do not change no matter how many participants there are (Maxwell & Delaney, 2004, p. 100). This makes effect sizes a valuable piece of information, much more valuable than the question of whether a statistical test is "significant" or not. Murphy and Myors (2004, p. 108) state that, "if power analysis did nothing more than direct researchers' attention to the size of their effects, it would be well worth the effort." Effect sizes are also useful to those who are doing meta-analysis. Currently, the only journal in the second language research field which requires effect sizes is *Language Learning*, but hopefully this situation will change in the future as more researchers (future editors) realize the importance of effect sizes.

Table 4.5 tries to illustrate the difference between statistical significance and effect sizes with fictional data (idea taken from "Primer on statistical significance and p values," 2007).

Table 4.5 shows that a study with a resulting p-value of $p = .08$ might have much more practical significance than one whose p-value was $p = .003$. This is because the

Table 4.5 An Illustration of the Importance of Effect Size

n, each group	Change in accuracy on cloze test for grammar		Main effect	p value	Appropriate conclusion
	Teaching method A	Teaching method B			
10	25 points	5 points	20 points	.08	Not statistical at an a=.05 level, but promising
1,000	6 points	4 points	2 points	.003	Statistical but unimportant in practice

first study had only 10 participants but was still able to find a large effect size (here looking at effect size as simply the difference between means and not worrying about standardizing it). This means that teaching method A is very promising for increasing grammatical accuracy on a cloze test, but it lacked the power to find a lower p-value because of the small sample sizes. On the other hand, the study with 1,000 participants did find a statistical difference between groups but the actual difference was quite small and probably not worth changing grammar teaching methods for.

I do not want to imply that small effect sizes are never worth taking notice of, however. At times, something with a small effect size may be important for advancing our understanding. Rosenthal (1990, cited in Breaugh, 2003) noted that the correlation found between taking aspirin and having a reduced chance of heart attacks was based on a study which found a correlation of .03 (a small effect, by Cohen's standards). The importance of effect sizes, as Cohen (1988) has himself noted, should very much depend on the field itself and not on his arbitrary conventions.

4.3.1 Understanding Effect Size Measures

Huberty (2002) divided effect sizes into two broad families—group difference indexes and relationship indexes—although it is important to note that in most cases there are algebraic calculations that can transform one kind into the other (Breaugh, 2003), and there are other kinds of effect sizes that do not fit into these categories, like odds ratios (Rosenthal & DiMatteo, 2001). Both the group difference and relationship effect sizes are ways to provide a standardized measure of the strength of the effect that is found.

A **group difference index**, or mean difference measure, has been called the **d family of effect sizes** by Rosenthal (1994). The prototypical effect size measure in this family is **Cohen's d**. Cohen's d measures the difference between two independent sample means, and expresses how large the difference is in standard deviations. Therefore, if Cohen's $d = 1$, the two means differ by one standard deviation. This means that the value of d can range higher than 1. Other group difference index measures include Cohen's f^2 and Hedge's g (this is similar to Cohen's d but adjusts for sample size).

Relationship indexes, also called the **r family of effect sizes** (Rosenthal, 1994), measure how much an independent and dependent variable vary together or, in other words, the amount of covariation in the two variables. The more closely the two variables are related, the higher the effect size. So, for example, the relationship between height and weight among adults is quite closely related, and would have a high r value. Squared indices of r (R^2) and related quantities such as eta-squared (η^2), omega-squared (ω^2), partial eta-squared, and partial omega-squared are also measures of association, but because they are squared they lack directionality (Rosenthal & DiMatteo, 2001). These squared measures indicate "the observed proportion of explained variance" (Kline, 2004, p. 100), and I will often call them **percentage variance effect sizes** (PV) in this book.

The reader may wonder which kind of effect size measure to use, the group difference or relationship effect size. In fact, either one can be used, and can even be easily converted into the other, but some effect sizes seem to be more associated with some statistical tests than others. For example, relationship indexes are almost always used with correlations or regression. Olejnik and Algina (2000) note that relationship indexes may seem easier to understand because they vary between the fixed values of 0 and 1, unlike the group difference indexes, which may go above 1. However, as Rosenthal and DiMatteo (2001) point out, because the group relationship measures are squared, they can sometimes look very small and unimportant. Therefore, there is no one overarching recommendation on which type to use.

4.3.2 Calculating Effect Sizes for Power Analysis

The biggest question in a researcher's mind for calculating power may be how to determine the effect size to expect. The best way to do this is to look at effect sizes from previous research in this area to see what the magnitude of effect sizes has been. If there is no previous research, or none that lists effect sizes, the researcher must make an educated guess of the size of the effect that they will find acceptable. Weinberg and Abramowitz (2002) say that one should "set the power of the test to detect a difference from the null hypothesis that is of practical importance" (p. 267).

In the case where there is no previous research to estimate effect sizes from, one may want to use Cohen's effect size guidelines as given in the tables in Section 4.3.3. Cohen (1988) notes that effect sizes are likely to be small when one is undertaking research in an area that has been little studied, as researchers may not know yet what kinds of variables they need to control for. Cohen admits that his proposed effect size magnitudes are subjective and based on his experience with the literature in the behavioral sciences. Still, he does have some general explanations for the guideline magnitudes. A small effect size is one that is not visible to the naked eye but exists nevertheless. Cohen (1988) says this would be equal to the difference in IQ between siblings who were twins and non-twins. A medium effect is one that is visible to the naked eye or apparent to the observer, and would be equivalent to the difference in IQ between clerical and semiskilled workers. Lastly, a large effect is one that would be "grossly perceptible" (p. 27) and correspond to the difference in IQ between typical college freshmen and persons with Ph.D.s.

When one understands the reasoning behind Cohen's proposed magnitude sizes, one also understands that there is no imaginary line which would label a $d = .49$ a medium effect while $d = .51$ would be labeled a large effect. Cohen also notes that effect size magnitudes depend on the area, so that what may be a small effect size in one area may in fact be a rather large effect size in another area.

4.3.3 Calculating Effect Sizes Summary

In Part II of this book, information will be given as to how to calculate effect sizes for each statistical procedure. In this chapter, however, I include a summary of effect sizes for each of the procedures outlined in this book. I imagine this section as more of a resource than something you will read through carefully all at one time. Do remember that you should try to give effect sizes for all associations that you report on, not just those that are statistical (Kline, 2004). It may be that those associations that are not statistical still have large enough effect sizes to be interesting and warrant future research.

In general, statistical tests which include a categorical variable that divides the sample into groups, such as the t-test or ANOVA, use the d family of effect sizes to measure effect size. The basic idea of effect sizes in the d family is to look at the difference between the means of two groups, as in $\mu_A - \mu_B$. However, if we just look at the mean difference, the scale of this effect will be different in every experiment. Therefore, we divide the mean difference by a standardizer. Olejnik and Algina (2000, p. 245) note three alternative methods for computing standardizers, found in Table 4.6.

For option C, the formula to derive the pooled standard deviation with any number of groups is: $S_{pooled} = \sqrt{\dfrac{(n_1 - 1)S_1^2 + \ldots + (n_J - 1)S_J^2}{(n_1 - 1) + \ldots + (n_J - 1)}}$ where S_J=the standard deviation of the jth group, and n_J=the number of participants or items in the jth group, and the formula for S_{pooled} with just two groups is: $S_{pooled} = \dfrac{SS_{within}}{df_{within}} = \dfrac{(n_1 - 1)S_1^2 + (n_2 - 1)S_2^2}{n_1 + n_2 - 2}$.

Table 4.7 contains a summary of the most useful formulas to use for the d family of effect sizes. In general, Olejnik and Algina (2000) recommend r family statistics for omnibus results of ANOVA tests, and these can be obtained as partial eta-squared statistics (r family effect sizes) through computer output and then converted into d family statistics.

If d family effect sizes are not normally used with certain statistical tests, I give a conversion from the r family to the d family. Note that the statistical tests in Table 4.7 do not go beyond one-way ANOVAs. Explanations for how to compute effect sizes for more complex kinds of ANOVA using d family statistics are beyond the scope of this book (interested readers should see works by Cohen, 1988; Grissom & Kim, 2005; and Olejnik & Algina, 2000), but, given Cohen's (1988) statement about analyzing power analysis for complex ANOVAs by examining a variable or interaction separately, effect sizes for separate variables or interactions in an ANOVA could also be calculated.

Table 4.8 summarizes effect size calculations for the r family. In statistical tests that deal with continuous variables, such as correlation or regression, the r family of effect sizes are generally used. If d family effect sizes are more commonly used with a particular test, conversion formulas are given.

Table 4.6 Options for Computing Standardizers (the Denominator for d Family Effect Sizes)

A	The standard deviation of one of the groups, perhaps most typically the control group
B	The pooled standard deviation of [only the groups] being compared
C	The pooled standard deviation [of all the groups] in the design

Table 4.7 Calculation of *d* Family of Effect Sizes

	d family	Cohen's guidelines
t-test (one-sample)	$d = \dfrac{\overline{X}_{sample} - \mu}{S_{sample}}$ (Weinberg & Abramowitz, 2002)	
t-test (independent-samples)	$d = \dfrac{\overline{X}_1 - \overline{X}_2}{\sigma}$ where $\overline{X}_k$ = the mean of group k, and σ = the appropriate standardizer from Table 4.6. A shortcut: $d = \dfrac{2t}{\sqrt{df_{err}}}$ (Murphy & Myors, 2004)	$d = .2$ (small) $d = .5$ (medium) $d = .8$ (large)
t-test (paired-samples)	$d_{paired} = \dfrac{\overline{X}_1 - \overline{X}_2}{\sqrt{2(S_1 - S_2)}}$ (Volker, 2006) where S_k = the standard deviation of group k.	
One-way ANOVA	$f = \dfrac{\sqrt{\dfrac{\Sigma(X_i - X_{grand})^2}{k - 1}}}{\sqrt{MS_{within}}}$ where $\overline{X}_i$ = mean of each group, $\overline{X}_{grand}$ = grand mean or average of all of the individual group means, k=number of means or groups, and MS_{within} is the within-group sum of squares divided by the within-group degrees of freedom (the number found in an ANOVA table). This formula should only be used when group sizes are equal (Volker, 2006). Cohen's *f* can be calculated in an easier way by using the ANOVA *F*-value and the degrees of freedom: $f^2 = \dfrac{(df_{hyp} \times F)}{df_{err}}$ or eta-squared: $f^2 = \dfrac{\eta^2}{1 - \eta^2}$ (Murphy & Myors, 2004)	$f = .10$ (small) $f = .25$ (medium) $f = .40$ (large)
Contrasts instead of omnibus ANOVA	Insert the appropriate mean estimates into the numerator of the effect size d equation. For example, to compare the average of Groups A and B with Group C, the numerator will be: $\frac{1}{2}(\overline{X}_{Group\,A} + \overline{X}_{Group\,B}) - \overline{X}_{Group\,C}$ For the denominator, we consider whether variances are equal (in which case, use the pooled sd across groups) or not (in which case, choose which one sd will be considered the control group's sd) (Volker, 2006).	
Post-hoc contrasts (after ANOVA)	In a post-hoc contrast, there are only two groups, so matters proceed as outlined above for independent-samples t-tests.	
Correlation	Normally, correlation effect size is reported in *r*, but to convert this to *d*: $d = \dfrac{2r}{\sqrt{1 - r^2}}$ (Murphy & Myors, 2004)	

Table 4.8 Calculation of *r* Family of Effect Sizes

	r family (also known as **percentage variance,** *or* **PV**)	Cohen's guidelines
t-test (independent-samples or paired-samples)	The t-test effect size is most often calculated with Cohen's *d*. In the case of a t-test, *r* will be the point-biserial correlation. To convert *d* to *r* if sample sizes are equal: $r_{pb} = \dfrac{d}{\sqrt{d^2 + 4}}$ (Volker, 2006)	*d* = .2 (small) *d* = .5 (medium) *d* = .8 (large)
One-way ANOVA (testing omnibus effects)	For eta-squared (η^2) and omega-squared (ω^2) with all factors **fixed** the general formulas are: $\eta^2 = \dfrac{SS_{between\text{-}groups}}{SS_{total}}$ where SS = sum of squares, found in ANOVA table $\omega^2 = \dfrac{SS_{between\text{-}groups} - (k - 1)MS_{error}}{SS_{total} + MS_{error}}$ where *k* = number of groups or means, and MS = mean square, found in ANOVA table (Volker, 2006). If ω^2 returns a negative value, it should be reported as zero (Olejnik & Algina, 2000).	η^2/ω^2 = .01 (small) η^2/ω^2 = .06 (medium) η^2/ω^2 = .14 (large)
Factorial ANOVA	For a design where all factors have **fixed effects**, the calculations for η^2 and ω^2 are the same as in the one-way ANOVA. For partial η^2 and ω^2: $_{partial}\hat{\eta}^2 = \dfrac{SS_{effect}}{SS_{effect} + SS_{error}}$ $_{partial}\hat{\omega}^2 = \dfrac{df_{effect}(MS_{effect} - MS_{error})}{df_{effect}MS_{effect} + (N - df_{effect})MS_{error}}$ (Olejnik & Algina, 2000) Another way to calculate partial η^2 is $\dfrac{df_{hyp}F}{df_{hyp}F + df_{error}}$ (Murphy & Myors, 2004, p. 62)	
Contrasts instead of omnibus ANOVA	For more complex designs with more than two means, Olejnik and Algina (2000) specify that the comparison sum of squares can be replaced by the contrast sum of squares: $SS_{contrast} = \dfrac{(c_1\bar{X}_1 + \ldots + c_j\bar{X}_j)^2}{\dfrac{c_1^2}{n_1} + \ldots + \dfrac{c_j^2}{n_j}}$ where *cj* = is the contrast coefficient for the *j*th condition in the contrast, $\bar{X}_j$ = the mean of the *j*th condition in the contrast, and n_j = the sample size of the *j*th condition in the contrast.	
Chi-square	Cohen (1988) gives *w* as an effect size for chi-square. In cases of 2 × 2 tables, $w = \varphi$(phi) (Howell, 2002). For larger designs, φ can be derived from Cramer's V by $w = V\sqrt{r - 1}$ where V = Cramer's V and *r* = the number of rows or columns (whichever is smaller of the two) (Volker, 2006). This type of effect size calculation is apparently only valid with naturalistic studies (no assigned groups trying to achieve random distribution); see Grissom and Kim (2005) for calculations when assignment is random.	*w* = .10 (small) *w* = .3 (medium) *w* = .5 (large)
Correlation	The correlation coefficient r is an effect size in itself. The squared r (R^2) expresses the percentage of variance of the dependent variable that the independent variable explains.	*r* = .10 (small) *r* = .30 (medium) *r* = .50 (large) R^2 = .01 (small) R^2 = .09 (medium) R^2 = .25 (large)

Although r and R^2 are most commonly used with correlation and regression, indices which are related to r are used quite frequently for ANOVA designs as well. These are eta-squared (η^2), omega-squared (ω^2), and partial eta-squared. Maxwell and Delaney (2004, p. 104) explain that eta-squared is a proportion which "indicates how much knowledge of group membership improves prediction of the dependent variable" (2004, p. 104). Kline (2004, p. 100) also explains that eta-squared is "the proportion of total population variance accounted for by an effect of interest when all factors are fixed." When sample sizes are small, however, there is a tendency for η^2 to be positively biased (larger), so ω^2 adjusts for this bias. Volker (2006) advocates reporting both η^2 and ω^2 to give readers a sense of the estimation bias.

Partial eta-squared (found in SPSS computer output and until SPSS version 11.0 labeled as "eta-squared") according to Pierce, Block, and Aguinis (2004) is used when there is more than one factor in the ANOVA design, and it gives a measure of the effect of the factor of interest when other factors in the design are controlled. Kline (2004) says that partial eta-squared (and partial omega-squared as well) removes the variance of other factors which are not currently of interest from the calculation. Kline notes that, if the samples are independent, partial eta-squared and eta-squared calculations will result in the same number. Olejnik and Algina (2000) observe that partial effect sizes are generally larger than their non-partialed counterparts, and Pierce, Block, and Aguinis (2004) mention that, if the effect sizes from main effects together add up to more than 100%, you know you are looking at partial effect sizes. Researchers may choose to report partial effect sizes or total effect sizes, but should clearly label their effect sizes so that readers know what they are looking at.

In considering which effect sizes to report for ANOVA designs, Kline (2004) recommends that researchers report on either **omnibus test** effects (the first test you do when you have more than two groups, such as an ANOVA or an RM ANOVA) or contrast effect sizes (where you get into the nitty-gritty of figuring out which groups, pairwise, differ from each other), but not both. For example, if you tested the hypothesis that three different kinds of treatments result in different test scores, an omnibus test would simply say whether the type of treatment was statistical, but would not indicate which groups were better than which other groups. Contrast effect sizes will be measured using **post-hoc tests** or **planned comparisons** and will specifically show which groups are better than which other groups.

One reason to report only the omnibus or contrast effect size is because omnibus effects will already include the effect sizes of the contrasts, so it is redundant to look at each. However, some authors, such as Volker (2006), recommend reporting effect sizes for both omnibus effects and post-hoc contrasts. Authors should look at their own data and decide what makes sense.

ANOVA effect size calculations also depend on whether factors are **fixed** or **random**, ideas which were explained in Chapter 2 (Olejnik & Algina, 2000). However, when eta-squared (not omega-squared) is calculated for multifactor ANOVA, Olejnik and Algina (2000, p. 269) say that the "distinction between random and fixed effects is not relevant" since eta-squared is a statistic that should not be used to make inferences to the population (for more on random and fixed effects see the Advanced Topics Section 2.1.6).

4.4 Confidence Intervals

Reporting confidence intervals, along with effect sizes, is something considered vital to improving researchers' intuitions about what statistical testing means (Kline, 2004; Wilkinson & Task Force on Statistical Inference, 1999). Reporting confidence intervals alongside (or in place of) *p*-values is recommended by many researchers, who point out that confidence intervals provide more information than *p*-values about effect size and are more useful for further testing comparisons (Kline, 2004; Maxwell & Delaney, 2004; Wilcox 2001, 2003; Wilkinson & Task Force on Statistical Inference, 1999). I have mentioned confidence intervals previously but try to explain them more in depth in this section.

The **confidence interval** represents "a range of plausible values for the corresponding parameter" (Kline, 2004, p. 27), whether that parameter be the true mean, the difference in scores, or whatever. With a 95% confidence interval, if the study were replicated 100 times, 95% of the time the parameter would be found within the confidence interval range. The *p*-value can show if the comparison found a significant difference between the groups, but the confidence interval shows how far from zero the difference lies—giving an intuitively understandable measure of effect size. In addition, the width of the confidence interval indicates the precision with which the difference can be calculated or, more precisely, the amount of sampling error. Higher power in a study will result in smaller confidence intervals and more precision in estimating correlations or mean differences in samples.

If there is a lot of sampling error in a study, then confidence intervals will be wide, and we must say that our statistical results may not be very good estimates. As an example, let's return to the fictional experiment in Table 4.5. Suppose that a mean difference of 20 vocabulary words was found between the groups receiving the two different teaching approaches. This is a big difference, but then when we look at the 95% confidence interval we see it ranges from .03 to 38.6. This would show us that the difference was statistical (because zero is not contained in the interval), but it would also show us that our estimate of 20 is not very accurate and not a good estimator. There is a possibility that the actual difference is as little as .03. If another researcher replicated this study with larger sample sizes, they might find a narrower confidence interval that would more accurately estimate the true size of the difference between groups. In each chapter in Part II, when it is possible using SPSS, I will show how to calculate confidence intervals for each statistic.

A visual representation of confidence intervals may also be helpful in understanding the concept. Below I will contrast *p*-value information with confidence interval information for data from a study by Lyster (2004). Lyster tested four groups which differed in the type of feedback they received on French grammatical errors. In one written test he looked at what articles they assigned to nouns in a text. We want to know which groups did better than which other groups. We can first look at the results of **pairwise comparisons** between each group. A pairwise comparison is simply a statistical comparison between two groups. These comparisons are found in Table 4.9.

Table 4.9 shows there were statistical differences (in other words, *p*-values below 0.05) for all pairs except for those between the "FFI only" and the "FFI recast" group and also between the "FFI only" group and the control group (who did not receive any

Table 4.9 Pairwise Comparisons between Four Conditions in Lyster (2004) on a Written Completion Task for Articles (Score is Gain Score between Pre-Test and First Post-Test, with 40 Points Possible on Test)

Comparison	Estimate of mean difference	Standard error	t-value	p-value
FFIprompt–FFIrecast	5.20	1.06	4.91	<0.001
FFIonly–FFIrecast	−2.20	1.10	−2.01	0.19
Comparison–FFIrecast	−4.30	1.05	−4.10	<0.001
FFIonly–FFIprompt	−7.40	1.03	−7.19	<0.001
Comparison–FFIprompt	−9.50	0.98	−9.70	<0.001
Comparison–FFIonly	−2.10	1.02	−2.06	0.17

feedback). The same information, plus more, can be gleaned by looking at the 95% confidence intervals of each of the comparisons in Figure 4.2.

In Figure 4.2, the comparisons where the line goes through zero are the non-statistical comparisons. Whether the difference is positive or negative doesn't much matter, as this just depends on which group gets subtracted from the other. However, all of the intervals are wide, covering about 5 points each. This shows how much precision the estimates of mean differences given in Table 4.9 have. In other words, there is some wiggle room around those estimates. Also, the pairwise comparison between the "FFI prompt" and "Comparison" groups is farthest from zero, meaning it has the biggest effect size (the estimate is nearly 10 points of difference, which may range from as little as 7 points of difference to as large as 12 points of difference). Thus, statistical significance, precision of the estimate, and effect size can all be gleaned quite quickly from confidence intervals (especially if they are visually presented, as they are here; I used the **plot(confint())** command associated with the **glht** procedure and the **multcomp** library from R to create the graphic, but the same information can be ascertained from numerical reports of confidence intervals).

4.4.1 *Application Activity with Confidence Intervals*

1   Larson-Hall (2008) examines scores on three tests by two groups of Japanese learners of English—those who studied English before age 12, and those who began their study of English at age 12 when it is compulsory in Japan. Please look at the confidence intervals for the mean differences between the two groups on each of the three tests and answer the questions that follow (confidence intervals have been changed slightly for teaching purposes).

   a.   Aptitude test (37 points possible): (−1.57, .99)
   b.   Grammaticality judgment test (200 points possible): (−5.62, .76)
   c.   Phonemic discrimination task (96 points possible): (−10.8, −.001)

   Are the groups statistically different from each other on any of the tests? What can you say about the precision of the estimates of mean difference (are they precise or not very precise)? Which test do you think has the largest effect size?

2   Ellis and Yuan (2004), which will be examined in more detail in Chapter 9, examined the complexity and accuracy of written language produced by three groups

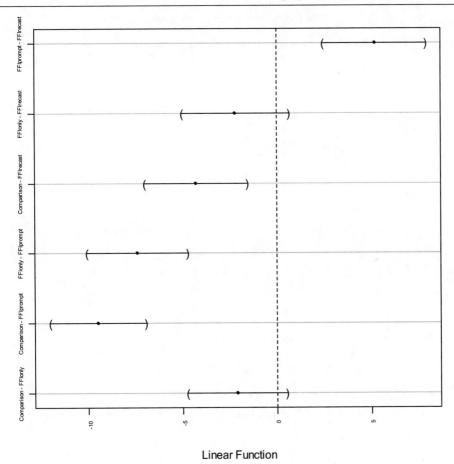

Linear Function

Figure 4.2 Visually representing 95% confidence intervals in pairwise comparisons on the Lyster (2004) data.

who differed in the amount of time they had available to perform the task. Please look at Figure 4.3 for the mean differences between pairs of groups on the number of disfluencies (word crossed out and reformulated in the writing) in the groups' production and answer these questions: Are the groups statistically different from each other on any of the tests? What can you say about the precision of the estimates of mean difference, given that the mean difference between groups' PTP-NP is 3.42, the mean difference between their OLP-NP is 3.38, and the mean difference between their OLP-PTP is 0.14 (are they precise or not very precise)? Which test do you think has the largest effect size?

3   Chapter 6 features data from DeKeyser (2000) and Flege, Yeni-Komshian, and Liu (1999), which both used correlations. Consider the differences between these ways of reporting correlations, one using the standard method (with *p*-values) and the other using confidence intervals. What do the confidence intervals tell you that *p*-values can't? In both cases, think of the *r* value (which is the estimate that the 95%

95% family-wise confidence level

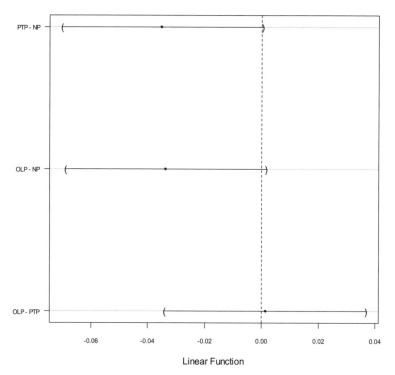

Figure 4.3 Ellis and Yuan's (2004) groups compared visually using 95% confidence intervals.

confidence interval is giving) as a measure of the strength of the relationship, where an $r = .50$ may be considered a strong relationship.

Variant 1a: DeKeyser (2000) found a statistical correlation between age of arrival and scores on the grammaticality judgment test ($r = -.62$, n = 57, $p < .001$).

Variant 1b: Flege, Yeni-Komshian, and Liu (1999) found a statistical correlation between age of arrival and pronunciation scores ($r = -.89$, n = 264, $p < .001$).

Variant 2a: DeKeyser (2000) found a statistical correlation between age of arrival and scores on the grammaticality judgment test (95% CI: $-.76, -.42$).

Variant 2b: Flege, Yeni-Komshian, and Liu (1999) found a statistical correlation between age of arrival and pronunciation scores (95% CI: $-.92$, $-.87$).

4.5 Summary

The field of second language research, like most other areas of scientific inquiry, would benefit from some changes in the way that statistics are reported in research articles. In this chapter I have noted some ways that researchers currently working in the area of applied statistics have proposed as ways to help researchers and journal readers better understand what they are doing when they use statistics to analyze their data.

A few easy steps that all researchers in the field of second language research could take is to report exact *p*-values (unless they are quite small), use confidence intervals, and give effect sizes. Subsequent chapters in this book will try to illustrate this approach to reporting statistics.

A step which is not much harder to do, but may be harder to implement, is to calculate the number of participants needed in a study in order to obtain sufficient power to find statistical results. The R statistical program can fairly easily help you calculate the number of participants you will need, using previously published effect sizes or estimating by using Cohen's (1988) guidelines, but actually gathering data from that number of people may sometimes be challenging. Nevertheless, I urge researchers to take the issue of power seriously and understand that many times power may be the real reason that the expected results were not found. Another step which would help in this area is for the field (mainly, journal editors) to raise the acceptable alpha level to $\alpha = 0.10$ instead of the current 0.05. This would provide a better balance between Type I (being overeager to find statistical results) and Type II (being overly cautious about finding statistical differences) errors, providing more power to find interesting results.

I'd like to conclude my summary by discussing the idea of replication studies, which would surely enhance the reliability of findings in the field and strengthen theoretical claims, and their relationship to the idea of power, one of the central ideas of this chapter.

4.5.1 Power through Replication and Belief in the "Law of Small Numbers"

Mackey and Gass (2005) and Polio and Gass (1997) have urged second language researchers to conduct more replication studies. Tversky and Kahneman (1971) point out that replication studies will ideally have a larger number of participants than the original study. With a sample size that is larger than the original, the experimenter will have a better chance of finding a significant result. Why? As discussed above, sample sizes play a direct role in the amount of power that a study has, and also directly affect the *p*-value of the test statistic.

Tversky and Kahneman note that most social science researchers have a "belief in the law of small numbers" (the title of their article). The law of large numbers says that given a sufficient number of observations, or participant measurements, the sample statistic (such as the average) will approach the population statistic more and more closely. Tversky and Kahneman's proposed law of small numbers states that "the law of large numbers applies to small numbers as well" (p. 106). In other words, researchers believe that even a small sampling should represent the whole population well, which leads to an unfounded confidence in results found with small sample sizes. Hopefully, through the discussion of effect sizes and the importance of group sizes, the reader has seen that studies with small sample sizes will have significant drawbacks, including low power to find results, and most likely wide confidence intervals, meaning that sampling error is large.

The "law of small numbers" leads researchers to believe that a statistical group difference found with groups of 40 participants each should still hold for groups of 20, when in fact the chances of finding a statistical group difference if this condition holds are only slightly above 50%! Researchers hold these erroneous assumptions because they do not understand power, and overestimate how much power a given study has. In fact, Tversky and Kahneman found that most of their colleagues in psychology would try to give an explanation for a non-statistical difference in such a replication study (where the original had 40 participants and the replication had 20) instead of noting differences in power as the most likely cause of the discrepancy and/or testing 20 more participants for the replication. The authors note that reporting effect sizes, which are not affected by sample size, and confidence intervals, which provide a range of sampling variability, and not just p-values, will help improve the statistical intuitions of researchers. I hope all of this just underscores the value of the ideas in this chapter, which we as researchers crucially need to understand well.

Part II

Statistical Tests

Chapter 5

Choosing a Statistical Test

> The hardest part of any statistical work is getting started. And one of the hardest things about getting started is choosing the right kind of statistical analysis. The choice depends on the nature of your data and on the particular question you are trying to answer.
>
> Michael Crawley (2007, p. 323)

Statistics is as much an art as a science. There is never just one way to analyze your data, which is why it's important to understand the reasoning behind the use of various tests. In my own research I often find myself revising my statistical analysis when I take a fresh look at it after setting it aside for some months. I may discover an alternative test, or a different idea for looking at the data. Part II of the text will cover in depth a number of basic statistical tests including correlation, regression, t-tests, ANOVA, and chi-square tests. These are by no means all of the statistical tools that are available for analyzing data, but they are the basic ones that are used most frequently in the second language research literature.

Of course, in getting started in analyzing your data, you do need to pick a statistical test. And getting started, as Michael Crawley suggests, may be the hardest part of statistical work. I have seen many approaches to trying to help students learn how to choose which test to use to analyze their data, but I'm not sure any approach works very well! One common type of approach is to provide a step-by-step decision tree like that provided in Porte (2002) (reprinted from Hatch & Lazaraton, 1991) or Field (2005). I have found that such charts are quite helpful once you have a good deal of experience with statistics, but I remember as a beginning statistics user I found such charts frustrating. For example, I didn't know if I wanted "to discover the effect of independent variables on dependent variables" or "discover a relationship between variables" (Porte, 2002, p. 248; this is the first question to divide the major types of statistical tests in Hatch and Lazaraton's flow chart).

So I have taken a different approach to the question of which test to choose in this chapter. Instead of providing a flow chart, this chapter is designed to give you a broad understanding of some basic types of statistical procedures illustrated by actual studies in the field that have used that test. The idea is to help you gain a feeling for the questions that various statistical procedures can answer. I hope an illustrative approach will *show* the difference between the types of tests instead of just tell it, but the fact of the matter is that understanding statistics does take some time and experience. This chapter will just be a first step in helping you figure out where to start.

5.1 Statistical Tests that Are Covered in This Book

A first step toward understanding what kind of statistical test you should choose is to understand the distinction between tests of relationships and tests of group differences, even though this dichotomy is somewhat of an oversimplification. Tests of relationships will look at questions of how strongly one variable influences another, or which variables can predict scores on another variable. Those covered in this book are correlation, partial correlation, and regression. Tests of group differences look at whether membership in a particular category or group influences the outcome of some test. Those covered in this book are chi-square tests, t-tests, and analysis of variance (ANOVA).

One way to tell if you want a test of relationships or a test of group differences is to look at the level of measurement of your variables. In general, you will want a test of relationships if all of your variables are **continuous**. In other words, they are measured on a scale where a difference of one point at the upper end of the scale is equal to the difference of one point on the lower end of the scale, and where a larger number has more of the quality than a smaller number. Examples include test scores, **Likert scale** scores (if the scale is wide enough), and age. If you have a mix of continuous and **categorical** variables you will probably want a test of group differences. Remember that categorical variables have labels which have no inherent numerical value, and these categories are often used to define the groups whose differences you want to explore. Examples of categorical variables are L1, experimental treatment group, and a division into young/old age (remember from Chapter 2 that such a scale for age might also be called **ordinal** because there is some inherent ranking in younger versus older, but in statistical tests we will have to decide whether to treat such variables as either continuous or categorical, and this variable is clearly too small to be labeled continuous). If you have *only* categorical variables, then you may want to use a chi-square analysis, which is a test of group differences.

Another thing to keep in mind as you decide which test to use is whether your variables are dependent or independent variables. Remember from Chapter 2 that this dichotomy involves which variable we hypothesize may be influencing another (the independent variable influences the dependent). However, it is not always the case that we can clearly identify causation or influence. In some cases we are looking at mutual influence of the variables on each other, and usually in these cases we will use a test of relationships.

The following sections of this chapter will lay out some information about the types of variables that are used in each type of test, whether they are dependent or independent variables, and give several examples from the SLA literature that have used this particular technique. I have come up with some mnemonic devices that might be helpful for remembering what test to use, and although these are somewhat cheesy they might be helpful, so I'll include them here. Also, I specify if there is a non-parametric alternative to the test.

5.2 A Brief Overview of Correlation

Correlation: A test of relationships

Correlation looks at how two measurements vary together. The meaning of correlation in a statistical sense is very much related to the meaning you would think of in ordinary life; you might notice that people in your neighborhood seem to wear heavy coats more in the winter than in the summer. If there is a relationship between type of coat and weather there is a correlation between the two variables, and this means there is some kind of discernible linear pattern among the data. A test of correlation is thus looking for a pattern of relationships among data.

If we think of a graph that charts the relationship between two variables, then a relationship that shows a correlation has a linear trend (such as graph A in Figure 5.1 on the left) rather than being a collection of scattered points (as in graph B on the right).

A correlation has the following attributes:

- There are exactly two variables.
- These variables do not have any levels within them.
- If you took averages of the variables, you would have only two averages.
- Both variables are continuous.
- The variables cannot necessarily be defined as independent and dependent (having a cause-and-effect structure), although they might be.

Mnemonic device: A correlation has two variables, so stick out your two index fingers. A correlation involves a relationship, so bend your fingers toward each other as if they are having a conversation. Turn your fingers on the side and you have a "C" for correlation.

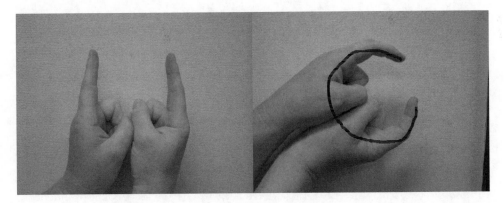

Research questions in SLA that have used correlation:

Robinson (2005)

Research question	How does intelligence relate to the ability to abstract rules unintentionally and without awareness (implicitly) or intentionally and with awareness (explicitly)?
Answer examines	Whether intelligence and scores on implicit/explicit tests are related.

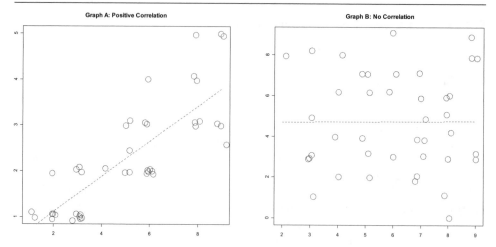

Figure 5.1 Scatterplots showing a correlation (A) or no correlation (B).

Pearson, Fernandez, Lewedeg, and Oller (1997)	
Research question	Does amount of input that a bilingual child receives matter to how much vocabulary they will learn in Spanish?
Answer examines	The relationship between input and amount of vocabulary in Spanish.

The non-parametric alternative to a (Pearson's) correlation test is Spearman's rank order correlation test.

5.3 A Brief Overview of Partial Correlation

Partial correlation: A test of relationships

Partial correlation looks at the way two measurements vary together when a third variable has been factored out of their relationship. For example, you may have noticed while administering a timed vocabulary test that your older students struggled more with this than your younger students. You are actually interested in the relationship between amount of vocabulary knowledge and scores on a reading test, but you decide you need to factor the effect of age out of the relationship to get an accurate view of it. For this you would use a partial correlation.

A partial correlation has the following attributes:

- There are three or more variables (you may factor out the influence of more than one variable at a time).
- These variables do not have any levels within them.
- If you took averages of the variables, you would have three or more averages.
- All variables are continuous.
- The variables cannot necessarily be defined as independent and dependent (having a cause-and-effect structure), although they might be.

Research questions in SLA that have used partial correlation:

Larson-Hall (2006)	
Research question	How does age at which a learner began studying English as a foreign language relate to scores on a grammaticality judgment test and a phoneme contrast test? Those who began studying earlier might have more total input, so this factor is statistically subtracted out of the equation by using **partial correlation**.
Answer examines	Whether there is a relationship between age and test scores when the amount of total input is factored out (in other words, input is partialled out).

There is no non-parametric alternative to a partial correlation test.

5.4 A Brief Overview of Multiple Regression

Multiple regression: A test of relationships

Multiple regression looks at the relationship among multiple variables to try to make a prediction about how some variables (the **independent** or **explanatory variables**) may predict scores on another variable (the **dependent** or **response variable**). This is often done with an aim toward building an explanative theory. Multiple regression tries to determine how much of the dependent variable can be explained by variation in the scores on the independent variables. What does it mean to explain the variance in scores? Basically, it means you are trying to explain why everyone did not get the same score. Why did some people get high scores and some get low scores? If you can explain the variance, you are explaining why people differ in their scores.

Figure 5.2 shows graphically how a nativeness rating in French might be explained to some extent by the age at which the participant began studying French, their level of motivation, and their phonological training. Notice that these explanatory variables do not explain *everything*! When dealing with human beings, we will rarely find a combination of variables that can explain 100% of the dependent variable.

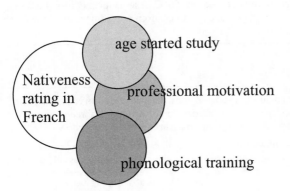

Figure 5.2 Visualizing how independent variables might help explain the dependent variable (areas of overlap show covariation).

A regression has the following attributes:

- It has two or more variables.
- These variables do not have any levels within them.
- If you took averages of the variables, you would have three or more averages.
- All variables are continuous.
- Unlike correlation, one variable *must* be dependent and the others are independent.

Mnemonic device: Regression usually has many variables, so hold out two fingers from each hand. Regression involves a relationship, so bend your fingers toward each other as if they are having a conversation. Join your forefingers and, if you were looking at yourself, you'd see an "M" for multiple regression.

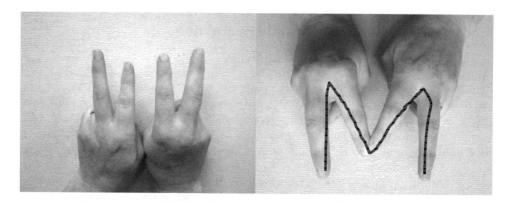

Research questions in SLA that have used multiple regression:

Dethorne, Johnson, and Loeb (2005)

Research question	How much of the variance in children's mean length of utterance can be accounted for by a syntactic measure of tense accuracy (TAC) and a vocabulary measure of the number of different words (NDW)?
Answer examines	Whether a morphosyntactic measure (TAC), a semantic measure (NDW), or both together can predict the length of children's utterances, and how much of that variance they predict.

Zareva (2005)

Research question	To what extent could self-reported vocabulary knowledge, vocabulary size, vocabulary difficulty, native-like associational knowledge, and number of associations made predict an actual measure of vocabulary knowledge?
Answer examines	Which measures of vocabulary knowledge can be used to predict actual vocabulary knowledge and create a model with the fewest possible predictors.

Paavola, Kunnari, and Moilanen (2005)	
Research question	Do the amount of maternal responsiveness and number of child's intentional communications predict early linguistic abilities?
Answer examines	How well maternal responsiveness and infant intention can predict language development.

There is no non-parametric alternative to a multiple regression.

5.5 A Brief Overview of the Chi-Square Test of Independence

Chi-square: A test of relationships

A **chi-square** test investigates whether there is a relationship between two categorical variables. The question is whether there is a relationship between the number of people in each category. For example, we want to see if males and females differ in their choice of foreign language to study in high school, where the school offers Japanese, Spanish, and French. The variable of gender (with two **levels** or two groups inside the variable) is categorical, as is choice of foreign language (with three levels). We might visualize this as a chart, as in Table 5.1.

Table 5.1 shows that the largest number of males chose Japanese and the largest number of females chose Spanish, but we also need to consider how many males and females took language classes overall, and how many of both genders chose each language to study.

A chi-square test for independence has the following attributes:

- It has exactly two variables.
- Each variable has two or more levels (categories) within them, so that the variable name is a word that generalizes (for example gender, experimental group, L1 background).
- You cannot calculate averages of the variables; you can only count how many are in each category.
- All variables are categorical.
- The variables cannot necessarily be defined as independent and dependent (having a cause-and-effect structure), although they might be.

Table 5.1 Visualizing a Chi-Square Test of Relationships

	Language		
	Japanese	Spanish	French
Males	25	16	10
Females	14	27	18

Research questions in SLA that have used chi-square for independence:

Geeslin and Guijarro-Fuentes (2006)	
Research question	Will three groups (Spanish L1, Portuguese L1, and Portuguese L1 Spanish L2) differ in their choice of copula (*ser, estar,* or both) in a contextual usage measure?
Answer examines	Whether first and second language knowledge plays a role in choice of *ser* versus *estar.*

Wharton (2000)	
Research question	Do high-proficiency learners use more of certain language learning strategies than low-proficiency learners, where use is measured as low, medium or high?
Answer examines	Whether proficiency and use of strategies are related.

The chi-square test of independence is a non-parametric test and there is no parametric alternative when both variables are categorical.

5.6 A Brief Overview of T-Tests

T-test: A test of group differences

The **t-test** is the simplest test of whether groups differ. Even if we tested two populations (or abstract groups of people under consideration, such as "ESL learners" and "native speakers") that we thought were exactly the same, there would be some variation in scores among the groups. Therefore, the t-test determines if the differences between groups are small enough to attribute them to the random variation in scores that would happen each time we take a new sample of the same population, or whether the differences are large enough that the two groups can be said to belong to two different populations.

In Figure 5.3 there are two distributions that have the same shape but have their peak at different places (meaning they have different mean scores). The t-test will tell us whether this amount of difference in mean scores (given the amount of variation that exists) is enough to say whether the scores come from the same population or from two different populations. There are two types of t-tests that we may be interested in. One is called the independent-samples t-test, when the groups consist of different people, and the other is the paired-samples t-test, when the groups consist of the same people sampled at different time periods.

Mnemonic device: A t-test has two mean scores, so hold out two fingers. T-tests involve tests of group differences or how one variable intersects with the other, so cross one finger over the other to make a "T" for t-tests.

Two groups with different means

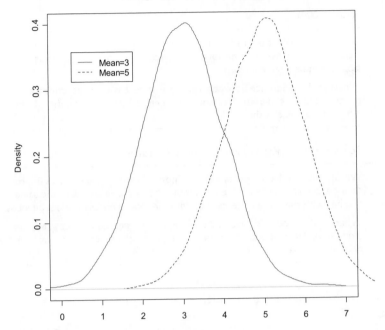

Figure 5.3 Two distributions with different means.

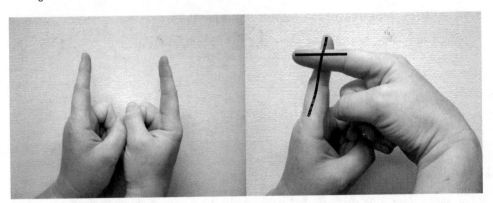

5.6.1 A Brief Overview of the Independent-Samples T-Test

An **independent-samples t-test** assumes that the two mean scores are independent of each other.

An independent-samples test has the following attributes:

- It has exactly two variables.
- One variable is categorical with only two levels and it is the independent variable.
  - People in each group must be different from each other.
- The other variable is continuous and it is the dependent variable.
- If you took averages of the variables, you would have only two averages.

Research questions in SLA that have used independent-samples t-tests:

Hirata (2004)	
Research question	Do English-speaking learners of Japanese who receive pronunciation training on a computer improve their performance on pitch and duration contrasts in Japanese more than controls?
Answer examines	Whether the difference between a group that received an experimental treatment and a group that did not is large enough to conclude the groups are different from each other.

Boers, Eyckmans, Kappel, Stengers, and Demecheleer (2006)	
Research question	Will instruction that helps learners to "notice" formulaic sequences improve their perceived fluency in L2 English more than a group taught by the same teacher with the same materials but without a focus on formulaic sequences?
Answer examines	Whether the group that focused on formulaic sequences and the group that didn't have different enough mean scores to be considered as coming from two different populations.

The non-parametric alternative to an independent-samples t-test is the Mann–Whitney U-test.

5.6.2 A Brief Overview of the Paired-Samples T-Test

A **paired-samples t-test** is used when the people who are tested are the same, so the two mean scores cannot be independent of each other.

A paired-samples test has the following attributes:

- It has exactly two variables.
- One variable is categorical with only two levels and it is the independent variable.
  - People in each group must be the same.
- The other variable is continuous and it is the dependent variable.
- If you took averages of the variables, you would have only two averages.

Research questions in SLA that have used independent-samples t-tests are found below. Note that the Hirata study is the same as the one examined above using independent samples, but the question is now slightly different.

Macaro and Masterman (2006)	
Research question	Would English-speaking students studying French benefit from a short, intensive burst of explicit grammar training in their L2? The students were tested before the training and then after the training.
Answer examines	Whether the scores of the same group at different time periods can be said to differ, meaning that the group improved over time.

Hirata (2004)	
Research question	Do English-speaking learners of Japanese who receive pronunciation training on a computer statistically improve their performance on pitch and duration contrasts in Japanese from a pre-test to a post-test?
Answer examines	Whether the group who received an experimental treatment performed differently enough on their second testing so we cannot say their scores reflect only random variation from test to test.

The non-parametric alternative to a paired-samples t-test is the Wilcoxon signed ranks test.

5.7 A Brief Overview of One-Way ANOVA

One-way ANOVA: A test of group differences

A logical extension of a t-test is the case where you have more than two groups. The **one-way analysis of variance** (ANOVA) is used when you want to test whether the scores of three or more groups differ statistically. Figure 5.4 shows the distribution of three groups on a measure of pronunciation. All the groups have similar variances (roughly understood as the spread of points in the box) but their mean scores all differ (actually, the boxplot shows the median but since these are perfectly symmetric distributions the mean and median will be the same). The one-way ANOVA will test the probability that the groups are different from each other.

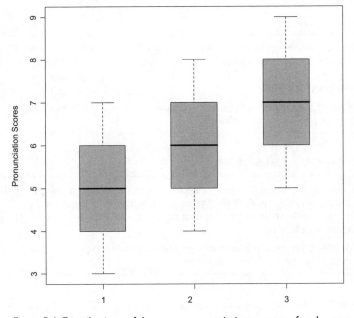

Figure 5.4 Distributions of data on a pronunciation measure for three groups.

A one-way ANOVA has the following attributes:

- It has exactly two variables.
- One variable is categorical with three or more levels and it is the independent variable.
- The other variable is continuous and it is the dependent variable.
- If you took averages of the variables, you would have three or more averages.

Mnemonic device: A one-way ANOVA has at least three mean scores, so hold out three fingers. ANOVAs involve tests of group differences, so cross one finger over the other two, which will make an "A" for ANOVA.

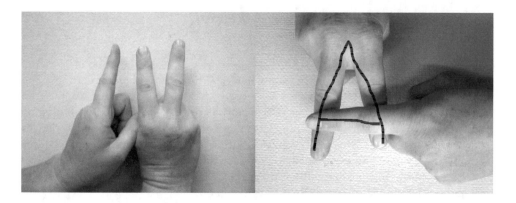

Research questions in SLA that have used one-way ANOVAs:

Schauer (2006)

Research question	"Do learners in English as a foreign language (EFL) and English as a second language (ESL) contexts display differences in their recognition and rating of pragmatic and grammatical errors?" (p. 269). The third group tested were native speakers of English.
Answer examines	Whether the three groups performed differently on correctly identifying pragmatic and syntactic violations.

Trofimovich and Baker (2006)

Research question	"Does the amount of L2 learners' experience influence their production of L2 suprasegmentals?" (p. 5). Three groups of Korean users of English were distinguished by their length of residence in the US, and native speakers of English were also tested.
Answer examines	Whether differences between four groups are large enough to say that the groups come from different populations.

The non-parametric alternative to a one-way ANOVA is the Kruskall–Wallis test.

5.8 A Brief Overview of Factorial ANOVA

Factorial ANOVA: A test of group differences

A factorial ANOVA expands from t-tests and one-way ANOVAs by including more than one independent variable (IV). If there are two IVs, we conduct a **two-way ANOVA**. If there are three IVs, it is a three-way ANOVA. As was seen in the one-way ANOVA section, each IV can have two or more levels. Therefore, these kinds of **factorial ANOVAs** are also sometimes labeled in a way that reports on the number of levels of the independent variables. A study which had the IV of gender (levels: male or female) and experimental condition (A, B, or C) could be called a 2 (gender) × 3 (condition) ANOVA.

One advantage of a factorial ANOVA over a simple t-test or one-way ANOVA is that the interaction between factors can be explored. For example, it may be the case that males respond better to treatment A while females respond better to treatment B, as seen in Figure 5.5. With factorial ANOVAs we are beginning to use multivariate data sets, and although these are more complex they often reflect the more complicated nature of real people and real situations.

A factorial ANOVA has the following attributes:

- It has more than two variables.
- Two or more variables are categorical and they are independent variables.
- Exactly one variable is continuous and it is the dependent variable.

Mnemonic device: A factorial ANOVA, like multiple regression, has many variables, so hold out two fingers from each hand. ANOVAs involve tests of group

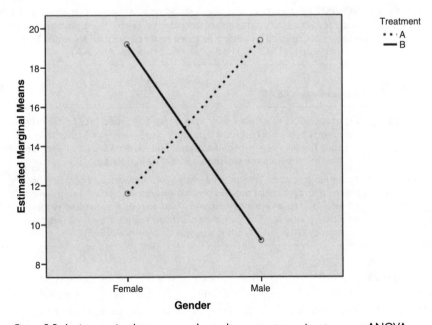

Figure 5.5 An interaction between gender and treatment type in a two-way ANOVA.

differences, so cross your fingers over the others. The result will look like a teepee, which you can think of as a "teepee factory" for *factorial* ANOVA (I know I'm getting desperate here—so it's the last one!).

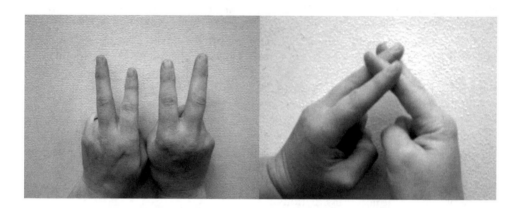

Two studies below reflect these more complicated research questions:

Juffs (2005)

Research question	Does the L1 of learners from different language backgrounds affect how they process grammatical and ungrammatical wh-extraction in English sentences? Learners from four different L1 backgrounds were tested. Is there any effect for the specific kinds of structures that the wh-word is extracted out of? Three different kinds of structures were tested.
Answer examines	Whether the factors of first language and type of sentence structure affect the accuracy with which participants can judge sentences to be grammatical (or ungrammatical), and whether these two factors interact. This would be a 4 (L1) × 3 (structure) ANOVA (in other words, a two-way ANOVA).

Kondo-Brown (2006)

Research question	Do groups of readers who differ in their reading proficiency (more proficient versus less proficient) perform differently depending on whether they are guessing the meaning or pronunciation of unknown words, and also depending on whether they see the words in context or in isolation?
Answer examines	Whether groups performed differently when the variables of task (guessing meaning or pronunciation) and context (words in isolation versus words in context) are taken into account, and whether task, context, and reading proficiency interact. This would be a 2 (task) × 2 (context) × 2 (reading proficiency) ANOVA (in other words, a three-way ANOVA).

There is no non-parametric alternative to a factorial ANOVA, but one could test the influence of each independent variable separately using the non-parametric Kruskall–Wallis test. You would not get any information about the interaction between the variables, however.

5.9 A Brief Overview of ANCOVA

ANCOVA: A test of group differences

A slightly more complicated case of factorial ANOVA arises when the author wants to statistically control for some variable. This is called an **analysis of covariance**, or ANCOVA. The method of analysis is the same as for the factorial ANOVA, in that the covariate is also included in the analysis as the means of controlling for it.

An ANCOVA has the following attributes:

- It has more than two variables.
- One or more variables are categorical and they are independent variables.
- Two or more variables are continuous.
  - Exactly one is the dependent variable.
  - The other variable or variables are the ones being controlled for (the covariates).

Dromey, Silveira, and Sandor (2005)	
Research question	Are there differences between groups with different language backgrounds (three groups) and different gender (two genders) in how accurately they recognize the affect in someone's voice when the participants' age is statistically controlled for?
Answer examines	Whether the factors of group membership and sex interact and have an effect on accuracy scores in recognizing affective prosody. Age is a covariate, meaning its effect is subtracted. This would be a 3 (LI) × 2 (gender) ANCOVA controlling for age.

There is no non-parametric alternative to an ANCOVA.

5.10 A Brief Overview of Repeated-Measures ANOVA

Repeated-measures ANOVA: A test of group differences

Repeated-measures ANOVAs are ANOVAs for data in which the same participants were tested at more than one time (a longitudinal design), with more than one measure, or participated in more than one experimental condition (and were tested repeatedly). In other words, we cannot assume the independence of scores in the design because the same people were tested more than once. This type of design is also sometimes called a "mixed between-within ANOVA."

A repeated-measures ANOVA has the following attributes:

- It has more than two variables.
- Two or more variables are categorical and they are independent variables.
  - At least one independent variable is within-groups, meaning the same people are tested more than once and are in more than one of the groups.
  - At least one independent variable is between-groups, meaning this variable splits people so each is found in only one group.

- Exactly one variable is continuous and it is the dependent variable.[1]

Mnemonic device: There is no mnemonic device for repeated measures, but here is a hint—if you have a test conducted with the same people at two different time intervals, it will be a repeated-measures test unless there are no other categorical variables besides the testing time (if the only variable is testing time, it would be a paired-samples t-test because there are only two mean scores).

Here is a research question in SLA that has used a repeated-measures ANOVA:

Toth (2006)

Research question	Will processing instruction provide any benefits over a communicative approach when participants must productively use Spanish se in a sentence-production task? There were three groups, who all received different types of input. Will there be differences on a delayed post-test (24 days later) as well as an immediate post-test? There was also a pre-test, resulting in three different times of test. The use of three tests of the same participants results in the need for a repeated-measures statistical analysis.
Answer examines	Whether groups that were taught using different teaching methods scored differently on a guided production test using a pre-test–immediate post-test–delayed post-test longitudinal design, and whether group and time of test had any interaction. This is a 3 (type of input) × 3 (time of test) repeated-measures ANOVA (repeated measures on time of test).

There is no non-parametric alternative to a repeated-measures ANOVA.

A **repeated-measures ANCOVA** can also be conducted by simply including the covariate in the analysis. In this way, the researcher can examine the effects of the desired variables and their interaction knowing that the effects of the covariates have been mathematically factored out. The study below illustrates how an ANCOVA can be used with a repeated-measures design:

Dewey (2004)

Research question	Do learners of Japanese progress more in their reading development in a situation of intensive immersion (where they do not leave the country where their LI is spoken) or in a study abroad context living in Japan, over the course of a semester? Each of the two groups was tested at two times, necessitating a repeated-measures ANOVA. In addition, because previous studies had shown that L1 and L2 reading ability affected reading development, measures of these constructs were also included in the analysis as covariates.
Answer examines	Whether two groups differ in their scores over time on a self-assessment task when two variables shown to affect reading development are factored out (the covariates). This is a 2 (context) × 2 (time of test) repeated-measures ANCOVA (repeated measures on time of test), controlling for reading ability in L1 and L2 (in other words, L1 and L2 are partialled out).

---

1 A design in which there is more than one dependent variable is called a multivariate analysis of variance (MANOVA). However, in the field of second language research, few actual MANOVAs are used. In my search for linguistic studies in the LLBA database (Language Learning Behavioral Abstracts), I found only

5.11 Summary

I have now given you a quick overview of the types of statistical designs that can be used to answer certain kinds of research questions in the field of second language research. Although there was a lot of information contained in this chapter, I hope you realized that the major criteria for choosing which statistical test to use include:

- whether you are trying to test a relationship between variables or look for group differences
- how many variables you have and how many levels or groups there are within the variable
- whether the variables can be considered continuous or categorical
- whether the variables are seen as independent or dependent (or not really either)

In the coming chapters you will see each of these statistical tests in turn, illustrated by more actual studies in the field of second language research. The following application activity will give you some practice in putting the brief overview of this chapter into use in trying to figure out which test to use.

5.12 Application Activity for Choosing a Statistical Test

1   A researcher is interested in studying whether men and women differ in how politely they make requests in a second language.

   a.   What kind of statistical test could be used if the requests are categorized as either "polite" or "non-polite" so that we count how many men there are in the "polite" category and how many are in the "non-polite" category, and do the same for the women?

   b.   What kind of statistical test could be used if the requests are rated for politeness on an eight-point scale so there is one mean score for men and one mean score for women?

2   Robb, Ross, and Shortreed (1986) studied Japanese learners of English to see how four different kinds of written feedback for grammatical errors on weekly written work would affect the grammatical accuracy on a pre-treatment and post-treatment cloze test.

   a.   What kind of statistical test could be used to compare the differences in the groups on the post-treatment cloze test, so there are four mean scores of the different groups on the test?

---

a few articles that claimed to use the MANOVA. Of those, none actually did. It may be that some authors are confused because the readout provided in SPSS when a repeated-measures ANOVA is performed is called "Multivariate" (there is both a "Univariate" and a "Multivariate" print-out provided; see Chapter 12 for more information). I personally can remember an article early in my career where I claimed to be using a MANOVA but I was actually doing repeated measures. Thankfully a reviewer corrected me! Because MANOVAs seem to be used so infrequently in the second language research field, I have not included them in this book.

b. What kind of test could be used to compare the differences in the groups on both the pre-treatment and the post-treatment cloze test, in order to test whether the groups were different and also whether there was any change from the pre-test to the post-test?

3   Taguchi (2007) wanted to see whether having English-speaking learners of Japanese learn chunks would make them sound noticeably more fluent in a speaking test at the end of the semester as compared to one at the beginning. What kind of statistical test could be used to compare the mean scores of the Japanese learners at the beginning of the semester to their scores on fluency at the end of the semester?

4   Ellis, Heimbach, Tanaka, and Yamazaki (1999) conducted several tests to examine the effectiveness of learning vocabulary through different types of input and interaction.

a. One study involved three groups, one group which had unmodified input and no interaction, one group with modified input and no interaction, and a third group with unmodified input and interaction. The authors measured how much vocabulary each group learned. What statistical test could be used to see whether the groups performed differently in the amount of vocabulary they learned?

b. Another study looked at children in a group and counted the number of times each child negotiated for interaction. The children's comprehension scores were then examined to see if there was a relationship to the number of times they interacted. What statistical test should be used?

5   White, Spada, Lightbown, and Ranta (1991) wanted to see whether drawing learners' attention to grammar in question formation in English would change how accurately learners of English could create wh-questions.

a. In Phase I, two groups, one which received form-focused instruction on question formation and another group which did not, were assessed on the accuracy of their question formation with a 15-item test. What kind of statistical test could examine whether there were differences in accuracy between the two groups?

b. In Phase II more participants were studied and a third group of monolingual English speakers was added for comparison. Also, the authors wanted to see whether tests changed from pre-test to post-test assessment. What kind of statistical test could examine whether the groups performed differently at the different time periods?

6   A researcher is interested in studying whether individual factors such as high language learning aptitude and strong motivation result in higher levels of tonal accuracy in second language learners of Thai.

a. The researcher wants to know whether there is a relationship between aptitude and scores on a 20-point tone identification test. Which statistical test can be used to examine the relationship between these two variables?

b. The researcher then examines how much of the difference in scores on the tone test can be explained by the factors of language learning aptitude and a motivation score. What kind of statistical test can be used to do this?

7 Bialystok, Craik, Klein, and Viswanathan (2004) performed a study to see whether being bilingual affected reaction time scores on a response task. The authors looked at a younger and an older bilingual group and also compared the bilinguals to monolinguals doing the same task. The task also involved congruent tasks (hitting a key on the keyboard that was on the same side as the stimulus on the computer) and incongruent tasks (hitting a key on the keyboard on the opposite side to the stimulus on the computer).

a. In order to see whether age, language group, and type of task affected reaction times, what kind of statistical test could be used?

b. The authors gave their participants an intelligence test. If they wanted to perform the same analysis as in (a) but factor out the possible effects of intelligence, what kind of statistical test could they use?

Chapter 6

Finding Relationships Using Correlation: Age of Learning

> Probably the *shortest true statement* that can be made about causality and correlation is *"Empirically observed covariation is a necessary but not sufficient condition for causality."*
> Edward Tufte (2003, p. 4)

In looking at individual statistical tests, I will start with **bivariate correlation**, which means the correlation between two variables. In my experience, correlation is the most intuitively understandable statistical test for those who are new to statistics because noticing that two properties are related is a common experience for all people. A correlation is thus looking for some relationship, some common variation, between two variables.

Correlation as a statistical test involves two variables which are both continuous. Some examples from daily life provide an intuitive feel for what correlation involves. For example, height and weight in individuals are usually highly correlated. The taller a person is, the more they will likely weigh. Although the area of IQ is controversial, there has also been research showing that IQ scores of parents and children are highly correlated (Plomin, 1999). The number of drinks you may choose to ingest on a given evening will directly affect (correlate with) your general sense of well-being the next morning.

Correlation can be either negative or positive. Figure 6.1 shows a positive correlation on the left side and a negative correlation on the right side. In the field of second language research, an example of a positive correlation would be the relationship between speaking and listening ability in a language. In other words, the larger the speaking ability, the larger the listening ability is. In a second language listening and speaking are highly related, although not exactly the same thing. An example of a negative correlation would be the topic of this chapter, which is a decline in test scores as second language learners become older. In other words, as age gets larger (older), test scores get smaller. However, even though a correlation is negative the relationship between the two variables can be equally strong (the strength of the relationships shown in Figure 6.1 are about $r = \pm .80$).

Human beings also like to search for causes and effects. Thus, if in your experience you have seen that the attitude of students affects how proficient they become in a second language, you may have concluded that a positive attitude causes higher achievement in language learning. However, establishing cause and effect is a trickier proposition than simply establishing correlation. A statistical test can tell us whether

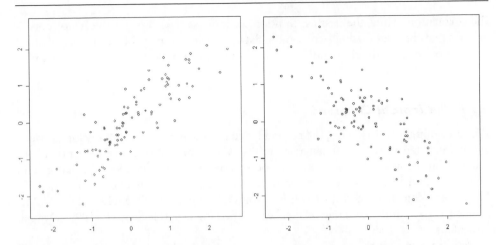

Figure 6.1 A scatterplot of a positive correlation (left side) and a negative correlation (right side).

two things we have measured have a relationship, but the test itself cannot tell us which one causes the other (or whether both mutually influence each other, as may be the case with language attitudes).

There is a well-known and justifiable caution in statistics that "Correlation does not equal causation." In other words, we cannot conclude just because two measurements vary together that one has caused the other. However, in many cases we are very interested in establishing causality when we do research, and there are ways to point toward a causal relationship even when using correlation. First of all, Maxwell and Delaney (2004) note that an experiment where the researcher manipulates some variable which groups differ on, such as the type of input received, will more convincingly show evidence of causality than one where the groups are divided based on an already-existing condition, such as age of learning. Second, one may use logic and reason. If you find a correlation between A and B, then logic dictates that A is the cause of B, B is the cause of A, or there is some external factor, C, which is the cause of both A and B. We can often make a good guess, depending on theory, previous research, or just common sense, about which way causality might be running (Shadish, Cook, & Campbell, 2002). For example, Moyer (1999) found a correlation between satisfaction with pronunciation and accent scores for second language learners of German. If we exclude the possibility that a third variable (C) is involved, common sense tells us that it is more likely that good pronunciation causes the satisfaction rather than the satisfaction causing the good pronunciation.

6.1 Visual Inspection: Scatterplots

Simple correlations tell us to what extent two variables are related or, in other words, vary together. If there is a correlation between two variables, we should be able to impose a line on the scatterplot data points, sloping either upwards or downwards through the data. The more tightly clustered around the line the data is, the stronger the correlation. Thus, the first assumption we must satisfy in order to test for correlation is that the relationship between the data is linear. It is possible to find a statistical correlation for data which do not have a linear relationship, so the first step in performing correlation is to take a graphic look at your data.

6.1.1 The Topic of Chapter 6

One area of interest in the field of second language research is the relationship between age and ultimate outcomes in language ability. Many studies have shown that there is a relationship between the age at which a person begins learning a second language and how well that person can perform on tests of grammatical judgment (DeKeyser, 2000; Flege, Yeni-Komshian, & Liu, 1999; Johnson & Newport, 1989; McDonald, 2000) or be judged to sound like a native speaker of the language (Flege et al., 1999; Oyama, 1976; Patkowski, 1980).

Data from two of these experiments will be used in this chapter. DeKeyser (2000) gave 57 Hungarian immigrants to the US a 200-point grammaticality judgment test of English. The participants varied in the age at which they first arrived in the US and started learning English. DeKeyser found a negative correlation, meaning that, as age of arrival increased, scores on the grammaticality test decreased. Flege, Yeni-Komshian, and Liu (1999) examined 240 Korean immigrants to the US on their ability to produce sentences as well as native speakers of English. The accent rating is the number from 1 to 9 that native English speakers gave to the learners' sentence-length productions. Again, the relationship here is negative in that, the older the learners were when they arrived in the US, the lower on average their accent scores tend to be. The line that Flege et al. (1999) fit to the data, however, is not linear, but a third-order (or cubic) non-linear fit to the data, which allows the line to change direction twice.

6.2 Creating Scatterplots

In this section I work with the DeKeyser2000.sav SPSS data file, and our first step in looking for a correlation between age and scores on DeKeyser's grammaticality judgment test will be to examine the data to see whether the relationship between these two continuous variables is linear. Scatterplots are an excellent graphic to publish in papers because they show all of your data to the reader.

I urge you to open up SPSS and follow the steps that I will show here. Create a scatterplot by clicking on GRAPHS > LEGACY DIALOGS > SCATTER/DOT (in SPSS 12.0 the additional LEGACY DIALOGS layer did not exist; in general, I still find the traditional way of doing graphs in SPSS more intuitive than the "Interactive" charts that SPSS 15.0 and 16.0 provide; you may want to experiment with them and see which you prefer). A dialogue box, shown in Figure 6.2, appears with several options for scatterplots. Pick the SIMPLE SCATTER scatterplot and then press DEFINE.

On the left side of the scatterplot dialogue box shown in Figure 6.3, all of your variables will be listed. Choose the two you want to plot and put them into the x-axis and y-axis boxes. Note: there is no good rule of thumb for which way to best plot your variables. If you decide to change the orientation afterwards, you can easily do this with the Chart editor.

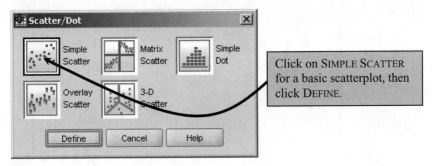

Figure 6.2 Choosing a scatterplot in SPSS.

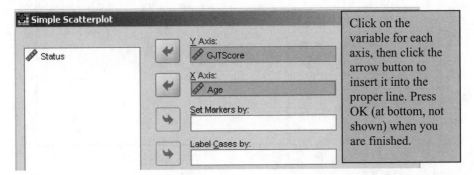

Figure 6.3 Scatterplot dialogue box in SPSS.

Tip: Note in Figure 6.3 that there is a ruler by all of the variables. The ruler means that the variables are numeric, or defined by numbers. Note that it does *not* mean that the variables are continuous. For example, the variable STATUS is a categorical variable with only two values, either the number "1" or the number "2." If your variable is not numerical, it is a string according to SPSS. You can use it in statistical calculations but only in places where you need a categorical variable, such as when you define groups. You would not be able to use a string variable in a correlation or scatterplot. You can change a variable's status by going to the VARIABLE VIEW tab and clicking on TYPE for the row (variable) you are interested in changing.

The scatterplot of the data in Figure 6.4 shows that, although the points do not lie in a perfect line, there is a general downward trend in the data. This means that, as participants started learning English at an older age, in general their performance on the morphosyntactic test grew worse. The inspection of the scatterplot shows that there is no other kind of non-linear relationship between the data, such as a U-shaped or curvilinear distribution. It is therefore appropriate to test for a linear relationship in the data by performing a correlation.

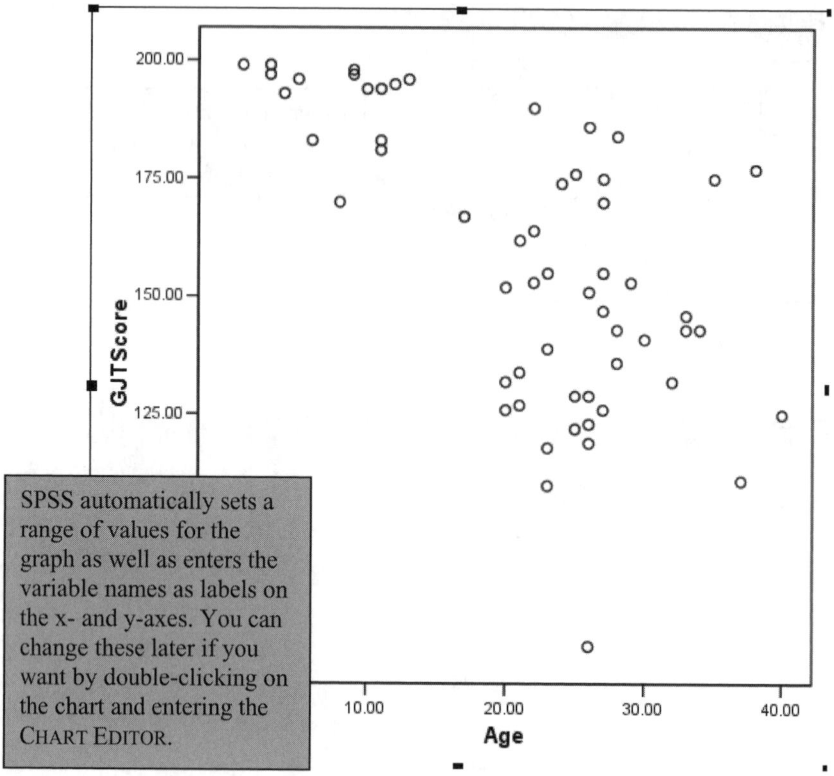
200.00
175.00
150.00
125.00
GJTScore
SPSS automatically sets a range of values for the graph as well as enters the variable names as labels on the x- and y-axes. You can change these later if you want by double-clicking on the chart and entering the CHART EDITOR.
10.00
20.00
30.00
40.00
Age

Figure 6.4 SPSS scatterplot of DeKeyser (2000) data.

Creating a Scatterplot in SPSS

1. On the drop-down menu, choose GRAPHS > LEGACY DIALOGS > SCATTER/DOT. When a dialogue box comes up, choose SIMPLE SCATTER for a two-variable scatterplot, and press the Define button.
2. Put one variable in the x-axis box and another in the y-axis box. Press OK.

6.2.1 Adding a Regression Line

Adding a **regression line** to a scatterplot can visually illustrate a linear relationship between variables. You may or may not want to include a regression line in published work, depending on your purposes for displaying the scatterplot. To add a regression line, first open the Chart Editor by double-clicking the graphic itself. The Chart Editor opens a reproduction of the graphic that you can change in a variety of ways (see Figure 6.5). All of the changes you make will be consolidated on your graph when you close the Chart Editor.

To fit a regression line, open the ELEMENTS menu as shown in Figure 6.6.

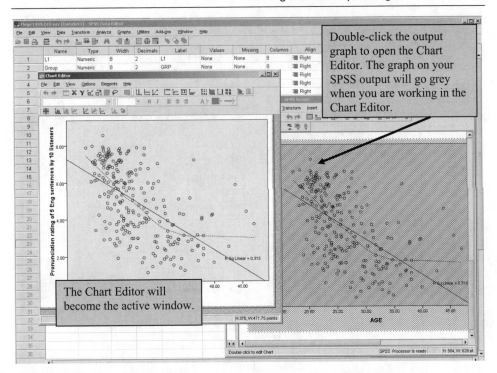

Figure 6.5 The Chart Editor in SPSS.

In SPSS 15.0 and 16.0 when you call on the Chart Editor to add a FIT LINE AT TOTAL, the PROPERTIES dialog box opens, as seen in Figure 6.6.

Tip: If you are working with older versions of SPSS like 12.0, you add a regression line by first clicking on a data point while in the Chart Editor and then opening the menu sequence ADD CHART ELEMENT > FIT LINE AT TOTAL. If you want to add lines for separate groups, you need to click twice, slowly, on a point within the group, and then open the menu option. Repeat this process with a different group.

The option for LINEAR is already chosen in the PROPERTIES box, so if you want a regression line all you need to do at this point is click CLOSE (see Figure 6.7 for examples of regression lines drawn on the scatterplot). Close the Chart Editor and you will see that the regression line has been drawn on your data, and that an "R Square Linear" value has been imposed on the chart. This is the size of the shared variance between the two variables, and ranges from −1 to 1. The closer this value is to ±1, the more variance the factors share. If a variable were correlated with itself, the value would be a perfect ±1.

Another useful type of line to draw on data is a Loess line. The **Loess** line is a locally weighted running-line smoother, and it considers only small chunks of the data at a

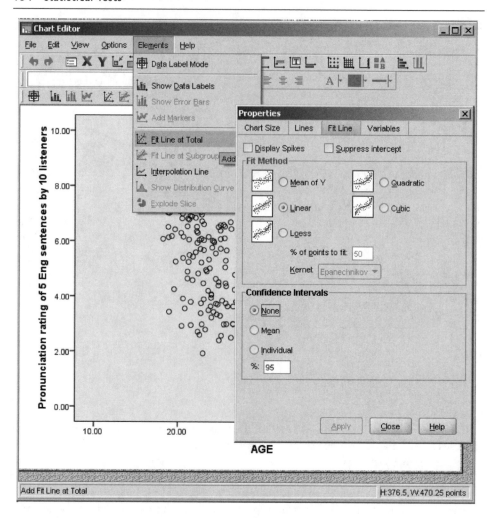

Figure 6.6 Using the Chart Editor to draw a regression line in SPSS.

time as it draws lines based on weighted least squares (Wilcox, 2001). In layman's terms, it fits the shape of the data by considering small intervals of the data at a time, instead of the overall pattern fit by a least squares regression line. The Loess line is a way to examine the assumption of **linearity** in the data (Everitt & Dunn, 2001). This assumption says that the relationship between the two variables should approximate a straight line. To examine this assumption, if the regression and Loess line match, this provides confidence in the assumption of a linear trend to the data. Most often you will use a Loess line for your own data analysis, although there may be cases when you would want to publish a graphic with a Loess line included as well.

Let's take a look at the Flege, Yeni-Komshian, and Liu (1999) data now, since the authors found that a non-linear (third order, or cubic fit) to the data was better than a straight regression line. First I create a scatterplot with the variables of age (the variable

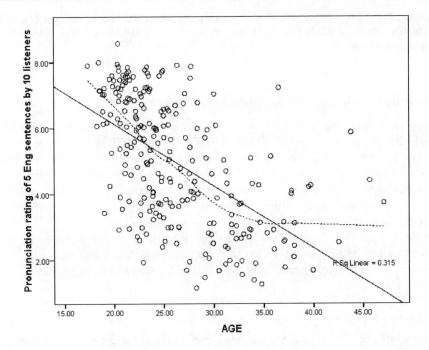

Figure 6.7 Scatterplot of Flege, Yeni-Komshian, and Liu (1999) pronunciation data, with a regression line (solid) and a Loess line (dotted) imposed on it.

is called "Age") and scores on a pronunciation measure in English (PRONENG) using the command shown in the previous section (GRAPHS > LEGACY DIALOGS > SCATTER/ DOT; then choose SIMPLE SCATTER). I double-click on the graph that is shown in the SPSS output to open the Chart Editor. Now from the Chart Editor's menus I choose ELEMENTS > FIT LINE AT TOTAL. To get a Loess line, I choose Loess from the Properties dialogue box. Figure 6.7 shows both a regression line and a Loess line on the Flege et al. data.

The Loess line shows that there is some curvature to the data, with younger starters scoring higher than the regression line predicts. Also, after about age 30 scores do not continue to decline but flatten out. It seems from the Loess line that there is ample reason to assume that a straight line is not the best fit for this data.

Adding a Fit Line to a Scatterplot in SPSS

1 Double-click on your created scatterplot. This will open the CHART EDITOR, giving you a replica of your plot.
2 From the Chart Editor drop-down menu, choose ELEMENTS > FIT LINE AT TOTAL. From the PROPERTIES dialogue box, choose the LINEAR option for a straight regression line, the LOESS option for a line that fits the data more closely.
3 When you are satisfied with the graph (and there are other options you may want to

> explore in the Chart Editor; just click on the area you'd like to change and you usually can change it), close the Chart Editor and you will now have a graph that can be copied and pasted anywhere.

6.2.2 Viewing Simple Scatterplot Data by Categories

You can in effect add a third variable to your graph by using the SET MARKERS BY option in the Scatterplot dialogue box (see Figure 6.8). DeKeyser (2000) had two categorical groups—participants who had begun to study English before age 15, and those who started after 15. To graphically see whether there appear to be differences between these two groups, we can use the SET MARKERS BY option to create a different look for each group. By entering a categorical variable into the SET MARKERS BY box, SPSS will then code the two groups with different colors and insert a legend.

The separate regression lines for the two groups in Figure 6.9 show that the negative correlation is quite slight if each group is considered separately, although it slopes downward more for the earlier group (before 15) than for the later group (after 15).

Splitting Data into Groups on a Scatterplot in SPSS

1   In the SIMPLE SCATTERPLOT dialogue box, add a categorical variable to the SET MARKERS BY box.
2   Customize the graph by adding fit lines, changing labels, or changing the properties of the plotting characters from the Chart Editor.

6.2.3 Application Activities with Scatterplots

1   Recreate the scatterplot for DeKeyser (2000). Use the file DeKeyser2000.sav. Create a simple scatterplot of the variables AGE and GJTSCORE. Draw a regression line over the scatterplot.
2   Draw a new scatterplot for the Flege, Yeni-Komshian, and Liu (1999) data. Use the file FlegeYeniKomshianLiu.sav. Create a simple scatterplot of the variables LOR

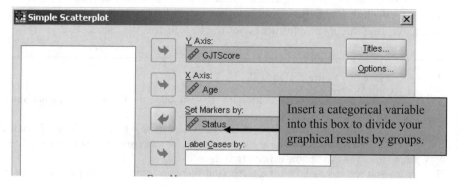

Figure 6.8 Dividing into groups in a scatterplot in SPSS.

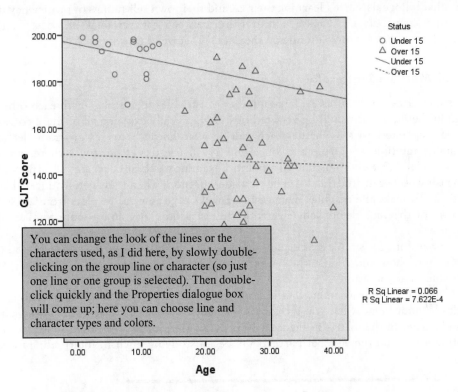

Status
○ Under 15
△ Over 15
⌒ Under 15
--- Over 15

R Sq Linear = 0.066
R Sq Linear = 7.622E-4

You can change the look of the lines or the characters used, as I did here, by slowly double-clicking on the group line or character (so just one line or one group is selected). Then double-click quickly and the Properties dialogue box will come up; here you can choose line and character types and colors.

Figure 6.9 Scatterplot of DeKeyser (2000) data with division into groups.

(length of residence) and PRON ENG. Draw a Loess line over the scatterplot. What trends do you see?

3   Use the data from Larson-Hall (2008). Use the LarsonHall2008.sav file. This data set was gathered from 200 Japanese college learners of English. The students took the same 200-item grammaticality judgment test that DeKeyser's (2000) partici-pants took. Create a simple scatterplot of the variables GJT SCORE and TOTAL HOURS of study to see whether students performed better on this test the more hours of study of English they had. Draw a regression line over the scatterplot. What trend can you see?

4   Using the same data set as in 3 above, graphically divide the data into two groups—early learners and later learners—using the variable ERLYEXP. I wanted to know whether students who had taken private English lessons before age 12 (early learn-ers) would ultimately perform better on morphosyntactic tests than Japanese learners who started study of English only in junior high school at age 12 (later learners). Separate your graph into these two groups, and draw regression lines over both groups. What trends can you see?

5   Dewaele and Pavlenko Bilingual Emotions Questionnaire (2001–2003). Use the BEQ.Swear.sav file. This data was gathered online by Dewaele and Pavlenko from a large number of bilinguals. Explore whether there is a correlation between the age

that bilinguals started learning their L2 and their own self-ratings of proficiency in speaking their L2. Create a scatterplot between the variables of AGESEC and L2SPEAK. Put a regression line on the data. What trend can you see?

6.2.4 Multiple Scatterplots

In some cases you may have a large number of variables to correlate with each other, and in these cases it would be very tedious to graphically examine all of these correlations separately to see whether each pairing were linear. Statistics programs let us examine multiple scatterplots at one time. I will use data from my own research, Larson-Hall (2008), to illustrate this point. I examine a subset of Japanese learners of English who began studying formally outside of school when they were younger than age 12. To make the graphics manageable, I will only show scatterplots from a 3 × 3 matrix of the variables of language aptitude test scores, age, and a score for use of English.

As was done for simple scatterplots, choose GRAPHS > LEGACY DIALOGS > SCATTER/ DOT. Now, however, choose the MATRIX SCATTER option and insert any number of variables that you want.

Note that in order to interpret the scatterplots you must look at the intersection of titles to understand what you are looking at. For example, the box in the lower left-hand corner of the matrix in Figure 6.10 is the scatterplot between total score on the aptitude test and the age that participants began studying English. Interpreting these

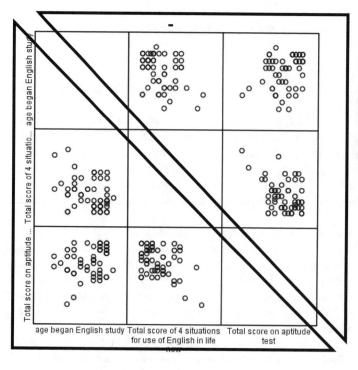

The top right half of the square and the bottom left are mirror images of each other; you only need to examine one side.

Figure 6.10 Multiple scatterplot of Larson-Hall (2008) data.

scatterplots may be more difficult than looking at individual scatterplots because the plots are smaller. However, at this point you should just be checking to make sure the data only have linear or randomly scattered patterns, not curvilinear or U-shaped patterns, so that you can ascertain whether the linearity assumption of the correlation test has been met. Therefore, a quick glance at the scatterplot matrix can be quite helpful when many variables are involved.

In Figure 6.10 we can see that there may well be linear relationships among the three intersections we are considering. The data do not appear to specifically follow a non-linear pattern, so we may proceed with further correlational analysis.

Creating a Multiple Scatterplot

1   On the drop-down menu, choose GRAPHS > LEGACY DIALOGS > SCATTER/DOT. When a dialogue box comes up, choose MATRIX SCATTER and press the DEFINE button.

2   Insert as many variables as you are examining into the MATRIX VARIABLES box. If you would like to split variables by groups, you can put a categorical variable in the SET MARKERS BY box. Press OK. Fit lines can be added by using the Chart Editor as explained in Section 6.2.1.

6.3 Assumptions of Parametric Statistics for Correlation

If you would like to conduct what is considered a "normal" type of correlation that you will see reported on in research in the field, you want to use a Pearson correlation. In this section I will discuss what assumptions you should fulfill to perform a parametric correlation (the Pearson). However, just a word of caution here. Statistics is about finding the best fit for the data, and it may turn out that a linear model of correlation may not be the best fit for your data. The previous sections have shown how to graphically examine your data to test the assumption of linear relationships between variables by using scatterplots. There is a variety of different models that may be used to characterize non-linear data, such as non-linear regression, non-parametric rank correlation (the Spearman correlation), tree models, and Loess models (a comprehensive look at all of these alternatives is beyond the scope of this book, but see Crawley, 2007, for a very clear exposition of these models). What I am trying to say is that you may be looking for relationships between variables, but if you use a correlation you are making an assumption that the best way to describe the relationship is with a straight line. A correlation is a linear model of the data. Chapter 7 on multiple regression will explore in more detail what a statistical model of the data entails.

The first assumption of correlation is that the data are related linearly. As seen above, this assumption must be tested by examining the data visually. Besides linearity, further assumptions for correlation are that the data should be independently gathered, normally distributed, and homoscedastic (Hatch & Lazaraton, 1991; Miles & Shevlin, 2001). Table 6.1 summarizes these assumptions.

Hatch and Lazaraton (1991) say that the assumption of **independence** means that the scores of one person must not influence the scores of another person in the data set. Thus the independence of variables needs to be addressed in the research design.

Table 6.1 Assumptions of Parametric Correlation (Pearson's r)

Meeting correlation assumptions		Correlation
1 Linear relationship between each pair of variables	Required?	Yes
	How to test assumption?	Examine scatterplots to rule out non-linear relationships; use multiple scatterplots to look at many variables at one time
	What if assumption not met?	1) Transform the variables to make the relationship linear; 2) try other kinds of models to better describe the data (cubic, quadratic, Loess models, etc.). Learn more about these in Chapter 8
2 Independence of observations	Required?	Yes, but should ideally be addressed in research design before experiment is conducted
	How to test assumption?	Plot residuals against case number (see Chapter 7)
	What if assumption not met?	Gather new data
3 Variables are normally distributed	Required?	Yes, both for individual variables and for the relationship between variables
	How to test assumption?	Examine plots for normality (histograms, Q-Q plots)
	What if assumption not met?	1) Transform variables to make distribution more normal; 2) use a non-parametric Spearman's rank test; 3) use robust methods in order to avoid assumption of normality and/or remove outliers while preserving independence of observations
4 Homoscedasticity (constant variance)	Required?	Yes
	How to test assumption?	Plot studentized residuals against fitted values and look for equal spread across entire graph (see Chapter 7)
	What if assumption not met?	1) Transform variables to make variances more equal; 2) use a non-parametric Spearman's rank test; 3) use robust methods in order to avoid assumption of homoscedasticity

The best way to satisfy the assumption of independence is to introduce randomness in how data is gathered, judged, or graded. Usually participants are not selected truly randomly in the second language research field, but one can strive to at least randomize assignment to groups, so that each volunteer for a study is randomly assigned to a specific group, but often intact classes are used in second language research and this is definitely not random assignment to groups.

The assumption of a normal distribution is not a trivial one but it has been addressed earlier in this book in Chapter 3. The assumption of **homoscedasticity** (sometimes also spelled homoskedasticity) means that the variance of the **residuals** (residuals are what is not accounted for in the model) for every pair of points on the independent variable is equal (Miles & Shevlin, 2001). This assumption is equivalent to the assumption of homogeneity of variance required for t-tests or ANOVAs (Miles & Shevlin, 2001). The way to check this assumption is by examining the residuals plot, but don't worry about how this can be done until you have read Chapter 7 on multiple regression. If the variances are not equal then the data are **heteroscedastic**.

Note that for the most part the statistical procedure is not going to tell you if you have violated any of these assumptions! It is up to you to check them, and to report this in your results. If the assumptions for a parametric test are not met, non-parametric versions of correlation include **Spearman's rho** (ρ) or **Kendall's tau-b** (τ) correlation tests. These non-parametric correlations are generally preferred when the data is ordinal, meaning that the measurements are ranked (Howell, 2002). For example, if you had 20 students perform an oral interview and did not give them a numerical score but instead ranked them relative to one another in proficiency level, you would have a rank ordering.

One more question might be whether there is any minimum sample size needed in order to perform a correlation. There is not, but one should keep in mind that the smaller the sample size, the larger the correlation coefficient (the r or rho) must be in order to maintain an adequate amount of power. For example, even with $r = .5$, a sample size of 15 would result in power of .47, which is low. What this means to researchers is that, even though there might be a statistical correlation, you might not have enough power to find it.

6.3.1 Effect Size for Correlation

The effect size that is calculated for correlations is R^2, which is usually described as a measure of how much of the variance in one variable is accounted for by the other variable. This definition can be confusing for those not yet familiar with statistics, however, and so I will borrow a very nice example from Crawley (2002, p. 235) which I think portrays what effect size means in a much clearer way.

Look at the two scatterplots in Figure 6.11 (produced using the TeachingDemos library in R). The two graphs have the same y intercept and slope of the line, but they differ in the amount of distance that the points are scattered from the regression line.

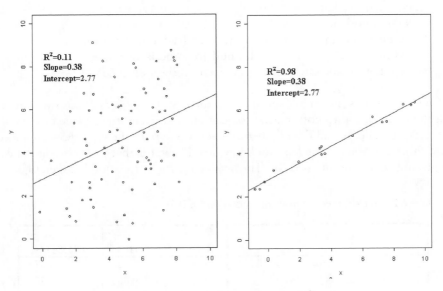

Figure 6.11 The effect of scatter on the correlation effect size (R^2).

R^2 is a measurement of how tightly these points fit the regression line. If the fit is perfect and all the points are lined up exactly on the regression line, R^2 will equal 1. In Figure 6.11, the scatterplot on the right has almost a perfect fit, meaning that almost all of the variance away from the line is accounted for. If there is a very poor fit and the points are widely scattered away from the regression line, R^2 will be low and close to 0. The scatterplot on the left in Figure 6.11 shows that the regression line does not account for a large amount of the variance between the variables, although it does account for some, because R^2 is greater than zero. This illustrates graphically how the variance in scores, or scatter away from the regression line, is accounted for by the R^2 statistic.

The R^2 is a percentage of variance (PV) effect size, from the r family of effect sizes. Cohen (1992) defined effect sizes for R^2 as $R^2 = .01$ is a small effect, $R^2 = .09$ is a medium effect, and $R^2 = .25$ is a large effect, but he also encouraged researchers to define effect sizes for their own fields. Thinking about some of the effect sizes that have been found with regard to age and language learning, DeKeyser and Larson-Hall's (2005) survey of Critical Period studies found age of arrival accounted for at least 50% of the variance in scores ($R^2 = .50$) in all studies, with other factors such as length of residence and motivation having much smaller effect sizes such as $R^2 = .05$ or less. Thus I would agree that an R^2 of 25% or more accounts for a large part of the variance (such as that seen with age in these studies), while an R^2 of 1–5% is seen as a small effect.

6.4 Calculating Correlation Coefficients

If you are satisfied that your data meet the requirements for the parametric Pearson's r correlation, the next sections tell you how to perform this test using SPSS. In the output for a correlation, you will want four pieces of information:

1   the correlation coefficient (Pearson's r, Spearman's rho, etc.)
2   the 95% confidence interval (CI) of the correlation coefficient
3   the number of items or participants (N) involved in the correlation
4   the p-value of a t-test testing the null hypothesis that there is no correlation between the variables (not strictly necessary if the CI is used)

Sample output is shown in Table 6.2 with three of these pieces of information. Each cell shows, from top to bottom, the correlation coefficient, the p-value of the correlation (Sig. (2-tailed)), and the number of cases where both the variables were present. Remember that the p-value lets you know how likely it is that if no correlation exists you would get the results you got. The p-value for the correlation between GJT score

Table 6.2 Sample Output from a Correlation Test in SPSS

		gjtscore	totalhrs	Total score on aptitude test
gjtscore	Pearson Correlation	1	.184**	.079
	Sig. (2-tailed)	.	.009	.267
	N	200	200	200

and total hours shows that it is highly unlikely that you would get these results if there were no correlation (the probability is less than one in 100). However, you should look at the effect size as well. The correlation coefficient for the correlation between GJT score and total hours is $r = .184$, so $R^2 = .03$. Thus, although the relationship is statistical, the importance of this relationship is rather small and does not explain much of the variance on scores on the test. SPSS does not provide 95% confidence intervals in the output.

Tip: This boxy output in Table 6.2 was the default for SPSS before version 16.0. After 16.0 the default is a Report style with minimal lines. To change the look of an individual table, double-click on the table. A new window called SPSS PIVOT TABLE will open. Choose a new look by going to FORMAT > TABLELOOKS (you can preview looks). Be careful though—even if you can change the format of the table, very rarely should you use the table as reported in SPSS as it is in a published article. You most likely will need to just extract the data and put it in an appropriate format yourself. To change the default look of all tables in your output, go to EDIT > OPTIONS > PIVOT TABLES. I still prefer the Box style that I show here in this book. I think it makes locating the data easier than the other styles.

6.4.1 Calculating Pearson's r, Spearman's ρ, or Kendall's τ Correlations

Perform a correlation in SPSS by choosing ANALYZE > CORRELATE > BIVARIATE. Enter any of the continuous variables that you want from the list on the left into the box on the right titled Variables, as shown in Figure 6.12.

Tip: In SPSS the order in which you transfer variables is the order in which you see them in your output. Therefore, I advise you to transfer the variables you are *most* interested in to the VARIABLES box first.

Using the Flege, Yeni-Komshian, and Liu (1999) data, I entered three variables into the correlation: English use (average of seven questions on a 5-point scale from 1=never to 5=always), Korean use (average of nine questions on the same 5-point scale), and the pronunciation rating.

The output in Table 6.3 shows that, for the correlation between English use and pronunciation rating, the effect size is $r = .61$, $p = .000$ (statistical at $a = .05$ level), and $n = 240$. This is a large effect size and shows there is a strong relationship between English use and the pronunciation rating each participant received.

To perform a Spearman's ρ or Kendall's tau-b correlation, the procedure is exactly the same as for a Pearson's r correlation, except that you should tick the appropriate boxes in the "Bivariate Correlations" box, and report your results by naming the test you used.

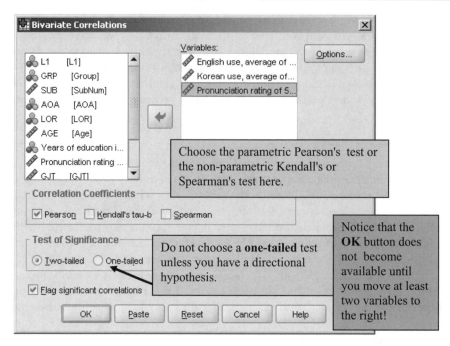

Figure 6.12 Obtaining correlations in SPSS.

Table 6.3 Output from a Pearson Correlation with the Flege, Yeni-Komshian, and Liu (1999) Data

Correlations

		English use	Korean use	Pronunciation rating
English use	Pearson Correlation	1	-.756**	.610**
	Sig. (2-tailed)		.000	.000
	N	240	240	240
Korean use	Pearson Correlation	-.756**	1	-.691**
	Sig. (2-tailed)	.000		.000
	N	240	240	240
Pronunciation rating	Pearson Correlation	.610**	-.691**	1
	Sig. (2-tailed)	.000	.000	
	N	240	240	240

**. Correlation is significant at the 0.01 level (2-tailed).

Calculating Correlations in SPSS

1   In the drop-down menu choose Analyze > Correlate > Bivariate.
2   Move variables on the left to the Variables box on the right. Choose whether you want Pearson's, Kendall's, or Spearman's correlation coefficients (you may pick one or more at a time). Decide if you are testing a one-tailed or two-tailed hypothesis and only change this box if you are sure you have a directional hypothesis.

6.4.2 Application Activities for Correlation

1   Use the file DeKeyser2000.sav. What correlation did DeKeyser (2000) find between age of arrival (AGE) and scores on the GJT (GJTSCORE) over the entire data set? What correlation did he find when the participants were divided into two groups based on their age of arrival (STATUS)? Before performing a correlation, check to see whether assumptions for parametric correlations hold (but still perform the correlation even if they do not hold; tick the non-parametric Spearman box though). Say something about effect size.

2   Use the file FlegeYeniKomshianLiu.sav. What correlation did Flege, Yeni-Komshian, and Liu (1999) find between age of arrival (AOA) and scores on an English pronunciation test (PronEng)? Before performing a correlation, check to see whether assumptions for parametric correlations hold (but still perform the correlation even if they do not hold; tick the non-parametric Spearman box though). If they do not, try to perform a correlation on just a subset of the data that appears to have a linear relationship. Do this by going to DATA > SELECT CASES and then choosing the button that says IF CONDITION IS SATISFIED. In the SELECT CASES: IF box write your own equation about which data to select. Leave the OUTPUT setting to FILTER OUT UNSELECTED CASES and press OK. Say something about effect size.

3   Use the file LarsonHall2008. There is a variety of variables in this file; let's look for relationships between use of English (UseEng), how much participants said they liked learning English (LikeEng), and score on the GJT test (GJTScore). In other words, we're looking at three different correlations. First, check for assumptions for parametric correlations. Do you note any outliers? Note which combinations do not seem to satisfy parametric assumptions. Then go ahead and check the correlations between these variables, checking both Pearson's and Spearman's boxes if assumptions for Pearson's are violated. What are the effect sizes of the correlations?

4   Dewaele and Pavlenko Bilingual Emotions Questionnaire (2001–2003). Use BEQ.Swear.sav file. What correlation was found between the age that bilinguals started learning their L2 (AGESEC) and their own self-ratings of proficiency in speaking (L2SPEAK) and comprehending their L2 (L2_COMP)? In other words, look at three different correlations. First, check for assumptions for parametric correlations. Do you note any outliers? Note which combinations do not seem to satisfy parametric assumptions. Then go ahead and check the correlations between these variables, checking both Pearson's and Spearman's boxes if assumptions for Pearson's are violated. What are the effect sizes of the correlations?

6.4.3 Reporting a Correlation

Report the correlation by including the name of the test used, the p-value, the r and/or R^2 value, and confidence intervals, if possible (SPSS does not report them but you can easily calculate them at the following web site just by typing in the r value and the sample size: http://glass.ed.asu.edu/stats/analysis/rci.html). Here is an example for the Larson-Hall (2008) data on Japanese learners of English:

A Pearson's r correlation between reported hours of study of English and scores on the GJT found the effect size of the correlation was small, and the CI fairly wide (95% CI: .05, .32; $r = .18$, N = 200, $R^2 = .03$), meaning the correlation coefficient is not highly reliable. The correlation between aptitude score and scores on the GJT was not statistical, with a negligible effect size and a confidence interval spanning zero (95% CI: −.06, .22; $r = .08$, $R^2 = .006$).

It can be seen that it takes a lot of words to report on correlations, and readers may be just as interested in the non-statistical correlations as in the statistical ones (effect sizes will play a role in what is important). For this reason, many writers report correlations in a tabular form when there are quite a number of variables involved. Here is an example using a number of variables from the Larson-Hall (2008) data, where correlations of the explanatory or predictor variables (the rows) with the GJT and phonemic discrimination tasks (the columns) are of most interest.

Table 6.4 shows that, while most of the effect sizes associated with the GJT are small (.01 to .14), those associated with phonemic discrimination are tiny (.00 to .03). Thus, whether an association is statistical or non-statistical (and any confidence interval which does not change sign from positive to negative is statistical) is not nearly so important to understanding what is happening as the effect size.

6.5 Other Types of Correlations (Advanced Topic)

6.5.1 Partial Correlation

Do you think that how well second language learners can pronounce words in their second language gets worse as they get older? I certainly didn't suspect this might be the case when I performed an experiment designed to see how well 15 Japanese speakers living in the United States for 12 years or more pronounced words beginning in /r/ and /l/ (Larson-Hall, 2006).

In every experimental condition the researcher wants to manipulate some variables while holding all other variables constant. One way to do this involves controlling for

Table 6.4 Correlation Table Example

Variable	GJT	N	CI	Effect size (R^2)	RLW phonemic discrimination	N	CI	Effect size (R^2)
Age began English study	−.37	61	−.58, −.13	.14	.07	61	−.19, .32	.00
English speaking ability (1–10, 10=native-like)	.29	196	.16, .42	.08	.13	196	−.01, .27	.02
English reading ability (1–10, 10=native-like)	.18	196	.04, .31	.03	.08	196	−.06, .22	.01
English usage	.31	187	.18, .44	.10	.09	187	−.05, .23	.01
How much like studying languages	.32	199	.19, .44	.10	.18	199	.04, .31	.03
Aptitude test score	.08	200	−.06, .22	.01	.12	200	−.02, .26	.01

the variable before experimental participants are chosen. If I had thought age was a concern for pronunciation accuracy, I would have set experimental parameters to exclude participants over, say, age 50. When I found, after the fact, that pronunciation accuracy as well as scores on a timed language aptitude test declined with age, the only way left to hold the age variable constant was to use partial correlation to subtract the effects of age from the correlations I was interested in.

I found a strong (as judged by effect size) and statistical negative correlation between length of residence (LOR) and production accuracy (as later judged by native speaker judges; $r = -.88$, $p = .00002$) as well as LOR and scores on a language aptitude test ($r = -.55$, $p = .035$). This meant that, as the participants lived in the US longer, their scores went down on both measures. However, I also found that *age* correlated negatively with both production accuracy and aptitude scores! Of course age also correlated positively with LOR (the longer a person had lived in the US, the older they were; $r = .74$, $p = .002$). Thus, in order to determine the true relationship between length of residence and production accuracy, I needed to use a partial correlation. The partial correlation can tell me how LOR and accuracy vary together by subtracting out the effects of age.

6.5.2 Calling for a Partial Correlation

In SPSS, call for a partial correlation by choosing ANALYZE > CORRELATE > PARTIAL command. If you want to follow along, I'm using the LarsonHallPartial.sav file. The dialogue box is almost the same as the one for regular correlations, except that it asks you to put factors you want to control for in the box labeled CONTROLLING FOR (see Figure 6.13).

The output shown in Table 6.5 is almost identical to the normal correlation matrix output except that degrees of freedom (df) are shown instead of N. The output shows

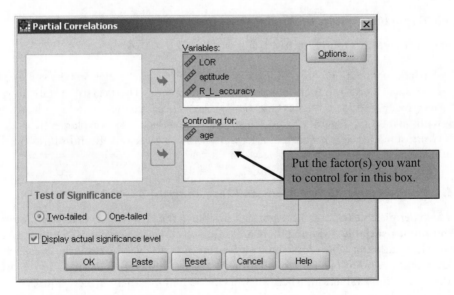

Figure 6.13 Calling for partial correlation.

Table 6.5 Output from a Partial Correlation

Correlations

Control Variables			LOR	aptitude	R_L_accuracy
age	LOR	Correlation	1.000	.027	-.753
		Significance (2-tailed)	.	.928	.002
		df	0	12	12
	aptitude	Correlation	.027	1.000	-.158
		Significance (2-tailed)	.928	.	.590
		df	12	0	12
	R_L_accuracy	Correlation	-.753	-.158	1.000
		Significance (2-tailed)	.002	.590	.
		df	12	12	0

that the correlations between length of residence (LOR) and production accuracy are now slightly smaller but still statistical ($r = -.75$, $p = .002$), while the correlation between the language aptitude score and LOR has become tiny and insignificant ($r = .03$, $p = .93$). This seems to imply that age played a large role in explaining the relationship of LOR and the aptitude scores, but not as great a role in the correlation between LOR and production accuracy. There is still a strong and statistical negative correlation between length of residence and production accuracy even when the effects of age are statistically subtracted.

Calculating Partial Correlations in SPSS

In the drop-down menu choose ANALYZE > CORRELATE > PARTIAL. Put the variable you want to control for in the CONTROLLING FOR box, and the other variables in the VARIABLES box.

6.5.3 Reporting Results of Partial Correlation

To report the results found for my data, I would say:

A partial correlation controlling for age found a strong correlation between length of residence and production accuracy of R/L words. The Pearson r statistic was negative ($r = -.75$, $p = .002$), meaning scores on production accuracy decreased with increasing length of residence, and the effect size was large ($R^2 = .56$). Controlling for age, no correlations were found between LOR and scores on the language aptitude test ($r = .03$, $p = .93$).

6.5.4 Point-Biserial Correlations and Test Analysis

It is also permissible to enter a categorical variable in the Pearson's r correlation if it is a **dichotomous variable**, meaning there are only two choices (Howell, 2002). In the case of a dichotomous variable crossed with a continuous variable, the resulting correlation is known as the **point-biserial correlation** (r_{pb}). Often this type of correlation is used in the area of test evaluation, where answers are scored as either correct or incorrect.

For example, in order to test the morphosyntactic abilities of non-literate bilinguals

I created an oral grammaticality judgment test in Japanese. The examinees had to rate each sentence as either "good" (grammatical) or "bad" (ungrammatical), resulting in dichotomous (right/wrong) answers. Since this was a test I created, I wanted to examine the validity of the test, and see how well individual items discriminated between test takers. One way to do this is by looking at a discrimination index, which measures "the extent to which the results of an individual item correlate with results from the whole test" (Alderson, Clapham, & Wall, 1995). Such a discrimination index investigates whether test takers who did well overall on the test did well on specific items, and whether those who did poorly overall did poorly on specific items. It therefore examines the correlation between overall score and score on one specific item (a dichotomous variable). Scores are ideally close to +1.

One way to determine item discrimination in classical test theory is to conduct a corrected point-biserial correlation, which means that scores for the item are crossed with scores for the entire test, minus that particular item (that is the "corrected" part in the name). In SPSS, this is easily done by choosing ANALYZE > SCALE > RELIABILITY ANALYSIS. Move the total test score and the dichotomous scores for each item to the ITEMS box on the right. Click the STATISTICS button, and be sure to check the box for "Scale if item deleted" under DESCRIPTIVES FOR. This will give you a box labeled Item-Total Statistics in the output, where you can see the Corrected Item-Total Correlation, which is the point-biserial correlation for each item. Oller (1979) states that, for item discrimination, correlations of less than .35 or .25 are often discarded by professional test makers as not being useful for discriminating between participants.

More modern methods of test item analysis have become more popular, however, now that computing power has increased. In particular, item response theory (IRT) provides a way to analyze test items by positing a latent or unmeasured trait that is linked to the dichotomous scores. Harvey (1998) lists a number of advantages that IRT holds over classical methods, and speculates that IRT will soon replace classical test methods. Although there is not space in this book to detail how IRT works, interested readers are directed to edited collections by Baker and Kim (2004) and van der Linden and Hambleton (1997).

In other cases where you may have a dichotomous variable such as gender (male versus female) or group membership with only two categories (student versus employed, for example) that you want to correlate with a continuous variable such as TOEFL scores, it generally does not make sense to conduct a correlation (whether Pearson or Spearman) because you have so little variation in the dichotomous variable (there are some exceptions; see Hatch & Lazaraton, 1991, p. 450, for additional information). It would be better in this case to compare means for the two groups using a t-test or one-way ANOVA.

Calculating Point-Biserial Correlations

In the drop-down menu choose ANALYZE > SCALE > RELIABILITY ANALYSIS. Put the score for the total test and also the individual items in the "Items" box. Open the STATISTICS button and tick "Scale if item deleted." If point-biserial correlations are low, you should probably think about eliminating these items from your test (but more modern methods of test analysis such as IRT are really better ways to consider your test data and I would urge you to find out how to use these).

6.5.5 Inter-rater Reliability

It often happens in second language research that you will have a set of judges who will rate participants. The judges may rate the participants' pronunciation accuracy or writing ability or judge the number of errors they made in past tense, for example. In this case you will have multiple scores for each participant that you will average to conduct a statistical test on the data. However, you should also report some statistics that explore to what extent your raters have agreed on their ratings.

If you think about what is going on with judges' ratings, you will realize that you want the judges' ratings to differ based on the participants that they rated. For example, Judge A may give Participant 1 an 8 and Participant 2 a 3 on a 10-point scale. You would then hope that Judge B will also give Participant 1 a high score and Participant 2 a low score, although they may not be exactly the same numbers. What you don't want is for judges' scores to vary based on the judge. If this happened, Participant 1 might get an 8 from Judge A but a 2 from Judge B and a 10 from Judge C. In other words, you want to see that the variability in scores is due to variation in the sample and not variation in the judges. Any variation that is seen in the judges' scores will be considered error, and will make the rating less reliable. DeVellis (2005) defines **reliability** as "The proportion of variance in a measure that can be ascribed to a true score" (p. 317). Mackey and Gass (2005) define reliability as consistency of a score or a test. They say a test is reliable if the same person taking it again would get the same score. You can see that these two definitions of reliability are similar, for they both address the idea that a test result can be confidently replicated for the same person. Therefore, the more reliable a measurement is, the more it will measure the right thing (the true score) and the less error it will have.

Howell (2002) says the best way to calculate **inter-rater reliability** for cases of judges rating persons is to look at the intraclass correlation. This will not only take into account the correlation between judges, but also look at whether the actual scores they gave participants differed. We will look at **Cronbach's alpha** as a measurement of intraclass correction. Cortina (1994) says that coefficient alpha is an internal consistency estimate, "which takes into account variance attributable to subjects and variance attributable to the interaction between subjects and items [on a test, or for our purposes here, judges]" (p. 98).

In this section I will use data from a study by Munro, Derwing, and Morton (2006). These authors investigated to what extent the L1 background of the judges would affect how they rated ESL learners from four different L1 backgrounds—Cantonese, Japanese, Spanish, and Polish. The judges themselves were native speakers also of four different backgrounds—English, Cantonese, Japanese, and Mandarin, but I will examine the data only from the ten Mandarin judges here. The judges rated the samples on three dimensions—their comprehensibility, intelligibility, and accentedness. I will examine only scores for accentedness here using the file MunroDerwingMorton.sav.

To calculate the intraclass correlation for a group of raters, go to ANALYZE > SCALE > RELIABILITY ANALYSIS. You will see the dialogue box for Reliability Analysis shown in Figure 6.14. Move the scores for your participants to the "Items" box. The columns you enter here should consist of the rating for each participant on a different row, with the column containing the ratings of each judge. Therefore, variable M001 contains the ratings of Mandarin Judge 1 on the accent of 48 speakers, M002 contains the ratings of

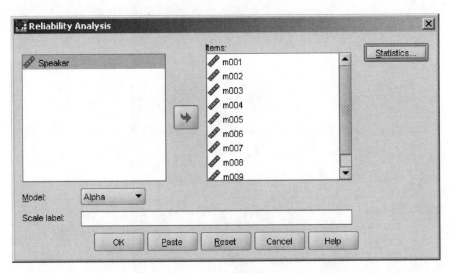

Figure 6.14 Dialogue box for Reliability Analysis with Munro, Derwing, and Morton's (2006) data.

Mandarin Judge 2 on the accent of the 48 speakers, and so on. Leave the "Model" menu set to ALPHA. Other choices here are SPLIT-HALF, GUTTMAN, PARALLEL, and STRICT PARALLEL, but what you want to call for is Cronbach's coefficient alpha.

Next, open the STATISTICS button and you'll see the box in Figure 6.15. The most important thing to do here is to tick the "Intraclass correlation coefficient" box. When you do this, two drop-down menus will become visible. In the first one choose TWO-WAY RANDOM. This choice specifies both the item effects (the judges/the columns) as random variable and the subject effects (the participants/the rows) as random as well. Since both the rows and the columns contain subjects, they are both random effects (we want to generalize to more than just the actual judges and more than just the actual participants; I discussed the difference between fixed and random effects in Section 2.1.6).

In the second drop-down menu you can choose whether you'd like a measure of CONSISTENCY or ABSOLUTE AGREEMENT, but in truth this doesn't matter for the Cronbach's alpha result so just leave the default of CONSISTENCY chosen. Also tick the boxes that say "Scale if item deleted" and "Correlations."

The first box you will see in the output will just be a summary of how many cases were analyzed. Of course you should check this to make sure that all the cases you thought were going to be analyzed actually were (there were 48 in the Munro, Derwing, & Morton data). The next box contains Cronbach's alpha, which is the major item you are interested in (see Table 6.6). For the Mandarin judges, Cronbach's alpha is 0.89. This is a high correlation considering that there are ten items (judges).

In general, we might like a rule of thumb for determining what an acceptable level of Cronbach's alpha is, and some authors do put forth a level of 0.70–0.80. Cortina (1994) says determining a general rule is impossible unless we consider the factors that affect the size of Cronbach's alpha, which include the number of items (judges in our case) and the number of dimensions in the data. In general, the higher the number of

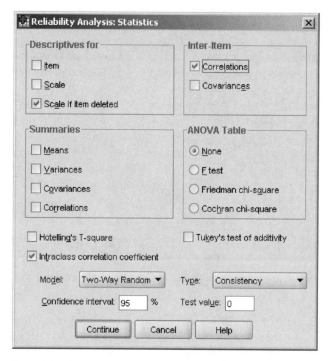

Figure 6.15 Statistics for the reliability analysis.

Table 6.6 Cronbach's Alpha Output from the Reliability Analysis

Reliability Statistics

Cronbach's Alpha	Cronbach's Alpha Based on Standardized Items	N of Items
.885	.892	10

items, the higher alpha can be even if the average correlations between items are not very large and there is more than one dimension in the data. Cortina says that, "if a scale has enough items (i.e. more than 20), then it can have an alpha of greater than .70 even when the correlation among items is very small" (p. 102). It is therefore important to look at the correlations between pairs of variables, and this is shown in the next part of the output, the inter-item correlation matrix, shown in Table 6.7.

By and large the paired correlations between judges are in the range of 0.30–0.60, which are medium to large effect sizes, and this Cronbach's alpha can be said to be fairly reliable. However, if the number of judges were quite small, say three, then Cronbach's alpha would be quite a bit lower than what is obtained with 10 or 20 items even if the average inter-item correlation is the same. Try it yourself with the data—randomly pick three judges and see what your Cronbach's alpha is (I got .65 with the three I picked).

Table 6.7 Inter-Item Correlation Matrix from a Reliability Analysis

Inter-Item Correlation Matrix

	m001	m002	m003	m004	m005	m006	m007	m008	m009	m010
m001	1.000	.352	.341	.413	.231	.236	.337	.385	.407	.323
m002	.352	1.000	.333	.530	.411	.478	.518	.614	.507	.538
m003	.341	.333	1.000	.599	.427	.411	.325	.393	.578	.606
m004	.413	.530	.599	1.000	.434	.615	.514	.497	.443	.619
m005	.231	.411	.427	.434	1.000	.366	.309	.250	.309	.481
m006	.236	.478	.411	.615	.366	1.000	.553	.551	.309	.672
m007	.337	.518	.325	.514	.309	.553	1.000	.577	.387	.586
m008	.385	.614	.393	.497	.250	.551	.577	1.000	.513	.580
m009	.407	.507	.578	.443	.309	.309	.387	.513	1.000	.547
m010	.323	.538	.606	.619	.481	.672	.586	.580	.547	1.000

Why don't we just use the average inter-item correlation as a measure of reliability between judges? Howell (2002) says that the problem with this approach is that it cannot tell you whether the judges rated the same people the same way, or just if the trend of higher and lower scores for the same participant was followed.

The last piece of output I want to look at is shown in Table 6.8. This has a column that shows what Cronbach's alpha would be if each item (judge) individually were removed. If judges are consistent then there shouldn't be too much variation in these numbers, and this is true for the Munro, Derwing, and Morton (2006) data. However, if there were a certain judge whose data changed Cronbach's drastically you might consider throwing out that judge's scores.

Overall test reliability is often also reported using this same method. For example, DeKeyser (2000) reports, for his 200-item grammaticality judgment test, that "The reliability coefficient (KR-20) obtained was .91 for grammatical items [100 items] and .97 for ungrammatical items" (p. 509) (note that, for dichotomous test items, the Kuder–Richardson (KR-20) measure of test reliability is equal to Cronbach's alpha). DeKeyser gives raw data in his article, but this raw data does not include individual dichotomous results on each of the 200 items of the test. These would be necessary to calculate the overall test reliability. Using the file LarsonHallGJT described in Section

Table 6.8 Item-Total Statistics Output from a Reliability Analysis

Item-Total Statistics

	Scale Mean if Item Deleted	Scale Variance if Item Deleted	Corrected Item-Total Correlation	Squared Multiple Correlation	Cronbach's Alpha if Item Deleted
m001	51.48	172.893	.449	.265	.889
m002	50.04	169.530	.668	.529	.870
m003	50.46	185.020	.613	.559	.877
m004	52.62	158.495	.732	.594	.864
m005	50.44	190.294	.484	.321	.883
m006	51.21	157.317	.660	.576	.872
m007	53.12	175.601	.655	.479	.872
m008	52.42	163.355	.690	.558	.868
m009	51.40	182.457	.608	.512	.876
m010	52.44	158.719	.776	.671	.861

6.5.4 I will show how to obtain an overall test reliability score if you have the raw scores (coded as 1s for correct answers and 0s for incorrect answers). I have deleted the scores of native speakers of Japanese on this test, as I think native speakers may score quite differently from learners of Japanese.

Use the same reliability analysis as for the inter-rater reliability (ANALYZE > SCALE > RELIABILITY ANALYSIS). Here I will enter all 40 of my items into the "Items" box as shown in Figure 6.16. If all I want is to get Cronbach's alpha, there is no need to open the STATISTICS button (the boxes you might tick in the STATISTICS button to look at item-total statistics and inter-item correlation would be a way of doing test analysis, which I have already explained in Section 6.5.4). The output gives a Cronbach's alpha of 0.67, which can also be reported as a KR-20 score of .67. This is not very high considering how many items I have, so it would be hard to call this a highly reliable test (I made it up myself and it clearly needs more work! I actually presented a conference paper at AAAL 2008 where I used the R statistical program to analyze the data with IRT methods, and I would be happy to send you this presentation if you are interested).

Calculating Inter-rater Reliability

In the drop-down menu choose ANALYZE > SCALE > RELIABILITY ANALYSIS. Put all the items which contain judges' ratings of the participants in the "Items" box. Open the STATISTICS button and tick the "Intraclass correlation coefficient" box. In the first drop-down menu choose TWO-WAY RANDOM, but leave the other drop-down menu alone. Also tick "Scale if item deleted" and "Correlations." Look for Cronbach's alpha in the output.

For **overall test reliability** simply put all of your dichotomous test items (coded as 0s and 1s) into the "Items" box in the Reliability analysis and obtain Cronbach's alpha, which you can also call the KR-20 measure of reliability.

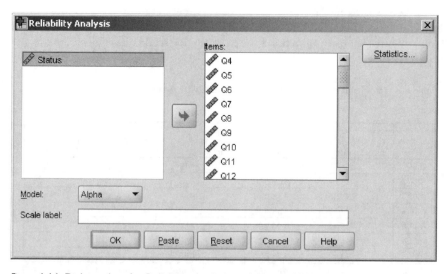

Figure 6.16 Dialogue box for Reliability Analysis with Larson-Hall's GJT data.

6.6 Summary

The main use of correlation in second language research studies is to examine whether two continuous variables show a relationship. In looking at variables, the most useful first step is to examine a scatterplot. The scatterplot can show visually how or whether the variables are related. A correlation assumes that the relationship is linear, in other words that it is best described by a straight line through the data. A Loess line, which follows the trend of the data closely, is a useful tool for visually ascertaining whether a straight line is a good approximation to the data.

In order to use the parametric correlation statistic (the Pearson's r), various assumptions such as normal distribution of the variable and a linear relationship between the variables should be examined. In the exercises you have seen that, in many cases, assumptions are not fulfilled but parametric statistics are still used. An alternative is to use non-parametric statistics such as Spearman's rho (or better yet to use robust statistics, but these are not currently available in SPSS).

I have suggested that the most important point to report in looking at a statistical association is the effect size. R^2 is a percentage of variance effect size, and indicates to what degree a straight line through the data effectively accounts for the variation between the two variables. The larger this number is, the more strongly the variables are related.

In the Advanced Topics section of the chapter several more uses of correlation that can be useful in the field were addressed. One was the use of partial correlation, which can factor out the effects of one variable which you may decide after the fact is interfering with revealing the true extent of the correlation between your variables. Another use of correlation, fast becoming outdated, is the use of the point-biserial correlation to determine which items are useful in test construction when answers are dichotomous (with only two choices, such as yes/no or correct/incorrect). Lastly, the question of reporting inter-rater reliability when judges are used in your experimental design was addressed. In these cases Cronbach's alpha can be obtained as a measure of inter-rater reliability. This same statistic can be used to report on the reliability of a test you have used if you have raw scores for each item in the test.

Chapter 7

Looking for Groups of Explanatory Variables through Multiple Regression: Predicting Important Factors in First-Grade Reading

Assuming that the regression [you fit] adequately summarizes the data does not make it so.

John Fox (2002, p. 28)

One of the goals of scientific research is to try to explain and predict phenomena. For example, if you are a teacher you know that some students in your classes excel, while others just can't seem to grasp the concepts you are teaching. In order to explain these differences, you might look for explanatory variables such as IQ, motivation, amount of time spent on homework, reading speed, socio-economic status, or any other number of variables. Regression is a technique that allows you to look at a number of **explanatory variables** and decide which ones have independent power to explain what's going on with the variable you have measured, for example scores on a TOEFL test. We'll call this property you measure the **response variable**, and the variables you think might explain what's going on the explanatory variables. The explanatory variables are also sometimes called independent variables, but we will avoid that since these variables are often correlated with the response variable, and thus not very "independent."

As a statistical test, multiple regression involves two or more continuous variables. One of the variables will be the response variable, and one or more variables will be the explanatory variables. As an example of how multiple regression might apply to the real world, say that you run a small business in Korea helping students to score highly on the TOEFL test. You know that how hard students work to learn grammar and vocabulary has an impact on how well they can do. But you also sense that some students are just more gifted than others at learning languages, and this also affects how highly they can score. You measure how much time the students spend per week in classes and studying English, and you also give them a language aptitude test. You can use multiple regression to determine whether these two factors do indeed independently affect scores on the TOEFL test, and how much they affect scores.

7.1 Understanding Regression Design

In this chapter, we will use the default settings in SPSS to analyze multiple regression. Mathematically, the default for a regression equation will be:

$$Y_i = a + \beta_1 x_{i1} + \cdots + \beta_k x_{ik} + \text{error}_i$$

To put this in terms of our example:

> TOEFL score = some constant number (the intercept) + time spent on English per week + aptitude score + a number which fluctuates for each individual (the error)

This mathematical equation is one that defines a line for a data set (although multiple regression does not always have to define a line, for this chapter it will). If it's been a while since you thought about how to draw a line, let me remind you that mathematically a line needs to be defined by a number representing its intercept (**alpha** or *a*) and a number representing its slope (**beta** or *β*). In Figure 7.1, you see how the line is formed by knowing just these two values—the intercept and the slope. In the regression formula, the *a* is the intercept and the *β* is the slope. The slope is divided up into different parts if there is more than one explanatory variable. These betas are thus called **partial coefficients** if there is more than one explanatory variable. The error part at the end of the equation is necessary to explain all of the other parts of the real data that don't actually land straight on this regression line. This error is also called the **residual**.

In multiple regression, then, we can try to see whether the explanatory variables we've posited explain very much of what is going on. For example, we might find that time spent on English per week plus aptitude scores explains about 60% of the variation in TOEFL scores (in other words, $R^2 = .60$). The rest, the part we can't explain,

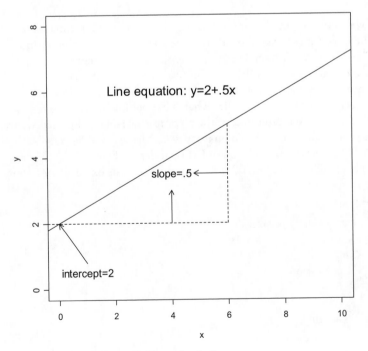

Line equation: y=2+.5x

slope=.5

intercept=2

Figure 7.1 The mathematical formula of a line.

gets dumped into the error, and we might want to add other variables to try to explain more later.

Besides seeing whether the explanatory variables we picked do a good job of explaining what is happening, we can also use multiple regression to predict how people in the future will score on the response variable. Since we can have an equation for the response variable, we can just plug in the x values for each individual (the scores on each of the explanatory variables) and calculate the y value mathematically (the response variable). In the TOEFL example, if it turns out that with my current students the combination of language aptitude and hours spent in study explains a lot of the variation in TOEFL scores, then with future students, if I know how many hours a week they are studying and I measure their language aptitude, the regression equation will spit out a predicted TOEFL score *for each individual* that should be fairly close to what they will actually score.

To put this into concrete terms, let's suppose one of our students, Jun, scored 486 on the TOEFL. He reported to us that he studies English five hours a week, and he got a score of 25 on the short form of the modern language aptitude test (MLAT). We have analyzed the data of our 20 students through multiple regression and found out that alpha = 29.2. The beta coefficient for hours of study is 10.1, and the beta coefficient for the MLAT is 12.6. If we were going to predict what score Jun would get, we could calculate it like this, putting the numbers we obtained into the TOEFL score equation found at the beginning of this section:

TOEFL score = 29.2 + 10.1 (Jun's hours of study = 5) + 12.6 (Jun's MLAT = 25)

TOEFL score = 29.2 + 51 + 315 = 395.2

In other words, if we were predicting Jun's score, we would predict he would score 395 on the TOEFL. But in fact he scored 486, so we have some error in the equation. The error for Jun is 486 − 395 = 91. You can see that, even though this regression equation explains a good deal of variation in TOEFL scores (60%), it is not perfect.

Although the regression equation is a linear equation, and the regression line we will draw is a straight line, another way to visualize what is happening in multiple regression is to look at a Venn diagram. We can think of the response variable being what we want to explain, and we can think of the explanatory variables as overlapping with the response variable. The overlapping portions of the circles in Figure 7.2 are areas of shared variance (Tabachnick & Fidell, 2001). Using our previous example of trying to

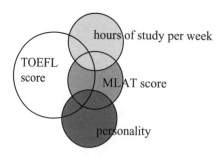

Figure 7.2 Venn diagram of regression variables.

explain TOEFL scores, we can add another variable to hours of study per week and MLAT score, that of personality, to try to improve the predictive ability of the model.

What we see is that there are overlapping areas of variance *among* the explanatory variables as well as with the response variable (the TOEFL score). For example, the score on the MLAT may correlate in part with how many hours an individual studies per week as well as with some part of the personality measure. The way these overlapping parts are measured is the basis for a division into two types of regression—**standard** and **sequential** (also called **hierarchical**). As I explain these types you should understand how the choice of **regression model** (the type of regression you do and what variables are included) can make a difference to the final conclusions that a researcher may draw, and will answer different questions.

7.1.1 Standard Multiple Regression

If **standard multiple regression** is used, the importance of the explanatory variable depends on how much it *uniquely* overlaps with the response variable. In Figure 7.3 then, MLAT score has the largest unique contribution to the variance of the TOEFL score (the area in c), because it overlaps most with the TOEFL score only and not with any of the other explanatory variables.

Thus in standard regression only the areas of each explanatory variable that overlap with the response variable, but not with any other variables, contribute to the overall estimation of how much the variables predict the response. In other words, each variable is evaluated "as if it had entered the regression after all other IVs [independent variables] had entered" (Tabachnick & Fidell, 2001, p. 131). Tabachnick and Fidell (2001) explain that standard multiple regression answers two questions:

1   What are the nature and size of the relationship between the response variable and the set of explanatory variables?
2   How much of the relationship is contributed uniquely by each explanatory variable?

If one of the explanatory variables is very highly correlated with another explanatory variable, it may appear to contribute very little to the overall regression equation in spite of being highly correlated with the response variable. For this reason, you should

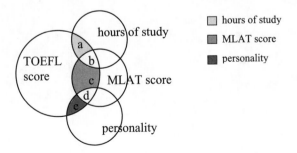

Figure 7.3 Venn diagram of standard regression design.

consider both the canonical correlation of the variables and the information about the unique contribution made by the explanatory variable from the regression analysis.

7.1.2 Sequential (Hierarchical) Regression

For **sequential (hierarchical) regression**, all of the areas of the explanatory variables that overlap with the response variable will be counted (unlike in standard regression), but the way that they will be included depends on the *order* in which the researcher enters the variables into the equation. Therefore, the importance of hours of study in our example will increase with sequential regression if it is entered first, because it will account for both areas a and b (shown in Figure 7.4). If MLAT score is added second, it will account for even more of the variance than it did in standard regression because it will be able to "claim" areas c and d.

The importance of any variable, therefore, can be emphasized in sequential regression, depending on the order in which it is entered. If two variables overlap to a large degree, then entering one of them first will leave little room for explanation for the second variable. Tabachnick and Fidell (2001) therefore advise researchers to assign the order of variables depending on a theoretical or logical reason.

Tabachnick and Fidell state that the main research question that a sequential regression can answer is:

> Do the subsequent variables that are entered in each step add to the prediction of the response variable after differences in the variables from the previous step have been eliminated? (2001, p. 139)

The data set illustrated in this chapter from Lafrance and Gottardo (2005) basically asked this question by examining whether differences in phonological awareness add to the prediction of first-grade L1 word reading performance after differences in non-verbal reasoning, L2 word reading ability in Kindergarten, L2 naming speed, and L2 working memory measures have been eliminated.

In fact, if the authors had done a standard regression, the only explanatory variable included in the model would have been phonological awareness. This is because apparently it is the only explanatory variable which overlaps with first-grade L1 reading scores in a unique way that does not overlap with any of the other explanatory

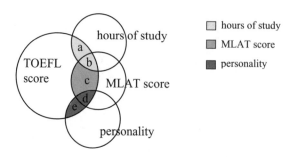

Figure 7.4 Venn diagram of sequential regression design.

variables. Thus to see the contributions of the other variables, the authors used a sequential regression with phonological awareness entered last.

7.1.3 Data Used in This Chapter

This chapter will use data from a study by Lafrance and Gottardo (2005) which tried to predict reading performance by French–English bilinguals, and took an uncommon look at whether L2 abilities affected L1 reading skills. The study was longitudinal and looked at the same children, being schooled in French, from Kindergarten to Grade 1.

The response variable is:

*   scores on L1 (French) word reading skills in Grade 1 (Woodcock-Revised test)

The five explanatory variables are:

*   L2 (English) phonological awareness measured in Kindergarten
*   L2 working memory measured in Kindergarten
*   L2 naming speed measured in Kindergarten
*   nonverbal reasoning ability (Matrix Analogies test)
*   L2 word reading skills in Kindergarten

7.2 Visualizing Multiple Relationships

Before you begin a multiple regression it is imperative that you examine your data graphically and get to know what is going on. Actually conducting a multiple regression is extremely easy using computer software, but multiple regression also has a large number of assumptions that must be met in order to be satisfied that the statistical techniques that are employed are going to give accurate results. These assumptions are traditionally examined *after* you have run the regression, however, since many of the assumptions involve looking at plots of the residuals, which cannot be determined until after the regression model has been determined (in other words, you have to decide which variables you will include in the model before you can test assumptions).

One assumption that can be examined before running a multiple regression is that of **linearity**. The assumption is that each explanatory variable has a linear relationship with the response variable. To examine this assumption let's take a look at a multiple scatterplot for the Lafrance and Gottardo (2005) data set (I've included only four of the five variables we will examine in the regression in this scatterplot for reasons of space). The scatterplot has the Loess line (not the regression line) on each graph, and a histogram of the distribution of the variable on the diagonal. Since Chapter 6 explained how to create scatterplots and scatterplot matrices, I will not explain how to perform any graphics in this section; I will merely comment on the Lafrance and Gottardo (2005) data.

Here are some of my thoughts on looking at the matrix scatterplot in Figure 7.5, where Grade 1 French (L1) word reading skills (L1G1WR) is the response variable and the others are the explanatory variables (I'm looking specifically down the far right column where L1G1WR is matched with the other variables):

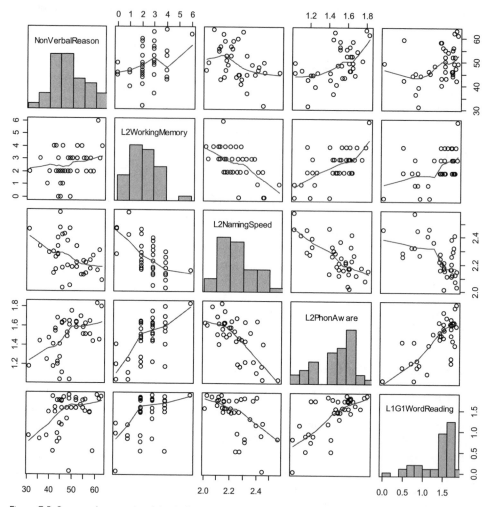

Figure 7.5 Scatterplot matrix of the Lafrance and Gottardo (2005) variables.

- The relationship between L1 word reading and L2 phonological awareness seems reasonably linear.
- The relationship between L1 word reading and the other variables does not seem as clearly linear but also does not seem to show any curvature or other defined patterns.
- There may be some outliers in the relationship between L1 word reading and nonverbal reasoning.

The one scatterplot not shown here, that between Grade 1 French (L1) word reading skills and Kindergarten English (L2) word reading skills, is shown in Figure 7.6 with a Loess line drawn over the data.

The scatterplot in Figure 7.6 shows some clear curvature. In this chapter I will recreate the regression as Lafrance and Gottardo (2005) conducted it, but it is worth

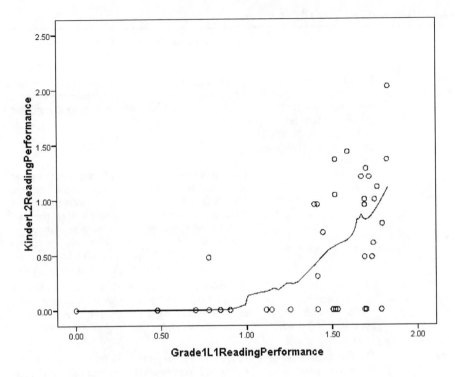

Figure 7.6 Scatterplot between Grade 1 L1 reading and Kindergarten L2 reading skills.

keeping in mind that, because the relationship between these two variables is not linear, a better approach might be to try a polynomial fit for this variable (see Section 7.5).

7.3 Assumptions of Multiple Regression

Regression presents a large number of assumptions that must be satisfied, and indeed this area is quite a complex one that cannot be totally covered in this book. I will focus only on the most basic assumptions and tests of the assumptions. Assumptions such as a normal distribution and linearity may be familiar from previous chapters, but the methods used to check them differ. Regression fitting is done *after* a regression model has been selected. Assumptions cannot be tested until the model has been decided on, because in many cases the variables you are testing are results from the model, such as the residuals (what is left over after the explanatory variables have done their part). Table 7.1 may thus not make sense until after you have gone through later sections of the chapter which show how to check assumptions of multiple regression.

7.3.1 Assumptions about Sample Size

There is a variety of "rules of thumb" for the number of samples that should be collected for a multiple regression. Porte (2002) recommends 30 participants per

Table 7.1 Assumptions for Multiple Regression

Assumptions		How to test assumption?	What if assumption is not met?
Normal distribution	Errors normally distributed (note that this is *not* the distribution of the variables, but rather the distribution of the error that should be examined)	Examine Q-Q plots	1) Transform variables; 2) use robust regression; 3) use bootstrap regression
	No outliers	Look at graphs of studentized residuals, Cook's D and Mahalanobis distances; look for values beyond usual ones	1) Remove outliers and rerun analysis; report on both results to your readers; 2) use robust methods to remove outliers while preserving independence of observations
Homogeneity of variances (constant variance)	"The variance of Y for each value of X is constant (in the population)" (Howell, 2002, p. 267)	Plot studentized residuals against fitted values and look for equal spread across entire graph	1) Transform to equalize spread (try square root or log); 2) use robust regression; 3) use bootstrap regression
Linearity	The relationship between X and Y is linear	1) Examine scatterplot matrices; 2) plot residuals against individual variables and look for curvature	1) Transform; 2) use a polynomial model instead (put in x^2 or x^3 terms to model the curvature)
Multicollinearity	*Explanatory* variables involved in the regression should not be highly intercorrelated	1) Look at numerical matrix of correlations; 2) check VIF	Delete a variable from the regression if it is highly correlated with another explanatory variable

explanatory variable. Tabachnick and Fidell (2001, p. 117) give the formula: $N \geq 50 + 8m$ where m = number of explanatory variables. Stevens (2002) recommends about 15 per variable based on his own experience and some statistical studies. Howell (2002, p. 548) cites (but does not necessarily support) a widespread rule of thumb of 10 observations for each variable. Thus, for Lafrance and Gottardo's regression with five explanatory variables, Porte would say they should have 150 participants, Tabachnick and Fidell would recommend 90, Stevens would say 75, and Howell's rule of thumb would ask for 50 (quite a difference!). Tabachnick and Fidell quote Green (1991), who gives a rule that includes effect size: $N \geq (8/f^2) + (m-1)$ where $f^2 = .01$, .15, and .35 for small, medium, and large effects, respectively. Given this rule and estimating a medium effect size from previous research with reading and phonological awareness, Lafrance and Gottardo would need $N \geq (8/.15) + (5-1) = 58$ participants (rounding up). Note that such a number would enable the authors to find a medium or large effect size, but not a small effect size. Cohen, Cohen, West, and Aiken

(2003, p. 93) combine both power and effect size to determine that, with five explanatory variables, for an $R^2 = .20$ and power of .80, 52 subjects would be required. This wide divergence of sample size recommendations is daunting, giving support for any number of observations, ranging in the case of five predictors from 50 to 150.

I include here Table 7.2, calculated from Cohen et al. (2003), for various levels of R^2 and various numbers of predictors, but all at the same $a = .05$ and power = .80 level.[1] It can be seen that the higher or more obvious you expect the effect size to be (the R^2), the fewer participants are needed. Because the effect size in Lafrance and Gottardo's study is so high ($R^2 = .58$ for the regression I am examining), their sample size of 40 turns out to be more than adequate.

However, one important idea to take away from this discussion is that you should not try to "throw in the kitchen sink" and include every variable you can think of. The more variables you have, the more observations or participants you will need in order to have a strong statistical case. The number of variables and your choice of them should include the costs of obtaining the data in sufficient numbers so as to be statistically valid. The best-case scenario would be if researchers chose a power level and estimated an effect size in order to have a principled reason for the number of participants in a study. Although this is something I have never seen addressed in any second language research study that I have read, I hope that this kind of statistical thinking may become more prevalent in the future.

7.4 Performing a Multiple Regression

Before doing a multiple regression, I need to explain one more type of regression that Tabachnick and Fidell (2001) discuss. In Section 7.1 I discussed standard and sequential types of regression. In the former case, only the unique contribution of the explanatory variable to the response variable was counted, while in the latter the entire amount of overlap of the explanatory variable with the response variable was counted, so that order of entry mattered.

Another type of regression mentioned in Tabachnick and Fidell (2001) is **stepwise**

Table 7.2 Sample Size Needed for Various Effect Sizes at 80% Power in Regression

Number of predictors	$R^2=.10$	$R^2=.15$	$R^2=.20$	$R^2=.25$	$R^2=.30$	$R^2=.50$
2	74	47	34	21	21	10
3	91	58	42	26	26	13
4	104	66	48	30	30	15
5	114	73	53	33	33	17
6	123	79	58	36	36	19
7	131	85	62	39	39	21
8	139	90	66	42	42	23
9	146	95	70	44	44	25
10	153	99	73	47	47	26

1 The formula is: $\frac{L}{f^2}$ + number of predictors; to calculate this you must use Cohen et al. (2003)'s table to look up values of L, and can then calculate $f^2 = R^2/1 - R^2$.

regression. Like sequential regression, this type of regression will count all of the area where the explanatory variables overlap with the response variable. However, what is called a stepwise regression in SPSS (actually, the descriptions stepwise, backward, and forward all apply to types of stepwise regression in SPSS) is not recommended. This is because using stepwise regression leaves the model determination up to the computer and the variables are entered based "solely on statistical criteria," which makes this a "controversial procedure" (Tabachnick & Fidell, 2001, p. 133). The choice for which variable is entered first is based on the strength of the correlation.

Let's say for the TOEFL example we were looking at in Section 7.1 that all three variables had nearly the same strength of correlation with the TOEFL score, but MLAT score had a slightly higher correlation with the TOEFL score than the other two explanatory variables (see Figure 7.7). In that case, MLAT score would be entered first, and thus b, c, and d would count for the variance of motivation. Next, the algorithm would evaluate whether the remaining variables contributed significantly to the R^2 (the part of the variance in the response variable that the explanatory variables account for). If they did not (because much of their variance has been claimed by motivation), they would not be entered in the equation, in spite of the fact that initially their correlation levels were about the same strength.

For the Lafrance and Gottardo (2005) data, we find fairly high correlations between naming speed and the response variable ($r = -.57$), kindergarten measures of reading and the response variable ($r = .55$), and working memory and the response variable ($r = .51$). If only these three variables were included in a regression model, a stepwise regression would pick naming speed first, even though the difference between $r = .57$, $r = .55$, and $r = .51$ may not be statistical.

Stepwise regressions can be done forward, backward, or both ways (the default method in SPSS). In all cases, you as the researcher are letting the computer pick the regression configuration based on purely statistical information, with no logical or theoretical assumptions involved. For this reason, most writers recommend against stepwise regression. Tabachnick and Fidell (2001, p. 135) caution that it should be used only if samples are "large and representative," and even then researchers should be cautious about generalizing results to a wider population. Howell (2002, p. 565) says that it can "capitaliz[e] on chance" and thus the computer may choose a model which is only slightly better than a more "logically appropriate model." It should not be used unless you truly "have no particular theoretical axe to grind" (p. 564).

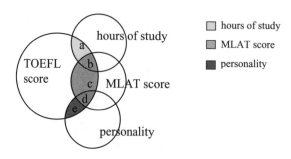

Figure 7.7 Venn diagram of stepwise regression design.

7.4.1 Starting the Multiple Regression

Before running the regression you should have examined your data set for linearity by using scatterplots. If the data look reasonably linear, you may begin your regression (note that Lafrance and Gottardo transformed some of their variables with the log transformation in order to correct for skewness). We will examine assumptions of multivariate normality and homogeneity of variances through residual plots called for in the regression analysis itself.

To perform a regression, choose ANALYZE > REGRESSION > LINEAR. Put your response variable in the box labeled "Dependent" (see Figure 7.8). A crucial step, and one that will determine how you enter the explanatory variables in the box labeled "Independent(s)," is determining which method you want to use to analyze the regression. Pull down the menu next to METHOD and use the explanations in Figure 7.8 to decide which

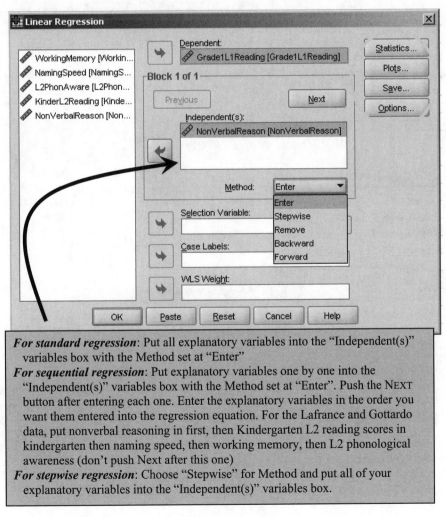

For standard regression: Put all explanatory variables into the "Independent(s)" variables box with the Method set at "Enter"

For sequential regression: Put explanatory variables one by one into the "Independent(s)" variables box with the Method set at "Enter". Push the NEXT button after entering each one. Enter the explanatory variables in the order you want them entered into the regression equation. For the Lafrance and Gottardo data, put nonverbal reasoning in first, then Kindergarten L2 reading scores in kindergarten then naming speed, then working memory, then L2 phonological awareness (don't push Next after this one)

For stepwise regression: Choose "Stepwise" for Method and put all of your explanatory variables into the "Independent(s)" variables box.

Figure 7.8 Main dialogue box for linear regression in SPSS.

method to choose. Also, open three of the buttons on the right-hand side of the dialogue box: STATISTICS, PLOTS, and OPTIONS.

Figure 7.9 shows all four sub-dialogue boxes you should open from the main Linear Regression dialogue box. From the STATISTICS button you will decide which statistics to receive in the output. From the PLOTS button you will choose to view graphs which will be used to assess the assumptions of the regression model (normality, homogeneity,

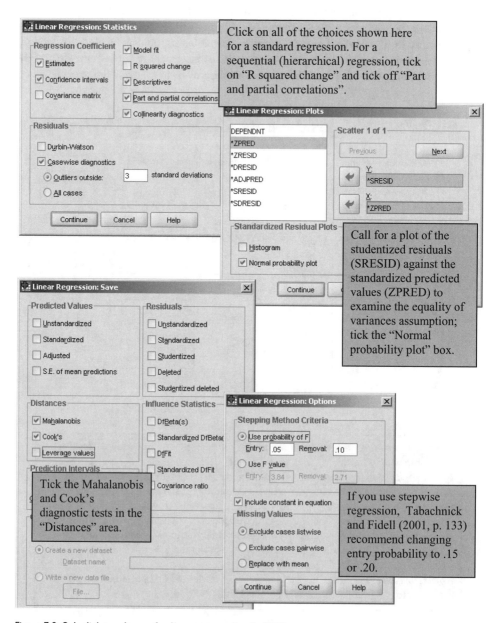

Figure 7.9 Sub-dialogue boxes for linear regression in SPSS.

etc.). From the SAVE button you will be able to call for some diagnostic tests. From the OPTIONS button you have the chance to choose how to deal with missing data and also to specify the stepwise criteria if you should choose this method of regression. For missing data, the default option is listwise exclusion, which is preferable to pairwise exclusion even though it may reduce sample size. Howell (2002) says that excluding pairwise in a regression can result in strange correlations. Replacing missing values with the mean can be appropriate if you have only a small amount of missing data that does not display any patterns for being missing. Remember from Section 3.6 that the APA task force has labeled both listwise and pairwise deletion the worst ways of dealing with missing data, and I suggested in that section that one good way to deal with missing data would be imputation. In fact, the LafranceGottardo.sav file that is used later in this chapter is one where I imputed a few missing values for the Naming Speed variable.

Once you have configured your regression as noted in Figure 7.8 and 7.9, press OK and run your regression.

7.4.2 Regression Output in SPSS

The first box in the regression output is the descriptive statistics (Table 7.3). Here we see that the mean scores are quite different for the different predictors. For example, the mean score for nonverbal reasoning is 48.9, but for naming speed it is 2.2. All this means is that the variables were measured on different types of scales. We also see that using listwise deletion means that we have only 37 cases for the regression, even though 40 participants were included in the experiment (to follow along with the analysis in this section, use the Lafrance5.sav file, which is not imputed, and will recreate Lafrance and Gottardo's (2005) results, Table 3, under L2 phonological processing variables, Grade 1 word reading L1).

The second box of the output is a correlation matrix. The format of this in SPSS is rather messy, so Table 7.4 shows the same data in a more readable form, giving the r-value, p-value, and N for each cell of the correlation matrix.

Although we will examine **multicollinearity** measures later (e.g. VIF; multicollinearity measures how much a number of variables vary together), it is important to note here whether there are any high correlations between the explanatory variables and the response variable (these are shown in the first row), or among the explanatory

Table 7.3 Regression Output: Descriptive Statistics

Descriptive Statistics

	Mean	Std. Deviation	N
Grade1L1Reading Performance	1.3669	.45215	37
NonVerbal Reasoning	48.9459	7.28753	37
Kinder L2 Reading Performance	.5464	.58691	37
Naming Speed	2.2414	.12846	37
Working Memory	2.6486	1.27402	37
Phonological Awareness in L2	1.4926	.20815	37

Table 7.4 Correlations between Variables in Lafrance and Gottardo (2005)

	Nonverbal reasoning	Kindergarten L2 reading performance	Kindergarten L2 naming speed	Kindergarten L2 working memory	Kindergarten L2 phonological awareness
Grade 1 L1 reading performance	.346	.550	−.572	.505	.730
	.029	.000	.000	.001	.000
	40	40	37	40	40
Kindergarten L2 reading performance	.442				
	.004				
	40				
Kindergarten L2 naming speed	−.407	−.404			
	.012	.013			
	37	37			
Kindergarten L2 working memory	.298	.536	−.607		
	.062	.000	.000		
	40	40	37		
Kindergarten L2 phonological awareness	.511	.712	−.699	.590	
	.001	.000	.000	.000	
	40	40	37	40	

variables themselves (shown in the second through fifth rows). Tabachnick and Fidell (2001) caution against correlations as high as or higher than $r = .70$, and a couple of correlations with Kindergarten L2 phonological awareness reach that level. However, Lafrance and Gottardo know from previous studies that phonological awareness is highly correlated with reading measures, and they want to see whether any other factors can be predictive before phonological awareness is added, so they probably do not want to throw out phonological awareness.

The next part of the output shown in Table 7.5 is the Variables Entered/Removed table. Because Lafrance and Gottardo performed a sequential (hierarchical) regression, this table importantly shows the order in which the variables were entered. If this were a standard regression, this table would just list the variables entered, as shown in the smaller table on the right.

The next part of the output, the Model Summary table, provides a summary of how much of the variance in the response variable is accounted for by the predictors (Table 7.6). In the sequential regression there are five models because SPSS tests each of the models listed as (a) through (e). Thus, in the first model (a), SPSS tests how much of the variance in word reading can be accounted for by just nonverbal reasoning. In other words, this equation is tested:

Grade 1 L1 word reading = intercept (Constant) + nonverbal reasoning + error

Model 2 tests how much of the variance can be accounted for by two factors:

Grade 1 L1 word reading = intercept (Constant) + nonverbal reasoning
+ Kindergarten L2 reading + error

Table 7.5 Regression Output: Variables Entered/Removed

Variables Entered/Removed

Model	Variables Entered	Variables Removed	Method
1	NonVerbal Reasoning [a]	.	Enter
2	Kinder L2 Reading Performance [a]	.	Enter
3	Naming Speed [a]	.	Enter
4	Working Memory [a]	.	Enter
5	Phonological Awareness in L2 [a]	.	Enter

a. All requested variables entered.

b. Dependent Variable: Grade1L1Reading Performance

Variables Entered/Removed

Model	Variables Entered	Variables Removed	Method
1	Phonological Awareness in L2, NonVerbal Reasoning, Working Memory, Kinder L2 Reading Performance, Naming Speed [a]	.	Enter

a. All requested variables entered.

b. Dependent Variable: Grade1L1Reading Performance

Table 7.6 Regression Output: Model Summary (Sequential Regression)

Model Summary[f]

Model	R	R Square	Adjusted R Square	Std. Error of the Estimate	Change Statistics				
					R Square Change	F Change	df1	df2	Sig. F Change
1	.335[a]	.112	.087	.43209	.112	4.422	1	35	.043
2	.582[b]	.339	.300	.37819	.227	11.686	1	34	.002
3	.683[c]	.467	.418	.34489	.127	7.884	1	33	.008
4	.688[d]	.473	.407	.34814	.006	.385	1	32	.539
5	.761[e]	.580	.512	.31585	.107	7.879	1	31	.009

a. Predictors: (Constant), NonVerbal Reasoning

b. Predictors: (Constant), NonVerbal Reasoning, Kinder L2 Reading Performance

c. Predictors: (Constant), NonVerbal Reasoning, Kinder L2 Reading Performance, Naming Speed

d. Predictors: (Constant), NonVerbal Reasoning, Kinder L2 Reading Performance, Naming Speed, Working Memory

e. Predictors: (Constant), NonVerbal Reasoning, Kinder L2 Reading Performance, Naming Speed, Working Memory, Phonological Awareness in L2

f. Dependent Variable: Grade1L1Reading Performance

By the end, Model 5 tests how much variance is explained by all five predictors added into the regression equation. You can see how the regression equation used in each model can easily be derived from the predictors listed underneath the model summary box in the lettered footnotes (the equation is just missing the error term and plus signs between the variables).

The number that we are most interested in from Table 7.6 is in the R Square column (or R Square Change column after the first row). The results tell us that Model 1 with just nonverbal reasoning accounts for $R^2 = 11\%$ of the variance, as seen in the R Square column in the Model Summary (the R^2 number can range from 0 to 1). This model has 35 degrees of freedom, because there are 37 rows of data, and we have to subtract 1 degree of freedom for the response variable and 1 for the one explanatory variable. The Adjusted R Square corrects for positive bias in the R^2 estimate, but few people report this number because it is usually lower than the R^2!

The second model tested adds the predictor of Kindergarten L2 Woodcock reading test results. Now the R^2 is .339, but what we really want to know is how much R^2 Kindergarten L2 reading independently added to the total model. To know this we just subtract .112 from .339 (.339 − .112 = .227) or simply look in the R Square Change column to see .227. In other words, Kindergarten L2 reading independently adds 23% of explanation for the variation in scores on the Grade 1 L1 reading test.

The model with five explanatory variables can explain 76% of the variance in scores on the Grade 1 L1 reading test. This is a very large amount! However, we should realize that there is a tradeoff between the amount of explanatory value and the number of predictors. Adding more predictors always results in a higher R^2, so if we fit the model with 37 predictors we might have an R^2 of 1 but we would have little explanatory value.

What Lafrance and Gottardo were interested in examining with this sequential regression was if other predictors besides phonological awareness have an independent ability to account for variance. The output in Table 7.6 shows that they did, except for working memory, which added only about .01% in explanation of the variation in scores on the Grade 1 L1 reading measure.

Going on to explain a couple more of the columns of output in Table 7.6, the F Change column of the sequential regression Model Summary gives the result of an ANOVA comparing the current model with the previous model to see whether the two models are statistically different. Model 2, for example, is statistically different from Model 1 ($F = 11.69$, $p = .002$). Model 1 is compared to the null model, which is just the average mean score of all of the variables. Model 4 is not statistically different from Model 3, as seen by the fact that the significance of the F change there is $p = .539$ (not less than $p = .05$). If you are interested in a good fit for predictors, you would probably want to leave out the predictor added in Model 4, which was working memory (WM).

Note that the Model Summary output, shown in Table 7.7, will not contain any part of the "Change Statistics" if the regression is a standard regression with all variables added at once. If you performed a standard regression, your Model Summary table will look much simpler, and you'll basically be interested in the R^2 statistic.

Moving on to the next part of the output, Table 7.8 shows a table which gives the results of an ANOVA performed on each model. The ANOVA tests the null hypothesis that the predictive power of the model is equal to zero. This is probably never a very realistic hypothesis, so a statistically significant result is not too much to get excited about, and there is probably nothing from this table you will want to report.

The next part of the output is the Coefficients table (Table 7.9). This is an important

Table 7.7 Regression Output: Model Summary (Standard Regression)

Model Summary

Model	R	R Square	Adjusted R Square	Std. Error of the Estimate
1	.761[a]	.580	.512	.31585

a. Predictors: (Constant), NonVerbalReason, WorkingMemory, KinderL2Reading, NamingSpeed, L2PhonAware

Table 7.8 Regression Output: ANOVA Table

ANOVA[f]

Model		Sum of Squares	df	Mean Square	F	Sig.
1	Regression	.826	1	.826	4.422	.043[a]
	Residual	6.534	35	.187		
	Total	7.360	36			
2	Regression	2.497	2	1.248	8.729	.001[b]
	Residual	4.863	34	.143		
	Total	7.360	36			
3	Regression	3.435	3	1.145	9.625	.000[c]
	Residual	3.925	33	.119		
	Total	7.360	36			
4	Regression	3.481	4	.870	7.181	.000[d]
	Residual	3.879	32	.121		
	Total	7.360	36			
5	Regression	4.267	5	.853	8.555	.000[e]
	Residual	3.093	31	.100		
	Total	7.360	36			

piece of the output. This table gives information about each explanatory variable in the equation. Here you find the unstandardized (**B**) and standardized **regression coefficients** (confusingly named Beta, symbol is β) for each of the five explanatory variables (plus 95% confidence intervals for the B). The unstandardized coefficients are the coefficients you would use to write the regression equation. For example, Model 2 would predict that scores in Grade 1 L1 reading performance could be modeled by:

Y = .795 + (.007)*nonverbal reasoning + (.404)*Kindergarten L2 reading performance

The .795 is the intercept (alpha), taken from the row named "Constant" under Model 2. The B coefficients are then multiplied by each factor in the equation. Unstandardized coefficients cannot be compared to each other well, however. Standardized coefficients give the coefficients that would result if they were fit to standardized data. Tabachnick and Fidell (2001) report both in their results.

The t-test associated with each line in the Coefficients table tests whether each explanatory variable contributes uniquely to the equation (Tabachnick & Fidell, 2001). In their paper, Lafrance and Gottardo reported, for each model, the total R^2 (from Model Summary output), the change in R^2 (from Model Summary output), the standardized coefficients for each model (from Coefficients output), and whether each coefficient was statistical (from the Sig. column next to the t-test in the Coefficients output) by putting stars next to the statistical coefficients.

In their paper, Lafrance and Gottardo (2005) noted that, when L2 phonological awareness was entered (Model 5), it became the only statistical predictor of Grade 1 L1 reading performance. They concluded that L1 and L2 phonological awareness were

Table 7.9 Regression Output: Coefficients (Sequential Regression)

Coefficients[a]

Model		Unstandardized Coefficients B	Unstandardized Coefficients Std. Error	Standardized Coefficients Beta	t	Sig.	95% Confidence Interval for B Lower Bound	95% Confidence Interval for B Upper Bound	Collinearity Statistics Tolerance	Collinearity Statistics VIF
1	(Constant)	.350	.489		.716	.479	-.643	1.342		
	NonVerbal Reasoning	.021	.010	.335	2.103	.043	.001	.041	1.000	1.000
2	(Constant)	.795	.447		1.777	.085	-.114	1.704		
	NonVerbal Reasoning	.007	.010	.116	.754	.456	-.012	.027	.825	1.212
	Kinder L2 Reading Performance	.404	.118	.525	3.418	.002	.164	.644	.825	1.212
3	(Constant)	4.415	1.352		3.265	.003	1.664	7.166		
	NonVerbal Reasoning	.000	.009	-.002	-.014	.989	-.019	.018	.757	1.320
	Kinder L2 Reading Performance	.315	.112	.409	2.806	.008	.087	.544	.760	1.316
	Naming Speed	-1.434	.511	-.407	-2.808	.008	-2.473	-.395	.768	1.302
4	(Constant)	3.868	1.624		2.382	.023	.561	7.176		
	NonVerbal Reasoning	.000	.009	.008	.053	.958	-.018	.019	.749	1.336
	Kinder L2 Reading Performance	.286	.123	.371	2.321	.027	.035	.536	.645	1.549
	Naming Speed	-1.242	.601	-.353	-2.066	.047	-2.466	-.018	.565	1.770
	Working Memory	.039	.062	.109	.621	.539	-.088	.165	.536	1.865
5	(Constant)	.156	1.980		.079	.938	-3.882	4.194		
	NonVerbal Reasoning	-.004	.008	-.057	-.418	.679	-.021	.014	.727	1.375
	Kinder L2 Reading Performance	.073	.135	.095	.542	.592	-.202	.348	.442	2.262
	Naming Speed	-.311	.638	-.088	-.487	.630	-1.613	.991	.412	2.426
	Working Memory	.025	.057	.071	.444	.660	-.090	.141	.532	1.878
	Phonological Awareness in L2	1.322	.471	.609	2.807	.009	.362	2.283	.288	3.471

a. Dependent Variable: Grade1L1Reading Performance

highly related and that cross-language transfer of phonological awareness was taking place.

Both Tabachnick and Fidell (2001) and Howell (2002) argue that the change in R^2 is a better measure of the "importance" of each variable than the regression coefficients, which do not really measure the effect of each variable independently of each other, vary greatly from sample to sample, and are affected by the size of their standard deviations. For a sequential regression, this "R Square Change" (found in the Model Summary output) is also called the squared semipartial correlation (sr^2). This measure "expresses the unique contribution of the IV to the total variance of the DV" (Tabachnick & Fidell, 2001, p. 140), and because of shared variances between the explanatory variables it often does not actually sum up to the total R^2 for the entire model.

The last column of the Coefficients table provides information about multicollinearity. The VIF column shows the variance inflation factor (Tolerance, the column before it, is just 1/VIF). Heiberger and Holland (2004, p. 243) say that VIF values of over 5 are evidence of collinearity, which would be evidence that the variables are too highly intercorrelated and may harm the model. Most of the VIF for this data set are around 1 or 2, and the highest value is for phonological awareness in L2 in Model 5 at 3.47. These are all under 5, so we do not find anything problematic.

If you do a standard regression, you will see additional columns in the Coefficients output, notably the columns under the "Correlations" section (see Table 7.10). These columns contain the partial and part correlations. The column labeled "Part" gives the squared semipartial correlations (sr^2) for each term, and these should be reported as a way of comparing the importance of each term in the model, as noted above. As you can see, if Lafrance and Gottardo's regression were done as a standard regression, L2 phonemic awareness would be the most important factor by far (with an sr^2 of .37).

Table 7.10 Regression Output: Coefficients (Standard Regression)

Coefficients[a]

Model		Unstandardized Coefficients		Standardized Coefficients	t	Sig.	Correlations			Collinearity Statistics	
		B	Std. Error	Beta			Zero-order	Partial	Part	Tolerance	VIF
1	(Constant)	-1.015	1.832		-.554	.583					
	NonVerbalReasoning	-.002	.009	-.037	-.270	.789	.346	-.046	-.031	.714	1.400
	WorkingMemory	.042	.057	.116	.735	.468	.505	.125	.085	.537	1.863
	NamingSpeed	.097	.599	.028	.162	.872	-.491	.028	.019	.465	2.151
	L2PhonemicAwareness	1.453	.452	.872	3.218	.003	.730	.483	.373	.308	3.247
	KinderL_2Reading	.029	.136	.037	.211	.834	.550	.036	.024	.442	2.260

a. Dependent Variable: Grade1L1Reading

Table 7.11 Regression Output: Residuals Statistics

Residuals Statistics(a)

	Minimum	Maximum	Mean	Std. Deviation	N
Predicted Value	.5996	1.9967	1.3669	.34430	37
Std. Predicted Value	-2.228	1.829	.000	1.000	37
Standard Error of Predicted Value	.076	.185	.124	.027	37
Adjusted Predicted Value	.5437	2.0857	1.3710	.34588	37
Residual	-.73580	.72589	.00000	.29309	37
Std. Residual	-2.330	2.298	.000	.928	37
Stud. Residual	-2.540	2.473	-.006	1.022	37
Deleted Residual	-.87468	.84074	-.00411	.35654	37
Stud. Deleted Residual	-2.808	2.716	-.012	1.078	37
Mahal. Distance	1.120	11.372	4.865	2.475	37
Cook's Distance	.000	.267	.037	.066	37
Centered Leverage Value	.031	.316	.135	.069	37

a Dependent Variable: Grade1L1ReadingPerformance

For a sequential regression, beyond the Coefficients table there will be two more tables included in the output (Excluded Variables and Residuals Statistics). We won't worry about excluded variables, but we will see in the next section that the Residuals Statistics are important for examining assumptions for the model. For a standard regression, there is no Excluded Variables table because all variables were entered at the same time and there are no excluded variables.

7.4.3 Examining Regression Assumptions

We have already examined the assumption of multicollinearity, but in this section we will look at the assumptions of normal distribution of data, including outliers, and the equality of variances (homogeneity of variances). The last table of the output before the charts is labeled Residuals Statistics. There are several tests here which look for outliers or influential points, and the output is shown in Table 7.11.

In examining the assumption of normality, there are two ideas we need to look at. The first is the distribution of data, but for a regression we do not look at the distribution of individual variables but instead at the distribution of the residuals. The first chart that will appear in the regression output (if you have followed my instructions to request one, as in Figure 7.9) is a P-P plot of the standardized residuals. The P-P plot is similar to the Q-Q plot in that the points should follow a linear distribution if they are normally distributed. Figure 7.10 shows this plot, and we can detect some distinct curvature of points in its distribution. This is evidence of some non-normality in the data distribution, although it does not appear too extreme.

The second idea we want to look at for normality is to check whether there are any outliers. One way to do this is to look at the row in the Residuals Statistics output (Table 7.11) that is labeled Std. Residual. No points should be above 3.0 or below −3.0 (because the numbers are standardized, they reflect the number of standard deviations they are away from the mean). The table tells us that there is nothing below −2.33, and nothing above 2.298, so in this test no signs of outliers are found.

Outliers which are influential data points can be checked for by looking in the Residuals Statistics output (Table 7.11) at the row for **Cook's distance**. A value over 1.0 would be cause for concern, but the largest value in this data set is .267. If you found a value over 1.0 you could then look at your data set and search for the value or values which are over 1.0 (when you call for this diagnostic a row is added to the Data Editor called COO_1). The **Mahalanobis distance** value is another diagnostic for influential outliers. Field (2005) summarizes Barnett and Lewis's (1978) recommendations by saying that if your sample size is very small (less than 30 and with only two explanatory variables) values greater than 11 would be cause for worry. In a case like this, where the data set is larger, values above 15 would cause worry. Again, Table 7.11 does not indicate any problems with influential points in the data using the Mahalanobis distance diagnostic.

The next assumption we want to check is for homogeneity of variances. The way to check this is to examine the scatterplot between the studentized residuals (what SPSS calls *SRESID) and the predicted value of the standardized residuals (*ZPRED). In the SPSS output, look at the section labeled "Charts" for this graph.

Figure 7.11 shows this graph. The shape of this scatterplot should show a cloud of data scattered randomly. Instead, the data here show a more restricted range on the

Dependent Variable: Grade1L1ReadingPerformance

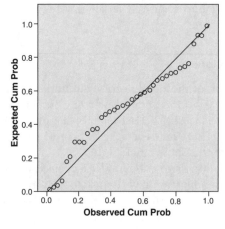

Figure 7.10 P-P plot for diagnosing normal distribution of data.

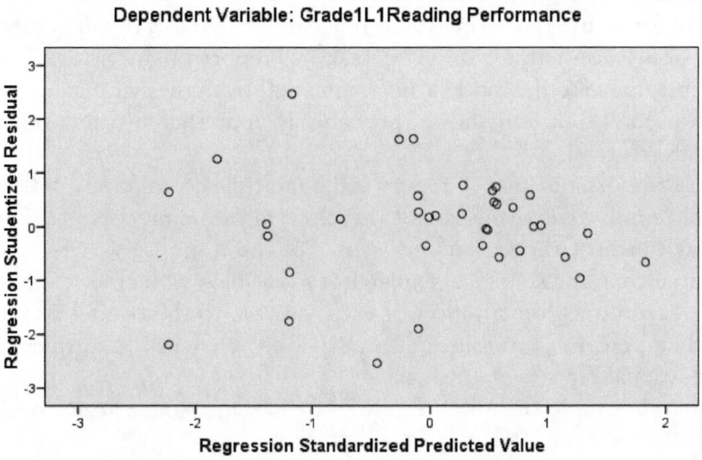

Dependent Variable: Grade1L1Reading Performance

Figure 7.11 Plot of studentized residuals crossed with fitted values.

right side of the graph, indicating that the assumption of homogeneity of variances has been violated. Often variables are transformed to correct this problem, but Lafrance and Gottardo already performed a log transformation on their variables, so it may be unlikely that further transformation would help.

The conclusion we can make after examining the various regression assumptions is that the data may be non-normally distributed and violate the homogeneity of variances assumption. There does not seem to be excessive multicollinearity, nor do there seem to be any obvious outliers or influence points. The assumption of linearity (seen in the scatterplot matrix at the beginning of the chapter) may not always be a good assumption either. There are many assumptions inherent in a regression analysis, and it seems that few researchers in the field report on whether these assumptions are satisfied. If you have access to the ability to perform a robust regression, this is a way to remedy the violation of assumptions. Another option would be to take out some of the variables that might be causing problems (such as the phonological awareness here) and try running the regression again.

7.4.4 Reporting the Results of Regression Analysis

One of the first things to report to your readers about a regression analysis is correlations between the explanatory variables and the response variable as well as correlations among the explanatory variables. If at all possible, a correlation matrix with r-values, p-values, and N should be provided to readers (such as that found in Table 7.4).

Next, you will want to tell your readers what kind of regression you performed, whether standard, sequential, or stepwise (not recommended). If you performed a sequential regression, you will want to detail the results of the R^2 and R^2 change for each step of the model. For all regression models you should report regression coefficients, especially the unstandardized coefficients (labeled B) which are necessary to write a predictive equation, including the coefficient for the intercept (labeled as

"Constant" in the SPSS output). If you can include 95% confidence intervals for these, that could be helpful for future researchers who replicate your study. If you performed a sequential regression I don't think it is necessary to report on the t-tests for the contribution of each variable to the model (this is apparent from the significance of the R^2 change for each model), but you should probably include this information when performing a standard regression.

Probably the most important thing to report is the multiple correlation coefficient, R^2, and the squared semipartial correlations for each term of the model (sr^2). This R^2 value expresses how much of the variance in scores of the response variable can be explained by the variance in the statistical explanatory variables, while the sr^2 provides a way of assessing the unique contribution of each variable to the overall R^2. These numbers are already a percentage variance effect size (of the r family), so there is no need to give any additional reports of effect sizes.

The following gives a sample of how the results of Lafrance and Gottardo (2005) could be reported:

Lafrance and Gottardo (2005) examined the question of whether phonological awareness (measured in L2) would add in predictive power for Grade 1 L1 reading performance after the variables of Kindergarten L2 reading performance, nonverbal reasoning, L2 measures of naming speed, and working memory were already added to the regression equation. There were correlations between the Grade 1 L1 reading measures and the five explanatory variables in the model (see Table 7.4), with the highest being L2 phonological awareness ($r = .73$). There were also inter-correlations among the five explanatory variables, with the highest being between phonological awareness and Kindergarten L2 reading measures ($r = .71$) and phonological awareness and naming speed ($r = -.70$).

It was assumed from previous research that phonological awareness (PA) would be the most significant factor in a standard regression, so a sequential regression was run to examine the effects of the other variables before PA was added. The variable of Kindergarten L2 reading measures added the most explanatory power to the model ($R^2 = .2$) when it was added before PA, as can be seen in the squared semipartial correlations for each factor (under the ΔR^2 column). After all other variables were added, PA accounted for 11% of the variance, but it was the only statistical variable in the regression model with all five explanatory variables. Total R^2 for the model, change in R^2, and unstandardized regression coefficients (B) and their 95% CIs are found in the table below.

Model	Total R^2	ΔR^2	Nonverbal reasoning B	Kindergarten reading B	Naming speed B	Working memory B	Phonological awareness B
1	.12*	.12*	.02 (.002, .04)				
2	.32*	.20*	.008 (−.011, .027)	.38 (.15, .62)			
3	.44*	.12*	.001 (−.02, .02)	.30* (.07, .53)	−1.43 (−.247, −.38)		

| 4 | .44 | .007 | .002
(−.02, .02) | .27*
(.02, .52) | −1.24
(−2.45,
−.03) | .04
(−.08, .17) | |
| 5 | .55* | .11* | .003
(−.02, .01) | .06
(−.22, .33) | −.38
(−1.65, .89) | .03
(−.09, .14) | 1.28
(.35, 2.21) |

* $p<.05$, Intercept for Model 5=.38 (−3.48, 4.24), with all five predictors, the regression equation is statistical, $F_{5,34}=8.2, p<.0005$.

Model 5, with all five predictors, accounted for 55% of the variance in first-grade L1 reading scores, but the only statistical predictor was PA. Certainly, PA is the most important variable for predicting reading performance.

The answer to the question of whether phonological awareness added to the prediction of first-grade L1 word reading performance after differences in other predictors were eliminated was yes. Phonological awareness added 11% to explaining the total variance of first-grade L1 reading scores.

7.4.5 Application Activity: Multiple Regression

1 Lafrance and Gottardo (2005) data. Using the Lafrance5.sav file, replicate the results I got in the text for the sequential regression using Grade 1 L1 reading scores as the response variable and the five explanatory variables shown in the text.

2 Lafrance and Gottardo (2005) data. Lafrance and Gottardo (2005) also looked at a multiple regression using Grade 1 L2 reading scores as the response variable and the same five explanatory variables (L2 measures) used in the text. Using the LafranceGottardo.sav file, perform a standard regression to determine what variables were statistical predictors of Grade 1 L2 reading scores, what their standardized regression coefficients were, and what the R^2 of the model is. Mention whether this model satisfies the assumptions of regression.

3 French and O'Brien (2008). Use the French and O'Brien Grammar.sav file. The authors examined French L1 children in an intensive English program and tested their phonological memory abilities. In order to see whether phonological memory predicted later abilities in learning vocabulary and grammar in English, the authors performed several hierarchical multiple regressions. We will look only at one where the response variable was Time 2 grammar (GRAM_2). The explanatory variables were, in the order they were entered, Time 1 grammar (GRAM_1), scores on an intelligence test (INTELLIG), language contact (L2CONTA), then an Arabic non-word phonological memory test at Time 1 (ANWR_1) and lastly an English non-word phonological memory test at Time 2 (ENWR_1). Perform this hierarchical regression and report the overall R^2, the change in R^2 for each of the explanatory variables, the unstandardized regression coefficients (with which you would write a regression equation), and which variables were statistical (using the t-test in the Coefficients output table). Also mention whether this model satisfies the assumptions of regression.

4 Howell (2002). Use the HowellChp15Data.sav file. Chapter 15 included a data set where students rated their courses overall and also aspects of the courses on a five-point scale (where 1 = very bad and 5 = exceptional). Using the OVERALL variable as the response variable and the other variables (teaching skills of

instructor, quality of exams, instructor's knowledge of subject matter, the grade the student expected in the course where F = 1 and A = 5, and the enrollment of the course) as explanatory variables. First take a look at a scatterplot matrix to make sure the relationships are linear. Perform a standard multiple regression and look at which factors statistically predict the response variable. Report the overall R^2 for the model. Run a new regression using just the statistical factors and report the regression equation, the R^2, and comment on regression assumptions.

5   Dewaele and Pavlenko Bilingual Emotions Questionnaire (2001–2003). Use the BEQ.Swear.sav file. An earlier analysis I performed showed that the variables that might help explain how frequently a person swears in their L2 (SWEAR2) are the frequency that the person uses their L2 (L2FREQ), the weight they give to swearing in their L2 (WEIGHT2), and their evaluation of their speaking and comprehension skills in L2 (L2SPEAK, L2_COMP). First take a look at a scatterplot matrix to make sure the relationships are linear. Conduct a multiple regression analysis to determine which of these variables effectively predicts frequency in swearing in an L2, and perform another regression with only statistical predictors. Report the unstandardized coefficients and the R^2 for the mode with only statistical predictors, and comment on regression assumptions.

6   Larson-Hall (2008). Are amount of hours of input in a foreign language (TOTAL-HRS), aptitude (APTSCORE), and scores on a phonemic task (RLWSCORE) useful predictors of scores on a grammaticality judgment test (GJT)? Perform a hierarchical regression using the GJT (GJTSCORE) as the response variable, and the three other variables as explanatory variables. There are six possible combinations, but try three by entering each variable as the first variable once. See which order gives the highest overall R^2, and which results in the highest change in R^2 for each of the three explanatory variables. Use the larsonhall2008.sav file.

7.5 Taking Regression Further: Finding the Best Fit (Advanced Topic)

The previous part of this chapter has acted as if there were only one way to conduct a regression analysis. The truth is that statisticians who understand how regression works know that the point is not in simply performing a regression, but in finding the regression model which best fits your data. Crawley says that "All models are wrong" (2007, p. 339). What Crawley means by this is that, whatever model you use to fit your data, there will be error. Thus all models are wrong, but some models are better than others. In general, a simpler model is better than a more complicated one, if they have the same explanatory value. A model with less error will be better than one with more error.

In order to find the best model for your data, Crawley (2007) recommends beginning with the maximal model and then simplifying your model where possible. What is the maximal model? It is the one that includes all of the **main effects** (the effect of the variable by itself) plus all of the **interactions** between the terms. A main effect is the effect due to a variable by itself. Going back to the TOEFL example considered at the beginning of this chapter with the two explanatory variables of MLAT and hours of study, a model with only main effects looks like:

TOEFL score = MLAT score + hours of study

In order to make this example more interesting, let's add a third variable of gender. Gender is of course a categorical variable with only two possible responses. It is perfectly acceptable to add a categorical variable to a regression but we will have to interpret the output for categorical variables a little differently than we did for continuous variables. So adding gender to the equation, this model has only main effects for the three explanatory variables:

TOEFL score = MLAT score + hours of study + gender

However, it may be the case that there is an interaction between gender and hours of study. It may be the case that females study more than males. In other words, the way that gender and hours of study vary is linked. If there is an interaction, then we will want to include that in our equation as well, in order to most effectively model what is happening. An interaction can be shown by putting a colon between the two variables, as in the following model with an interaction between gender and hours of study shown:

TOEFL score = MLAT score + hours of study + gender + gender:hours of study

As stated above, the way a professional statistician would approach a question of regression is to consider the model that has the best fit. The statistician would start with the maximal model, which would include all of the possible interactions. In a model with three explanatory variables, there will be three two-way interactions and one three-way interaction:

Two-way interactions: MLAT score:hours of study
                        MLAT score:gender
                        Gender:hours of study

Three-way interaction: MLAT score:hours of study:gender

Putting all of the main effects and interactions into one regression model, then, would look like this:

TOEFL score = MLAT score + hours of study + gender + MLAT score:hours of study + MLAT score:gender + gender:hours of study + MLAT score:hours of study:gender

You can see that, if you have more than three explanatory variables, this model can very quickly get very complicated! In addition, you might want to add some quadratic terms, which are variables that are squared or raised to the cubic power. Why would you want to do this? If there is some curvature in your data then squared powers of a variable can help account for that curvature.

The problem with trying to conduct this type of regression analysis in SPSS is that it does not provide an easy way for us to evaluate model fit. In the R program different models can easily be compared using an ANOVA which tests the difference in something called "residual deviance" between the two models. If there is a statistical difference between the residual deviance of two models, you pick the model with the smaller deviance as the simpler model. In R there are also commands that help automate the process of testing each model against simpler ones (I like bootStep AIC). Because SPSS cannot really conduct this type of analysis, in this section I can only recommend that, if you think there might be an interaction, you can try including it in a regression analysis and see whether it helps improve the size of your R^2 and also whether the parameter coefficients for each part of the regression equation are statistical. You won't be able to formally test whether one model is better than another, but you can still take a good shot at heading toward the minimally adequate model.

The way to include an interaction term in a regression model is to simply create one yourself. I will illustrate this process with a file called TOEFLexample.sav which I made up to illustrate the TOEFL example in this chapter. Go to TRANSFORM > COMPUTE VARIABLE. In the box called "Target Variable" call the interaction between MLAT score and hours of study "MLAT_Hours" (the colon is an illegal character so I used the underscore). Then move the MLAT variable to the box labeled "Numeric Expression." From the keypad in this screen put a "*" after MLAT to show multiplication. Then add the Hours of Study variable and press OK. In the data set there is a new variable. I went ahead and made up interaction terms for the rest of the possible interactions with the three variables. Now I'll create a regression with all three main effects (MLAT, Hours of Study, Gender) and all four interactions (MLAT_Hours, MLAT_Gender, Hours_Gender, MLAT_Hours_Gender). I'm interested in finding out the nature and size of the relationship between the TOEFL scores and my explanatory variables, so I'll use standard regression (so the METHOD is "Enter"), and this procedure is shown in Figure 7.12.

This model explains 68% of the variance ($R^2 = .68$), but none of the terms is statistical! You can tell this by looking at the column in the Coefficients table of output that gives the significance of the t-test (Table 7.12). None of these numbers is less than .05, meaning that none of the terms is statistical. This model is thus not a very good one. We want to get to the sparest equation we can where all of the terms have a statistical coefficient.

Crawley's recommendation is to look at the maximal model first and then simplify by taking out the largest interaction terms first. So I'll run the regression again, taking out the three-way interaction. R^2 is still 68%, but none of the terms have statistical coefficients. Therefore, the next step would be to take out the two-way interactions, one at a time. Choose the one with the highest p-value for the t-test (the Sig. column), which is Hours_Gender. When I run the regression now without this term, the $R^2 = .65$, but still none of the coefficients is statistical. The next highest p-value for the two-way interactions is for MLAT_Gender. However, I don't see a statistical coefficient appear until I have taken out all of the interactions. With all of the interactions gone, I see that MLAT has a statistical coefficient, and $R^2 = .61$. I still want to simplify the model as much as I can, so I'll take out the main effect which has the highest p-value, which is Gender (see Table 7.13).

It turns out that with just MLAT and Hours of Study in the equation, the p-value of Hours of Study is still .163, not statistical. I therefore continue to reduce the equation to its simplest value, an equation with just the MLAT. My final regression accounts for

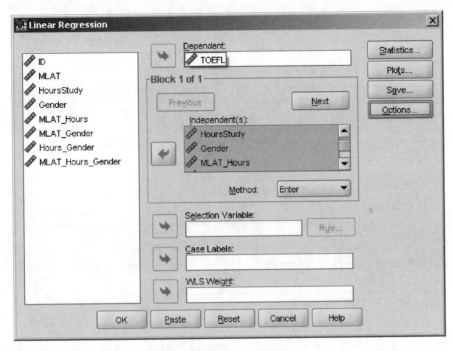

Figure 7.12 Regression with interaction terms.

Table 7.12 Output for a Maximal Regression

Coefficients[a]

Model		Unstandardized Coefficients		Standardized Coefficients	t	Sig.
		B	Std. Error	Beta		
1	(Constant)	136.551	828.447		.165	.872
	MLAT	-.419	35.978	-.024	-.012	.991
	HoursStudy	8.189	166.904	.183	.049	.962
	Gender	210.312	561.972	1.018	.374	.715
	MLAT_Hours	1.680	6.803	1.162	.247	.809
	MLAT_Gender	-3.488	23.087	-.486	-.151	.882
	Hours_Gender	-56.662	120.197	-2.490	-.471	.646
	MLAT_Hours_Gender	1.303	4.724	1.578	.276	.787

a. Dependent Variable: TOEFL

56% of the variance in TOEFL scores. The Coefficients output for this minimally adequate model is shown in Table 7.14.

You might wonder why you shouldn't stick with the regression that includes Hours of Study since it accounts for a higher amount (60%) of the variance, but the fact is that, the more variables you include, the higher the R^2 will always go. What you are looking for is the minimally adequate model. It might be that if we had been able to check model fit there would be no difference between the model with two terms and

Table 7.13 Output for a Regression with Only Main Effects

Coefficients[a]

Model		Unstandardized Coefficients		Standardized Coefficients	t	Sig.
		B	Std. Error	Beta		
1	(Constant)	48.261	88.478		.545	.593
	MLAT	12.688	2.844	.712	4.462	.000
	HoursStudy	9.503	7.286	.212	1.304	.211
	Gender	-12.454	33.223	-.060	-.375	.713

a. Dependent Variable: TOEFL

Table 7.14 Output for a Minimally Adequate Regression

Coefficients[a]

Model		Unstandardized Coefficients		Standardized Coefficients	t	Sig.
		B	Std. Error	Beta		
1	(Constant)	61.652	69.029		.893	.384
	MLAT	13.263	2.801	.745	4.735	.000

a. Dependent Variable: TOEFL

that with one, in which case we would keep both Hours of Study and MLAT, but with SPSS we do not have a good way to determine that. I will also note that the model with only one term doesn't seem to have the troubles with non-constant variances (heterogeneity of variances) that previous models did (as seen in the chart plotting studentized residuals against fitted values), so the model seems to adhere to assumptions better than previous models.

My final regression equation will be:

TOEFL score = 61.7 + 13.3*MLAT + error

I have barely scratched the surface here of the many things that would need to be kept in mind when doing this type of model simplification, but hopefully this will give you an idea of how you can take charge of your regression model and look for the minimally adequate model.

7.6 Summary

There are two main uses of regression in second language research studies. One is to decide to what extent the explanatory variables the researcher has measured can account for some response variable of interest. To answer this question the researcher will use standard regression and report on the R^2 statistic, letting readers know how much of the variance in the response variable can be accounted for by the combination of the explanatory variables. In a standard regression the researcher can also provide information about how much each explanatory variable uniquely contributes to the equation. Rather than use the standardized coefficients for this, I have suggested that researchers provide information about the semipartial correlation (sr^2) of each term of the equation. The semipartial correlation provides information about the relative importance of each term of the regression equation.

The other main use of regression analysis in second language research studies is to try to find a predictive model which will best account for the variance in the response variable. Using a sequential (hierarchical) regression can help answer this question by examining whether the addition of a term adds to the predictive power of the equation. It is up to the researcher to specify in what order terms are added, and we have seen in this chapter that order does matter when using a sequential regression.

I have suggested that stepwise regression is probably not a type of regression that most researchers will be looking for, as it lets the computer decide which terms to eliminate, often based on non-statistical differences between terms of similar importance. It is better for researchers to have a theoretical reason to examine the addition or elimination of terms in a regression.

Consumers of research on regression ought to realize that the order that variables are entered into a sequential regression matters, and that those variables that are entered first will account for the most variance. It is also important to note the correlations among variables as a consumer of research. If the author has included several variables which are highly intercorrelated, it is highly likely that one of those variables will be seen as inconsequential. This is not because it really is necessarily inconsequential, but because the regression gets rid of terms which substantially overlap with each other.

Last of all, in the section on advanced statistics I have suggested that the lock-step format for conducting a regression analysis that SPSS forces upon the user can be circumvented. The best use of standard regression, given what I have read in the statistical research, is for users of regression to find the minimally adequate regression model and report on that. SPSS users will have to do this by manually adding interaction and possibly quadratic (squared or cubic) terms to the regression equation themselves, but I have provided some simple rubrics for helping to decide which terms to keep and which to discard.

Chapter 8

Finding Group Differences with Chi-Square when All Your Variables Are Categorical: The Effects of Interaction Feedback on Question Formation and the Choice of Copular Verb in Spanish

> Statistics is a subject of amazingly many uses and surprisingly few effective practitioners.
>
> Bradley Efron and R. J. Tibshirani (1993, p. xiv)

Chi-square is a simple statistical test that is used in a variety of ways. The very variety may lead to some confusion over what the test is good for, but the basic idea behind the test is that you calculate the difference between the scores you observed and the scores you would expect in that situation and then see whether the magnitude of the difference is large or small on the chi-square distribution. Chi-square is a non-parametric test, which means there are fewer assumptions for its use than there are for parametric tests. However, as we will see in this chapter, and as noted in Saito (1999) and Hatch and Lazaraton (1991), chi-square is a much-abused test in second language research studies, and often one of its assumptions (that of independence of data) is violated as a matter of course.

This chapter will discuss what kinds of statistical tests should be used when you have one or two categorical variables. In the case where you have three or more categorical variables, you should use logistic regression, which is not covered in this text.

8.1 Two Types of Chi-Square Tests

This chapter will discuss two main uses of the chi-square test:

- test for goodness of fit of the data
- test for group independence

The first type of test, goodness of fit, is used when we have only **one** categorical variable with two or more levels of choices. The test for group independence is used when there are **two or more** variables, and all of the variables are categorical. I will illustrate the difference between these two tests in the following sections.

8.1.1 Chi-Square for Goodness of Fit

If we think of the data being partitioned according to its categories, and if we have only one variable, we will think of a one-row table that will list counts. As a con-

Table 8.1 Fictional Data on Desired Foreign Language at One University

Chinese	Spanish	French	German	Japanese
23	20	15	13	29

crete example, suppose we looked at a survey question that asked college freshmen what foreign language they wanted to study out of five choices: Chinese, Spanish, French, German, or Japanese. In this study there is only one variable, that of language choice, but it has five levels. Suppose we randomly surveyed 100 college freshmen at our local Hometown University and this resulted in the data in Table 8.1.

Our question for this kind of data is whether this distribution is the one we would expect given what we think is the probability of each choice. For simplicity's sake, at this point let us hypothesize that every choice is equally likely, which would mean a 20% chance of choosing each one. Of course, in every sample there is random variation. So do the frequencies we observed match with what we would expect if every chance were equally likely?

To answer this question we will use the chi-square for goodness of fit. This test is used when there is only one categorical variable with two or more levels and we want to measure how good the fit is to the probabilities that we expect. Notice that we surveyed 100 students, and each student falls into only one category or cell in our table.

A chi-square goodness-of-fit test for this data shows that the chi-square statistic (χ^2) is 8.2. The probability of obtaining a statistic this large or larger on the 4 degrees of freedom that we have (the number of levels less 1) is $p = .09$. If we have set our alpha level to .05, we could not reject the null hypothesis that all choices were equally likely, and we would conclude that no one preferred any one of the language groups over any of the others, but the low p-value might make us think that we were on to something here, and seek to improve the power of the test by gathering additional data.

8.1.2 Chi-Square for Testing Group Independence

You may easily imagine the case where you would have not just one but two categorical variables. To extend the previous example, let us say we randomly survey 100 more freshmen, this time from Big City University, and we now want to know whether there is any difference in the two populations (Hometown University and Big City University) in their choice of preferred language to study. We can construct a table that shows a cross-tabulation of both variables, like the one in Table 8.2.

Table 8.2 is called a **contingency table**, because it shows all the events that could happen (Crawley, 2002, p. 180). Notice that 200 people were surveyed, and we find 200 points of data in the table. Each person's data goes into only one cell of the table.

The question that is being asked here is whether there is any association between the two variables, in this case a university population and their choice of language to study.

Table 8.2 Fictional Data on Desired Foreign Language at Two Universities

		Language					
		Chinese	Spanish	French	German	Japanese	Total
Population	Hometown U	23	20	15	13	29	100
	Big City U	14	25	10	26	25	100
Total		37	45	25	39	54	200

Table 8.3 Observed and Expected Frequencies for the Foreign Language Survey

	Chinese	Spanish	French	German	Japanese
Expected frequencies:					
Hometown University	$\frac{100*37}{200} = 18.5$	$\frac{100*45}{200} \equiv 22.5$	$\frac{100*25}{200} \equiv 12.5$	$\frac{100*39}{200} \equiv 18.5$	$\frac{100*54}{200} \equiv 27$
Big City University	$\frac{100*37}{200} = 18.5$	$\frac{100*45}{200} \equiv 22.5$	$\frac{100*25}{200} \equiv 12.5$	$\frac{100*39}{200} \equiv 18.5$	$\frac{100*54}{200} \equiv 27$

The chi-square test will calculate the difference between the scores you observed and the scores you would expect in a particular situation and divide by the expected score.

I will just quickly walk you through the process of determining the chi-square statistic for a chi-square test of group independence. My reason for showing this to you, even though you do not have to calculate it by hand, is to demonstrate how simple this test really is. Sometimes you can start thinking that statistics is magic because you don't see the calculations behind the output. Since chi-square is so simple, it is easy to see what is going on in the calculations.

Expected scores are determined by multiplying the total row score by the total column score of any given cell and then dividing by the total number of observations. Thus, the expected score for Chinese at Hometown University is 100 (the total row score for Hometown University) times 37 (the total column score for Chinese) divided by 200 (the total number of observations). Table 8.3 shows the observed and expected frequencies of the fictional language choice experiment. Notice that the expected frequencies for both rows are the same because the row totals are exactly the same in this experiment (exactly 100 students were surveyed at each school).

The chi-square value is now calculated by summing up the difference between the observed (O) and expected (E) score (and squaring it so no negative numbers arise) and then dividing by the expected score:

$$\chi^2 = \sum \frac{(O - E)^2}{E}.$$

This will give the following calculation:

$$\frac{(23 - 18.5)^2}{18.5} + \frac{(20 - 22.5)^2}{22.5} + \frac{(15 - 12.5)^2}{12.5} + \frac{(13 - 18.5)^2}{18.5} + \frac{(29 - 27)^2}{27} +$$
$$\frac{(23 - 18.5)^2}{18.5} + \frac{(20 - 22.5)^2}{22.5} + \frac{(15 - 12.5)^2}{12.5} + \frac{(13 - 18.5)^2}{18.5} + \frac{(29 - 27)^2}{27} \equiv 8.374$$

This chi-square statistic is then checked against the chi-square distribution (with 4 degrees of freedom) to determine the probability of obtaining a chi-square value that is as large as or larger than 8.374. The probability is $p = .07$. Although technically this goes above $p = .05$ it is quite low, and as an author I might argue that it shows evidence that there is a difference between choice of language at both universities, evidence that could be bolstered by gathering additional data.

8.1.3 Other Situations that May Look like Chi-Square but Are Not

There may be times when you want to measure the same person more than once on a categorical variable. I have been careful to note that, for the chi-square tests, each person contributes only once to each cell of the table. However, let's imagine some scenarios where the variables are still categorical, but a person may contribute to a cell more than once. As Saito (1999) points out, if you perform a chi-square analysis when the data are dependent in this way, your p-value will be positively biased, meaning more results will be positive than really should be.

Scenario One: Case Study, Only One Participant

First, let's imagine that we have data from one person in a case study on a grammaticality judgment test (GJT). Our GJT is formulated so that the respondent labels each sentence as either grammatical or ungrammatical, and we want to examine the difference in how the respondent performed on the grammatical and ungrammatical items. Our question is whether there is any association between the number of correct responses and the fact that the item was grammatical or ungrammatical. There were 200 items on the test, with the fictitious data in Table 8.4.

There are 200 responses in the table but they were all made by the same person. Therefore, although this looks very much like Table 8.3 where we used the chi-square for group independence, the data are not independent of one another (one of the requirements of chi-square) and should not be analyzed with a chi-square. The best way

Table 8.4 Data from a Fictitious Case Study with One Participant

	Grammatical	Ungrammatical	Total
Correct	80	56	136
Incorrect	20	44	64
Total	100	100	200

to handle this data would be to say we have two categorical independent variables (grammaticality and correctness) and an interval-level dependent variable (score on test for each of the four cells). With just one participant, we could not use a two-way ANOVA (which is what we would use if we had a number of different participants), and the best approach might be to use two binomial tests (explained in Scenario Two below), one to test the split between grammaticality and ungrammaticality, and the other to test the difference between correct and incorrect answers. We would not be able to test for interaction.

Scenario Two: Binary Choice, Only One Variable with Exactly Two Levels

Second, let's imagine a case where we had 30 participants who were tested on their ability to correctly form the past tense on 15 verbs that were presented as 15 separate picture description tasks. The research question is whether the proportion of successes is statistically higher than one would expect by chance, given the null hypothesis of both choices being equal. We sum up over all 15 items and obtain the results in Table 8.5.

Here we might assume that we could use a goodness-of-fit chi-square to test the assumption that the participants formed the verbs correctly more often than we would expect if each choice were equally likely. The problem is that we have only 30 participants but we have 450 responses. Each participant contributed more than once to each cell. One solution is to use a **binomial test**. The binomial test answers the question of what the probability is of getting 339/450 answers correct if both answers are equally likely. The p-value is interpreted in the same way as other p-values—if the p-value is small (below .05) then the probability of getting this distribution by chance is very small, and we would reject the null hypothesis that the distribution of answers is random.

You can perform the binomial test in SPSS by using the ANALYZE > NONPARAMETRIC TESTS > BINOMIAL menu option. You would then enter only one variable (one column) into the "Test Variable List" box, and press OK. If you had already entered in a value for each of the 450 total cases (say, a 1 for the correct formation and a 0 for incorrect as shown in Column A of Figure 8.1) you would then just run your analysis. If, however, you just had summary data like I have here (as shown in Column B of Figure 8.1), you would have to weight your cases to tell SPSS these were summary counts *before* running the analysis.

To weight your data, go to DATA > WEIGHT CASES. Move the variable with the summary data to the box that says "Frequency Variable" as shown in Figure 8.1. This tells SPSS to consider these as counts of data, not as the data itself.

Now I can run the binomial test, putting column B in the "Test Variable List." I want to consider both options as equally likely so I leave the "Test Proportion" at .50. SPSS

Table 8.5 Data from a Test with Only Two Choices (Binary Choice)

Correct formation	Incorrect formation
339	111

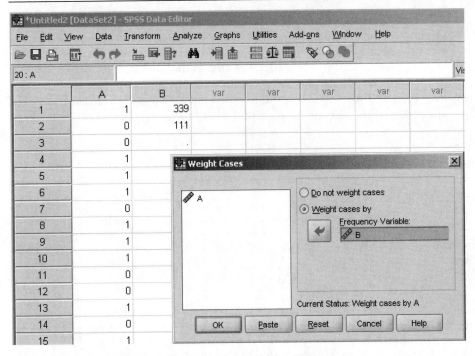

Figure 8.1 Weighting data for summary counts.

output tells me that the probability of getting these summary counts if both choices are equally likely for a two-tailed test is $p = .000$, which I would interpret as $p<.0005$ (this value is found in the "Asymp. Sig." column). In other words, it is highly unlikely that there would be 339 correct formations if both choices were equally likely, so we reject the null hypothesis that both choices are equally likely. It is also easy to calculate a binomial test online; I found a quick calculator at the website http://www.graphpad.com/quickcalcs/binomial1.cfm.

Scenario Three: Matched Pairs with Categorical Outcome

Let's imagine a third scenario that uses repeated measures with categorical data. Let's imagine a researcher is interested in motivation, and asks 500 incoming Spanish-major freshmen just one question on the very first day of class—"Are you excited about learning Spanish, yes or no?" as a measure of motivation. These students are distributed into the classes of five different teachers, and on the last day of class the researcher asks the students the same question. Table 8.6 gives a made-up reporting of the data.

Our question would be whether the variable of teacher influenced the excitement students had for Spanish. We can imagine that, if we only wanted to look at the first day or the last day separately, this would very much fit our profile for a chi-square for independence of groups. With separate chi-squares, each person would fit into only one cell of the table. However, this is repeated measures (matched pairs), since each person was surveyed twice. In the case of repeated measures with two categorical variables, the McNemar test can be used (Saito, 1999).

In SPSS, the McNemar test is accessed by using the ANALYZE > DESCRIPTIVE STATISTICS > CROSSTABS menu and then opening the Statistics button and ticking off the McNemar test. For my three variables, I entered them in this order: FIRST in Row, LAST in Column, and TEACHER in Layer 1. With this order, I got the output in Tables 8.7 through 8.9.

Table 8.7 shows the order that the variables were put in, and correctly shows that there were only 500 participants, although there are 1,000 pieces of data. Table 8.8 shows the results of the statistical test, with the last box giving the *p*-value for each test

Table 8.6 Data from a Fictitious Motivation Survey

	Excited—yes		Excited—no		
	First day	Last day	First day	Last day	Total
Teacher A	95	88	5	12	200
Teacher B	97	54	3	46	200
Teacher C	87	89	13	11	200
Teacher D	89	63	11	37	200
Teacher E	91	99	9	1	200
Total:	459	393	41	107	1,000

Table 8.7 Motivation Experiment Summary with the McNemar Procedure

Case Processing Summary

	Cases					
	Valid		Missing		Total	
	N	Percent	N	Percent	N	Percent
first* last* teacher	500	100.0%	0	.0%	500	100.0%

Table 8.8 Motivation Experiment Results with the McNemar Test

Chi-Square Tests

teacher		Value	Exact Sig. (2-sided)
1	McNemar Test	100	.016[a]
	N of Valid Cases	100	
2	McNemar Test	100	.000[a]
	N of Valid Cases	100	
3	McNemar Test	100	.500[a]
	N of Valid Cases	100	
4	McNemar Test	100	.000[a]
	N of Valid Cases	100	
5	McNemar Test	100	.008[a]
	N of Valid Cases	100	

a. Binomial distribution used.

Table 8.9 Motivation Experiment Crosstabs with the McNemar Procedure

first* last* teacher Crosstabulation

Count

teacher			last yes	last no	Total
1	first	yes	88	7	95
		no	0	5	5
	Total		88	12	100
2	first	yes	54	43	97
		no	0	3	3
	Total		54	46	100
3	first	yes	87	0	87
		no	2	11	13
	Total		89	11	100
4	first	yes	63	26	89
		no	0	11	11
	Total		63	37	100
5	first	yes	91	0	91
		no	8	1	9
	Total		99	1	100

(five McNemar tests are run, one for each of the teachers). For four out of the five teachers, there was a statistical difference in the answers that students gave from the first day to the last, since p-values are below $p = .05$. Only for Teacher 3 did students not change from the beginning to the end of the semester in answer to the question of whether they were excited about learning Spanish (since the probability of seeing the scores on the first and last days given the hypothesis that there was no difference between those days is 50%). However, just knowing the statistical results does not give us a lot of information. We don't know, for example, whether scores were high and remained high for Teacher 3's students, or maybe they started low and remained low.

To get answers to what was happening, whether it was statistical or not, we need to look at the patterns of data in crosstabs, shown in Table 8.9. This table divides the data into tables of scores for the individual teachers (each teacher is in a separate row). Looking at the crosstabs, Teacher 3 had no students who were in the first–yes, last–no box, meaning no students had decreased motivation with this teacher, but quite a few were first–no and last–no, meaning the teacher had not had success in increasing motivation for some students. Teacher 5 had the highest number of students whose motivation increased (first–no, last–yes), while Teacher 2 had 43 students whose motivation decreased (first–yes, last–no).

The McNemar test can thus answer the question of whether repeated data which represents pairs of related points (beginning and end, test 1 and test 2) measured with a categorical scale (yes/no, high/low) are different. Note that the McNemar test is not for all types of repeated measures, just paired measures.

Scenario Four: Summary over a Number of Similar Items by the Same Participants

Last, let's imagine a case like the one in Scenario Two where participants were scored on whether they had correctly formed the past tense, but with the addition of the variable of regular or irregular verbs. Let's say there were 45 participants. We'll pretend our theory predicted that participants would be much less likely to provide the correct formation on irregular verbs than regular ones. Let's say we had data like that found in Table 8.10.

Our question here is whether there is any association between the type of verb and the way the participant formed the verb. Here we might assume, since we have two categorical variables, that we can perform a chi-square independent-group comparison. This would be in violation of the assumptions for chi-square, however, since each participant contributes more than once to each cell. One solution for this kind of data would be to examine each of the 15 items in the test with a separate chi-square group-independence test. This would probably not be the best solution, because it inflates the overall error rate and, as Saito (1999) points out, it does not give the researcher any chance of checking for interactions. Saito (1999) recommends using logistic regression on this kind of data, but notes that such an approach would still not correct the fact that the data are not independent. In other words, in this experiment there was a total of 450 pieces of information, but there were not 450 different participants, all tested on only one item. In fact, there were only 45 participants, and they were each tested on ten items. This means that some people may influence one cell of the contingency table more than others, leading to dependence and an increased chance of a Type I error (rejecting the null hypothesis when it is in fact true: in other words, finding more "statistical" results than you should).

A better approach to this type of data is beyond the scope of this book to show but I want to present a possible solution because I believe this type of data is common in our field. My friend Richard Herrington, a statistical consultant, suggests that this is in fact a linear mixed-effects design with nested categorical data (count data). A mixed-effects design has both fixed and random factors. Because the data set here aggregates answers over the individuals, there is a random effect due to participant. This random effect is nested within the "treatment" factor of regular versus irregular verb (in other words, each participant has multiple data for both regular and irregular verbs). The mixed model can take account of the correlations that occur in the data because the same participants are tested more than once (Crawley, 2007).

The linear mixed-effects design to use here will need to be a generalized mixed-effects model which will let us specify the distribution. We will use the binomial distribution

Table 8.10 Data from a Fictitious Study of Past-Tense Formation

	Correct formation	Incorrect formation	Total
Regular verbs	144	81	225
Irregular verbs	176	49	225
Total	320	130	450

since the dependent variable has only two choices (correct or incorrect formation of the verb) and because there is a fixed number of observations (in other words, it is not count data where the number of trials is not fixed; in that case a Poisson distribution would be used).

In SPSS the way to choose such an analysis would be to use ANALYZE > GENERALIZED LINEAR MODELS > GENERALIZED LINEAR MODELS. When specifying the model you would use the Binary Logistic, which specifies the Binomial as the distribution and the Logit as the link function. However, understanding how to set up a linear mixed-effects model and interpret its output is beyond the scope of this book.

8.1.4 Application Activity: Choosing a Test with Categorical Data

Read the following descriptions of possible linguistic experiments. Decide whether you would use a goodness-of-fit chi-square, independent-group chi-square, or some other test (fill in the name of the test if you can).

1   Native speaker friends. An instructor in the foreign language department noticed that the students who performed best in her Spanish classes often had friends who were native speakers of Spanish. She surveyed her students to determine whether they had friends who spoke Spanish natively or not (yes/no answer), and then grouped her students into those who received As and Bs in class (successful), those who received Cs (moderate), and those who scored lower grades (unsuccessful). The research question is whether having a friend who speaks the language is related to success in the classroom.

Choose one: goodness of fit   group independence   other _____

2   Bilingualism and language dominance. Dewaele and Pavlenko (2001–2003) conducted an online Bilingualism and Emotion Questionnaire (BEQ). All respondents had at least two languages, and 31% of the sample had five languages (the maximum investigated in the questionnaire). They also asked respondents which language they considered to be their dominant language, and answers were coded as YES (dominant in L1), NO (dominant in another language besides L1) or YESPLUS (dominant in more than one language). Investigate the possibility that the number of languages a person speaks has a relationship to their answer on the dominance question.

Choose one: goodness of fit   group independence   other _____

3   Self-ratings of proficiency. One thousand students at a university in France were surveyed and asked to self-rate their proficiency in English as Poor, Fair, or Good. Researchers wanted to know whether each of these choices was equally likely in a large sample.

Choose one: goodness of fit   group independence   other _____

4   Extroversion and proficiency. The same researchers wanted to know whether extroversion had any relationship to self-perceived proficiency ratings. A subset of the 1,000 students took the EPI (Eysenck Personality Inventory), and were rated as either Extroverted or Introverted. The researchers investigated whether personality and proficiency ratings were related.

Choose one: goodness of fit   group independence   other _____

5   Lexical storage. In order to investigate how the lexicon is constructed, 50 native speakers of English were provided with 12 pictures representing actions involving verbs that participate in the dative alternation and asked to describe the picture in real time (using the present progressive). The utterances were then classified as being either DO or IO based on whether the direct object or indirect object directly followed the verb (Example: "He's giving his girlfriend a gift" versus "He's giving a gift to his girlfriend"). The research question was whether speakers preferred one order over the other for each verb.

Choose one: goodness of fit   group independence   other _____

6   LI background and success in ELI. Your university's English Language Institute wants to know whether the number of students who pass the exit exam come from a balanced mix of the LI of the students who enter. The enrollment last year was composed of students who speak as their LI: French, 30; Spanish, 20; Arabic, 35; Japanese, 60; Korean, 43; Mandarin, 16. The students who passed the exit exam included: French, 23; Spanish, 19; Arabic, 12; Japanese, 47; Korean, 40; Mandarin, 16. You want to investigate whether the proportion who passed the exam from each LI is approximately the same, assuming that all groups should have an equal chance of passing.

Choose one: goodness of fit   group independence   other _____

7   Foreign accent and study abroad I. Two English teachers at a Japanese university suspect that the foreign accent of their students is greatly improved by a study abroad session. The teachers survey all of the English majors in their school and categorize students into those who have done a study abroad and those who have not. The researchers also ask the teachers to listen to their students read a paragraph and rate the accent of their students as Poor, Fair, or Excellent.

Choose one: goodness of fit   group independence   other _____

8   Foreign accent and study abroad II. The researchers who looked at foreign accent and study abroad wrote a paper and were roundly criticized for their unreliable measure of foreign accent. The researchers went back and gathered recordings of the students reading a paragraph and then asked five native speakers of English to rate each sample as Poor, Fair, or Excellent. The researchers then again investigated the relationship between study abroad and foreign accent.

Choose one: goodness of fit   group independence   other _____

8.2 Data Inspection: Tables and Crosstabs

With categorical data, tables are a useful tool for seeing a summary of the data and getting a quick view of the patterns that may be present. In the case of goodness-of-fit data, because there is only one variable, a simple tabular summary is the best way to examine the data. For group comparison data, variables can be cross-tabulated to produce a contingency table of the data.

8.2.1 Summary Tables for Goodness-of-Fit Data

In producing a table to summarize patterns with a goodness-of-fit situation, data from Geeslin and Guijarro-Fuentes (2006) will be used. The authors wanted to know whether Spanish speakers (both L1 and L2), in a given context, preferred the Spanish verb *ser, estar,* or the use of both. The dependent variable was the choice of verb, which is categorical and has no inherent ranking or value. Note that the dependent variable is a count of how many times each of the three possibilities of verbs was chosen. The independent variable was also categorical and consisted of membership in one of the three populations (Spanish L1 speaker, Portuguese L1 speaker, or Portuguese L1 learner of Spanish L2). The data set you will use is one I calculated by using the report for percentage use of the verbs in Appendix B of Geeslin and Guijarro-Fuentes's paper and knowing how many participants were in each group. Note that a summary of the data over all of the items would result in a situation like that of Scenario Four (in Section 8.1.3), so only the responses of native speakers of Spanish from Item 3 will be examined (this portion can be found in the GeeslinGF3_5.sav file).

To make a frequency table, open ANALYZE > DESCRIPTIVE STATISTICS > FREQUENCIES. When you do you will see a dialogue box like that in Figure 8.2. All you need to do is move your variables to the VARIABLE(S) box.

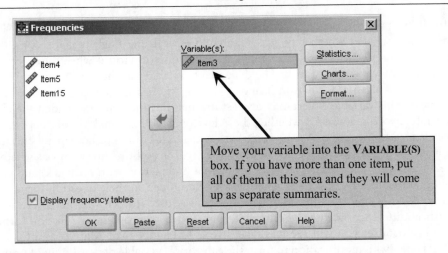

Figure 8.2 Frequency table dialogue box.

Table 8.11 Output from Goodness-of-Fit Summary

		Frequency	Percent (%)	Valid Percent (%)	Cumulative Percent (%)
Item 3					
Valid	Estar	13	68.4	68.4	68.4
	Ser	4	21.1	21.1	89.5
	Both	2	10.5	10.5	100.0
	Total	19	100.0	100.0	

The main output will be labeled with your variable name as shown for Item 3 in Table 8.11.

The output in Table 8.11 shows that, although the majority of native speakers chose to use *estar* in the situation for Item 3 (68.4%), there was some variation with the other two choices as well.

Creating a Frequency Table with One Categorical Variable

1   On the drop-down menu, choose ANALYZE > DESCRIPTIVE STATISTICS > FREQUENCIES.
2   Move the variable or variables you want into the box labeled VARIABLE(S). Press OK.

8.2.2 Summary Tables for Group-Independence Data (Crosstabs)

When you have two or more categorical variables, a simple frequency table will not be adequate to capture the complexity of the situation, especially the interactions of the variables. In this case, a cross-tabulation (crosstabs) is used. In SPSS, crosstabs is the first step toward performing an independent-groups chi-square.

I will illustrate the use of crosstabs using data from Mackey and Silver (2005). The authors investigated whether Singaporean children learning English as a second language in primary schools produced more advanced question forms when they received interactional feedback on a task. The dependent variable was the developmental level of the child's question formation (using levels 1–5, where 5 is the most developed and complex). This variable is certainly at least ordinal, but the authors divided the children into two categories of whether they developed or not, making the dependent variable a categorical one. Again, note that the data are counts of how many children are in each category (developed or not developed). The authors' question was whether there was a difference between the experimental (interaction with feedback) and control (interaction only) groups in whether they developed in their question-formation ability. A chi-square for group independence was used to see whether there were statistical differences across the groups in their ability to progress in question formation. The data set you will see was taken from Appendix A of Mackey and Silver's (2005) paper (with modification to form the categorical variable of development or not) and is found in the MackeySilver2005.sav file.

To inspect the data numerically, use the ANALYZE > DESCRIPTIVE STATISTICS > CROSSTABS menu. You'll see the dialogue box in Figure 8.3. Put one variable each in the ROW(S) and COLUMN(S) boxes. If you have more than two variables, add the additional variables one by one in the LAYER box.

The main part of the output results in a table such as that seen in Table 8.12.

The crosstabs table shows, at least on first glance, that there doesn't seem to be much difference between groups in who developed higher-level question formation

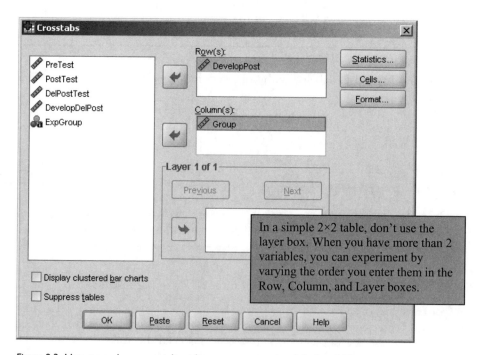

Figure 8.3 How to make a crosstab with two or more categorical variables.

Table 8.12 Output from a Crosstabs Command

DevelopPost* Group Crosstabulation

Count

		Group		Total
		Control	Experimental	
DevelopPost	Developed	7	9	16
	Not developed	5	5	10
Total		12	14	26

and who didn't, since 7 out of 12 in the control group developed while 9 out of 14 in the experimental group developed. To test this intuition, however, we will need to conduct the chi-square test of group independence. We will do this further on in the chapter.

Creating a Cross-Tabulated Table with Two or More Categorical Variables

1 On the drop-down menu, choose ANALYZE > DESCRIPTIVE STATISTICS > CROSSTABS.
2 Move the variable or variables you want into the boxes labeled ROW, COLUMN, and LAYER (use LAYER if you have more than two variables). In order to get the data in a format that is easy to understand you might need to experiment with changing the order of the variables in these areas. Press OK.

8.2.3 Application Activities with Tables of Categorical Variables

1 Use the Mackey and Silver (2005) data set and examine the frequency of the differing developmental levels of question formation in the pre-test (use the MackeySilver2005.sav file). What is the most frequent developmental level? What is the least frequent?
2 Use the Mackey and Silver (2005) data set to examine whether there is any difference between experimental groups on the pre-test data. From just eyeballing the data, does it appear that students in both experimental groups had roughly the same distribution of developmental levels for question formation?
3 Use the Dewaele and Pavlenko BEQ data (BEQ.Dominance). By eyeballing the crosstabs, examine whether the number of languages someone speaks has any relationship to whether they choose their first language as their dominant language (YES), their non-dominant language (NO), or a co-dominant language (YESPLUS). Use the categorical variables "CatDominance" and "NumberOfLang."
4 Further calculate the three-way intersection of number of languages known, dominance, and sex in the BEQ.Dominance file. Does the pattern noted in Question 3 seem to hold equally well for both males and females?

8.3 Visualizing Categorical Data

Categorical data consist of counts of frequencies, so a traditional way of visualizing such data has been with barplots. In this section I will show you barplots, but I'd also like you to be aware that there are new and very exciting ways to visualize categorical data. Friendly (2000) notes that, while methods for visualizing quantitative data have a long history and are widely used, methods for visualizing categorical data are quite new. I'll show you two plots, called a mosaic plot and a doubledecker plot. While these graphs are not yet available in SPSS, I think they will be in the future. They are available now with a statistical program like R.

8.3.1 Barplots with One Categorical Variable

There may not be a lot of reason to make a barplot when you have only one variable (it does not really provide a lot more information than what you can get from a tabular account), but, if you really want to do it, of course you can. I will illustrate how a barplot can be made with just one variable by looking at the Geeslin and Guijarro-Fuentes (2006) data. The variable "Item 3" in the GeeslinGF3_5.sav file records whether participants chose to use the verb *estar*, the verb *ser*, or said both verbs were equally plausible in that context.

To make a barplot with one variable, choose GRAPHS > LEGACY DIALOGS > BAR (in Version 12.0 the LEGACY DIALOGS step is absent). A dialogue box will appear. Choose SIMPLE and then SUMMARIES FOR GROUPS OF CASES, as shown in Figure 8.4.

The resulting barplot in Figure 8.5 shows graphically that *estar* is by far the most frequent response to Item 3.

8.3.2 Barplots with Two Categorical Variables

In order to look at barplots with two categorical variables I will use the Mackey and Silver (2005) data set. The authors wanted to examine the relationship of experimental groups on the question development of the students. For two categorical variables, again choose GRAPHS > LEGACY DIALOGS > BAR from the menu, but this time pick the CLUSTERED box with SUMMARIES FOR GROUPS OF CASES, as shown in Figure 8.6.

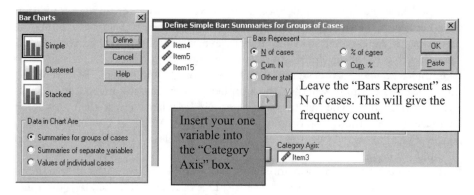

Figure 8.4 Creating a barplot with one variable.

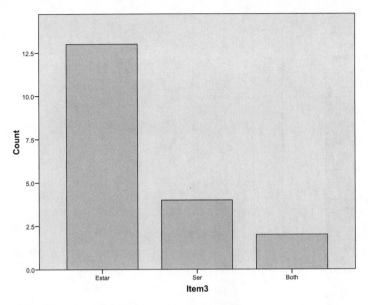

Figure 8.5 A barplot with one categorical variable.

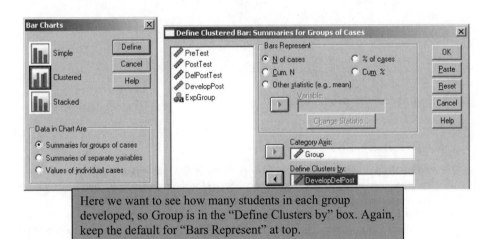

Here we want to see how many students in each group developed, so Group is in the "Define Clusters by" box. Again, keep the default for "Bars Represent" at top.

Figure 8.6 Creating a barplot with two variables.

I personally find the terminology for the Bar Charts dialogue box confusing, but one way to understand it better is to realize that if you want counts (or frequency data) you should choose the SUMMARIES FOR GROUPS OF CASES option. On the other hand, if you want mean scores, choose the SUMMARIES OF SEPARATE VARIABLES option (see—does that make any logical sense? I think not). For two categorical variables, the barplot in Figure 8.7 is obtained (this plot has been modified slightly for format). It shows clearly that the number of students who developed in their question-formation ability (the white box) was greater in the experimental group than in the control group.

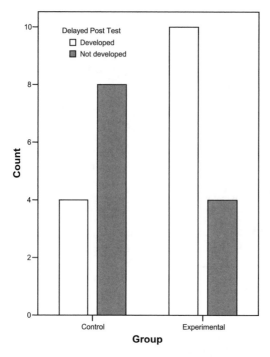

Figure 8.7 A barplot with two categorical variables.

8.3.3 Summary: Barplots in SPSS

Creating a Barplot in SPSS

1   On the drop-down menu, choose GRAPHS > LEGACY DIALOGS > BAR.
2   If you have one categorical variable, choose SIMPLE for the type of barplot, and SUMMARIES FOR GROUPS OF CASES. Put your variable into the "Category Axis" box.
3   If you have two categorical variables, choose CLUSTERED for the type of barplot, and SUMMARIES FOR GROUPS OF CASES. Put the variable that will define clusters on the x-axis in the "Category Axis" box and the variable that will contrast bars in the "Define clusters by" box.

SPSS has no good way to layer three categorical variables in a barplot. Activity 2 in the application activities in Section 8.3.4 has three variables but I will ask you to look only at two variables at a time. It would be possible, of course, to put the two barplots side by side for a comparison. The newer graphics I will show you in Sections 8.3.5 and 8.3.6 are able to integrate three or more categorical variables at one time.

Tip: In this book I do not show you how to make barplots when you have interval-level variables. This is because I do not think there is a reason to use barplots when you have interval-level variables. Instead, use boxplots (see Larson-Hall & Herrington, forthcoming, for an explanation).

If you do insist on making a barplot when you have one categorical and two interval-level variables and the bars represent mean scores instead of counts, choose the CLUSTERED, SUMMARIES OF SEPARATE VARIABLES in the BAR CHARTS dialogue box. If you do this, please add error bars through the Options button to give your reader more information.

8.3.4 Application Activities with Barplots

1   Using the fabricated data set of LanguageChoice.sav, create a barplot that shows the distribution of which language students choose to study, based on which university (POPULATION) they come from. Comment on big differences in language preference between the two universities.

2   Using the fabricated data set Motivation.sav, create one barplot that shows the distribution of YES and NO responses for the five teachers at the beginning of the semester (FIRST). Then create another barplot that shows the distribution of responses at the end of the semester (LAST). What do you notice from the visual data?

3   Use the Mackey and Silver (2005) data set and create a barplot that examines the development of questions on the immediate post-test (DEVELOPPOST), categorized by experimental group (GROUP). We saw in Figure 8.7 from the delayed post-test that more students in the experimental group developed than students in the control group. Does that pattern hold true for the immediate post-test?

4   Use the Dewaele and Pavlenko BEQ data (BEQ.Dominance). Graphically explore the question of whether the number of languages someone speaks has any relationship to whether they choose their first language as their dominant language (YES), their non-dominant language (NO), or a co-dominant language (YESPLUS). What do you think, from looking at the data?

8.3.5 Mosaic Plots

In mosaic plots "the variables are nested into rows and columns using recursive conditional splits. . . . The result is a 'flat' representation that can be visualized in ways similar to a two-dimensional table" (Meyer, Zeileis, & Hornik, 2007, p. 5). In Figure 8.8 I show a mosaic plot for the data from the Dewaele and Pavlenko (2001–2003) BEQ data file (you should have worked with this and made a barplot for this data in Activity 4 of the application activities in Section 8.3.4). This plot was created using the statistical program R and the **vcd** library.

If you could see Figure 8.8 in color, you would see that all of the boxes with solid lines are blue and all of the boxes with dotted lines are red. The boxes with solid lines are places where there are more answers in that category than we would expect, while the

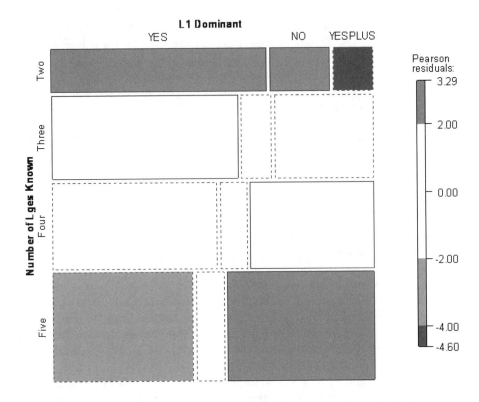

Figure 8.8 Mosaic plot with two categorical variables (Dewaele and Pavlenko data).

boxes with dotted lines are places where there are fewer answers in that category than we would expect. The area of the boxes gives an indication of their proportion to the whole.

What this plot shows is that there are more persons with two languages who say their L1 is their dominant language (YES) or is not their dominant language (NO) than expected, while there are fewer persons with two languages (dotted lines) who say they are dominant in more than one language (YESPLUS) than we would expect if there were no relationship between number of languages and language dominance (the null hypothesis). The departure from expected is not so striking for those with three and four languages as evidenced by a lack of color, but we again see some striking differences for persons with five languages. There are fewer persons (dotted lines) with five languages who say their L1 is their dominant language (YES), and there are more persons (solid lines) with five languages who say they are dominant in more than one language (YESPLUS) than would be expected if the variables were independent.

The Pearson residuals plot shown to the right of the mosaic plot uses both color and saturation to indicate inferences that can be made from the data. The most saturated hue (the one below −4.00) for the red (dotted line) allows you to identify areas where the null hypothesis that the variables are independent can be rejected (Meyer, Zeileis, & Hornik, 2007). Residuals above 4 or below −4 indicate a difference that means the null hypothesis can be rejected. Residuals between 2 and 4 (and −2 and −4) are medium-sized and do not indicate a statistical rejection of the null hypothesis (Meyer, Zeileis, & Hornik, 2007). Therefore, in Figure 8.8, the only cell which we can see is individually statistical is the one between persons with two languages and L1 dominance in more than 1 language (YESPLUS).

Mosaic plots can easily incorporate a third categorical variable by adding divisions to another side of the square.

8.3.6 Doubledecker Plots

The doubledecker plot is a very nice visual when you have three or more categorical variables and you want to visualize conditional independent structures. For this section I will illustrate with data for the *Titanic* (the ship that sank). There are three predictor factors that are included in the *Titanic* survival tables: sex (male or female), age (child or adult), and class (first, second, third, or crew). The doubledecker plot in Figure 8.9 gives labels in layers underneath the table. The darker shadings are for those who survived (the skinny key that shows this is on the far right of the graph).

As your eye moves from left to right over this plot, first you can see that proportionally more people in first class survived than in third class or crew (width of boxes represents proportions of numbers). Among first-class passengers (almost all of whom were adults; the children are a slim black line to the left of the adults in first class), proportionally more females than males survived. There were very few children at all, but it appears that children survived at a very high rate in first and second class, and usually at a higher rate than adults in third class (except among females, where slightly more adult women survived than female children).

I assume that excellent summaries of categorical variables such as the mosaic plot and doubledecker plot will be common for visualizing data in the not-too-distant future. If you would like to use R to create these plots I highly recommend

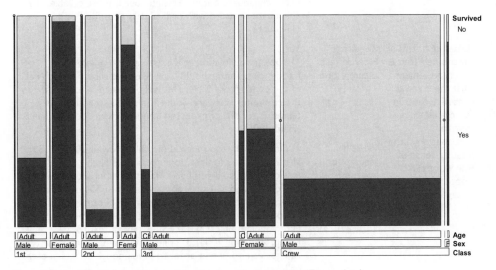

Figure 8.9 Doubledecker plot using three categorical variables (*Titanic* data).

reading Meyer, Zeileis, and Hornik (2007), who explain the syntax for creating these plots.

8.4 Assumptions of Chi-Square

Chi-square is a non-parametric test, so it has fewer assumptions than parametric tests. However, chi-square does have some basic assumptions that must be met in order to make the results valid.

Meeting chi-square assumptions		
1 Independence of observations	Required?	Yes
	How to test assumption?	Make sure that number of participants will be equal to the number of observations in the contingency table (so there are no repeated measures)
	What if assumption not met?	1) If data is not independent, use a different statistical test (see Section 8.1.3 for ideas of other tests that could be used) or rearrange the data into a format that is independent; 2) if you have paired data (before/after treatment measurement) you can use the McNemar test
2 Nominal data (no inherent rank or order)	Required?	Not strictly; interval or ordinal data may be collapsed into categories but this results in data loss and so cannot be recommended
	What to do if assumption is not met?	If you have ordinal data, then the ordering of the rows and columns will make a difference to the outcome; Howell (2002, pp. 311–312) says one approach to this type of data is to use the linear-by-linear association reported in the chi-square output. This number is more reliable as a chi-square measure with ordinal data than the Pearson chi-square
3 Data are normally distributed (this is the requirement that there are at least five cases in every cell, since normal distribution in the regular sense of the word can't happen with categorical data)	Required? How to test assumption?	Yes 1) Look for a violation of the assumption of expected frequencies. There should be at least five cases for each cell of the contingency table. This will be tested automatically by the computer software. Some authors say that in larger tables up to 20% of expected frequencies can be less than 5 (Field, 2005)
	What if assumption not met?	1) Don't worry too much about this (Howell, 2002, p. 159). With small sample sizes, your problem is likely to be a loss of power, so if you find a statistical difference then you don't need to worry about this. If you do not find a difference, then be aware that it may be because your sample sizes are too small and thus you lack power to find real differences; 2) use Fisher's exact test (Brace, Kemp, & Snelgar, 2003); 3) collect more data or collapse two categories into one in order to have enough counts in each cell

4 Non-occurrences must be included as well as occurrences	Required?	Yes; an example of this mistake would be counting the number of students with high motivation levels who earned a 2 (advanced) on the Oral Proficiency Interview scale in French, Russian, and Japanese, and then conducting an independent-groups chi-square on whether there was a relationship between motivation and high achievement, with a contingency table like this:

	French	Russian	Japanese	Total
Obs.	15	6	9	30
Exp.	10	10	10	30

In counting only those students with high motivation, we would leave out the students we surveyed with non-high levels of motivation

	How to test assumption?	Make sure that the number of participants in the study is equal to the grand total of observations in the contingency table
	What if assumption not met?	Include the non-occurrences as well as the occurrences; in our example above, we'll need to know how many people in total from each language group were surveyed:

	French	Russian	Japanese	Total
High	15	6	9	30
Non-high	63	6	19	88
Total	78	12	28	118

With only occurrences included, it seemed that more students of French who were highly motivated became advanced speakers, but that was before we knew how many speakers in total were tested. In fact, 50% of the Russian speakers with high motivation scored highly, while only 19% of the French speakers with high motivation scored highly.

I would like to emphasize one more time that the first assumption of chi-square listed here is often violated in research studies I have seen from applied linguistics and sociolinguistics. To give another example of this type of violation, assume that we do a study on the number of times our participant supplies a third person singular –s on a verb appropriately. For example, say we have five participants and they were observed for how many times they put a third person –s on the 20 obligatory instances in a cloze test. We want to know if our participants supplied the –s more times than would be predicted by chance (so we are interested in a goodness-of-fit chi-square). We might have the following type of table:

	Supplied –s	Omitted –s	Total
Participant 1	15	5	20
Participant 2	7	13	20
Participant 3	12	8	20
Participant 4	3	17	20
Participant 5	10	10	20
Total	47	53	100

If we now performed a chi-square for goodness of fit, assuming that each choice is equally likely, $\chi^2 = .36$ on 1 degree of freedom, which has an associated p-value of .55, meaning there is no evidence here that our participants performed any differently from chance. However, we can clearly see that some participants appeared to do much better or worse than chance (such as Participants 1 and 4). The problem with using chi-square in this case is that we have 100 pieces of data in our contingency table but only five participants. Each person has contributed more than once to a cell and thus the data are not independent. This type of data analysis is similar to that shown in Scenario Two of Section 8.1.3, and separate binomial tests for each participant would be one way to evaluate if each person's answers differed statistically from chance.

8.5 Chi-Square Statistical Test

There are two types of chi-square statistical tests. One is used when you have only one variable, and want to examine whether the distribution of the data is what is expected. This is called the one-way goodness-of-fit chi-square.

The other type of chi-square is used when you have two variables, with two or more levels each. This is used when you want to examine whether there is a relationship between the variables. This is called the two-way group-independence chi-square.

8.5.1 One-Way Goodness-of-Fit Chi-Square in SPSS

To look at a goodness-of-fit chi-square test I will use the data set extrapolated from the appendix of Geeslin and Guijarro-Fuentes (2006), although I am not answering the questions they asked in their study. Instead, I will look only at three items to determine whether the choices (of the verbs *ser* and *estar* or both verbs equally) are distributed equally.

Using the data set GeeslinGF3_5.sav, answers are coded to reflect the choice that native speakers of Spanish used in Items 3–5. To examine the distribution of answers with a one-way goodness-of-fit chi-square, open ANALYZE > NONPARAMETRIC TESTS > CHI-SQUARE. You will see a dialogue box like that in Figure 8.10.

The print-out from the one-way chi-square is seen in Table 8.13. First we see the summary of observed and expected counts for Items 3 through 5. The chi-square was done using the hypothesis that all categories were equally likely to have been chosen, as can be seen in the "Expected N" column. Notice that for Item 4, where there was no variation (all of the speakers chose the verb *ser* for this situation), a chi-square cannot be performed.

The next part of the printout (Table 8.14) shows the results of the goodness-of-fit chi-square test.

The "Test Statistics" box shows that the chi-square statistic for Item 3 is 10.8 at 2 degrees of freedom, which gives a very low probability ($p = .004$). Item 5 likewise has a very low p-value. We can thus conclude that it is very unlikely we would obtain these results if the null hypothesis were true. The null hypothesis is that all choices are equally likely. Notice that the chi-square does *not* tell us whether two of the choices (of the verb *ser, estar,* or both) are the same and one is different, or if all three are different. However, in this case for all three items the number of native speakers of Spanish who chose *ser* is quite large, so if Items 3 and 5 are statistical this means that statistically

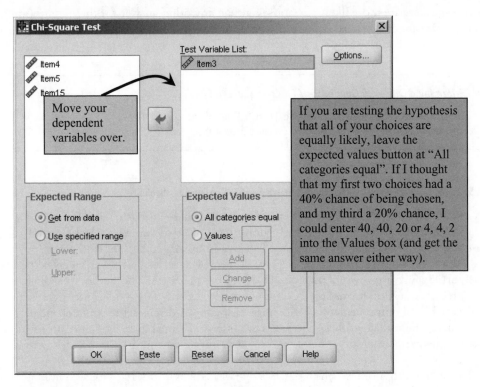

Figure 8.10 Dialogue box for a one-way goodness-of-fit chi-square test.

Table 8.13 Output on Descriptives from a One-Way Goodness-of-Fit Chi-Square Test

Item3

	Observed N	Expected N	Residual
Estar	13	6.3	6.7
Ser	4	6.3	-2.3
Both	2	6.3	-4.3
Total	19		

Item4

	Observed N	Expected N	Residual
1	19	19.0	.0
Total	19[a]		

a. This variable is constant. Chi-Square
Test cannot be performed.

Item5

	Observed N	Expected N	Residual
1	13	6.3	6.7
2	5	6.3	-1.3
3	1	6.3	-5.3
Total	19		

Table 8.14 Chi-Square Test Results Output from a One-Way Goodness-of-Fit Chi-Square Test

Test Statistics

	Item3	Item5
Chi-Square[a]	10.842	11.789
df	2	2
Asymp. Sig.	.004	.003

a. 0 cells (.0%) have expected frequencies less than
5. The minimum expected cell frequency is 6.3.

native speakers are more likely to choose *ser* than any other answer for these items (for Item 4 this cannot be tested statistically because it is the only choice, but logically this must be true for Item 4 as well).

Performing a One-Way Goodness-of-Fit Chi-Square in SPSS

1   Choose ANALYZE > NONPARAMETRIC TESTS > CHI-SQUARE.
2   Put variable in "Test Variable List" box and press OK.

8.5.2 Two-Way Group-Independence Chi-Square in SPSS

In order to illustrate a group-independence chi-square test (this is also called a multidimensional chi-square, although note that only two variables can be tested at one time) I will use data presented in Mackey and Silver (2005). The authors wanted to know whether being in an experimental group where feedback was given helped the participants improve in their ability to form questions. The authors calculated the pre-test question-formation developmental level, and then coded for a categorical variable of improvement or no improvement. In doing a group-independence chi-square, the null hypothesis is that there is no relationship between group membership (experimental or control group) and improvement in question-formation level.

To test the null hypothesis, choose ANALYZE > DESCRIPTIVE STATISTICS > CROSSTABS, just as we did in Section 8.2.2 in order to obtain the crosstabs tables—the only additional step is to open up the STATISTICS button. In the Crosstabs dialogue box seen in Figure 8.11, I put the Group (splitting) variable in the "Column(s)" box, and the delayed post-test developmental categorization into the "Row(s)" box. I also ticked the "Display clustered bar charts" box to get barplots to appear in the output. In the dialogue box shown when the STATISTICS button is pressed (also in Figure 8.11), I ticked the box

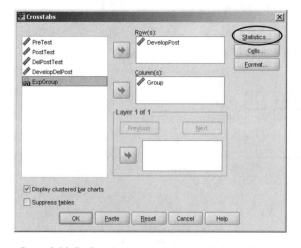
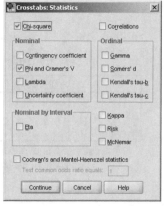

Figure 8.11   Performing a two-way group-independence chi-square in SPSS.

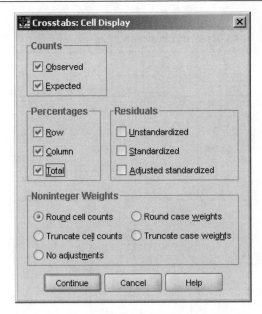

Figure 8.12 Dialogue box for Cells in group-independence chi-square.

labeled "Chi-square" to call for the test, and then the box labeled "Phi and Cramer's V" in order to ask for an effect size. Note that, if you wanted to do a McNemar test (when you have paired data), this box would be the place to ask for it.

Also open the CELLS button from the main Crosstabs dialogue box and click the boxes that I have clicked on in Figure 8.12.

The first part of the output, shown in Table 8.15, gives a summary of how many cases are included. This table shows that no cases are missing, which is good.

The next part of chi-square test output gives the crosstab table with expected counts and all of the row and column percentages. Table 8.16 shows just the first part of this crosstab, since we have already examined these tables in Section 8.2.

Table 8.16 shows that, in the delayed post-test, four participants in the control group developed. This is 33% of the control group (of 12), 29% of those who developed (14), and 15% of the total number of participants (26). The next part of the output, shown in Table 8.17, gives the chi-square tests.

The statistic normally reported for the chi-square test is the first row of Table 8.17, the Pearson chi-square. The χ^2 value is 3.77 with 1 degree of freedom (because there are two variables), with a p-value just barely above the .05 statistical level ($p = .052$).

Table 8.15 Case Processing Summary Table in Chi-Square Output

Case Processing Summary

	Cases					
	Valid		Missing		Total	
	N	Percent	N	Percent	N	Percent
Group * DevelopDelPost	26	100.0%	0	.0%	26	100.0%

Table 8.16 Crosstab Summary in Chi-Square Output

Group ' DevelopDelPost Crosstabulation

			DevelopDelPost		
			Developed	Not developed	Total
Group	Control	Count	4	8	12
		Expected Count	6.5	5.5	12.0
		% within Group	33.3%	66.7%	100.0%
		% within DevelopDelPost	28.6%	66.7%	46.2%
		% of Total	15.4%	30.8%	46.2%
	Experimental	Count	10	4	14
		Expected Count	7.5	6.5	14.0

Table 8.17 Chi-Square Test Results in Chi-Square Output

Chi-Square Tests

	Value	df	Asymp. Sig. (2-sided)	Exact Sig. (2-sided)	Exact Sig. (1-sided)
Pearson Chi-Square	3.773[b]	1	.052		
Continuity Correction	2.396	1	.122		
Likelihood Ratio	3.862	1	.049		
Fisher's Exact Test				.113	.060
Linear-by-Linear Association	3.628	1	.057		
N of Valid Cases	26				

a. Computed only for a 2x2 table

b. 0 cells (.0%) have expected count less than 5. The minimum expected count is 5. 54.

Footnote b is important to notice at once, because it informs us whether expected counts are less than 5, which could be problematic. None are in this case. The likelihood ratio is an alternative test to the chi-square, which also uses the χ^2 distribution (it is also called a g-test). Howell (2002) asserts that this test is gaining in popularity and that its results should be equivalent to the chi-square when sample sizes are large. Since we notice in the case of the Mackey and Silver data that the likelihood ratio statistic has a *p*-value of .049, we might choose to report this statistic instead of the Pearson chi-square.[1] The linear-by-linear association test assumes that both variables are ordinal. Report this if your variables have inherent rank.

---

1 You might wonder whether this is cheating. I don't think it is, especially since the *p*-values differ by 3 one-hundredths of a point, but one just happens to come down on the easy side of *p* = .05. In either case you could argue that it was a statistical result, and still the most important measure would be its effect size, not its *p*-value!

Tip: If you have only two levels in each variable (a 2 × 2 contingency table) you will see two more tests in the chi-square test print-out than if you have three levels or more. One is the Continuity Correction, which some authors argue should be used for a 2 × 2 contingency table. Howell (2002) gives good arguments against it, and I would recommend against it as well. The other line is Fisher's exact test. This can be used when cells do not have the minimum number of counts, although it does not have to be used in those cases.

Although the Pearson *p*-value is slightly above .05, I would personally argue that the test showed that there was a strong likelihood that the variables of experimental group and developmental progress are independent of one another. We can deduce which group is better than the other by looking at the pattern of results on the contingency table. Ten out of 14 people in the experimental group (71%) developed while only 4 out of 12 people in the control group (33%) developed. Therefore we may conclude that, by the time of the delayed post-test, the experimental treatment had helped statistically more participants progress in their question-formation abilities than the control treatment.

Howell (2002) notes that good measures of effect size to use for the chi-square test are phi (φ), which is used for 2 × 2 contingency tables with only two levels per each variable, and Cramer's V, which is used for tables larger than 2 × 2 (when there are more than two levels per variable). Table 8.18 shows the part of the output that gives these effect size numbers. **Phi** (or **Cramer's V**) is a percentage variance effect size (from the *r*-family) and would indicate that the experimental treatment accounted for 38% of the variance in the data. Phi can only be used as an effect size when there is a 2 × 2 contingency table, but Cramer's V is an extension for tables with more levels.

The last part of the output is the barplot, which is the same as was seen in Figure 8.5, so I won't reproduce it here.

Performing a Two-Way Group-Independence Chi-Square

I   ANALYZE > DESCRIPTIVE STATISTICS > CROSSTABS. If you want a barplot, tick the "Display clustered bar charts" box.
2   Open the STATISTICS button and tick the "Chi-square" and "Phi and Cramer's V" boxes.
3   Open the CELLS button and tick the "Expected values" and all of the boxes under "Percentages."

Table 8.18 Effect Size Result in the Chi-Square Output

Symmetric Measures

		Value	Approx. Sig.
Nominal by Nominal	Phi	-.381	.052
	Cramer's V	.381	.052
N of Valid Cases		26	

8.5.3 Application Activities with Chi-Square in SPSS

1   Using the Geeslin and Guijarro-Fuentes (2006) data (GeeslinGF3_5), analyze Item 15 to see whether the native speakers of Spanish chose each possibility with equal probability. Additionally, generate a barplot to help you better understand the data, and describe what you have found.

2   Using the same data as in 1 above, test the hypothesis that there is only a 10% probability that speakers will choose answer 3 ("both verbs equally"), while the probability that they will choose the other two choices is equal.

3   Using the Mackey and Silver (2005) data, investigate the question of whether there was any relationship between question development and experimental group for the immediate post-test (use the DevelopPost variable). We saw in Section 8.5.2 that there was a relationship between experimental group and delayed post-test. Does this hold true for the immediate post-test? Be sure to report on effect size.

4   We saw in previous sections that there seemed to be some statistical associations in the Dewaele and Pavlenko data between the number of languages people knew and their answer as to which language was dominant. Use the BEQ.Dominance.sav file (variables: CatDominance, NumberOfLang) to investigate this question using the chi-square test.

5   Bryan Smith (2004) tested the question of whether preemptive input or negotiation in a computer-mediated conversation was more effective for helping students to learn vocabulary. Smith considered the question of whether these strategies resulted in successful uptake. He found that 21 participants who heard preemptive input had no uptake, while 2 had successful uptake. He further found that 37 participants who heard negotiated input had no uptake and 6 had successful uptake. Assuming that these data are independent, is there any relationship between the way the participants heard the vocabulary and whether they had successful uptake? Since we have only summary data here, you'll have to do something a little special in SPSS to test this out. Open a new data file in SPSS and enter the data as shown in Figure 8.13. To make SPSS understand that this is summary data, go to Data > Weight Cases and put the variable Result into the line that says "Weight cases by." This will tell SPSS the data are summary data, and you can now run an independent-groups chi-square test by putting the variables Input and Uptake into the crosstab.

8.5.4 Testing for Independence in Chi-Square when There Are More than Two Levels in Each Factor (Advanced Topic)

Up to this point I have assumed that, if you have a contingency table where there are more than two levels in each of the two variables (a 2 × 2 table), you will simply get an overall chi-square result and look at the contingency table to make further inferences. In fact, if you are working with data that is larger than 2 × 2 (but still only has two variables), you can do further testing to find out which groups are different from each other. You can partition the contingency table and then test the smaller 2 × 2 tables (Agresti, 2002). In order to demonstrate this idea, let us suppose Mackey and Silver had had three different experimental groups (this data is now made up) as shown in Table 8.19.

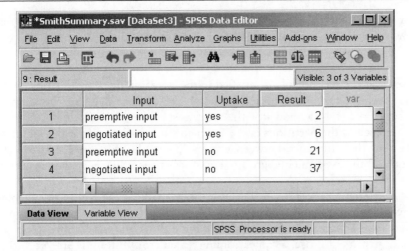

Figure 8.13 Typing in summary statistics for a chi-square analysis.

An overall chi-square test for group independence (results: $\chi^2 = 6.6$, df = 2, $p = .04$) would not tell you which groups were different from each other. If we have a 2×J component table (where J = 3 in this example), then one can partition the table into (J–1) tables (two in this case). Partitioning is done by computing first a 2 × 2 table using the first two rows and first two columns of the original table. The next partition will combine the first two rows and compare them to the third row. Thus we will have two partition tables to test with the group-independence chi-square test. Table 8.20 shows this partitioning of the made-up data in Table 8.19.

In order to keep the tests independent, the rules for doing this partitioning are (Agresti, 2002, p. 84):

1 "The df for the subtables must sum to df for the full table."
2 "Each cell count in the full table must be a cell count in one and only one subtable" (the other times the original cell of the full table will be combined with another cell).

Table 8.19 An Example of a 2×3 Contingency Table

Group	Developed	Did not develop
Experimental 1	10	4
Experimental 2	9	2
Control	4	8

Table 8.20 Partitioning the 2×3 Table into 2×2 Tables

Group	Developed	Did not develop	Group	Developed	Did not develop
Experimental 1	10	4	Experimental 1 + Experimental 2	19	6
Experimental 2	9	2	Control	4	8

3   "Each marginal total [the row or column total] of the full table must be a marginal total for one and only one subtable" (but this rule will be upheld if 2 above is upheld).

You can see that the second rule is satisfied in the partitioning shown in Table 8.20. If we ran a chi-square for these two partitions, the results are that, for the leftmost table, $\chi^2 = .36$, df = 1, $p = .55$ and, for the rightmost table, $\chi^2 = 6.3$, df = 1, $p = .01$. Thus the df for each of the partitions is $1 + 1$, which sums to the 2 df for the full table. We also see that the difference between groups lies in the difference between the control group and the experimental groups, and not between the experimental groups themselves.

At this point, you might wonder how to test these smaller 2 × 2 contingency tables. Will you have to rearrange your data in SPSS? There is a way to get SPSS to recognize summary data (see Activity 5 in Section 8.5.3), but I think the easiest way to do the testing would just be to use a quick online calculator. I found one at http://www.graphpad.com/quickcalcs/Contingency1.cfm that calculates a 2 × 2 contingency table. To get the same results as I get with SPSS (using the Pearson's chi-square row of the output), choose the "Chi-square without Yates' correction" button (even though this website recommends Fisher's exact test). This site will return a p-value.

Returning to the question of analyzing even larger contingency tables, we would follow the same rules. Let's say our larger contingency table has I number of columns and J number of rows. As an example, take the Dewaele and Pavlenko data we have looked at in this chapter, which is a 3×4 contingency table, so I = 3 and J = 4. There will be (I-1)(J-1) partitions, which in this case means $(3–1)(4–1) = (2)(3) = 6$ (see Table 8.21).

To further examine differences, we would look at the first two columns and first two rows. Next we add together either the first two rows or the first two columns and compare them to the next row or column. This may become clearer as you look at what I do in Table 8.22. The second 2 × 2 table adds together the first two columns, YES + NO, and compares them to the third column, still for the first two rows. The third 2 × 2 table then adds the first two rows together and compares them to the fourth row, and so on. The bolded numbers indicate original numbers from Table 8.21.

This was a little complicated to set up, but actually it's very helpful to check Agresti's Rule 2 above that every cell of the original table is found once in the partitioned tables (each original cell *must* be found once in a partitioned table). I've bolded the original cells in the partitioned table. The original table had a df = 6, and each of these six 2 × 2 tables will have a df = 1, which will sum to 6.

Table 8.21 An Example of a 3×4 Contingency Table

No. of languages	LI dominant (YES)	Other dominant (NO)	LI + other(s) dominant (YESPLUS)
Two	94	26	17
Three	159	26	83
Four	148	23	110
Five	157	30	163

Table 8.22 Partitioning the 3×4 Table into 2×2 Tables

	YES	NO		YES+NO	YESPLUS		YES+NO	YESPLUS
Two	94	26	Two	120	17	Two+ Three	305	100
Three	159	26	Three	185	83	Four	171	110

	YES+NO	YESPLUS		YES	NO		YES	NO
Two+ Three+ Four	476	210	Two+ Three	253	52	Two+ Three+ Four	401	75
Five	187	163	Four	148	23	Five	157	30

8.5.5 Effect Sizes for Chi-Square

Because one-way goodness-of-fit chi-squares are just looking at fit, there are no measures of effect size for this test.

For the chi-square group-independence test, one type of effect size you can use is phi (φ) and Cramer's V. These two numbers are the same when the test has only two levels for each factor (2 × 2), but Cramer's V should be used when there are more than two levels. This number is a correlation (percentage variance, r-family effect size) and its value can range from 0 to ±1.

The effect size that Cohen (1988) uses for chi-square is called w. Volker (2006) says that w is equal to φ with 2 × 2 tables, and that $w = V \sqrt{r-1}$ when there are more than two levels to a variable, where V=Cramer's V and r=the number of rows or columns, whichever is smaller. For the Mackey and Silver (2005) data, we can obtain phi from the SPSS output ($\varphi = -.38$), so $w = \varphi = .38$, which is a medium effect size (we don't need to consider the negative sign if we think about this as an effect size). Calculating the effect size for the Dewaele and Pavlenko group-independence chi-square, we can obtain V from the print-out (V = .17) and the smallest number of levels is 3, in the "Categorical Dominance" variable, so $w = .17\sqrt{3-1} = .17\sqrt{2} = .24$, which could be considered a small to medium effect size.

Howell (2002) also notes that an **odds ratio** can be an intuitively understandable way to present results and understand the strength of the effect. Heiberger and Holland (2004) further note that odds ratios are not much affected by group size, unlike the chi-square statistic. I'll show how an odds ratio could be calculated. Table 8.23 shows the crosstab output for the Mackey and Silver (2005) data in the delayed post-test condition.

For the Mackey and Silver (2005) data, which was a 2 × 2 table, if we look at the odds of developing on question formation given that a person was in the experimental group, this is equal to the number of people in that group who developed divided by the number of people in that group who did not develop, so the odds equal 10/4 = 2.5. The odds of developing in the control group are 4/8 = .5. Now we make an odds ratio with both of these odds: 2.5/.5= 5. You are five times more likely to develop your question-making ability if you were in the experimental group than if you were in the

Table 8.23 Crosstabs for Mackey and Silver (2005)

Group ' DevelopDelPost Crosstabulation

Count

		DevelopDelPost		Total
		Developed	Not developed	
Group	Control	4	8	12
	Experimental	10	4	14
Total		14	12	26

Table 8.24 Table Subscripts

N_{11}	N_{12}
N_{21}	N_{22}

Table 8.25 Dewaele and Pavlenko 2×2 Contingency Table

	Five languages	Fewer than five languages
Dominant One	187	476
Dominant Two	163	210

control group. An even easier way to calculate this odds ratio is to calculate the cross-product of the contingency table, as $\frac{n_{11}n_{22}}{n_{12}n_{21}}$, where the subscript on the n refers to position in the table, as shown in Table 8.24.

You just need to make sure that the ratio you are testing for is the one in the N_{11} position. With the Mackey and Silver data we need to flip Table 8.23 on its head so that the experimental group that developed is in the N_{11} position, and then we have $\frac{10*8}{4*4} = \frac{80}{16} = 5$.

To calculate odds ratios for contingency tables larger than 2 × 2 you need to collapse some categories to get to a 2 × 2 contingency table. Let's say that, with the Dewaele and Pavlenko data, we want to know the odds of being dominant in more than one language if you know five languages. We will then collapse the two categories of "Dominant in L1" and "Dominant in LX" into one category. For number of languages that a person knows we will collapse this into "Knows five languages" and "Knows fewer than five languages." This collapsing results in the contingency table in Table 8.25.

The odds of being dominant in two (or more) languages given that you speak five languages is equal to $\frac{163*476}{187*210} = \frac{77588}{39270} = 1.97$ (again, we will consider the data in the intersection of two (dominant languages) and five (known languages) as our N_{11} position). You are about twice as likely (as bilinguals, trilinguals, and quadrilinguals) to be dominant in two languages than just one if you know five languages.

8.5.6 Reporting Chi-Square Test Results

For chi-square tests, it is imperative that you provide a contingency table with a summary of your data as well as the statistical results. We have seen in this chapter that, since chi-square is not a directional test, it is impossible to understand the statistical results without seeing the contingency table as well.

For the chi-square test itself, you should report the type of test that was performed, the chi-square value, the degrees of freedom, and the *p*-value of the test. If you have done a test for group independence, you should report effect sizes as phi (or Cramer's V if the table is larger than 2 × 2) or *w*. You might want to calculate odds ratios as well, as these are quite intuitive to understand.

For a one-way goodness-of-fit chi-square, let's consider a report about the Geeslin and Guijarro-Fuentes (2006) data:

A one-way goodness-of-fit chi-square was conducted to see whether native speakers of Spanish were choosing each of the three choices for verbs equally in Items 3, 4, and 5. The frequency counts for each choice for each item are given in the following table:

Item	Estar	Ser	Both	Total
3	13	4	2	19
4	19	0	0	19
5	13	5	1	19

A separate chi-square for each item revealed that native speakers of Spanish chose *estar* more frequently than would be predicted if all speakers were randomly picking one of the three choices (Item 3: $\chi^2 = 10.8$, df = 2, $p = .004$; Item 4: could not be tested because only *estar* was chosen; Item 5: $\chi^2 = 11.8$, df = 2, $p = .003$).

For a two-way group-independence chi-square, we will report the result of the Mackey and Silver (2005) data:

A two-way group-independence chi-square was performed to assess the relationship between group membership and development in question formation. A contingency table for these data is shown below:

Group	Developed	Did not develop
Experimental	10	4
Control	4	8

The results were statistical (likelihood ratio $\chi^2 = 3.86$, df = 1, $p = .049$), with an effect size of $w = .38$, which is a medium size effect. The odds of developing in the question-formation hierarchy for participants in the experimental group were five times greater than for participants in the control group (odds ratio$=\dfrac{\frac{10}{4}}{\frac{4}{8}} = \dfrac{2.5}{.5} = 5$).

8.6 Summary of Chi-Square

In this chapter we have seen that chi-square is a test used when all of your variables are categorical. There are several situations when it is inappropriate to use chi-square, however, even if all of your variables are categorical. All of the situations involve a violation of the assumption that each person will contribute only once to each cell of a contingency table summarizing the data.

When looking at a situation that satisfies this assumption, there are two types of chi-square tests that can be used. These tests differ in the number of variables that they require, and in hypotheses they make. The one-way goodness-of-fit chi-square test requires only one variable. It tests the hypothesis that every choice in the variable is equally likely (as a default, although other percentages can be specified).

The two-way group-independence chi-square test requires two variables. It tests the hypothesis that there is no relationship between the two categorical variables. This is probably the more common chi-square test in the field of second language research. Further sections of this chapter showed how to analyze differences between levels of variables statistically (by partitioning them into 2 × 2 tables and testing them) and also how to calculate odds ratios as well as report effect sizes for these tests.

If you have more than two categorical variables you would like to test then you cannot use a chi-square test. Field (2005) recommends loglinear analysis, and I refer you to his book for more information.

Chapter 9

Looking for Differences between Two Means with T-Tests: Think-Aloud Methodology and Phonological Memory

> Far better an approximate answer to the *right* question, which is often vague, than an *exact* answer to the wrong question, which can always be made precise.
>
> Quote attributed to Tukey (1962)

T-tests answer a very simple question—are two scores the same or different? In spite of the apparent simplicity of this test, it is widely useful in a variety of settings. All of the statistical tests investigated in this chapter involve looking at two mean scores on the same testing instrument. Owing to random chance, scores from two groups on the same test are unlikely to be exactly the same, even if the two scores come from the same set of people. A t-test can tell us if the differences between the two scores are big enough that we can assume they come from two different groups, or that scores at Time 1 differ from scores at Time 2. If the differences are not big enough we will assume that the scores come from the same group or that there are no differences between Time 1 and Time 2 scores. This chapter will look at two main types of t-tests which are very frequently used in second language research studies:

1   the independent-samples t-test
2   the paired-samples (or matched-samples) t-test

9.1 Types of T-Tests

This section will help you understand how to choose which t-test to use. The independent-samples t-test is used when you perform an experiment and you have obtained mean scores from two independent groups. You have measured both scores yourself, and you only have two of them (if you had three groups, you could not use a t-test). For example, you might assign students randomly to one of two treatments, and then at the end of the experiment you would test them and have two mean scores. You want to know whether one group performed better or worse than the other group.

An example of the independent-samples t-test that will be used in this chapter comes from Leow and Morgan-Short (2004). These researchers addressed the methodological question of whether doing a think-aloud while completing a task affected learners' comprehension ability and subsequent production ability. Leow and Morgan-Short had a think-aloud group and non-think-aloud group who were compared on their scores, which is why the independent-samples t-test was needed. For example, on the comprehension task, there was one mean score from the think-aloud group and one mean score from the non-think-aloud group. There were thus two mean scores to be compared, and the question was whether there was any difference between the two groups.

The **paired-samples t-test**, or **matched-samples t-test**, is used when you have performed an experiment and you have two mean scores but the groups are not independent of each other. This may be because you measured the same group at two different time periods, and you want to see if they perform better or worse at the second time period. Or maybe you measured the same group on two related measures, such as a morphosyntactic and phonological measure, and you want to see if they performed better on one type of test than the other. In these cases, because you are measuring the same people more than once, you cannot assume the groups are independent, and a paired-samples t-test takes this lack of independence into account.

Data from French and O'Brien (2008) will illustrate the paired-samples t-test in this chapter. One of French and O'Brien's main questions was whether young language learners would improve in their phonological memory over the course of an intensive English immersion. One of the phonological memory measures they used was an English non-word repetition test. The language learners were tested after one month of immersion and then after five months. There were thus two mean scores to be compared, and the question was whether there was any difference over time. Since the two means came from the same participants, however, a paired-samples t-test needed to be used.

There is actually another type of t-test called the one-sample t-test, but it is much less common in second language research data than the other two types of t-tests. The one-sample t-test is used when you have measured only one mean score, but you would like to compare this mean to some idealized mean or otherwise already known mean score. For example, let's say that you know from literature put out by your college that incoming graduate students have an average of 600 on the GRE. You want to compare the GRE scores of the group of graduate students coming into your program to this known mean to see whether your students are better or worse than the average students entering the university. A second language example would be that you measured students' reactions to a new curriculum change on a scale of 1–7. You want to know whether there is a statistical difference in the result from a purely neutral attitude (which would be 4 on this scale). You can use a one-way t-test to see whether the results are statistically different from neutral. This type of t-test will not be highlighted in this chapter but I will briefly explain how to perform it in Section 9.7.

9.1.1 Application Activity: Choosing a T-Test

Read the following descriptions of possible linguistic experiments. Decide whether you would use an independent-samples or paired-samples t-test.

1 Reading attitudes. ESL students randomly received either a scripted or a non-scripted version of a reading program. Twenty students from the scripted version were interviewed about their attitudes about reading before the semester started, and near the end of the semester. You want to know whether the students' attitudes toward reading changed over the course of the year.

Choose one: independent   paired

2 Reading ability. In the study above, you also want to know whether students using the scripted version of the reading program performed better on a reading test at the end of the year than the ESL learners who used the non-scripted version.

Choose one: independent   paired

3 Listening comprehension. One group of advanced French as a second language (FSL) users and another group of beginning FSL users performed a listening comprehension task that had two components. One component was linguistic processing ability and the other was pragmatic processing ability. You want to know whether the beginning and advanced learners differed from each other in their ability to process pragmatic information on the test.

Choose one: independent   paired

4 Pitch. A group of English–Spanish bilinguals were recorded speaking to monolingual English and monolingual Spanish speakers. Their average fundamental frequency (pitch) was recorded in each language. You want to know whether these bilinguals use a different pitch when speaking in each of their languages.

Choose one: independent   paired

5 Learning strategy instruction. A group of ESL learners in Taiwan received a class detailing how to ask higher-order questions and give more elaborated responses. The learners were measured as to the accuracy of their questions before this training, and again at the end of the course. You want to know whether the students improved in their accuracy over the course of time.

Choose one: independent   paired

6 Vocabulary learning I. Students in an English Language Institute were randomly assigned to watch one episode of either *Friends* or *Seinfeld* each day for eight weeks. A recorded interview with an unknown but same-sex and same-age native English speaker was recorded for every participant before and after the term. You want to know whether students used more slang terms at the end of the semester.

Choose one: independent   paired

7 Vocabulary Learning II. You also want to know whether there were any differences between the *Friends* and *Seinfeld* groups in the number of slang terms used in the final interview.

Choose one: independent   paired

9.2 Data Summaries and Numerical Inspection

The first data set featured in this chapter is that of Leow and Morgan-Short (2004), who wanted to know whether performing a think-aloud task while also performing a language task would affect scores on the language tasks. Leow and Morgan-Short thus had two independent groups of students, and they compared scores from the two groups using an independent-samples t-test. The SPSS file used here from Leow and Morgan-Short contains scores from two language measures—one a recognition task measure and the other a controlled written production measure.

Table 9.1 contains the mean scores and standard deviations of the two language

Table 9.1 Summary Data for the Leow and Morgan-Short (2004) Data

	Receptive post-test			Production post-test		
	Mean	sd	N	Mean	sd	N
Think-aloud	5.89	6.04	39	1.34	3.45	38
Non-think-aloud	3.92	4.31	39	1.15	3.11	39

measures from Leow and Morgan-Short (2004).[1] Consider the mean scores of the think-aloud and non-think-aloud groups on the receptive post-test. The total number of points on the test was 17, and one group scored 5.89 while the other scored 3.92. This is not a very big difference in the context of 17 points. Notice that the standard deviations are also quite large, even bigger than the mean score, indicating skewness in the data (since, if the data were normally distributed, we would expect to be able to find two to three standard deviations in either direction from the mean; we will look at the distribution visually in the next section). Notice that mean scores for the production test are quite low overall, showing very little improvement from pre-test to post-test.

Remember that summary scores when there is more than one group can be obtained in several ways. Here I used ANALYZE > DESCRIPTIVE STATISTICS > EXPLORE and put the GROUP variable into the "Factor List" box and the test variables into the "Dependent List" box.

The second data set featured in this section comes from French and O'Brien (2008). The authors examined 104 French Canadian students in Grades 4 and 5 who were taking a five-month intensive English course. These students were measured at the one-month mark and again at the end of the five months. French and O'Brien had an interest in finding out whether scores on two measures of phonological memory would improve at the end of the five months of study. Phonological memory is an ability which has been shown in some studies to predict vocabulary development and fluency in learning both an L1 and an L2. Since children's phonological memory has been shown to develop as children get older and cognitively more mature, French and O'Brien wondered if they would be able to find a statistical difference in phonological memory abilities from the beginning of the immersion experience to the end of it. They wondered whether they could find a measure of phonological memory which would not be influenced by changes in language proficiency (in other words, a measure which was language independent). Two phonological memory measures were used, one using English non-words (ENWR) and the other using Arabic non-words (ANWR). Arabic was a language unknown to the children.

Table 9.2 shows the mean scores and standard deviations on the two phonological memory measures from Time 1 to Time 2. To obtain the summary I used ANALYZE > DESCRIPTIVE STATISTICS > DESCRIPTIVES menu and put the variables ANWR_1, ANWR_2,

Table 9.2 Summary Data for the French and O'Brien (2008) Data

	Time 1			Time 2		
	Mean	sd	N	Mean	sd	N
ANWR	16.36	5.22	104	16.61	4.81	104
ENWR	16.34	4.13	104	19.44	3.74	104

---

1 Leow and Morgan-Short did in fact make both pre-test and post-test measures, but in order not to confuse the reader at this point I will include just the comparison at the post-test. Leow and Morgan-Short conducted their analysis of the groups by comparing them at the post-test point, so this analysis is in keeping with the spirit of their paper.

ENWR_1 and ENRW_2 into the "Variable(s)" box. In looking at the data it is clear that the mean score hardly changed from Time 1 to Time 2 for the Arabic non-word test, but did seem to improve for the English non-word test. It is always important to examine the data both numerically and visually before conducting any statistical summaries in order to have an intuitive sense of what is going on with your data.

9.2.1 *Visual Inspection: Boxplots*

Two good ways to visually examine data where group differences may occur are the **histogram** and the **boxplot**. Histograms have been explained in Chapter 3, so this chapter will show how to call up boxplots. I have found that boxplots are fairly rare in second language research reports. Larson-Hall and Herrington (forthcoming) report that, in looking at three years of publications in *Language Learning* and *Studies in Second Language Acquisition*, out of 68 studies which contained data that could have been visually represented with boxplots, 27 used barplots, one used a boxplot, and the rest presented no graphics. Boxplots are far superior to barplots because they provide much more data. While a barplot usually provides only a mean score, boxplots provide information about group centers, spread, and shape of a distribution. Boxplots are also a useful device for spotting outliers in your data—points which distort group means, especially in groups with small sizes.

However, because many readers may not be familiar with boxplots, I would like to discuss them in a little more detail here. Figure 9.1 shows a boxplot with a skewed distribution (on the left) and a normal distribution (on the right). The line drawn in the box marks the median, which is the point at which 50% of scores are above and 50% of scores are below. For the skewed distribution, you can see that this median is not in the middle of its box—it is somewhat off-center—while for the normal distribution the line is directly in the center of the box.

The shaded box is called the interquartile range (IQR) and contains the scores that fall within the 25th to 75th percentile. If two distributions have equal variance, the length of their boxes (or IQR) will be very similar. For these two distributions we see that the skewed distribution has a much longer box than the normal distribution, so we could not say these two distributions had equal variance.

Lines called whiskers extend out from the box. These whiskers extend to the minimum and maximum points of the data set, unless those lie beyond a point that is one and a half times the length of the box. Points that lie outside one and a half times the length of the box are identified as outliers with a circle in Figure 9.1. These whiskers show the range of the data, excluding outliers. The range is certainly much wider for the skewed distribution than for the normal distribution.

In summary, the boxplot, at a glance, gives us the following information:

- the midpoint of scores (at the median)
- the area that contains the central scores (the box) and gives a visual sense of the variance
- the minimum and maximum points, which show the range of data
- whether outliers are present
- if the distribution is symmetrical

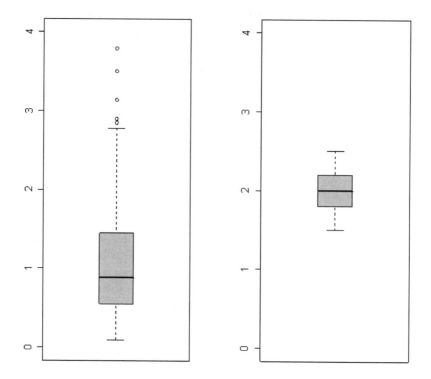

Figure 9.1 Boxplot of a skewed and a normal distribution.

9.2.2 Boxplots for an Independent-Samples T-Test (One Dependent Variable Separated by Groups)

To look at the data from the Leow and Morgan-Short (2004) experiment, we will want to look at a boxplot that shows distributions on one variable for the two different groups. Let's look then at scores on the recognition post-test. To make a boxplot, open GRAPHS > LEGACY DIALOGS > BOXPLOT. When you define the boxplot, put the dependent variable (RECPOSTSCORE) into the line labeled "Variable." Put the group variable (GROUP in this case) into the line labeled "Category Axis." Additionally, if you put your ID variable in the "Label Cases by" box, any outliers will be labeled with their ID number. These steps are shown in Figure 9.2.

Figure 9.3 shows the boxplot for the post-test scores on the recognition test. Notice that, although the median scores do not seem to be that different between the think-aloud and non-think-aloud groups, the distributions are clearly not normal because the boxes and whiskers of the boxplot are not symmetrical around the median lines. Both are positively skewed (meaning the tail extends to the right if we were looking at a histogram, or if we turned the boxplot on its side), with the majority of scores concentrated toward the lower end of the scale. In the think-aloud group, the median line is clearly non-symmetric in relation to the box. The whiskers are also non-symmetric. For the non-think-aloud group, although the median seems symmetric to

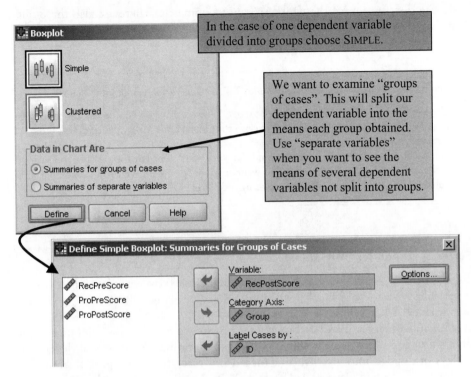

Figure 9.2 How to make a boxplot of one variable separated into groups.

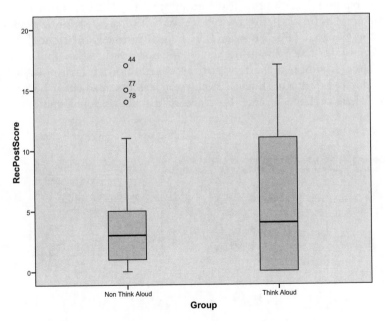

Figure 9.3 A boxplot of Leow and Morgan-Short's (2004) post-test receptive measure.

the box, the distribution of the whiskers is not symmetric. There are also three out-liers in the non-think-aloud group, identified by their subject numbers (44, 77, and 78).

Creating a Boxplot for an Independent-Samples T-Test (One Variable Split into Groups)

1   Choose GRAPHS > LEGACY DIALOGS > BOXPLOT. When a dialogue box comes up, choose SIMPLE for a one-variable boxplot, and choose the "Summaries for groups of cases" radio button. Press the DEFINE button.
2   Put the group or splitting variable in the "Category Axis" box. Put the variable you have measured in the "Variable" box. If you want to identify outliers with row names, put a column of ID numbers in the "Label cases by" box. Press OK.

9.2.3 Boxplots for a Paired-Samples T-Test (a Series of Dependent Variables)

To look at the data from the French and O'Brien (2008) study, we will want to look at four variables—scores on the ENWR and ANWR at Time 1 and Time 2. To see these variables side by side in a boxplot, choose GRAPHS > LEGACY DIALOGS > BOXPLOTS, and when the Boxplot box comes up choose SIMPLE plus "Summaries of separate variables." This choice will let you look at summaries of several dependent variables not divided into groups; thus there is no place to enter a group variable in the dialogue box seen in Figure 9.4. The "Label Cases by" box will simply label outliers in the boxplot if you put an identifier label in it (SUBJECT for the French and O'Brien data).

   The boxplot in Figure 9.5 shows the distribution of all four variables that measure phonological memory in this experiment. Notice that all of the distributions except for the English non-words at Time 2 (ENWR_2) look fairly normally distributed. There are no outliers identified. The medians for the Arabic non-word test are quite similar at Time 1 and Time 2, although the range of the distribution at Time 2 is slightly smaller than at Time 1. For the English non-word test the median at Time 2 is definitely higher than at Time 1, and the range of distribution at Time 2 is also smaller.

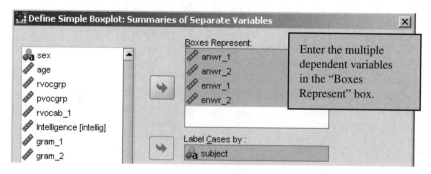

Figure 9.4 How to make a boxplot of several variables side by side (not separated into groups).

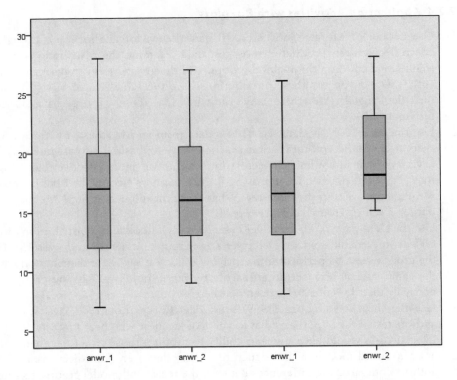

Figure 9.5 A boxplot of French and O'Brien's (2008) phonological memory measures.

Tip: What will you get if you try the other choices in the Boxplot dialogue box?

- If you choose a Clustered boxplot with "Summaries for groups of cases" you will need to have three variables: the dependent variable and *two* grouping variables, such as group membership *and* sex. You will see the results of one variable split by two different groupings.
- If you choose a Clustered boxplot with "Summaries of separate variables" you will need one categorical grouping variable and one or more dependent variables. You will see multiple dependent variables separated by one independent variable such as group membership.

Creating a Boxplot for a Paired-Samples T-Test (Several Variables Side by Side)

1 Choose Graphs > Legacy Dialogs > Boxplot. When a dialogue box comes up, choose Simple, and choose the "Summaries of separate variables" radio button. Press the Define button.
2 Put the dependent variables in the "Boxes represent" box. If you want to identify outliers with row names, put a column of ID numbers in the "Label cases by" box. Press OK.

9.2.4 Application Activities with Boxplots

1   Use Leow and Morgan-Short's (2004) data (LeowMorganShort.sav). Using the controlled written production post-test data, examine the distributions of the think-aloud and non-think-aloud groups. Did the groups seem to perform differently? Would you say these distributions have the same size of box (the interquartile range)? Are there any outliers? Do these groups have normal distribution?

2   Use the Yates2003.sav data set. This is data from an MA thesis by Yates which examined whether pronunciation practice that emphasized suprasegmentals (by having participants mimic the actors in *Seinfeld*) was more effective than laboratory segmental practice in improving English learners' accent. Did the lab group seem to improve over the semester? What about the mimicry group? Are there any outliers? Which group has more spread?

3   Use the DeKeyser (2000) data (DeKeyser2000.sav). Look at the distribution of the GJT score variable split by DeKeyser's age groups (under 15 and over 15). Did the groups seem to perform differently? Would you say these distributions have the same size of box (the interquartile range)? Would you say the groups are normally distributed? Are there any outliers?

4   Use the Inagaki and Long (1999) t-test data (InagakiLong1999.Ttest.sav). The authors tested the hypothesis that learners of Japanese who heard recasts of target L2 structures would have a greater ability to produce those structures than learners who heard models of the structures. These data were for adjectives, and the authors compared the differences between the recast and model groups. Examine the distributions. Did the groups seem to perform differently? Would you say these distributions have the same size of box (the interquartile range)? Are there any outliers? Do these groups have normal distribution?

5   Use the Larson-Hall and Connell (2005) data (LarsonHall.Forgotten.sav). These are data from an experiment with Japanese speakers who lived in the US when they were children (early), as adults (late), or never (non), or were native speakers of English (NS). I had them produce words beginning in /r/ and /l/ and then judges judged whether they thought they heard an /r/ or /l/. Let's look at their judged accent on words beginning with /r/ (AccentR) and /l/ (AccentL), splitting the data into the four groups according to the Status variable (hint: this case is different from the others; see the tip in Section 9.2.3). In this case a higher accent score is more native-like. Did the learners in general produce words beginning with /r/ or /l/ better? Would you say the variances are equal across the groups? Which boxplots represent approximately normal distributions?

9.3 Assumptions of T-Tests

There are four main assumptions for t-tests:

1   The dependent variable should be measured in interval-level measurements.
2   The data should be independent.
3   The data should be normally distributed.
4   Groups should have equal variances.

The first two assumptions are covered well in most books about general research design (Hatch & Lazaraton, 1991; Mackey & Gass, 2005; Porte, 2002) and will not be discussed further in this chapter. The last two assumptions are ones that can be examined through the use of statistical software.

The assumption of equal variances is very often violated in second language research studies if a group of native speakers versus non-native speakers is included, since the native speakers usually have a far smaller variance than the group of non-native speakers. Fortunately, for t-tests there are estimators that can take unequal variances into account.

Although there are statistical tests to check for both the normality of your data and equal variances, Wilcox (2003) notes that a basic problem with such tests is that these tests "do not always have enough power to detect situations where the assumption should be discarded" (p. 241). He does not recommend using them. Table 9.3 shows the assumptions for each test, and alternatives that can be used if the assumptions do not hold.

9.3.1 Adjustments for Multiple T-Tests (Bonferroni, FDR)

Another type of assumption associated with doing any statistical testing is the alpha level (a), the level of tolerance for Type I errors. Remember that a Type I error is a false positive—when you mistakenly conclude there was an effect for a treatment when there in fact was not one. In our field alpha is generally set to $a = .05$ (although I have argued

Table 9.3 Assumptions for T-Tests

Meeting t-test assumptions		Independent-samples t-test	Paired-samples t-test
1 Normal distribution of data	Required?	Yes	Yes
	How to test assumption?	Examine boxplots, plot normal curve over histogram; use Q-Q plots (see Chapter 3)	Examine boxplots, plot normal curve over histogram; use Q-Q plots (see Chapter 3)
	What if assumption not met?	1) Use non-parametric Mann–Whitney U test; 2) use a robust method with means trimming and/or bootstrapping	1) Use non-parametric Wilcoxon signed ranks test; 2) use a robust method with means trimming and/or bootstrapping
2 Equal variances	Required?	Yes; homogeneity especially important if group size unequal (Maxwell & Delaney, 2004)	Assumed to be true for paired-samples
	How to test assumption?*	Examine boxplots; look at summary statistics for variance (see Chapter 3)	
	What if assumption not met?	1) Choose Welch procedure readout (equal variances not assumed); 2) use robust methods	

* Note that SPSS provides a test called Levene's test for the independent-samples t-test which is supposed to check whether the variance of two groups is similar enough to satisfy this requirement. The problem is that, if sample sizes are small, large differences in variances may not be seen as problematic, while, if sample sizes are large, even small differences in variances may be counted as a problem (Clark-Carter, 2005).

that it may be better to set it to $a = .10$ in Section 4.1.3). In many cases, however, researchers do not perform only *one* statistical test; in fact, they perform many! This is often the case when t-tests are used. For example, Leow and Morgan-Short (2004) looked at t-tests comparing their think-aloud and non-think-aloud groups on three different language measures, and then, because they did pre-tests and post-tests, they also did comparisons across time.

The problem with conducting multiple statistical tests is that the possibility of a false positive increases. In other words, each time you conduct a statistical test such as a t-test, you have a 5% chance of getting a false positive error. If you have ten t-tests, then we can imagine that this 5% chance gets added together ten times to give a 50% chance overall that you will get a false positive somewhere in your batch of tests (the truth of what exactly this chance is is a little more complicated, but it's close enough for us).

One way to address this conceptual problem is with a **Bonferroni adjustment**. A Bonferroni adjustment corrects the problem by decreasing the acceptable alpha rate depending on how many tests are done. Bonferroni found that the Type I error rate (the false positive) is less than or equal to the number of comparisons done, multiplied by the chosen alpha level. Again, for ten t-tests at an $a = .05$, this would be $10 \times .05 = .50$. To correct for this increase in false positive error, Bonferroni advised the researcher to divide the desired alpha level by the number of comparisons. In other words, you're distributing the chance of finding a false positive equally over all of your t-tests. Thus, if you had ten t-tests, you should not consider the t-test to be statistical unless the alpha level was less than $a = .05/10 = .005$.

Herrington (2002) points out that this approach is much too conservative when many comparisons are being made. Herrington advocates using Benjamini and Hochberg's (1995) **False Detection Rate (FDR)** method. FDR has more power than the Bonferroni adjustment, as it seeks only to control the proportion of errors that are found in tests where the null hypothesis was rejected, but keeps the overall number of decision errors at the 5% alpha level. To calculate the FDR you can use the R statistical program (SPSS will not calculate it presently). Appendix B contains the commands that are necessary to run the FDR. Just open up R to see the R Console window and type in the lines exactly as you see them in Appendix B on the left side of the table, except for lines one and three, where you will insert your own values. In line one you will put the original p-values that you received after conducting your statistical test. When you type the third-to-last line, "p.cutoff," this will show the cut-off level, at or below which p-values will be statistical. When you type the final "p.sig" you will see listed only those original p-values which are statistical.

9.3.2 Data Formatting for Tests of Group Differences (the "Wide Form" and "Long Form")

Up to this point in the book we haven't worried about how your data were set up because there really wasn't anything to worry about—variables were all entered into the SPSS Data Editor with the variables in columns and the rows representing individual cases (see Section 1.1.2). However, with the advent of tests which examine group differences (where you need to divide the data into groups) you'll need to be aware that you may have to reformat in order to have your data in the correct format.

There are two basic ways that you might have your data set up in a spreadsheet:

1   Data is split so that the results for each group for each variable are found in different columns. We'll call this the "wide" format because the columns are shorter than they would be in the "long" format, thus making the whole file wider (see Table 9.4).

2   All the data for one variable is in one column, and there is another column that codes the data as to which group it belongs to. Everitt and Dunn (2001) call this the "long" form because the columns will be longer in this case (see Table 9.4).

Table 9.4 is an example of the data in the wide format. Let's say we are looking at the correlation between test scores of children and adults on regular and irregular verbs. We would have one column that represented the scores of the children on regular verbs, another column containing the scores of adults on the regular verbs, another one with scores of children on irregular verbs, and finally a column with scores of adults in irregular verbs. In the wide format, we do not need any indexing (or categorical) variables, because the groups are already split by those variables (adult versus child and regular versus irregular verbs in this case) into separate columns.

This data can be put into the long format (see Table 9.5). We put all of the irregular verb scores together, in the same order (let's say children first and then adults). Then the group membership column indexes the scores on both verb columns so we know which group the data came from, children (=1) or adults (=2). If it were necessary for our analysis, we could even reduce this further, so that all of the interval data were in one column, and the group column would then have to index both adult versus child and regular versus irregular (say, with a scheme such as 1 = child, regular; 2 = adult, regular; 3 = child, irregular; 4 = adult, irregular).

Table 9.4 Data in the "Wide" Format

ChildRegVerb	AdultRegVerb	Child/IrregVerb	Adult/IrregVerb
14.00	13.00	14.00	15.00
13.00	15.00	15.00	15.00
15.00	15.00	11.00	15.00
15.00	13.00	15.00	14.00
13.00	8.00	14.00	15.00
8.00	13.00	14.00	15.00
13.00	13.00	14.00	13.00

Table 9.5 Data in the "Long" Format

RegularVerbs	IrregularVerbs	Group
15.00	11.00	1.00
14.00	13.00	1.00
12.00	8.00	1.00
15.00	13.00	2.00
14.00	9.00	2.00
15.00	15.00	2.00
11.00	6.00	2.00

Although there is a special function that is supposed to be able to help you switch from wide to long format in SPSS (DATA > RESTRUCTURE; then the "Restructure Data Wizard" opens), I have yet to understand how to use it, so I cannot recommend it! I have found the easiest way to set up my data in the long format is just to do it by cutting and pasting, and then creating the categorical group variable myself.

For t-tests (and for ANOVA analysis in the chapters to follow), the data should be arranged in the "long form." This means that, if you have entered your data in the "wide" format, you'll need to combine columns and also make up a separate variable that indexes groups. If you don't have a categorical group variable, you will not be able to run a t-test or an ANOVA using SPSS commands.

9.4 The Independent-Samples T-Test

Leow and Morgan-Short (2004) tested 77 learners of Spanish on their knowledge of the Spanish impersonal imperative using two receptive tasks (one reading passage comprehension and the other recognition of correct imperative forms) and one productive task (produce the correct imperative forms). The learners were divided into a think-aloud group (n = 38) and a non-think-aloud group (n = 39). The authors essentially performed three independent-samples t-tests in order to see whether there were any differences in scores on each of the three tasks depending on which group the learners belonged to. In this analysis we will consider only the receptive recognition task and the productive task (not the reading comprehension task).

We have seen previously in the chapter that the data may not be normally distributed. Figure 9.6 shows boxplots of both the recognition and the productive task side by side. Both tasks had 17 points. Figure 9.6 shows that scores on the productive task were quite low overall, and heavily skewed. Scores on the receptive task were more varied, but the distributions are still somewhat skewed (since the whiskers are not symmetric around the boxes). There are some outliers in each task, especially for the very positively skewed production task. In summary, neither one of these tasks has perfectly normally distributed data, but to illustrate how t-tests work I will analyze the receptive task with an independent-samples t-test.[2] You can see how the productive task is analyzed with a non-parametric test in Chapter 14.

As regards the assumption of homogeneity of variance, the boxplots indicate that the variances are different in the receptive task because the width of the boxes is highly different. Also, numerically the variances are quite different. The variance is just the standard deviation squared, and the standard deviation (found in Table 9.1) for the think-aloud group was about 6, making its variance around 36, while the standard deviation for the non-think-aloud group was about 4, making its variance around 16. Thus, numerically and visually we can see that the two groups in the receptive task do not have homogeneous variances. However, we do have a procedure in the t-test to take unequal variances into account, so we will proceed with the analysis.

---

2 Leow and Morgan-Short (2004) noted that neither of these variables was normally distributed and in fact analyzed both of them with the non-parametric Mann–Whitney U test.

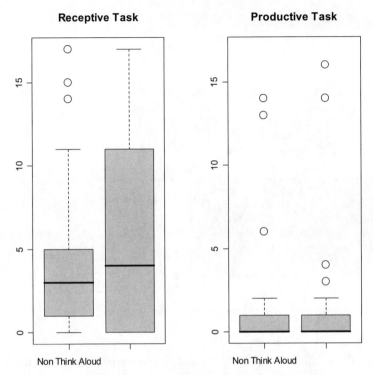

Figure 9.6 Boxplots of Leow and Morgan-Short's (2004) variables.

9.4.1 Performing an Independent-Samples T-Test

To perform an independent-samples t-test, go to ANALYZE > COMPARE MEANS > INDEPENDENT SAMPLES T-TEST (see Figure 9.7). In the dialogue box, move the dependent variable (RECPOSTSCORE in this case) into the "Test Variable(s)" box. Move the categorical grouping variable (GROUP in this data) into the "Grouping Variable" box. You should then be able to click on the DEFINE GROUPS button. If you can't, just click on your categorical variable to get it to highlight, and then the DEFINE GROUPS button should work.

Tip: In order to "Define groups" correctly you will need to use a variable with categories specified by numbers, not names (SPSS "strings"). If you have only strings you will need to recode your variable (Section 1.2.3). It is, however, perfectly valid to have *values* for your numbered categorical variables. These can be entered in the "Variable View" tab, in the Values column. These will describe the variable while still keeping it classified as numerical in SPSS.

The reason you have to define groups in the "Independent Samples T-Test" dialogue box is that you may want to perform t-tests among different pairs of groupings. For

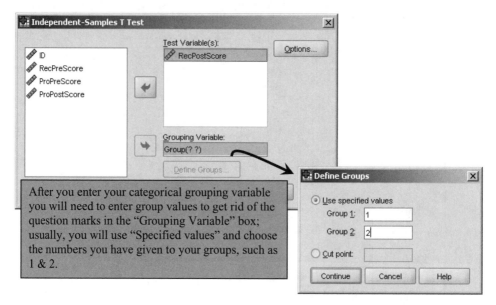

Figure 9.7 Performing an independent-samples t-test in SPSS.

example, if you had three different groups but decided to use t-tests to test them, you could do this by specifying that Group 1 = 1 and Group 2 = 2 the first time you run it, then Group 1 = 1 and Group 2 = 3 the second time you run it, and finally Group 1 = 2 and Group 2 = 3 the last time you run it.

Notice that the data for the independent-samples t-test need to be in the "long" format. That is, you must have one interval-level variable which contains data for both groups, and then a categorical grouping variable.

There are two tables produced as the output to this test, and these are seen in Table 9.6. The first table, titled "Group Statistics," shows descriptive statistics. You should always check descriptive statistics first to get a sense of your data and make sure the N is correct. However, I have already commented on numerical summaries for this data so we will not look at this any further.

The second table in the output is labeled "Independent Samples Test," and this table has the results of *two* different tests, and *two* columns labeled Sig. Be sure not to interpret the first significance level as the t-test! The first test is Levene's test for equality of variances. You can see that the Independent Samples Test table has two rows—one if you assume that variances are equal, and another if you assume they are not. The Levene's test for equality of variances will indicate whether you can use the line labeled "Equal variances assumed." If the p-value is *greater* than .05, you can use the first line; if not, use the second line.

The output in Table 9.6 shows that the p-value for the Levene's test is $p = .002$, which means that the variances of the two groups are not equal. In this case, Levene's result lined up with our intuitions gained from looking at the boxplots and the numerical summaries, namely that in the receptive task the group variances were not equal. You should be aware that there can be problems of power in testing assumptions of

Table 9.6 Output from the Independent-Samples T-Test

Group Statistics

	Group	N	Mean	Std. Deviation	Std. Error Mean
RecPostScore	Non Think Aloud	39	3.92	4.313	.691
	Think Aloud	38	5.89	6.044	.980

Independent Samples Test

		Levene's Test for Equality of Variances		t-test for Equality of Means					95% Confidence Interval of the Difference	
		F	Sig.	t	df	Sig. (2-tailed)	Mean Difference	Std. Error Difference	Lower	Upper
RecPostScore	Equal variances assumed	10.565	.002	-1.651	75	.103	-1.972	1.194	-4.350	.407
	Equal variances not assumed			-1.644	66.808	.105	-1.972	1.199	-4.365	.422

Note: The *p*-value of Levene's test is *lower* than $a=.05$, so we cannot assume equal variances.

parametric tests as the Levene's test does (Wilcox, 2003), so it may be safer to always use the second line with equal variances *not* assumed, which is also called Welch's procedure.

Tip: Because it might seem counterintuitive to look for a significance value *greater than* 0.05 for the Levene's test, here's an explanation. For the Levene's test, the null hypothesis is that the variances are equal. If the *p*-value is less than $p = 0.05$, you reject this hypothesis. Therefore you will assume that the variances are not equal.

The results of the t-test for independent samples is found under the part of the table labeled "t-test for Equality of Means." However, we can get all of the important information out of the 95% CI for the difference between groups. The CI ranges from −4.37 to .42. This means that the actual difference in scores between the groups will lie, with 95% confidence, in this interval. Since zero is found in this confidence interval, we know that we should not reject the null hypothesis. We also see that the interval is wide and so we do not have a precise estimate of the mean difference between groups.

Leow and Morgan-Short concluded that doing a think-aloud concurrent with a language task made no difference to participants' scores. However, remember that failing to reject the null hypothesis (not finding a *p*-value under 0.05) does not necessarily mean there was no difference between groups. In fact, I calculate (with $n = 38$ and $d = .46$) that the power for this test was only .51. In other words, there was only about a 50% chance that, even if differences between groups existed, the t-test would find it. To attain 80% power with the same effect size, 76 participants in each group would need to be tested. However, Leow reports that follow-up studies confirmed the original findings as well.

Performing an Independent-Samples T-Test

1   Choose Analyze > Compare Means > Independent-Samples T-Test. When a dialogue box comes up, put your independent variables into "Test Variable(s)" box. Put your categorical grouping variable in the "Grouping Variable" box.

2   Define which two groups you will compare in the Define groups button. If you have only two groups, you will just put "1" and "2" in these boxes (if those are the labels you have used in the "Data View").

9.4.2 Effect Sizes for Independent-Samples T-Tests

Unfortunately, at this time SPSS does not calculate the effect size for independent-samples t-tests. In some cases you can find a quick calculation using the internet, but first I need to explain the idea of a standardizer so you can know what your best choice for an effect size is.

Cohen's index of effect size for independent samples called d can be calculated as $d = \dfrac{\bar{X}_1 - \bar{X}_2}{\sigma}$, where $\sigma =$ the appropriate standardizer, selected from the following choices (Olejnik & Algina, 2000, p. 245):

    A. The standard deviation of one of the groups, perhaps most typically the control group (Glass, 1976)

    B. The pooled standard deviation of [only the groups] being compared (Cohen, 1988)

    C. The pooled standard deviation [of all the groups] in the design (Hedges, 1981)

If the groups do not have equal variances, then A is considered the best choice for a standardizer (Olejnik & Algina, 2000). This variant is sometimes called Glass's δ (delta) because Glass (1976) proposed this method. Leow and Morgan-Short's (2004) receptive task did not have equal variances, so we will use the standard deviation of the non-think-aloud group as the standardizer. When you have to pick one group's standard deviation as the standardizer, Olejnik and Algina note that the control group, or the group least affected by the experiment, should be the one used as the standardizer. This makes calculation of the effect size for the receptive task rather easy: $d = \dfrac{3.92 - 5.89}{4.31} = -.46$ (we can ignore the negative sign as it is an arbitrary result of which mean is put first). This effect size is medium, according to Cohen (1992) (see Table 4.7 for a list of Cohen's guidelines for effect size).

If the groups do have equal variances, then with only two mean scores there is no difference between choices B and C, and a way to save time is to use an online calculator. I found one at web.uccs.edu/lbecker/Psy590/escalc3.htm. This calculator lets you compute Cohen's d if you know the means and standard deviations of two groups. Another shortcut is to use the equation found in Table 4.7, which requires only the t-value and the degrees of freedom: $d = \dfrac{2t}{\sqrt{df_{err}}}$.

For Leow and Morgan-Short's productive task, here are the summary statistics:

	mean	sd	0%	25%	50%	75%	100%	n
Non Think Aloud	1.153846	3.108041	0	0	0	1	14	39
Think Aloud	1.342105	3.450627	0	0	0	1	16	38

An effect size calculator online returns $d = -0.06$, which is a negligible effect size.

The calculation for the pooled standard deviation for any number of groups, for anyone without online access, is $S_{pooled} = \sqrt{\dfrac{(n_1 - 1)S_1^2 + \cdots + (n_J - 1)S_J^2}{(n_1 - 1) + \cdots + (n_J - 1)}}$.

For Leow and Morgan-Short's productive task, the calculation for the standardizer (the denominator for d) is

$$S_{pooled} = \sqrt{\frac{(39 - 1)3.11^2 + (38 - 1)3.45^2}{(39 - 1) + (38 + 1)}} = \sqrt{\frac{367.54 + 440.39}{75}} = 3.28.$$

With the correct standardizer we can now calculate the effect size for the production task:

$$d = \frac{1.15 - 1.34}{3.28} = -.06.$$

9.4.3 Application Activities for the Independent-Samples T-Test

1 Larson-Hall (2008) examined 200 Japanese college learners of English. They were divided into two groups, one called early learners (people who started studying English before junior high school) and the other later learners (people who only started studying English in junior high). Open the Larsonhall2008.sav file and see whether the groups (divided by the variable ERLYEXP) were different in their language learning aptitude (APTSCORE), use of English in everyday life (USEENG), scores on a grammaticality judgment test (GJT), and scores on a phonemic listening test (PRONS-COR). Be sure to explore whether the data are normally distributed and have equal variances. Report results for all variables regardless of meeting assumptions: 95% CIs, means, standard deviations, Ns, hypothesis testing results (t- and p-values), and effect sizes. Discuss what the numbers mean.

2 Use the Inagaki and Long (1999) t-test data (InagakiLong1999.Ttest.sav). Test the hypothesis that learners of Japanese who heard recasts of adjectives would have a greater ability to produce this structure than learners who heard models of the structure. Remind yourself of whether this data is normally distributed and has equal variances by looking back to your answer on Activity 4 in Section 9.2.4. Report results regardless of meeting assumptions: 95% CIs, means, standard deviations, Ns, hypothesis testing results (t- and p-values), and effect sizes. Discuss what the numbers mean.

9.5 The Paired-Samples T-Test

French and O'Brien (2008) investigated several questions, one of which was the question of whether measures of phonological memory improve over time as learners grow more proficient in a second language. Two tests of phonological memory, one

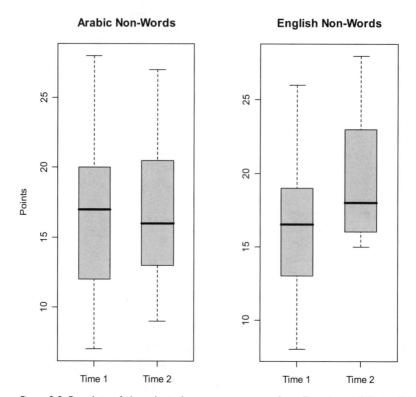

Figure 9.8 Boxplots of phonological memory measures from French and O'Brien (2008).

involving nonsense words which resembled English phonologically (the ENWR test) and one involving real words from Arabic (ANWR), were given to French Canadian children in Grades 4 and 5 learning English. The children had entered five months of intensive English immersion in school, and these tests of phonological memory were administered after one month and then after five months of study. Thus the learners in this study were given the same tests at two different time periods. French and O'Brien conducted paired-samples t-tests for the ENWR and the ANWR to see whether the participants improved from Time 1 to Time 2. Because the same children were tested at both time periods, an independent-samples t-test cannot be used. We expect that there will be some correlation between the two samples, and a paired-samples t-test explicitly takes this into account.

Figure 9.8 shows a boxplot of the distribution of scores on both tests, which contained 40 items each. There are no outliers in the data and distributions look fairly normal (Time 2 for the ENWR is slightly positively skewed). The sizes of the boxes are fairly similar so we assume variances are approximately equal as well (numeric reports of the standard deviations in Table 9.2 also confirm this).

9.5.1 Performing a Paired-Samples T-Test in SPSS

To perform a paired-samples t-test, go to ANALYZE > COMPARE MEANS > PAIRED SAMPLES T-TEST. You will see the dialogue box that is shown in Figure 9.9 (this box looked

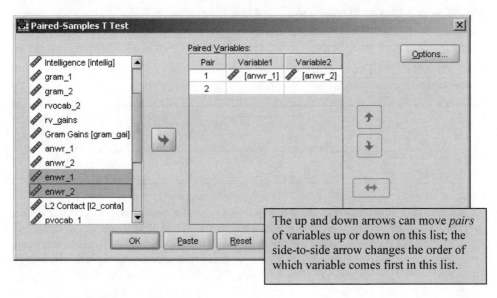

The up and down arrows can move *pairs* of variables up or down on this list; the side-to-side arrow changes the order of which variable comes first in this list.

Figure 9.9 Performing a paired-sample t-test.

slightly different before SPSS Version 16.0; specifically, it did not have two columns to show the pairing in the "Paired Variables" box). Because the paired-samples test must have a pairing of variables, the first variable you click from the list of variables on the left will go into the area labeled "Variable1" and the second will go into the area labeled "Variable2" (in previous versions of SPSS you needed to hold down the Ctrl key to select two variables at once to move to the right; you don't need to do that now).

Note that because I am comparing variables measured at two different times, and they are both in separate columns, I can do the paired-samples t-test in SPSS with no further modification to the data. The data as I received it from French and O'Brien is the "wide" form of the data because the scores from Time 1 are in their own column and separate from the scores at Time 2.

The output from this test is shown in Table 9.7. The first box of the output gives summary statistics (mean, standard deviation, sample size) which we saw previously in Table 9.2, so that table is not reproduced here. The second table of the output is labeled "Paired Samples Correlations" and shows the strength of the correlation between the two measures. Remember that the paired t-test assumes that the variables will be correlated, and that it could be problematic if they are not. You will want to examine the correlation assumption in this table, but don't be confused— this is not the t-test itself! Here we see there are very large correlations between both sets of variables. Notice that, if you have given the variable a label (usually longer and more descriptive than your variable name), it will be shown in the output as it is here.

The third table of the output (the lower table shown in Table 9.7) contains the results of the paired-samples t-test. The first column is the mean difference between the two scores. If it is quite small in terms of the scale used, you would not expect to

Table 9.7 Output from the Paired-Samples T-Test

Paired Samples Correlations

		N	Correlation	Sig.
Pair 1	Arabic Time 1 & Arabic Time 2	104	.965	.000
Pair 2	English Time 1 & English Time 2	104	.846	.000

Paired Samples Test

		Paired Differences							
					95% Confidence Interval of the Difference				
		Mean	Std. Deviation	Std. Error Mean	Lower	Upper	t	df	Sig. (2-tailed)
Pair 1	Arabic Time 1 - Arabic Time 2	-.250	1.392	.136	-.521	.021	-1.832	103	.070
Pair 2	English Time 1 - English Time 2	-3.106	2.216	.217	-3.537	-2.675	-14.292	103	.000

see a statistical difference for the *t*-test. Looking at the confidence intervals, we see that the 95% CI for the mean difference between the ANWR at Time 1 and Time 2 is −.52, .02. This just barely goes through zero, but means that the difference between mean scores could be as large as .52 or as small as zero (or go .02 in the other direction) with 95% confidence. For a 40-point test this is not a wide CI but it is quite close to zero. If we just considered the *p*-value of *p* = 0.07, we might argue that we could reject the null hypothesis that there was no difference between measurements, but the CI argues for the differences being quite small. On the other hand, the differences between mean scores for Time 1 and Time 2 for the ENWR are larger. The CI is −3.53, −2.68, meaning that the differences between groups might be as large as three and a half points or as small as about two and a half points, with 95% confidence. This is much further from zero than the difference between Time 1 and Time 2 on the ANWR, and we can conclude that the participants statistically improved in their performance on the ENWR over time. French and O'Brien concluded that scores on the ENWR improved because the participants were becoming more proficient at English, but the fact that scores did not improve statistically on the ANWR shows it is a language-independent measure of phonological memory (for people who do not know Arabic!).

Notice that for both the paired-samples and the independent-samples *t*-test, SPSS gives confidence intervals and significance levels for the two-tailed case; there is no way to specify the one-way hypothesis using the drop-down menus. If you want to test a one-tailed hypothesis (meaning you want to see only if there are differences in one direction), you could report a *p*-value that has been divided by 2. However, this is not true for the 95% CI; the calculated two-tailed CI cannot be halved to get the appropriate one-tailed CI.

Performing a Paired-Samples T-Test in SPSS

On the drop-down menu, choose ANALYZE > COMPARE MEANS > PAIRED-SAMPLES T-TEST. When a dialogue box comes up, move your variables to the box labeled "Paired Variables." Make sure the pairs of variables are put together in the way you want to test. Any number of paired groups can be selected.

9.5.2 Effect Sizes for Paired-Samples T-Tests

To calculate effect size for paired-sample t-tests, Volker (2006) notes that for descriptive purposes in published research it is acceptable to use the same calculations as were used for the independent-samples t-test (Section 9.4.2). Here are the summary statistics for the ANWR and ENWR tests:

	mean	sd	n
ANWR_1	16.35577	5.215582	104
ANWR_2	16.60577	4.807798	104
ENWR_1	16.33654	4.125720	104
ENWR 2	19.44231	3.736014	104

Entering the means and standard deviations into an online calculator (http://web.uccs.edu/lbecker/Psy590/escalc3.htm) returns a $d = -0.05$ for the ANWR and $d = -0.8$ for the ENWR. The ENWR has a large effect size but the effect size for the ANWR is negligible.

9.5.3 Application Activities with Paired-Samples T-Tests

1   French and O'Brien (2008) also performed paired-samples t-tests to see whether the participants in the study improved on receptive vocabulary (RVOCAB), productive vocabulary (PVOCAB), and grammar measures (GRAM). Maximum points were 60 on both vocabulary measures and 45 on the grammar measure. Perform three t-tests to investigate whether the schoolchildren made progress on these measures over the course of their English immersion. First comment on the distribution of the data by using boxplots; then report on the t-tests no matter whether distributions are normal or not. Use the French and O'Brien grammar.sav file.

2   Yates (2003). You examined boxplots from this data in Section 9.2.4. Compare the accent scores of the lab group before and after training, and also the mimicry group before and after training. Be sure to look at effect sizes. How might you explain the results?

3   The Larson-Hall and Connell (2005) data (LarsonHall.Forgotten.sav) that you examined in Section 9.2.4 can be analyzed with a paired-samples t-test. A paired-samples t-test will answer the question of whether the participants performed the same way with their accent on words beginning with /r/ (ACCENTR) and /l/ (ACCENTL). Be sure to look at effect sizes. What are the results?

9.6 Reporting T-Test Results

For a parametric t-test, you will want to make sure to report on the appropriateness of assuming normality and homogeneity of variances in order to do a parametric test. You will want to report a confidence interval for the mean difference, a t-value, associated p-value, the N, the mean and standard deviations of the groups, and effect sizes along with an interpretation of their magnitude.

A report on the study we examined in Section 9.4 by Leow and Morgan-Short (2004) might say:

> An independent-samples t-test was conducted to see if the think-aloud (TA) and non-think-aloud (NTA) groups differed on the receptive post-test. An examination of the data indicated that these data are not normally distributed—some data was skewed and contained outliers, and variances were unequal for the groups.[3] For the test (TA mean = 5.89, sd = 6.04, N = 38; NTA mean = 3.92, sd = 4.31, N = 39) the 95% CI for the difference in means is −4.37, 0.42 (t = −1.64, p = .11, df = 66.8 using Welch's procedure). The null hypothesis that the true difference in means was zero could not be rejected, although there was a medium effect size for the difference between groups (d = .46).

Another approach to reporting might be to list all of the details in a table and then comment briefly on them. This might be especially useful if you have a large number of variables to report on. Doing this for the paired-samples t-test from French and O'Brien (2008), I would say:

> The difference in the Arabic non-word repetition task (ANWR) and the English non-word repetition task (ENWR) from Time 1 (one month) and Time 2 (five months) was tested with a paired-samples t-test. Results are shown in Table 9.8. Results show a large effect size and a statistical effect for difference between testing times in the ENWR, but negligible effect sizes and a non-statistical effect for differences in the ANWR.

Table 9.8 Summary Results from French and O'Brien (2008) for ANWR and ENWR

Variable	95% CI	Mean Time 1 (SD1)	Mean Time 2 (SD2)	N1/N2	t-value	p-value	Effect size
ANWR	−.52, .02	16.36 (5.22)	16.61 (4.81)	104	−1.83	p=.07	d=.05
ENWR	−3.54, −2.68	16.34 (4.13)	19.44 (3.74)	104	−14.29	p<.0005	d=.8

9.7 Performing a One-Sample T-Test (Advanced Topic)

The one-sample t-test is not used as frequently as the independent-samples or paired-samples t-test in second language research, but as it could from time to time be useful I will outline briefly here how it can be done.

9.7.1 When to Use a One-Sample T-Test

To determine whether some obtained value is statistically different from a neutral value, from a previously published population mean, from zero, or from some other externally dictated mean score, a one-sample t-test can be used. The one-sample t-test

---

3 For this reason, in their actual research paper Leow and Morgan-Short used a non-parametric test for this comparison, but just to illustrate the process I will report the results of the parametric test.

asks whether the mean score from the sample you have tested is statistically different from the externally determined mean score you are using to compare it to. I use Torres's (2004) study as an example of how the one-sample t-test works (although it is possible that polytomous IRT methods, which are beyond the scope of this book, would be a better way to analyze these data).

Torres gave a 34-item five-point Likert scale questionnaire to 102 adult ESL learners to determine whether the students preferred native or non-native teachers. Torres wanted to know whether the learners would prefer one type of teacher over the other both in general and in specific skill areas such as pronunciation and grammar. In the scale a 5 indicated a preference for native speaking English teachers (NEST), a 1 indicated a preference for non-native English speaking teachers (non-NEST), and a 3 indicated no particular preference. In order to test whether the mean scores that were recorded were substantially different from a mean of 3, a one-sample t-test was conducted for each of the areas of investigation.

9.7.2 Performing a One-Sample T-Test

We will examine the question of whether ESL learners preferred NESTs or non-NESTs in the areas of culture and speaking in this example. I use the Torres.sav file. For a one-sample t-test choose ANALYZE > COMPARE MEANS > ONE-SAMPLE T-TEST, and the dialogue box in Figure 9.10 will appear.

When you call for the one-sample t-test, the output shown in Table 9.9 will appear in the SPSS Viewer.

The first thing we notice is that, for culture, the mean score is 3.5, meaning there is some preference for NESTs, but the standard deviation is fairly large as well. For speaking, the mean score is even more towards the neutral level, and the standard deviation is even higher.

The results of the t-test are found in the "One-Sample Test" table (the second in the output). This output looks very similar to that for the other t-tests found in this chapter, so I will not elaborate on the results except to note that both t-tests are statistical so we may reject the null hypothesis that preferences in culture and speaking do not significantly differ from the neutral value. However, note that we have large Ns

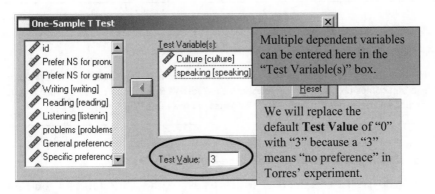

Figure 9.10 Performing a one-sample t-test.

Table 9.9 Output from a One-Way T-Test

One-Sample Statistics

	N	Mean	Std. Deviation	Std. Error Mean
Culture	102	3.5229	.76862	.07610
speaking	102	3.3039	.94700	.09377

One-Sample Test

	Test Value = 3					
					95% Confidence Interval of the Difference	
	t	df	Sig. (2-tailed)	Mean Difference	Lower	Upper
Culture	6.870	101	.000	.52288	.3719	.6738
speaking	3.241	101	.002	.30392	.1179	.4899

The first table contains summary statistics.

here, so the fact that the tests are statistical is not surprising. We will need to look at effect size to get an idea of how important the difference from the neutral score is.

Effect sizes can be determined similarly to how they were for the other two types of t-tests; basically just take the mean difference listed in the output (because this already shows the external mean subtracted from the group mean) and divide by the standard deviation of the group you have, just as you would do if the variances were not equal (see Section 9.4.2 if you do not remember this). The effect size for culture is thus 0.52/0.77 = 0.67, and the effect size for speaking is 0.30/0.95 = 0.32. These are small to medium effect sizes, with the effect for culture being bigger than the one for speaking.

> Tip: If we had had a directional alternative hypothesis (also called a one-tailed test), such as "The true mean is greater than 3," then we would have had to divide the p-value that SPSS returns by 2 in order to obtain the correct p-value result.

> **Performing a One-Sample T-Test in SPSS**
>
> On the drop-down menu, choose ANALYZE > COMPARE MEANS > ONE-SAMPLE T-TEST. When a dialogue box comes up, put your variables into the "Test Variable(s)" box. Also be sure to put the correct externally determined comparison mean in the "Test Value" box.

9.7.3 Application Activities for the One-Sample T-Test

1   Torres (2004) data. Use the data set Torres.sav. Although technically you should not use a parametric test because the data are not normally distributed, calculate

one-sample t-tests for the variables of LISTENING and READING using a one-sample parametric test. Comment on the size of the effect sizes.

2   Dewaele and Pavlenko Bilingual Emotions Questionnaire (2001–2003) data. Use the BEQ.sav data set. Test the hypothesis that the people who took the online Bilingualism and Emotions Questionnaire will rate themselves as fully fluent in speaking, comprehension, reading, and writing in their first language (ratings on the variable range from 1, least proficient, to 5, fully fluent). Use the variables L1SPEAK, L1COMP, L1READ, and L1WRITE. Calculate effect sizes.

9.8 Summary of T-Tests

In this chapter we started out by noting that t-tests are used when you have exactly two mean scores to compare, and your research question is whether the two groups those mean scores come from are different from each other (or whether the same group performed differently at different times or on different tests). One good way for visually examining the distribution of scores from two groups is to use a boxplot. Boxplots provide more information than barplots and are able to be a quick visual check on the assumptions of normality and homogeneity of variances that are necessary for using a parametric t-test.

In the independent-samples t-test, scores from two different groups on the same measure are compared. As always, I emphasized the importance of effect sizes over p-values in looking at t-test results, since p-values are greatly influenced by sample size while effect sizes are not. In the paired-samples t-test, scores from the same group at two different times or on two related measures are compared. Paired t-tests take into account the violation of the assumption of independence to report on whether the two mean scores are considered to be different from one another.

In the Advanced Topic section I also explained how to use one-sample t-tests, which are used when you have measured only one group but want to compare that group's scores to another, externally devised standard.

Chapter 10

Looking for Group Differences with a One-Way Analysis of Variance (ANOVA): Effects of Planning Time

> Most of the time, when you get an amazing, counterintuitive result, it means you screwed up the experiment.
>
> Michael Wigler, quoted by Angier (2007, p. 206)

In the previous chapter we examined t-tests, which look for group differences when there are only two groups. Although it was not framed this way when talking about t-tests, essentially we had one variable that was independent and measured categorically (the group splitting factor) while we had another that was dependent and measured on an interval or continuous scale (the measurement we took from the groups). When we want to ask the same question of whether the groups come from the same or different populations but we have more than two groups, we will use a one-way **analysis of variance** (ANOVA). For example, in this chapter we will look at the question of whether groups who differed in the kind of time they got to plan and write an essay performed differently on an evaluation of that essay. In this case there is one dependent variable, which is the evaluation of the essay, and one independent variable, which is group membership. In Ellis and Yuan's study (2004) there were three different levels of planning/writing time, so we cannot use a t-test; we must use a one-way ANOVA.

10.1 Understanding ANOVA Design

You might wonder why ANOVA is called an analysis of *variance*. Aren't we looking to see whether the mean scores of the groups are different from one another? The fact is, the mathematics of ANOVA indeed compares the variances of groups; an ANOVA compares the variances *within* the group to the **variance** *between* the groups to see whether the differences between groups are "big enough" to say that the groups come from different populations. A graphical example may help illustrate this idea and make the process of ANOVA seem less mystical (this example and the code to generate the figures are borrowed with permission from Crawley, 2002, p. 244).

First, let's say we have two groups, A and B. Figure 10.1 plots the data from both Group A and Group B, and the horizontal line is the mean score for both groups taken together. The vertical lines from the mean to the points represent the variance, or error, between the mean and the actual points. We subtract this error from the mean, and square it, in order to get a sense of the magnitude of how much the actual points differ from our estimate of their middle point. This is called the **total sum of squares**, or

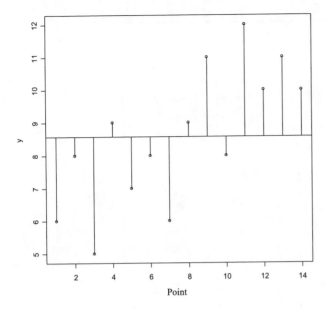

Figure 10.1 Total variance illustrated graphically (one total line for Groups A and B).

SST, and is written mathematically as $SST = \Sigma (y_i - \mu)^2$, where y_i=each point and μ=the overall mean score. This measures the total variance, and this number is what is found in the "Total" row of an ANOVA table in SPSS (see Table 10.5).

Next, we can divide the groups up and calculate a mean score for each group. Figure 10.2 shows that the mean for Group B is larger than the mean for Group A. Again, we will calculate the difference between the mean inside each group (the horizontal line) and the actual fitted points and square the result, which becomes what is called the **error sum of squares (SSE)**: $SSE = \Sigma (y_A - \mu_A)^2 + \Sigma (y_B - \mu_B)^2$, where y_A=each point in the A group and μ_A=the mean of Group A, and y_B=each point in the B group and μ_B=the mean of Group B. This number represents the variance *within* the groups, and shows the variability in scores due to the treatments. This measure is the variance *within* groups, and it is found in the "Within" row of an ANOVA table in SPSS (see Table 10.5).

The value of the variation between groups, the part that is explained by your independent variable (something like "Group"), is actually the total sum of squares (SST) minus the error sum of squares (SSE). In other words, take the overall variance (SST), subtract from it the variance due to the differences within groups (SSE), and you have the treatment sum of squares, or the variance that is explained. This number is found on the "Between" row of an ANOVA table in SPSS (see Table 10.5).

If the means of the Groups A and B were the same (which they are not in Figures 10.1 and 10.2), then the SST (the calculations illustrated in Figure 10.1) would be the same as the SSE (Figure 10.2). However, if the mean values are quite different, SSE will be less than SST because the separate group fits will be more accurate (and thus the difference between the mean and the points less), and the F value will end up being

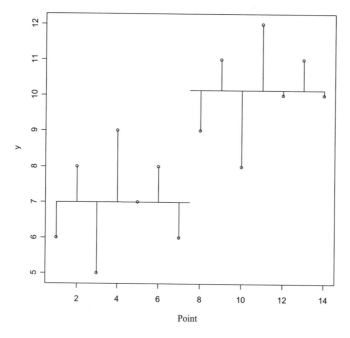

Figure 10.2 Variance *within* groups illustrated graphically (one line each for Group A and Group B).

large, which will mean we can reject the null hypothesis.[1] Hopefully this explanation will help make sense of why we are most concerned about *variances* in the analysis of variance. Crawley claims that we can "make inferences about differences between means by looking at variances" (2002, p. 245). A visual table you can play with, changing the variances and means to see the effects on F, can be found at http://www.psych.utah.edu/stat/introstats/anovaflash.html.

10.2 The Topic of Chapter 10

The data set used in this chapter comes from Ellis and Yuan (2004), who examined the effect of planning on writing—would planning time help writers produce more fluent, accurate, or complex language on a writing instrument? The population investigated was Chinese foreign language learners of English. The dependent measure was a story, written according to visual story prompts, and the groups differed in how much planning time they received for their writing, how much time they had to write, and whether they had a length requirement. The different levels in this dependent variable were:

---

1 Note that the actual ratio that gives the F-value is between the explained variance (the "Between groups" line in the SPSS print-out) and the unexplained variance within groups (SSE, the "Within groups" line in the SPSS print-out, illustrated in Figure 10.2). The total variance is used in order to make calculations about the explained variance, but is not used in calculating the F-ratio.

- no planning group: had 17 minutes to write and were asked to write at least 200 words
- pre-task planning group: had 10 minutes to plan what they would write and 17 minutes to write, and were asked to produce at least 200 words
- online planning group: had as long as they wanted to write and had no minimum word requirement

For the dependent measure, fluency, complexity, and accuracy on the writing task were measured by means of seven different measures. This means that there were seven dependent variables in the study. A one-way ANOVA has only one dependent and one independent variable, so Ellis and Yuan (2004) conducted a series of seven separate one-way ANOVAs. The box in Figure 10.3 represents one of the seven one-way ANOVAs.

The design box in Figure 10.3 shows that a one-way ANOVA has one dependent variable which will be continuous (interval-level) and one independent variable which will be categorical. The IV will have at least three levels. If it only had two levels, we could analyze it using a t-test. If there is more than one IV the test that will be needed is a factorial ANOVA, treated in the next chapter.

10.2.1 Numerical and Visual Inspection of the Data in This Chapter

To get a sense first of what is happening with the Ellis and Yuan (2004) data, let's take a look at a numerical summary of the dependent variable of syntactic variety. To get means and standard deviations in a more compact form I split the data by Group (DATA > SPLIT FILE, then click the radio button "Compare groups" and move the GROUP variable to the "Groups Based on" box) and then called for descriptive statistics using ANALYZE > DESCRIPTIVE STATISTICS > DESCRIPTIVES. I put SYNTAXVARIETY in the "Variable(s)" box. Table 10.1 shows the means and standard deviations for each of Ellis and Yuan's three groups.

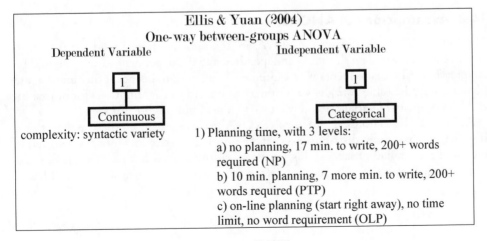

Figure 10.3 Design box for Ellis and Yuan one-way ANOVA.

Table 10.1 Numerical Summary for Ellis and Yuan's (2004) SYNTAXVARIETY

	Mean	Standard deviation	N
No planning (NP)	16.2	4.1	14
Pre-task planning (PTP)	22.1	3.6	14
Online planning (OLP)	18.9	3.2	14

We can see that the group that received the planning time scored the highest on the amount of syntactic variety they included in their writing (PTP). The group that scored the lowest was the group with no planning and also a strict time limit (NP). This is clear from the numerical summary, but we will be looking to a statistical summary to tell us whether the differences between groups are large enough to say that there are statistical differences between the groups.

Another thing we can note from the numerical summary is that there were the same number of participants in each group, and their variances are roughly equal.

Turning now to visual examination of the data, boxplots would be good for examining whether the distribution of the data was normal and whether variances look similar. Chapter 9 has already explained how to call for boxplots so we will not discuss any new ways of visualizing data in this chapter. To make the boxplot I chose GRAPHS > LEGACY DIALOGS > BOXPLOT and then SIMPLE and "Summaries for groups of cases." I put SYNTAXVARIETY into the "Variable" box and GROUP into the "Category Axis" box. I found when I did this I still had the data split and I got three different boxplots, so I went back and told SPSS to analyze all groups together (DATA > SPLIT FILE, "Analyze all cases"). A boxplot of the data is in Figure 10.4.

The boxplots show visually that none of the distributions is exactly normal; the NP group has an outlier, and none of the groups has a perfectly symmetrical median or whiskers. The size of the box is approximately the same for all three groups, which is one indication that variances are equal.

10.3 Assumptions of ANOVA

The four main assumptions for ANOVA are the same as those found for the t-test. Again, the first two (data should be independent and the dependent variable should be an interval-level measurement) are requirements that need to be met at the time you are planning a study. Table 10.2 gives a summary of how to test assumptions for normality and homogeneity of variances and what to do if assumptions are not met.

As Howell (2002) notes, the logic of ANOVA makes sense given these assumptions. If we have two or more distributions that are normally distributed (not skewed) and if they all have similar variances, this means all of the groups have similar shapes and dispersions, so that the only question left to ask is whether their mean values differ.

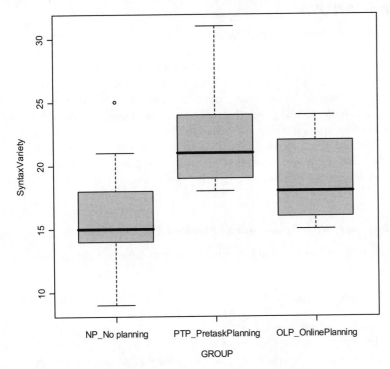

Figure 10.4 Boxplot of SyntaxVariety from Ellis and Yuan (2004).

Table 10.2 Assumptions for a Parametric One-Way ANOVA

Meeting assumptions		One-way ANOVA
1 Normal distribution of data (looking at the data according to groups)	Required?	Yes
	How to test assumption?	Examine boxplots, plot normal curve over histogram (see Chapter 3); use boxplots and Q-Q plots to check for outliers
	What if assumption not met?	1) Use non-parametric Kruskal–Wallis test if variances are fairly equal and data is not heavily skewed; 2) use 20% trimmed means and bootstrap
2 Equal variances (looking at the data according to groups)	Required?	Yes
	How to test assumption?	Examine side-by-side boxplots; look at summary statistics for variance (see Chapter 3); Howell (2002) notes that if sample sizes are unequal *and* variances are unequal it leads to an appreciable loss of robustness (pp. 340–341); use Levene's test for homogeneity*
	What if assumption not met?	1) Try transformation with a log function; 2) use robust regression analysis

* Be careful in trusting the results of this test (see note under Table 9.3 for more information).

10.4 One-Way ANOVA

A one-way ANOVA asks whether the differences between mean scores of three groups or more are so great that we could not just ascribe the differences to chance fluctuations in scores. This question is exactly analogous to that of the t-test, and in fact a one-way ANOVA could be used in place of the t-test if there were only two mean scores, and the results would be the same (the t-test statistic squared is equal to the F-value of the one-way ANOVA). The difference between a one-way ANOVA and a t-test, of course, is that, since there are more than two mean scores, a statistical outcome on a one-way ANOVA does not really end the question of exactly how the groups differ. Because there are more than two mean scores, we still are not sure whether all mean scores are different or whether some are different but others are the same.

10.4.1 Omnibus Tests with Post-Hocs or Planned Comparisons

In a one-way ANOVA we test the null hypothesis that any number of mean scores are equal:

$$H_o = \mu_1 = \mu_2 = \mu_3 = \ldots = \mu_k$$

If we reject this null hypothesis, we still want to know which mean scores are different from others. Wilcox (2003) notes that there are two ways to test the means of more than two groups. One way is the traditional and popular way of conducting an overall (or **omnibus**) test to see whether the means of all the groups are equal (the null hypothesis shown above). If this test is statistical, then researchers generally go on to perform so-called **post-hoc** tests, which test all of the possible pairings of groups for statistical differences. This may seem equal to performing a series of t-tests, but post-hoc tests are different in that they control the **familywise error rate (FWE)**, the overall level of Type I error in all tests of a related research question. If, instead of an ANOVA, a large number of t-tests were performed, the Type I error rate of $a = .05$ for each test would be compounded, and the overall familywise error rate would be larger than $a = .05$. Post-hoc tests employ different methods to reduce this FWE. The other way to test the mean is to use **planned comparisons**. In planned comparisons you do not conduct all of the possible tests of groups but instead focus on only a subset of groups.

Although an omnibus (overall) test followed by post-hocs is the traditional way of testing more than two groups, there is usually nothing to be gained by performing the omnibus test itself (Howell, 2002), as the researcher is most likely interested in the actual comparison between groups. In this case, performing an omnibus test (the initial test of the ANOVA) actually reduces the power to find differences between groups because an additional test is performed and has to be controlled for in order to not increase the familywise error rate.[2]

The major reason to use planned comparisons is to increase the power you have to find statistical differences between groups. You will gain power if you have a large

---

2 Actually, when conducting one-way tests and post-hocs, SPSS does not adjust the post-hoc alpha value to take the omnibus test effect into account; that would have to be done by the author, something I have never actually seen done in the literature, so in practice this point may be moot.

number of groups but you don't care about testing all possible comparisons. For example, if you had several groups who differed on their first language, and what you were interested in was how various groups differed from native speakers (NS) (but not among themselves), you could use planned comparisons to effectively increase your power. Do note, however, that the planning for such comparisons needs to be done before you conduct your statistical analysis. It should not be used to fish for a way to make your comparisons statistical! Both omnibus tests with post-hocs and comparisons without an overall test will be illustrated in this chapter.

10.4.2 Testing for Group Equivalence before an Experimental Procedure

Many researchers would like to show *before* experimental treatment is begun that the groups used in their studies are not different when they are compared on some proficiency measure, such as a TOEFL test. The goal is to show that any differences found after the experimental treatment can be attributed to the actual effects of the treatment and not to inherent differences between groups.

Although this kind of pre-testing for group homogeneity or heterogeneity is a common practice in our literature, Rietveld and van Hout (2005) assert that it does not make statistical sense and is pointless because it does not generalize to an entire population (p. 48, Exercise 5 and answer on p. 235). However, the real problem with testing for group equivalence before an experimental procedure is that just because a statistical test does not find evidence to reject the null hypothesis does not mean that the groups are indeed equal. It could be that the groups are different but the test does not have enough power to find this difference (Clark-Carter, 2005). Indeed, in general the absence of evidence does not mean that there is evidence of absence (Kline, 2004). Possibly the best that can be said after using the conventional **NHST** method is that a lack of statistical difference between groups before experimental testing is "comforting" (Howell, 2002, p. 500). If we did see a statistical difference between groups before an experimental procedure, we would want to then use the pre-test as a covariate in order to subtract its effect out of the equation.

There is in fact a way to test for equivalence of groups and this method is widely used in medical or clinical studies to show that some drug or treatment is "close enough" to an already established drug or treatment that it can be substituted for it (Kline, 2004; Streiner, 2003). Readers interested in using this technique for equivalence testing are referred to Streiner (2003) for the technical details.

10.5 Performing Omnibus One-Way ANOVA Tests in SPSS

There are two ways to perform a one-way ANOVA in SPSS. Both use the ANALYZE drop-down menu, but one uses the COMPARE MEANS > ONE-WAY ANOVA and the other uses the GENERAL LINEAR MODEL (GLM) > UNIVARIATE choice. One difference is that the GLM procedure offers the chance to specify independent variables as **random** or **fixed** (just briefly, this distinction has to do with whether the levels cover all possible divisions; more will be said on this topic in Chapter 11). Since the GLM approach will be needed for two-way and higher ANOVA and will be shown in Chapter 11, in this chapter I will illustrate the use of the COMPARE MEANS > ONE-WAY ANOVA menu. Be aware, though, that you could equally well use the univariate method for a one-way ANOVA.

10.5.1 Calling for a One-Way ANOVA

I will illustrate how to perform a one-way ANOVA using Ellis and Yuan's (2004) variable of Syntax Variety, which was explored graphically in the beginning of this chapter. The research question we are interested in is whether the groups with differing amounts of planning time are statistically different in the amount of syntactic variety they produce. The independent variable is experimental group. To conduct a one-way ANOVA in SPSS, open ANALYZE > COMPARE MEANS > ONE-WAY ANOVA. Put your dependent variable in the "Dependent List" box and your independent variable in the "Factor" box as shown in Figure 10.5.

You will also need to open the POST HOC button and the OPTIONS button on the one-way ANOVA dialogue box, as shown in Figures 10.6 and 10.7. In the Post Hoc area you will choose which post-hoc tests to use. You have a choice of tests if equal variances are assumed, and there are also tests to use if equal variances are not assumed.

Howell (2002) recommends the LSD test as the most powerful post-hoc test to find differences if you only have three means. If you have more than three, both Howell (2002) and Maxwell and Delaney (2004) recommend Bonferroni or Tukey's post-hocs, and Howell also likes the REGWQ. Bonferroni has more power to find differences if fewer tests are performed, while Tukey's has more power if more tests are performed. Both Tukey's and Bonferroni are conservative tests and strictly control the familywise error rate. If you would like more power to find differences, I recommend using the LSD post-hoc, which performs no adjustments for multiple tests at all, or the REGWQ. Take the p-values returned there and then use the Benjamini and Hochberg's FDR to adjust p-values (this is discussed in more detail in Section 9.3.1, and the FDR code is found in the Appendix). Maxwell and Delaney (2004) also like the FDR, but it was not easily implementable when they wrote their text. If variances are not equal, Howell (2002) recommends Games–Howell, and Maxwell and Delaney (2004) like it too.

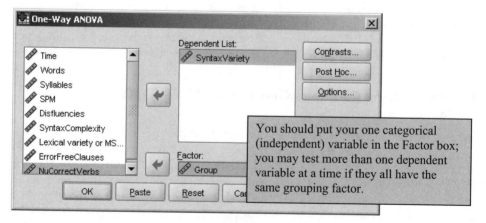

Figure 10.5 Opening a one-way ANOVA dialogue box.

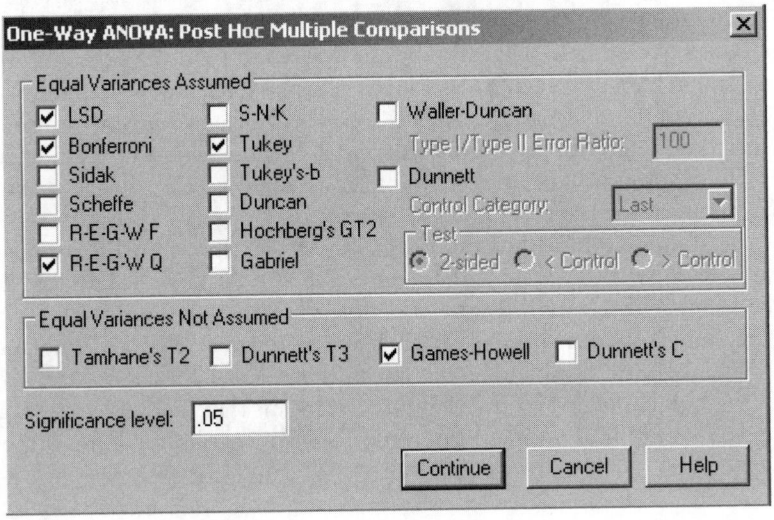

Figure 10.6 Post-hoc comparisons for a one-way ANOVA.

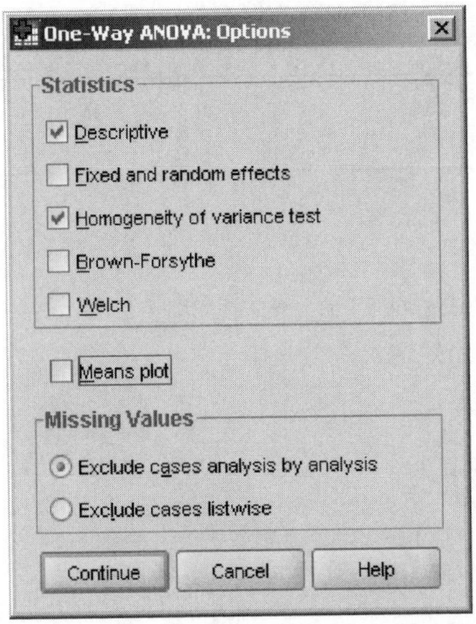

Figure 10.7 Options for a one-way ANOVA.

For the OPTIONS button, click on the boxes I show in Figure 10.7.

After you have finished all of these choices, you will run the ANOVA. The first piece of output you'll see, shown in Table 10.3, consists of descriptive statistics about your data, and you should check the sample size in the first column to make sure all the participants you expected were included. Notice that the Ellis and Yuan (2004) data has equal numbers of participants in each group.

The next piece of output, shown in Table 10.4, is the test for homogeneity of variance. There is some controversy in the literature about whether such formal tests have enough power to test their own assumptions. More informal ways of testing equal variances are probably better, such as looking at boxplots and numerical summaries, but, if you use Levene's test, a significance level above .05 means that you do not reject the hypothesis that the groups have equal variances. For the Ellis and Yuan data, the Levene's test does not contradict the assumption of equal variances that we already gained from looking at the boxplots in Figure 10.4.

The next part of the output is the omnibus ANOVA test, shown in Table 10.5.

For the variable of SYNTAXVARIETY, the omnibus ANOVA shows a statistical difference between groups. To report this you will note the value of the F-test (9.05), the degrees of freedom between groups (2) and within groups (39), and the p-value ($p = .001$). Remember, the p-value does *not* mean that there is, for this case, a 0.1% chance that the result happened by chance; rather, it means that there is less than a 1 in 1,000 chance you would find a value more extreme than the observed one if the null hypothesis were true.

Table 10.3 Output from the One-Way ANOVA: Descriptives

Descriptives

SyntaxVariety

	N	Mean	Std. Deviation	Std. Error	95% Confidence Interval for Mean		Minimum	Maximum
					Lower Bound	Upper Bound		
NP_No planning	14	16.21	4.098	1.095	13.85	18.58	9	25
PTP_PretaskPlanning	14	22.07	3.583	.958	20.00	24.14	18	31
OLP_OnlinePlanning	14	18.86	3.207	.857	17.01	20.71	15	24
Total	42	19.05	4.305	.664	17.71	20.39	9	31

Table 10.4 Output from the One-Way ANOVA: Levene's Test

Test of Homogeneity of Variances

SyntaxVariety

Levene Statistic	df1	df2	Sig.
.290	2	39	.750

Table 10.5 Output from the One-Way ANOVA: Omnibus One-Way ANOVA

ANOVA

SyntaxVariety

	Sum of Squares	df	Mean Square	F	Sig.
Between Groups	240.905	2	120.452	9.051	.001
Within Groups	519.000	39	13.308		
Total	759.905	41			

> Tip: When reporting the results of main effects from an ANOVA, you need to report two numbers for degrees of freedom. The first is the degrees of freedom for your independent variable (such as "Group" or "Gender"), which is shown as the "Between groups" row for a one-way ANOVA. The second is the degrees of freedom of the error, which is listed as the "Within groups" row for a one-way ANOVA. Do not get confused and report the total degrees of freedom for this second number. For example, for the output in Table 10.5 you could say: "The main effect of group was statistical, $F_{2,39} = 9.05, p = .001$."

Technically, if your omnibus ANOVA is not statistical then you should stop your analysis and not continue with post-hocs. Since you have called for post-hocs before seeing the omnibus test, however, SPSS will provide them, so just ignore them if the omnibus is not statistical.

The next piece of the output, shown in Table 10.6, contains the results of the requested post-hoc comparisons. Since there were three groups, three unique comparisons are made (NP versus PTP, NP versus OLP, and PTP versus OLP). The post-hoc comparisons show that choice of post-hoc test can matter (I have not included Bonferroni here but the results are the same as for Tukey)! The Multiple Comparisons table shows that, for the Tukey HSD post-hoc test, there is a statistical difference between the NP and PTP groups (the significance level is shown as .000, but because the difference is not really zero we can say that $p < .0005$). None of the other comparisons is statistical below $a = .05$. The results are different for the LSD test, reflecting more power to find differences. The LSD post-hoc finds statistical differences for the PTP versus OLP

Table 10.6 Output from the One-Way ANOVA: Post-Hocs

Multiple Comparisons

Dependent Variable:SyntaxVariety

	(I) Group	(J) Group	Mean Difference (I-J)	Std. Error	Sig.	95% Confidence Interval Lower Bound	95% Confidence Interval Upper Bound
Tukey HSD	NP_No planning	PTP_PretaskPlanning	-5.857*	1.379	.000	-9.22	-2.50
		OLP_OnlinePlanning	-2.643	1.379	.147	-6.00	.72
	PTP_PretaskPlanning	NP_No planning	5.857*	1.379	.000	2.50	9.22
		OLP_OnlinePlanning	3.214	1.379	.063	-.14	6.57
	OLP_OnlinePlanning	NP_No planning	2.643	1.379	.147	-.72	6.00
		PTP_PretaskPlanning	-3.214	1.379	.063	-6.57	.14
LSD	NP_No planning	PTP_PretaskPlanning	-5.857*	1.379	.000	-8.65	-3.07
		OLP_OnlinePlanning	-2.643	1.379	.063	-5.43	.15
	PTP_PretaskPlanning	NP_No planning	5.857*	1.379	.000	3.07	8.65
		OLP_OnlinePlanning	3.214*	1.379	.025	.43	6.00
	OLP_OnlinePlanning	NP_No planning	2.643	1.379	.063	-.15	5.43
		PTP_PretaskPlanning	-3.214*	1.379	.025	-6.00	-.43
Games-Howell	NP_No planning	PTP_PretaskPlanning	-5.857*	1.455	.001	-9.48	-2.24
		OLP_OnlinePlanning	-2.643	1.391	.160	-6.11	.83
	PTP_PretaskPlanning	NP_No planning	5.857*	1.455	.001	2.24	9.48
		OLP_OnlinePlanning	3.214*	1.285	.049	.02	6.41
	OLP_OnlinePlanning	NP_No planning	2.643	1.391	.160	-.83	6.11
		PTP_PretaskPlanning	-3.214*	1.285	.049	-6.41	-.02

*. The mean difference is significant at the 0.05 level.

Table 10.7 Output from the One-Way ANOVA: REGWQ Post-Hoc Results

SyntaxVariety

	Group	N	Subset for alpha = .05	
			1	2
Ryan-Einot-Gabriel-Welsch Range	NP_No planning	14	16.21	
	OLP_OnlinePlanning	14	18.86	
	PTP_PretaskPlanning	14		22.07
	Sig.		.063	1.000

Means for groups in homogeneous subsets are displayed.

group as well as the NP versus PTP group. The comparison between the OLP and NP groups also has a low *p*-value, although it is not below .05. We can also look at the confidence intervals here for the mean difference between the pairs. In this case, because visually from the boxplot and also numerically from Levene's test we did not find a reason to suspect heteroscedasticity, we don't need to use the results from the Games–Howell post-hoc, but this test also returns more statistical results than Tukey's HSD.

The very last piece of the output from the one-way ANOVA is titled "Homogeneous subsets." This shows the results of the REGWQ test (Table 10.7). The REGWQ post-hoc groups the NP and OLP together (the difference between them is $p = .063$, just like the LSD, so the difference is not below $p = .05$). The fact that the PTP group is in a different column from the others means that there is a statistical difference between PTP and the other groups at the $p = .05$ level. Therefore the REGWQ result is exactly the same as the LSD result.

The question may then arise—which post-hoc results will you report? I would report the LSD results since these have the most power. Now the LSD post-hoc really consists just of separate t-tests without any adjustment for familywise error rate, so some authors recommend against them. As you have seen, I favor methods that provide more power, and Howell (2002), a source I trust, also recommends the LSD if you have only three groups, so I would go with the most powerful post-hocs that I could.

Performing a One-Way ANOVA

1   ANALYZE > COMPARE MEANS > ONE-WAY ANOVA (or use ANALYZE > GENERAL LINEAR MODEL (GLM) > UNIVARIATE; this method is explained in more detail in Chapter 11).

2   Put dependent variable(s) into "Dependent List" (move more than one variable in if you are doing multiple one-way ANOVAs at one time). Put your independent variable into the "Factor" box.

3   Open the POST HOC button and tick Tukey or REGWQ (or LSD if you have only three means). Open the OPTIONS button and tick "Descriptive" and "Homogeneity of variances test."

10.5.2 More on Post-Hocs in ANOVA

In the previous section I recommended that you use only five types of post-hoc tests. Because SPSS offers you such a wide array of post-hocs, in this section I will explain a little more about the post-hocs that are available. Maxwell and Delaney (2004) discuss post-hoc tests in quite some detail, and assert that some post-hoc tests indicate only that means are different but do not indicate which one of the means is higher than the other (these are tests that are lower on their "levels of inference" scale). Thus, in Table 10.8 I will indicate whether Maxwell and Delaney recommend using the tests at all under the "Apprvd?" column (which stands for "Approved?").

Post-hoc tests also differ in how much control they put over the familywise error rate. In general, Maxwell and Delaney favor a stricter control over FWE than I do. I would rather use a more liberal test to gain more power than worry about committing a Type I error.

Different post-hoc tests can be better than others in some situations. For example, probably most of the time if you run a post-hoc test you are interested in testing all of the pairwise comparisons which you have (if you aren't, then you probably should run some planned comparisons, discussed in Section 10.5.3). However, some post-hocs will be better for other situations, such as when you want just to compare all of the groups with a control.

Another factor to consider is whether sample sizes are equal and whether variances are equal. Some tests will work better than others when sample sizes are unequal and when variances are unequal. These factors will be noted in Table 10.8, which lists the 18 post-hocs available in SPSS and gives more information about them.

10.5.3 Conducting a One-Way ANOVA Using Planned Comparisons

If you would like to perform the post-hoc tests without the omnibus F-test (as recommended by Wilcox, 2003, as a way of increasing the statistical power of the test), the easiest way to set this up is through the one-way ANOVA procedure. You could also, of course, just use a series of t-tests. However, if you did this you might be concerned about inflating the error rate by having multiple tests. Since I have argued in Chapter 4 that the alpha level cannot really be set too high, this may or may not be a factor in your considerations. Howell (2002) opines that if you have only one or two comparisons to make then the t-test approach is not unreasonable, but if you have a really large number of comparisons then using planned comparisons is better.

To illustrate this procedure we will look again at the comparison among the three groups of the Ellis and Yuan (2004) data for the Syntactic Variety variable without doing the omnibus F-test. Suppose that we wanted to test all of the possible comparisons among the groups. In this case, there are three groups, so there will be three possible comparisons. In each comparison, we want to ignore one of the groups and compare the other two. Study Table 10.9 to examine the pattern of coefficients that need to be used in order to do an ordinary comparison of the three groups.

From Table 10.9 you can see that you put a number in the row of the groups you want to compare. The number could be 1, 2, or 1,000, but there needs to be an equally large number to be subtracted so that, when the columns are added up, they add up to zero. Any row of the column which contains a non-zero number will be included in the comparison. For the planned comparison shown in Table 10.9, only two groups at a time are being compared. All possible pairings are made (that is, NP versus PTP, NP versus OLP, and PTP versus OLP).

Table 10.8 Post-Hocs Available in SPSS

Post-hoc test	Apprvd?	Liberal/ conservative	Good when . . .	Notes
LSD	No	Liberal	you plan to apply the FDR later and you want the unadjusted p-values	Howell (2002) allows this test without adjustment if you have 3 or fewer comparisons
Bonferroni	Yes	Conservative	testing planned comparisons	Has more power than Tukey when fewer tests are done
Sidak	Yes	Conservative	testing planned comparisons	Slightly more powerful than Bonferroni
Scheffe	Yes	Conservative	testing some complex comparisons like A+B+C versus D	SPSS does not allow use of the Scheffe in planned comparisons, precisely where one would need them!
REGWF	No			
REGWQ	No	Liberal		Should not be used when groups sizes are different
S-N-K	No	Liberal		
Tukey	Yes	Conservative	testing all pairwise comparisons	Has more power than Bonferroni when more tests are done
Tukey's-b	No			
Duncan	No			
Hochberg's GT2	Yes	Conservative	testing all pairwise comparisons and also unequal sample sizes	Don't use when variances are not equal; generally less powerful than Tukey's
Gabriel	Yes	Liberal	testing all pairwise comparisons and also unequal sample sizes	Generally less powerful than Tukey's
Waller-Duncan	N/A			
Dunnett	Yes	Conservative	testing group means against a control mean	
Tamhane's T2	N/A	Conservative		
Dunnett's T3	Yes	Conservative	testing all pairwise comparisons	Use when variances unequal
Games–Howell	Yes	Liberal	testing all pairwise comparisons and also unequal sample sizes	Use when variances unequal
Dunnett's C	N/A	Conservative		

To translate this idea to SPSS, we will bring up the dialogue box for the one-way ANOVA (ANALYZE > COMPARE MEANS > ONE-WAY ANOVA). The same variables are moved into the same boxes as shown previously in Figure 10.5 and now in Figure 10.8. The difference is that now we open the CONTRASTS button.

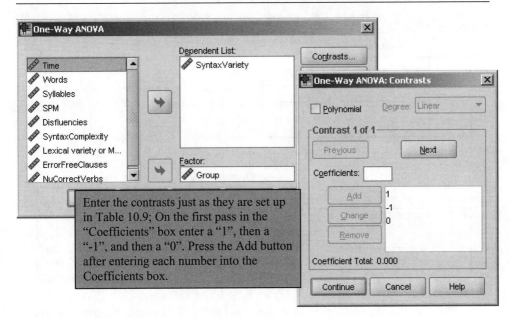

Figure 10.8 Calling for planned comparisons.

Table 10.9 Planned Comparison Coefficients for Two-Way Comparisons

Groups	Compare Group 1 to Group 2	Compare Group 1 to Group 3	Compare Group 2 to Group 3
NP=Group 1	1	1	0
PTP=Group 2	−1	0	1
OLP=Group 3	0	−1	−1

In the CONTRASTS dialogue box we enter the coefficients for each of our planned comparisons. Figure 10.8 shows the coefficients added for the first contrast. To call for all of the planned comparisons in Table 10.9, I would need to then press the NEXT button to move to "Contrast 2 of 2," where I would then enter the coefficients 1, 0, and −1. Pressing the NEXT button again moves me to "Contrast 3 of 3," where I would enter the final set of coefficients, 0, 1, −1.

The output we are interested in from this planned comparison is shown in Table 10.10. The first table shows the contrast coefficients you have entered. The main output of interest is labeled "Contrast Tests" and shows the results of our three planned comparisons.

The results from this planned comparison are, unsurprisingly, the same as were found with the LSD or REGWR post-hocs in Section 10.5.1, since the same three comparisons were made. However, let's say what we really wanted to know was whether having planning time made a difference or not, and whether having unlimited time made a difference or not. For the question of planning time, we could compare the group with planning time (PTP) to the two others without planning time (NP and

Table 10.10 Output from a Planned Comparison

Contrast Coefficients

	Group		
Contrast	NP_No planning	PTP_ Pretask Planning	OLP_ Online Planning
1	1	-1	0
2	1	0	-1
3	0	1	-1

Contrast Tests

		Contrast	Value of Contrast	Std. Error	t	df	Sig. (2-tailed)
SyntaxVariety	Assume equal variances	1	-5.86	1.379	-4.248	39	.000
		2	-2.64	1.379	-1.917	39	.063
		3	3.21	1.379	2.331	39	.025
	Does not assume equal variances	1	-5.86	1.455	-4.026	25.545	.000
		2	-2.64	1.391	-1.900	24.579	.069
		3	3.21	1.285	2.501	25.686	.019

Table 10.11 Planned Comparison Coefficients for Multiple Comparisons with Ellis and Yuan (2004)

Groups	Compare PTP to NP and OLP	Compare OLP to NP and PTP
NP=Group 1	−1	−1
PTP=Group 2	2	−1
OLP=Group 3	−1	2

Table 10.12 Planned Comparison Coefficients with L1 Groups

Groups	Compare Latinate groups to NS	Compare Japanese group to NS	Compare all NNS groups to NS
Native speakers	2	1	3
Spanish L1	−1	0	−1
Portuguese L1	−1	0	−1
Japanese L1	0	−1	−1

OLP). For the question of unlimited writing time, we could compare the group with unlimited time (OLP) to the groups who only had 17 minutes of writing time (NP and PTP). Study the coefficients in Table 10.11 to see how we could call for these comparisons.

Table 10.12 shows coefficients that could be used in a study with four groups and various research questions.

Performing Multiple Comparisons

1   ANALYZE > COMPARE MEANS > ONE-WAY ANOVA.
2   Move the DV and IV into appropriate boxes. Open the CONTRASTS button. Enter comparison coefficients in Coefficients box; press ADD after every number, and NEXT after each comparison is finished. Make sure that the "Coefficient Total" at the bottom of the dialogue box equals zero for every contrast. Press CONTINUE and then OK.

10.5.4 Effect Sizes in One-Way ANOVAs

When you do a one-way ANOVA you have a choice as to what effect size you will report—that of the omnibus ANOVA F-test, or that of the post-hoc or planned comparisons tests. Kline (2004) recommends reporting on only one or the other. For the omnibus test you will use a percentage variance (PV) effect size, while for the post-hocs or planned comparisons you will use Cohen's d. When researchers in second language research do report effect sizes, I have mostly seen the effect sizes for the individual comparisons, not for the omnibus test, and my feeling is that this is the most appropriate place to look at effect sizes.

However, if you'd like to report the omnibus PV effect size, you can use the ANOVA output. The formula is to divide the number for the sum of squares (SS) of the independent variable (found in the "Between Groups" row of SPSS output) by the total sum of squares (found in the "Total" row in the SPSS output). Thus, for the Ellis and Yuan (2004) omnibus test, looking at the output in Figure 10.10, PV = 240.9/59.9 = .32, meaning the between-groups differences account for 32% of the variance in scores.

To calculate Cohen's d effect sizes for post-hoc tests or planned comparisons, use the same approach as was used for independent-group t-tests in Chapter 9 (you can also use an online calculator, such as that at web.uccs.edu/lbecker/Psy590/escalc3.htm). In other words, you will divide the mean difference between groups by a standardizer, which can be either the pooled standard deviation, if variances are equal, or the standard deviation of the control group, if variances are unequal.

Since the Ellis and Yuan (2004) data had equal variances, I calculate:

$$d\,(NP - PTP) = \frac{16.2 - 22.07}{\sqrt{\dfrac{13(4.1)^2 + 13(3.58)^2}{13 + 13}}} = -1.53.$$

The effect size for the comparison between NP and OLP is $d = -.72$, and the effect size for the comparison between PTP and OLP is $d = .95$. These are all fairly large effect sizes, considering that Cohen (1992) suggests that $d = .8$ is a large effect size. If we think only about effect sizes and forget the statistical tests, it seems that each of the planning conditions provided the participants with a good opportunity to increase their statistical variety, although the effect was stronger for pre-task planning than for the online planning.

10.5.5 Application Activity with One-Way ANOVAs

1   Using the Ellis and Yuan data (EllisYuan.sav), look at the variables of error-free clauses, MSTTR (a measure of lexical variety), and speed per minute (SPM). First examine the data visually. What do you find with regard to normality, homogeneity of variances, and outliers? Next, perform a one-way ANOVA on each of the three variables along with post-hocs. Report omnibus F-results; find 95% confidence intervals for the difference in means, and calculate effect sizes for the contrasts. What would you remark upon here?

2   Pandey (2000) conducted research on how well native speakers of different English dialects performed on the TOEFL and reported the raw data scores in her article. Pandey's research design is shown in the following diagram:

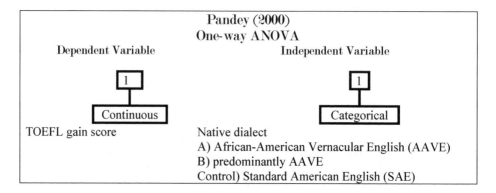

Pandey did not perform statistics on her data, but merely observed the trend that both focus groups had quite low TOEFL scores the first time they were tested (mean for Focus Group A—443; mean for Focus Group B—429), but, with comparative instruction, both focus groups improved their scores over time. In comparison, the control groups' scores hardly changed at all the second time they took the test. Using the Pandey2000.sav file, investigate statistically the research question of whether Groups A and B are different from each other in their first gain scores (GAIN1), and also whether Group A and B *together* are different from the control group in the first gain scores. You'll need to use planned comparisons to answer this question. Be sure to first visually examine the data (even if it does not fit assumptions, go ahead and analyze it here).

3   Thought question. Imagine a research design that investigates the pragmatic development of Chinese learners of Russian. The researcher asked participants to complete discourse completion tasks at three separate times during the semester. The participants were in three different classes, and each class received each of the three treatments (Control—no pragmatic discussion; explicit pragmatic discussion; and implicit pragmatic discussion), with five weeks between each treatment. Immediately following the treatment, participants took the discourse completion task. The researcher wants to know whether the groups differed depending on their treatment, and plans to conduct a one-way ANOVA with GROUP as the IV and score on the discourse completion task at every time period as the DV, as is shown in the table below. What is wrong with this research design?

	Participant	Group	Time	DCTScore
1	ChiWei	1	1	68
2	ChiWei	1	2	49
3	ChiWei	1	3	87
4	TsiWen	1	1	53
5	TsiWen	1	2	56

4   Inagaki and Long (1999) conducted an experiment with Japanese learners to see whether asking participants to repeat a correct model after they heard it would be as effective as recasting after an incorrect utterance (and whether these would differ from a control condition where participants simply studied *kanji* characters). Two structures, that of correct adjective formation when there are multiple adjectives, and subject placement after a locative phrase, were examined with 24 participants. If possible, conduct two separate one-way ANOVAs to determine whether there was any difference between the three experimental groups on each of the two structures. Be sure to first visually examine the data. Use the InagakiLong.sav file.

5   Dewaele and Pavlenko Bilingual Emotions Questionnaire (2001–2003). Use the BEQ.Context.sav file. Multilinguals who answered the questionnaire rated their proficiency in L2 speaking, comprehension, reading, and writing on a 1–5 scale (where 5 = fully fluent). Multilinguals also differed in the context in which they had acquired their L2, if it was naturalistic, instructed, or both. Examine the question of whether there are differences in proficiency on L2 speaking and L2 reading depending on the context of instruction. Be sure to first visually examine the data, and report effect sizes.

10.5.6 Reporting the Results of a One-Way ANOVA

The pieces of information that you will want to report from a one-way ANOVA depend on whether you decide to include the omnibus F-test. In most cases, it makes little sense to include an omnibus test, as what most researchers are interested in is not whether the groups differ or not, but specifically how each group differs from the others, or sometimes an even more constrained hypothesis (such as whether Groups A and B together are different from Group C).

In reporting the results from an omnibus test, include at least the degrees of freedom between groups (also called the hypothesis df), the degrees of freedom within groups (also called the error df), the F-value, and the p-value. Some people like to report the entire ANOVA table, with sums of squares and mean squares as well, but I prefer just to report the raw data so that people can recreate my analysis or, if the sample size is too large, tell people I would be happy to send them the raw data.

The information that should be reported from the post-hocs should start with means, standard deviations, and counts for each group. The type of comparison used (post-hoc or planned comparison) and method used for controlling the familywise error rate (for example, Tukey, FDR, etc.) should also be specified. Include the 95% confidence interval for the mean difference between the tests, and the p-value for the test. Depending on which way the comparison was made (for example, NP–PTP or

PTP–NP), the mean difference will be negative or positive. You can use either one to report on.

Effect sizes should also be reported, but statisticians specify that you should give the effect size for either the omnibus test *or* the comparisons, not for both. Most readers will probably be more interested in the effect size of the comparisons, not of the omnibus test. Here is an example of reporting the results of the test for syntactic variety from the Ellis and Yuan (2004) data, ignoring the omnibus test and focusing instead only on planned comparisons:

> In looking at the amount of syntactic variety produced by the participants in the groups with differing levels of planning time, planned comparisons were made among all three groups. The descriptive statistics for the groups were: no planning (NP), $\bar{X} = 16.2$, sd = 4.1, $n = 14$; online planning (OLP), $\bar{X} = 18.9$, sd = 3.2, $n = 14$; and pre-task planning (PTP), $\bar{X} = 22.1$, sd = 3.6, $n = 14$. Comparisons using Tukey's contrasts found a statistical difference between the NP and PTP groups (mean difference = 5.9, 95% CI = 2.5, 9.2, p < .001), but not between the NP and OLP (mean difference = 2.6, CI = –0.7, 6.0, $p = .15$) or the PTP and OLP groups (mean difference = 3.2, CI = –6.6, .14, $p = .06$). Effect sizes for all the comparisons, however, showed quite strong effects for each comparison: NP–PTP, $d = 1.53$; NP–OLP, $d = .95$; PTP–OLP, $d = .72$. This indicates that amount of planning time had a noticeable effect on the amount of syntactic variety produced in writing, with pre-task planning producing the largest amount of syntactic variety.

10.6 Summary of One-Way ANOVAs

A one-way ANOVA is just one conceptual step away from a t-test. T-tests are used when you want to examine whether two groups differ; one-way ANOVAs are used when you want to examine the effect of groups and you have three or more groups to examine. There is only one dependent variable and only one independent variable.

We saw at the beginning of the chapter that ANOVAs mathematically compare the difference in the fit of a line between all the data points (the within-subjects effects) to the fit of lines for each of the groups (the between-subject effects). If the groups are not very different this ratio will be close to one, but if they are different from each other the ratio will be larger than one and the p-value will be statistical.

The assumptions of the parametric one-way ANOVA are the same as those of the t-test, and include a normal distribution and homogeneous variances. In going through the examples and doing the exercises you will have probably noticed that there are very few if any instances when data is exactly normally distributed. I have basically ignored this problem; I did not do this because it does not matter—in fact, I think it matters a great deal (see Larson-Hall & Herrington, forthcoming). The problem is that I think the best way to deal with non-normal distributions is to use robust tests, which SPSS cannot yet do. The next best way would be to use non-parametric tests, but I am not illustrating those tests in this chapter, so I have just forged ahead with the analysis even with non-normal data. As for the assumption of homogeneous variances, with SPSS we do have some adjustments we can make if variances are not equal, so this assumption was not such a worry.

A new concept we discussed in regard to ANOVAs was the difference between an omnibus test and post-hocs or planned comparisons. Because ANOVAs look at three or more groups, a statistical ANOVA result (reporting an F-value) will not really tell us all that we need to know. If this F-test, or omnibus test, is statistical, we may proceed to look at post-hoc tests that compare only two groups at a time. Indeed, I asserted that we may want to ignore the omnibus test altogether and go straight to the comparisons we are interested in so as to retain more power to find real differences. This is possible by using planned comparisons. If you are not interested in all the possible pairings of groups, it is always a good idea to use planned comparisons.

As always, where possible effect sizes and confidence intervals should be reported. For one-way ANOVAs we saw that there are effect sizes for both the omnibus test and the comparisons. I suggested that most readers would be more interested in the effect sizes for comparisons than for the omnibus effect, and this effect size is calculated in much the same way as we saw for t-tests. In this chapter we saw several examples where effect sizes showed interesting effects even when p-values were not low.

Chapter 11

Looking for Group Differences with Factorial Analysis of Variance (ANOVA) when There is More than One Independent Variable: Learning with Music

> Although statistical analysis can objectify, to some extent, the process of looking for patterns in data, statistical methods . . . do not assure that the most appropriate ways of organizing the data will be found.
>
> Maxwell and Delaney (2004, p. 5)

A one-way ANOVA examines group differences when there is one independent variable and one dependent variable. However, sometimes we may be interested in a more complex situation where the dependent variable can be explained by several different independent variables. When we conduct an ANOVA with two independent variables it is called a two-way ANOVA (see that? The one-way ANOVA had one IV and the two-way ANOVA has two IVs—makes sense!). In general, once we get past the one-way ANOVA, these types of models are called factorial ANOVAs. Table 11.1 lists the terminology of ANOVAs that we use and then tells how many dependent and independent variables each type of ANOVA has.

Table 11.1 Types of Factorial ANOVAs

One-way between-groups ANOVA
   IV: 1 categorical variable
   DV: 1 continuous variable

Two-way between-groups ANOVA
   IV: 2 categorical variables
   DV: 1 continuous variable

. . .

K-way between-groups ANOVA
   IV: K categorical variables
   DV: 1 continuous variable

In this chapter we will look at a study by Obarow (2004) that asked whether music affected how much vocabulary ESL children learned, and also whether picture book illustrations affected vocabulary learning. These ANOVAs can be called "factorial," because we have more than one factor or independent variable. In fact, because there are two independent variables that split the participants into separate groups we can also call this a two-way **between-groups design**.

11.1 ANOVA Design

There are several factors to consider when thinking about the design of factorial ANOVAs and how to interpret output. One factor we will explore in this section is interaction. Another is distinguishing between the number of variables and the number of levels in a variable. If these two areas are not clear, it will be difficult to understand the ANOVA design.

11.1.1 ANOVA Design: Interaction

Although one-way ANOVAs and higher-order ANOVAs are very similar in many ways, one reason to treat them in different chapters is that, once we have more than one independent variable, there is a chance of **interaction** between the variables. An interaction is when one level of a variable affects the levels of a second variable differently. To give a concrete example, in the Obarow (2004) study, if there were no interaction between the independent variables of music and pictures, this would mean that the scores of the participants showed a parallel pattern across both variables. The graph on the left of Figure 11.1 represents a situation where participants learned more vocabulary when there was no music, no matter whether there were pictures present or not (and vice versa—they also learned more when pictures were present than when they were not regardless of whether music was played or not).

However, if the two independent variables show an interaction, then participants do not score the same way on both variables. The means plot on the right in Figure 11.1

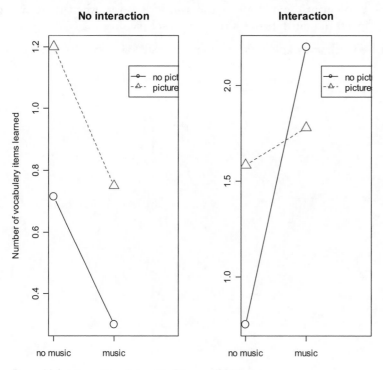

Figure 11.1 Interaction plots with Obarow (2004) data.

represents a situation of interaction where the effect of music did not make much difference when there were pictures present (the dashed line), but, when there were no pictures, music helped improve scores. In an interaction we cannot really talk about the effect of just one variable, because its effect depends on the other variable. So for the graph on the right of Figure 11.1 we can't really just say that the effect of music was important but that the effect of pictures wasn't, because the effect of music was only important when pictures were not present.

> Tip: As the number of independent variables becomes larger, the number of possible interactions becomes larger too. Many statistical experts recommend not including more independent variables in an ANOVA than you are able to understand if the highest possible number of interactions occurs. This often means you should stick to three independent variables at the most.

11.1.2 Application Activity in Understanding Interaction

Look at the graphs in the following exercises, which show an interaction between variables. Try to state the interaction in your own words. All of this data is invented. First, here's an example of what I want you to do. I'll describe the interaction in Figure 11.1 (right-hand graph):

> Interaction: When there were pictures present, it didn't matter if music was present or not—participants scored about the same. However, when there was no music, participants did much better if they could see pictures.

1   The use of feedback and explicit versus implicit instruction and its effect on test scores

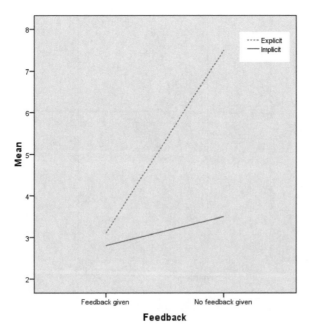

2 Type of pronunciation input and type of production data examined (segmental or intonation) and their effect on pronunciation accuracy

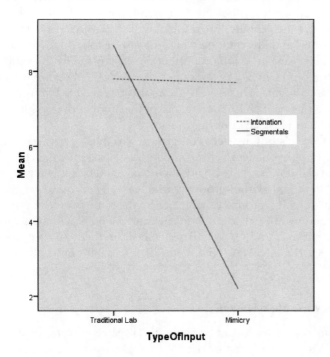

3 The effects of length of immersion, language aptitude, and motivation on the proficiency levels of study abroad learners

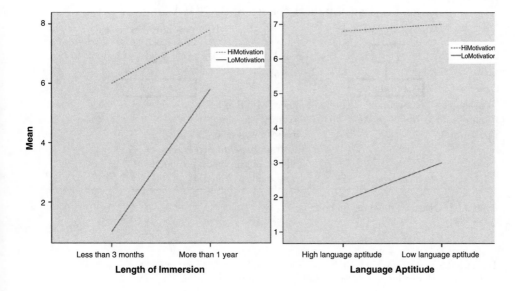

11.1.3 ANOVA Design of the Obarow (2004) Study

The study featured in this chapter is one done by Obarow (2004). Obarow investigated whether the method of presenting storybooks to young children would influence how much vocabulary they would incidentally learn. Obarow had two independent variables: music (singing the story) and illustrations. Thus, there were four different conditions that the story could be heard in—with or without music, crossed by the variable of with or without illustrations. This is a two-way factorial ANOVA because there is more than one independent variable. This ANOVA can also be called a 2 (music) × 2 (illustration) ANOVA (two-by-two ANOVA), to represent the number of levels in each factor. The design box in Figure 11.2 lays out this design.

Both variables in the Obarow study are **between-groups variables**. This means that each person participated in only one level of the variable. For example, the children tested either had music or did not have music with their story, and either had pictures or not.[1] In fact, if you have any **within-groups variables** you will need to use a repeated-measures design. A within-groups variable, where the same people repeat the experiment in different conditions (such as everyone hearing the book with music and later everyone hearing it without music), would result in more than one dependent variable. Therefore, for factorial ANOVA, the independent variables must always be between-groups variables.

11.1.4 ANOVA Design: Variable or Level?

Once we have more than one independent variable it can get confusing to distinguish between separate IVs and the levels of the IVs. I suggest that if the measurement applies to all of the participants in the study then it is a separate variable, while

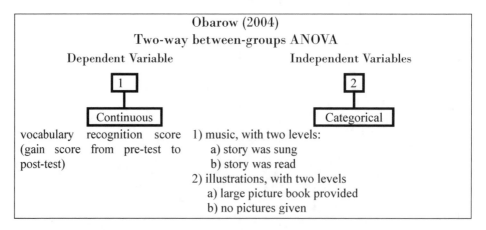

Figure 11.2 Obarow (2004) design box.

---

1 In fact, this statement is not accurate, as we will see in Chapter 12 on RM ANOVA, since actually Obarow tested the children on four different stories and each time they did it she varied the experimental group they were in, but for purposes of this chapter and this part of the data I will maintain this assertion.

conditions. Actually the least number of words that any children knew in the first story was 11, so there were not actually 20 words to learn for any children. Also, it appears that in every category gains were larger when considered in the delayed post-test (one week after the treatment) than in the immediate post-test (the day after treatment ended). The numerical summary also shows that standard deviations are quite large, in most cases larger than the mean.

For the visual summary, since we are looking at group differences, boxplots would be an appropriate way of checking the distribution of data. Figure 11.3 shows boxplots of the four different groups, with the left side showing the first gain score and the right side showing the second gain score (boxplots were obtained through GRAPHS > LEGACY DIALOGS > BOXPLOT; then I chose CLUSTERED and "Summaries for groups of cases." I put the gain score in the "Variable" box, PICTUREST1 in the "Category Axis" box, and MUSICT1 in the "Define clusters by" line).

The boxplots show a number of outliers for three of the four groups (note that there

Table 11.2 Numerical Summary from Obarow (2004) Story 1

		N	Mean	SD
Immediate gains:				
No pictures	No music	15	.73	1.62
	Music	15	.93	1.80
Pictures	No music	17	1.47	1.01
	Music	17	1.29	1.72
Delayed gains:				
No pictures	No music	15	1.40	1.88
	Music	14	1.64	1.50
Pictures	No music	17	1.53	2.12
	Music	17	1.88	2.03

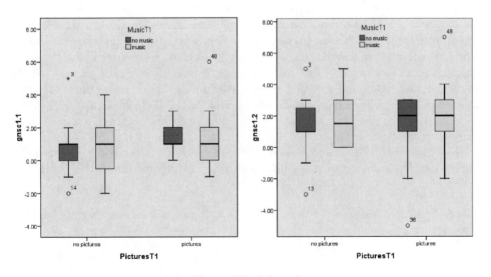

Figure 11.3 Boxplots of gain scores for Obarow (2004) Story 1.

is an outlier with a star in the first gain score boxplot, in the "No pictures, no music" condition; this is an extreme outlier), meaning that the assumption of normality is already violated. One or two of the boxplots look symmetric but there is definitely some skewness as well in most distributions. The variance of the "No pictures, music" group is largest of all four for the immediate gain score (GNSC 1.1).

11.2.1 Means Plots

One type of graphic that is often given in ANOVA studies is a means plot. Although this graphic is useful for discerning trends in the data, it often provides only one piece of information per group—the mean. As a way of visualizing an interaction, means plots can be helpful, but they are not graphically very informative. These types of plots will only be appropriate with two-way and higher ANOVAs (since a means plot with a one-way ANOVA would have only one line). A more informative graph (the parallel coordinate plot) will be shown in Chapter 12 on repeated-measures ANOVAs, and could be used with factorial ANOVAs as well.

11.2.2 Creating a Means Plot

You can create a means plot outside of the ANOVA analysis by using the GRAPHS menu and choosing a LINE graph. The problem is that in order to have two lines (when you have two independent variables) you would need to rearrange your variables differently from how they need to be arranged for the ANOVA.[3] However, the ANOVA process allows you to call for means plots, so there would not be much use in showing you how to call for a means plot when you have to rearrange your data. Thus, in this section, I will show the means plots which are generated by the Plots button when I run the ANOVA on the immediate and delayed post-tests, and discuss how to interpret them.

The left panel of Figure 11.4 shows the gain scores from the vocabulary test conducted immediately after testing. The figure shows that those who saw pictures overall did better (the dotted line is higher than the straight line at all times). However, there does at least seem to be a trend toward interaction because when music was present this was helpful for those who saw no pictures while it seemed to be detrimental for those who saw pictures. We'll see in the later analysis, however, that this trend does not hold statistically, and we can note that the difference between the mean of pictures with no music (about 1.5) and the mean of pictures with music (about 1.3) is not a very large difference. Our graph makes this difference look larger. If the scale of your graph is small enough, the lines may not look parallel, but when you pull back to a larger scale that difference can fade away.

The right panel of Figure 11.4 shows the gain scores from the vocabulary test conducted one week after testing. Again, those who saw pictures did better overall and

---

3 To create the plot where music and lack of it are separate lines and pictures and lack of them are on the x-axis, you would need to create two columns, one called GAIN1NoMUSIC and the other GAIN1MUSIC, copying over from the GNSC1.1 column but only the parts that correspond to "no music" (the first 32 cases) and "music" (the next 31 cases). In GRAPH > LEGACY DIALOGS > LINE, you would choose MULTIPLE and "Summaries of separate variables" and then put the GAIN1NoMUSIC and GAIN1MUSIC in the "Lines Represent" box, and PICTUREST1 in the "Category Axis" box.

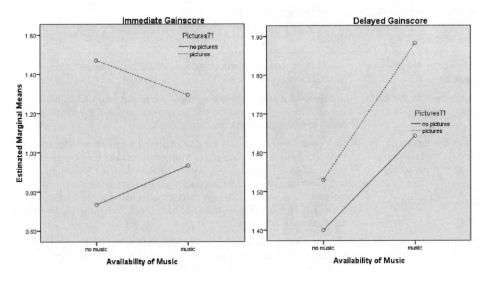

Figure 11.4 Means plots of gain scores from Obarow (2004) Story 1.

here there is no hint of interaction—receiving music is always better no matter if the participants saw pictures or not (and please note that the point scale of the graph on the right panel is different from the scale of the graph on the left panel, so that actually scores overall were higher for the delayed gain score).

11.2.3 Changing the Appearance of Graphs in the Chart Editor

There may be times when the graph that SPSS returns to you is not exactly what you want. It is easy to change many of the parameters of the graph in SPSS. Just double-click on the graph in the SPSS Viewer (the Output) and the Chart Editor will open. Table 11.3 explains various ways you can change different aspects of the graph.

Close the Chart Editor. You can now copy and paste this chart into any word processing document.

11.3 Assumptions of Factorial ANOVA

The four main assumptions for ANOVA are the same ones we've seen for the t-test and the one-way ANOVA, but, with factorial ANOVAs, meeting the assumptions is more complicated because the model is more complicated. For factorial ANOVAs the residuals are often examined as to how well they meet these requirements, as was done in the case of multiple regression. The four assumptions are:

1   The dependent variable should be measured in interval-level measurements.
2   The data should be independent.
3   The data should be normally distributed.
4   Groups should have equal variances.

Table 11.3 Changing Graphical Properties in Chart Editor

If you want to. . .	do this. . .
change titles, subtitles, or legend names	slowly click directly on the title twice. You can then erase the previous title and write a new one
change the orientation of the axis labels	double-click on the label and a Properties box appears. Click on the LABELS AND TICKS tab and choose an orientation from the drop-down menu for Label orientation
change the format of numbers measuring your variable on the y-axis	click once slowly on a numerical label on the y-axis so it is highlighted in blue and go to EDIT > PROPERTIES from the menu bar (or double-click quickly). Go to the SCALE tab. Untick the Auto box for Minimum and Maximum to insert your custom points. Customize the increments as well. Grid marks can be manipulated in the LABELS AND TICKS tab. Number format (number of decimal places) can be adjusted in the NUMBER FORMAT tab
change the lines so they will be visible in black and white	click on a line twice slowly so it is highlighted in blue and go to EDIT > PROPERTIES from the menu bar (or double-click quickly). Change the weight, style, and color of the line in the LINES tab
rearrange the order of the categories listed on the x-axis (when you have a categorical variable)	click on a line twice slowly so it is highlighted in blue and go to EDIT > PROPERTIES from the menu bar. The CATEGORIES tab will allow you to change the order of categories

The last two assumptions are the ones that can be tested before parametric ANOVA statistics are run and should also be examined by residual plots after the ANOVA is run. Just as for multiple regression, creating an ANOVA involves making a model, and that model needs to be examined for normal distribution and equal variances as well.

The first two assumptions listed above need to be addressed in the design of the study. Table 11.4 gives a summary of assumptions that can be tested for the ANOVA. Assumptions 1 and 2 can be tested before the model is run, and assumptions 3 and 4 can be tested only after the model is run.

11.4 Factorial ANOVAs: Extending Analyses to More than One Independent Variable

When we move to two-way and higher ANOVAs, we are finally moving into the world of multivariate analyses for groups. Factorial ANOVAs allow us to test for the effects of more than one independent variable at a time. For example, in the data set that will be used in this section, that of Obarow (2004), the factor of both music and pictures was used to investigate how well these two factors would facilitate vocabulary acquisition among Kindergarten and first-grade children who were being read stories containing some unfamiliar words. Although Obarow only included these two factors in her analysis, for purposes of illustrating a higher-level ANOVA (and because the inclusion of this factor leads to interesting interactions) I will also include the factor of gender.

One important reason for doing a factorial ANOVA, in this case, a 2 (levels of music) × 2 (levels of pictures) × 2 (levels of gender) ANOVA, is to uncover possible interactions among the variables. In other words, if we performed a t-test separately on

Table 11.4 Assumptions for Factorial ANOVA

Meeting assumptions		Factorial ANOVA
1 Normal distribution of data (looking at the data according to groups)	Required?	Yes
	How to test assumption?	Examine boxplots; plot normal curve over histogram (see Chapter 3); use Q-Q plots, robust diagnostics to check for outliers
	What if assumption not met?	1) Use non-parametric Kruskal–Wallis test; 2) use 20% trimmed means and bootstrap
2 Equal variances (looking at the data according to groups)	Required?	Yes
	How to test assumption?	Examine side-by-side boxplots; look at summary statistics for variance (see Chapter 3); examine spread versus level plot (called for in ANOVA)
	What if assumption not met?	1) Try transformation with a log function; 2) use robust regression analysis
3 Normal distribution of residuals	Required?	Yes
	How to test assumption?	Call for residuals and then examine a histogram of their distribution
	What if assumption not met?	1) Use non-parametric Kruskal–Wallis test; 2) use 20% trimmed means and bootstrap
4 Equal variances of residuals	Required?	Yes
	How to test assumption?	Examine scatterplot of predicted values versus studentized residuals. Should see random horizontal scatter and no patterns of data
	What if assumption not met?	Use robust regression analysis

the data by investigating the performance of males versus females, or by those who heard the stories sung (with music) versus those who heard it read (without music), we would not know whether these factors worked together. As we will see, in the Obarow data there is a difference in how males and females react to the presence of music in how well they learn vocabulary. This result could not be uncovered in separate t-tests or separate one-way ANOVAs.

Obarow was extending a previous study by Medina (1990), which found that second-grade second language learners had higher vocabulary gain scores in conditions where they heard a story either sung or read with illustrations, and had the highest scores of all when both conditions were in effect. Medina's results were not statistical; however, there were only seven students in each group. Obarow thus hoped to find statistical differences between groups by using a higher number of participants in each group (originally about 20 in each experimental condition, although through attrition her final numbers were lower). She also had each child participate in each of the four conditions, once for each of four stories. Obarow thus in essence had a repeated-measures ANOVA because each child participated in each condition. However, Obarow's original analysis was to run separate factorial ANOVAs for each of the stories, and that is what we will look at here (you can look at Obarow's results again in the exercises for Chapter 12 on repeated-measures ANOVA).

This chapter introduced the idea of **main effects** and **interaction** in an ANOVA. The variance of a factorial ANOVA is partitioned into different parts, including main (or simple) effects and interaction. In the Obarow example I will show, we have three IVs—music, pictures, and gender. The ANOVA will partition variance into seven separate parts:

1 effects due to music alone
2 effects due to pictures alone
3 effects due to gender alone
4 effects due to the interaction between music and pictures
5 effects due to the interaction between music and gender
6 effects due to the interaction between pictures and gender
7 effects due to the interaction between music, pictures, and gender

Effects 1 through 3 in this list are called **main effects** or **simple effects**. Effects 4 through 7 are called **interaction effects**. If we find an interaction effect, then very rarely will the main effect still be of interest. This is because the main effects can only be interpreted in light of how they interact together. For example, we wouldn't care that musical delivery of vocabulary was more effective than non-musical delivery if we knew that, when there were pictures, music was effective but, when there were no pictures, music was not effective.

11.4.1 Making Sure Your Data is in the Correct Format for a Factorial ANOVA

The Obarow data set provides a good example of the kind of manipulations one might need to perform to put their data into the correct format for an ANOVA. A condensation of Obarow's original data set is shown in Figure 11.5.

It can be seen in Figure 11.5 that Obarow had coded students for gender, grade level, reading level (this was a number from 1 to 3 given to them by their teachers), and then treatment group for the particular story. Obarow then recorded their score on the pre-test, as it was important to see how many of the 20 targeted words in the story the children already knew. As can be seen in the pre-test columns, most of the children already knew a large number of the words. Their scores on the same vocabulary test were recorded after they heard the story three times (immediate post-test) and then again one week later (delayed post-test). The vocabulary test was a four-item multiple choice format.

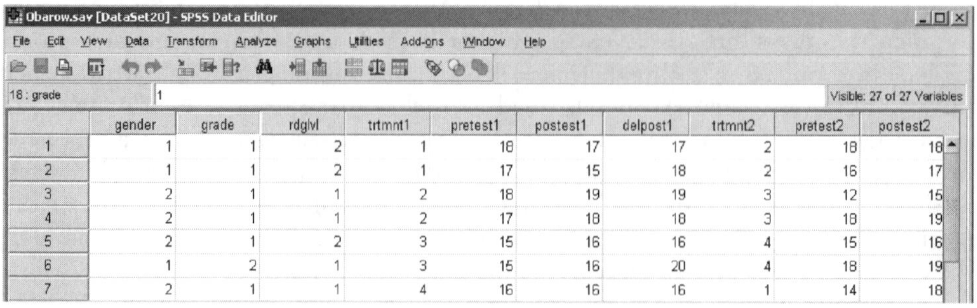
Obarow.sav [DataSet20] - SPSS Data Editor
File Edit View Data Transform Analyze Graphs Utilities Add-ons Window Help
18 : grade 1 Visible: 27 of 27 Variables

	gender	grade	rdglvl	trtmnt1	pretest1	postest1	delpost1	trtmnt2	pretest2	postest2
1	1	1	2	1	18	17	17	2	18	18
2	1	1	2	1	17	15	18	2	16	17
3	2	1	1	2	18	19	19	3	12	15
4	2	1	1	2	17	18	18	3	18	19
5	2	1	2	3	15	16	16	4	15	16
6	1	2	1	3	15	16	20	4	18	19
7	2	1	1	4	16	16	16	1	14	18

Figure 11.5 Original data entry for a complex experiment (Obarow, 2004).

The format found here makes perfect sense for entering the data, but it is not the form we need in order to conduct the ANOVA. First of all, we want to look at gain scores, so I am using the Obarow.Original.sav file. I used TRANSFORM > COMPUTE VARI- ABLE to create a new variable called GNSC1.1, which involves subtracting the PRETEST1 variable from the POSTTEST1 variable (GNSC1.2 is calculated by subtracting PRETEST1 from DELPOST1).

Then there is an issue we should think about before we start to rearrange the data. Although the vocabulary words were chosen to be unfamiliar to this age of children, there were some children who achieved a perfect score on the pre-test. Children with such high scores will clearly not be able to achieve any gains on a post-test. Therefore, it is worth considering whether there should be a cut-off point for children with certain scores on the pre-test. Obarow herself did not do this, but it seems to me that, unless the children scored about a 17 or below, there is really not much room for them to improve their vocabulary in any case. I do not think it violates the independence assumption to throw these cases out because it is equal to excluding children from the experiment if their pre-test scores are too high. With such a cut-off level, for the first story there are still 64 cases out of an original 81, which is still quite a respectable size. I will demonstrate how I cut out these cases.

To cut out some of the rows of the data set, go to DATA > SELECT CASES. We will select the cases we want to *keep* (I often get confused and work the opposite way, selecting the cases I want to get rid of!). We need a conditional argument, so I select the "If condition is satisfied" radio button. Figure 11.6 shows the SELECT CASES dialogue box and the dialogue box that opens when you press the IF button.

The next thing to rearrange in the original data file is the coding of the independent variables. Because music and pictures are going to be two separate independent vari- ables, we will need two columns, one coded for the inclusion of music and one coded for the inclusion of illustrations in the treatment. The way Obarow originally coded the data, TRTMNT1, was coded as 1, 2, 3, or 4, which referred to different configurations of music and pictures. Using this column as it is, we would be able to conduct a one- way ANOVA (with TRTMNT1 as the IV), but we would not then be able to test for the presence of interaction between music and pictures.

To add the two extra columns, I used the TRANSFORM > RECODE INTO DIFFERENT VARI- ABLES command. I set the recoding up knowing that 1 and 2 indicated the absence of music, and 3 and 4 the presence of music. After I created these variables I again tabbed to the Variable View, where I added Values so I would know later whether 1 meant music was present or not. I then did recoding for pictures.[4]

After all of this manipulation, I am ready to get to work on my ANOVA analysis! Notice that I now have a gain score (GNSC1.1), and two columns coding for the presence of music (MUSICT1) and pictures (PICTUREST1). There are only 64 rows of data. I have called this file Obarow.Story1.sav.

---

4 Actually, when I was trying this I found that TRTMNT1 could not be coded into two different codings in SPSS (one for whether music was present and another for whether pictures were present). What one would need to do then is to copy the TRTMNT1 column and call it something like TRTMNT1COPY2, and then recode using TRANSFORM > RECODE INTO SAME VARIABLES. The directives for transforming pictures are: 1 = 1, 2 = 2, 3 = 1, 4 = 2, where 1 =no pictures and 2=pictures.

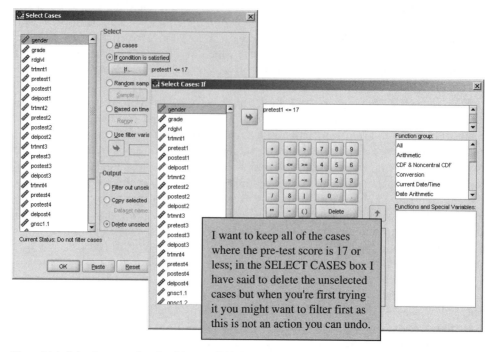

Figure 11.6 Selecting cases for the Obarow (2004) data set.

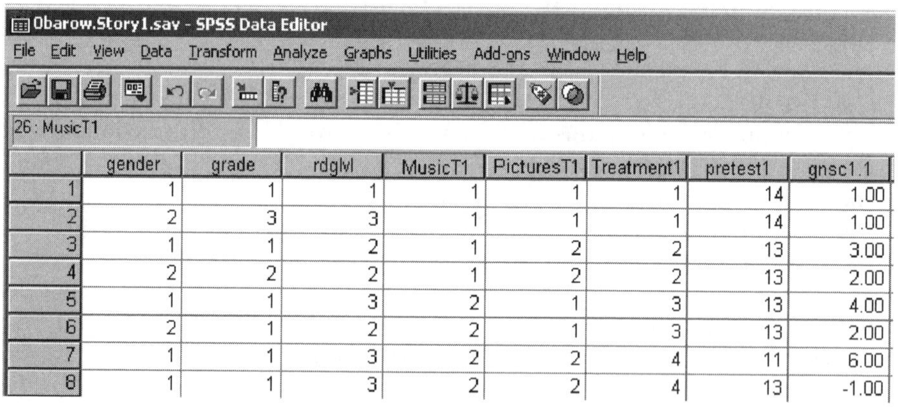

Figure 11.7 The Obarow data set ready for analysis.

11.4.2 Performing a Factorial ANOVA with SPSS

To perform an ANOVA when you have more than one independent variable, use the univariate ANOVA in SPSS (this can be used to analyze one-way ANOVAs with only one independent variable as well). The call for this is ANALYZE > GENERAL LINEAR MODEL > UNIVARIATE. The dialogue box that appears is shown in Figure 11.8. I have put all three independent variables into the "Fixed Factors" box.

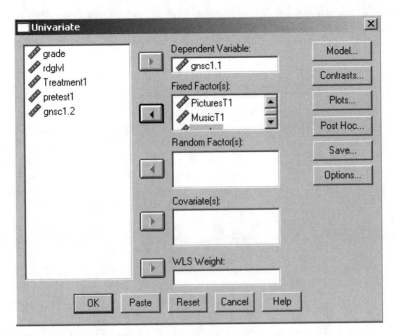

Figure 11.8 Performing a factorial ANOVA in SPSS.

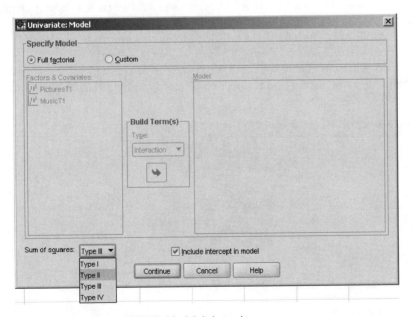

Figure 11.9 Univariate ANOVA: Model dialogue box.

You should also open the MODEL, PLOTS, POST HOC, SAVE, and OPTIONS buttons, which are found on the right-hand side of the UNIVARIATE dialogue box. In the MODEL box (Figure 11.9), change the type of Sum of Squares from Type III to Type II and press

CONTINUE (for a justification for this, see Section 11.4.3). SPSS uses Type III Sums of Squares as a default but from my readings I think it is better to use Type II.

Next, open the PLOTS box (Figure 11.10) and call for several different types of means plots, since you may find one configuration is more easily understandable than another. Just put the independent variables in the boxes and press the ADD button.

Figure 11.11 shows the Post Hoc dialogue box. You should move the variables that you are interested in seeing post-hoc tests for to the right, and then tick the post-hoc test you want to use. Repeating the recommendations given in Chapter 10 for the one-way ANOVA, I suggest you use the LSD along with the FDR adjustment or the REGWQ if you want the most power. For control of the FWE rate use Tukey's or Bonferroni's adjustments, and if your variances are unequal then use the Games–How-ell test. Note that, for the Obarow data, post-hoc tests cannot actually be performed because each factor has only two levels. If there is a statistical difference for the main effect, it will be clear from mean scores which group was better. Please note that these post-hocs are not doing anything to help interpret the interactions, just the main effects.

Last of all, open the SAVE and OPTIONS buttons and click on the boxes that I have clicked on (see Figure 11.12). In the OPTIONS box, if you would like to get confidence intervals for the mean scores of any of the levels of the variables by themselves (such as the 95% CI for the mean score on the dependent variable by males and females if you put in gender) or in concert with another variable (such as the 95% CI for the mean score on the dependent variable by males who hear no music in the treatment if you put in gender*MusicT1), move the correct term over to the right (under "Display Means for").

After opening all of the side buttons indicated here, you are ready to press OK on the main UNIVARIATE dialogue box and get your factorial ANOVA output.

The first two tables in the output will be descriptive statistics, telling you what your independent variables are, how many levels each variable has, and how many

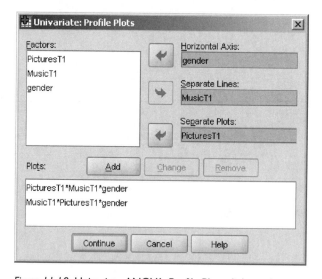

Figure 11.10 Univariate ANOVA: Profile Plots dialogue box.

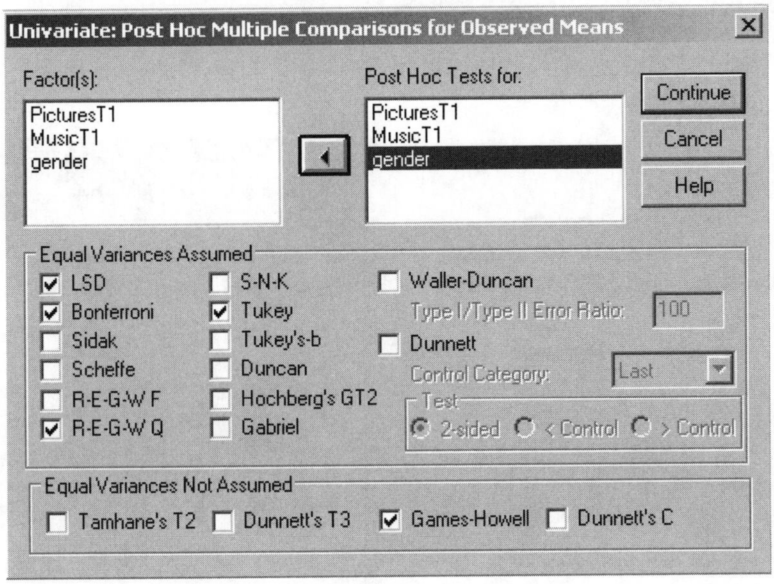

Figure 11.11 Univariate ANOVA: Post Hoc dialogue box.

participants are in each level (in the table labeled "Between-Subjects Factors"), and giving the mean, standard deviation, and N for each intersection of your variables (this table is labeled "Descriptive Statistics"). As always, be sure to look at these tables to make sure everything is set up the way you thought.

The next piece of output is Levene's test for homogeneity of variances, shown in Table 11.5. It is not statistical ($p > .05$), meaning that the assumption of homoscedasticity is not violated (or, at least, that's what Levene's test says). The other thing to notice about Levene's test is that in footnote (a) the regression equation is given explicitly. In just the same way that multiple regression used an equation, ANOVA uses an equation as well. The difference is that, for multiple regression, SPSS included only main effects, while, for an ANOVA, SPSS automatically includes main effects and all interactions as well. You can see the equation for the ANOVA has all seven parts of the variance which I said we would test in the ANOVA in Section 11.4.

The next table will be the heart of our analysis, and this is the Tests of Between-Subjects Effects table (Table 11.6). The first two and last two lines of this table are generally of no interest to us. The "Corrected Model" specified in the first line is a test of "the null hypothesis that performance is a function of the full set of effects (the main effects and the interactions)" (Howell, 2002, p. 464), and if group sizes are exactly equal this line will be exactly equal to the sum of squares of all the main effects and interactions (SS_{model}). The second line, "Intercept," tests the hypothesis that the grand mean is equal to zero (Howell, 2002), and we are generally not interested in this question. The information of interest is the between-groups factors (the three main effects of gender, music, and pictures, and the four interaction effects with these fac-

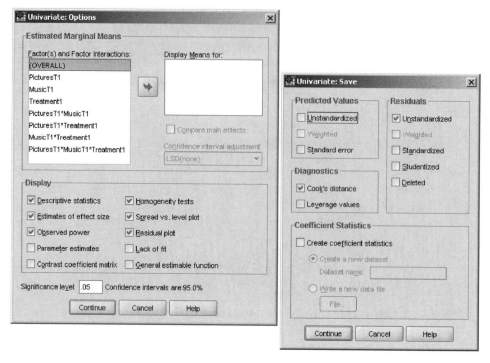

Figure 11.12 Univariate ANOVA: Options dialogue box.

Table 11.5 Univariate ANOVA Output: Levene's Test

Levene's Test of Equality of Error Variances

Dependent Variable: gnsc1.1

F	df1	df2	Sig.
1.882	7	56	.090

Tests the null hypothesis that the error variance of the
dependent variable is equal across groups.

a. Design:
Intercept+gender+PicturesT1+MusicT1+gender
* PicturesT1+gender * MusicT1+PicturesT1 *
MusicT1+gender * PicturesT1 * MusicT1

tors) and the within-groups factor, which is also called the "Error" (since the variation within and not across the groups represents variation we can't account for, and thus this is all put into the error term).

The error line is important because it tells us what mean square each of the previous seven lines was divided by. For example, the F-value for the pictures × music interaction is equal to the mean square of the interaction (1.669) divided by the mean square of the error (2.296). The significance of the F-value is determined by looking up that value of F using the degrees of freedom from the interaction (df = 1) and the error

Table 11.6 Univariate ANOVA Output: Test of Between-Subjects Effects

Tests of Between-Subjects Effects

Dependent Variable: gnsc1.1

Source	Type II Sum of Squares	df	Mean Square	F	Sig.	Partial Eta Squared	Noncent. Parameter	Observed Power[b]
Corrected Model	22.399[a]	7	3.200	1.393	.226	.148	9.754	.539
Intercept	81.000	1	81.000	35.272	.000	.386	35.272	1.000
PicturesT1	2.388	1	2.388	1.040	.312	.018	1.040	.171
MusicT1	.365	1	.365	.159	.692	.003	.159	.068
gender	9.990	1	9.990	4.350	.042	.072	4.350	.536
PicturesT1 * MusicT1	1.669	1	1.669	.727	.398	.013	.727	.133
PicturesT1 * gender	.270	1	.270	.117	.733	.002	.117	.063
MusicT1 * gender	5.551	1	5.551	2.417	.126	.041	2.417	.333
PicturesT1 * MusicT1 * gender	1.369	1	1.369	.596	.443	.011	.596	.118
Error	128.601	56	2.296					
Total	232.000	64						
Corrected Total	151.000	63						

a. R Squared = .148 (Adjusted R Squared = .042)

b. Computed using alpha = .05

(df = 56). A large sum of squares in the Error line relative to the main effects and interaction effects tells us our model has not accounted for very much of the variation in the model (which is true in this case).

Now let's look at how to interpret the main effects. The third line of Table 11.6 tests for the main effect of pictures, ignoring all other variables. The main effect is not statistical ($F_{1,56} = 1.04$, $p = .312$, partial eta-squared=.018, power=.17). One reason this effect may not be statistical is that the power is very low. Recall that we would like power to be at least .80 so that we have a four in five chance of finding a statistical effect. Here we have less than a one in eight chance of finding a statistical effect, even if it exists. Likewise, the main effect of music is also non-statistical, but again power to find real effects is quite low.

The fifth line of Table 11.6 tests for the main effect of gender. This main effect is statistical ($F_{1,56} = 4.35$, $p = .042$, partial eta-squared=.07, power=.55). The descriptive statistics (not given here) show that females scored higher than males, so we conclude that Kindergarten and first-grade females learn more vocabulary in an experiment like this than males. However, if there are any interactions, the main effect may be of little interest to us, as what will be important is how males and females perform differently in the presence of music or pictures.

The four lines with interactions in Table 11.6 do not point to any statistical two-way or three-way interactions. Notice that the partial eta-squared information for the Corrected Model entry is the same as the R-squared term given in footnote (a) below the table (.148). The adjusted R squared (.042) is equal to the omega-squared statistic. We may say that either the full factorial model accounts for 14.8% of the variation or, correcting for bias, the model accounts for 4.2% of the variation in the number of vocabulary items learned by the participants.

The univariate approach can also provide a post-hoc estimate of power. Although an a priori estimate is much preferable for determining sample sizes, a post-hoc estimate of power can also demonstrate whether there was enough power to fairly test the hypothesis. In the case of the overall model (the Corrected Model line) the power was not very good, at 54%. It is reasonable to say that there was not much power to find differences in this model.

If you have post-hoc tests (remember that I don't because all my variables have only two levels), then the next important part of the print-out will be the multiple comparisons. If none of the main effects are statistical, you would not go on to look at the post-hoc tests. Also, if you found that an interaction was statistical, you would be more interested in what was going on with the interaction, and the post-hoc tests for the main effect would not be very interesting.

Somewhere after the tests of between-subjects effects you will find a few plots which have been called for to check the assumptions of the ANOVA model. Figure 11.13 shows the spread versus level plot and the residuals plot.

There are two spread versus level plots, one comparing standard deviations and the other comparing variances. Both plots test the assumption of equal variances for the data and should show no pattern of data, just random scattering. This is true of the spread versus level plots seen here. For the residual plot, the Predicted versus Std. Residual box (center column, bottom row of the graph on the left in Figure 11.13) tests the homogeneity of variances of the residuals. This should also just show horizontal noise and no pattern of data.

To test the assumption of normality of the residuals, I called for the unstandardized residuals to be added to the end of the Data Editor. Find the column that says Res_1. We can make a histogram to see if the residuals are normally distributed. I will not show this graph, but the residuals appear to be fairly normally distributed. Cook's distance is a measure of influential outliers, and values over 1 would be cause for concern. There are many ways you could check this but I just went ahead and did another histogram and saw that the largest value of Cook's was only 0.2, so it seems the assumptions for the residuals are also satisfied.

If you called for profile plots you will find them at the end of your output. I showed the interaction plots for music and pictures in Figure 11.3. Now, adding gender to the

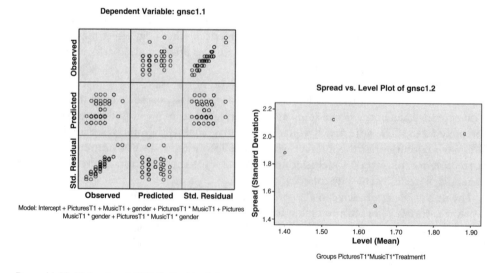

Figure 11.13 Univariate ANOVA: Residual plots.

analysis, we do find an interesting plot. The interaction plot between music and gender for males shows that, for boys, when pictures are present the presence or absence of music does not make a difference. However, when there are no pictures, having music is much more helpful for boys than no music.

Although the interaction looks large in Figure 11.14, the difference for boys between the presence of music when there are no pictures is only about a point and a half, a difference of one and a half words. This is the reason nothing is statistical in the ANOVA—the differences are not large enough to be statistical, not when the power levels are low.

One point to take away from the Obarow data is that, when expected results fail to materialize, it often pays to explore your data a bit to look for other explanatory variables. Obarow (2004) looked at her data using only the music and pictures variables and found no statistical results. Although only the main effect of gender was statistical when this third factor was added in, the effect sizes and interaction plot suggest that in testing more participants we might find that gender does play a small role in the effect of music and illustrations on how well young children learn vocabulary.

Performing a Factorial (Two-Way and Higher) ANOVA

1   ANALYZE > GENERAL LINEAR MODEL > UNIVARIATE.
2   Put dependent variable into "Dependent Variable" box. Put IV into the Fixed Factor(s)" box.
3   Open the MODELS button; change Sum of Squares from Type III to Type II.
4   Open the PLOTS button and call for different means plots using various configurations of your variables.
5   Open the POST HOC button, move factors with three or more levels into right-hand box, and tick Tukey or REGWQ (or LSD if you have only three means).
6   Open the SAVE button and tick Cook's distance under Diagnostics and Unstandardized under Residuals.
7   Open the OPTIONS button, move any factors whose confidence intervals you want to obtain to right-hand box, and tick Descriptive statistics, Estimates of effect size, Observed power, Homogeneity tests, Spread Vs. Level plot, and Residuals plot.

11.4.3 Excursus on Type II versus Type III Sums of Squares (Advanced Topic)

It is mainly when we are examining ANOVA tables that the issue of what types of sums of squares (SS) are used will arise. Within ANOVA, four methods of partitioning error into sums of squares have been distinguished. However, it is only when experimental designs are unbalanced, meaning that the group sizes are not all equal, that differences according to the type of sums of squares used will arise. Langsrud (2003) notes that most major statistical programs use Type III SS as the default in calculation, and this includes SPSS. Many researchers, including Maxwell and Delaney (2004), have concluded that Type III SS are best. However, several other researchers have argued strongly that, as a general rule, Type II SS are best, provide the most power, and generally test more interesting hypotheses than Type III sums of squares (Fox, 2002; Langsrud, 2003; Nelder, 1994; Nelder & Lane, 1995).

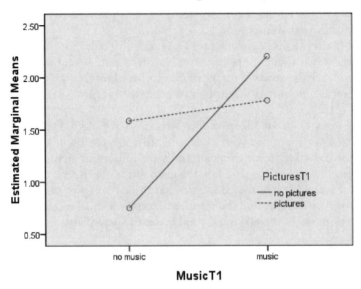

Figure 11.14 Interaction plot between music and pictures for males only (Obarow, 2004).

With all types of sums of squares, differences in analysis will arise only in conjunction with the analysis of the main effects, not of the interaction effects. Therefore, say we have factor A and factor B. The differences in what sums of squares are reported for the effect of A and the effect of B will differ according to the type of sums of squares used (if the design is unbalanced), but the effect of AB will be the same whatever the type of sum of squares used.

Type II sums of squares consider the main effects of variables A and B by assuming that any interaction involving them is not statistical. This results in each effect being adjusted for all other terms in the model except for terms which contain the effect. Langsrud (2003, p. 163) gives the following example: "in a three-way table (A, B and C) the main effect for factor A is not adjusted for the interaction AB, AC, and ABC. And the two-factor interactions are not adjusted for ABC." In contrast, using the Type III sum of squares adjusts for all other factors in the model, which means that, when looking at the main effect of A, adjustments are made for the interactions of AB, AC, and ABC as well as for all other factors. In practice this means that Type III SS evaluate the main effect of A regardless of whether the interaction is statistical or not.

Although it may at first seem logical to use Type III sums of squares because you don't want to assume that interactions are not statistical, Langsrud gives a convincing argument for the superiority of Type II SS. He says that, "[i]f a main effect is found to be significant, this result is correct if there is no interaction. If the interaction is present, both main effects will also be present. In any case, the statement about a significant main effect will be correct" (2003, p. 165). The logical argument, then, actually favors Type II SS because it is not logical to assume that the interaction AB could be statistical without the main effects A and B also being statistical (Langsrud,

2003). For this reason, several authors have argued that the hypotheses that Type III SS test are unrealistic or uninteresting hypotheses.

Langsrud (2003) also notes that one would like to choose the most powerful test. He says that, when there is no interaction, Type II SS will be the most powerful. When there is an interaction, some limited simulation studies have concluded that on average Type II is still more powerful than Type III. Therefore, when one is choosing between a Type II and Type III test, my advice is to prefer the Type II test, which means changing the default in SPSS.

Summary of a Comparison between Type II and Type III Sums of Squares

A Type II SS approach looks at a main effect A without adjusting for the higher-order factors that A is involved in, such as AB, AC, and ABC. The hypothesis that is tested is whether the main effect of A is statistical given the other interactions that A is involved in.

A Type III SS approach looks at a main effect A by adjusting for all higher-order factors that A is involved in, such as AB, AC, and ABC. The hypothesis that is tested is whether the main effect of A is statistical whether or not the interactions that A is involved in are statistical.

It was pointed out that logically it does not make sense to ignore an interaction if it is statistical. Fox (2002) claims that, thus, Type III SS test uninteresting hypotheses.

11.4.4 Performing Comparisons in a Factorial ANOVA with SPSS

Section 11.4.2 presented data from Obarow (2004), and showed how to conduct a $2 \times 2 \times 2$ ANOVA on the data. However, because each variable had only two levels, we did not need to do any further work to tell which group outperformed the other if the variable was statistical. This section will illustrate a factorial ANOVA where we will need to perform comparisons among groups inside a variable. The data I will be using in this section are adapted from a data set called "ChickWeight" from the R statistical program built-in library. These data provide the complex analysis that I want to show here, but I have renamed the data set in order to better help you understand the types of analyses that we would do in second language research. I call this data set "Writing.txt," and we will pretend that this data describes an experiment which investigated the role of L1 background and experimental condition on scores on a writing sample.

The dependent variable in this data set is the score on the writing assessment, which ranges from 35 to 373 (pretend this is an aggregated score from four separate judges who each rated the writing samples on a 100-point score). The independent variables are first language (four L1s: Arabic, Japanese, Russian, and Spanish) and condition. There were three conditions that students were asked to write their essays in—"correctAll," which means they were told their teachers would correct all of their errors; "correctTarget," which means the writers were told only specific targeted errors would be corrected; and "noCorrect," in which nothing about correction was mentioned to the students.

First of all, we want to examine the data before running any tests, so Table 11.7 gives a numerical summary of the data. The very highest scores within each L1 were obtained in the condition where no corrections were made, and the lowest scores in the condition where writers were told everything would be corrected. Standard deviations

Table 11.7 Descriptive Statistics for the Writing Data Set

L1	Condition	N	Mean	SD
Arabic	CorrectAll	59	48.2	7.1
	CorrectTarget	76	87.0	26.1
	NoCorrect	85	154.4	52.1
Japanese	CorrectAll	30	50.0	8.2
	CorrectTarget	40	101.7	30.9
	NoCorrect	50	182.9	66.0
Russian	CorrectAll	30	52.4	9.9
	CorrectTarget	40	116.7	27.4
	NoCorrect	48	202.5	42.7
Spanish	CorrectAll	30	51.1	9.2
	CorrectTarget	40	109.5	30.3
	NoCorrect	50	224.8	67.0

certainly have a large amount of variation within each L1. Clearly the numbers of participants in each group are unbalanced but there are a large number of them at least.

Next, a barplot, shown in Figure 11.15, will help in visually getting a feel for the multivariate data (I use a barplot here instead of a boxplot because there are so many data points that it's just a bit too much to have them all together in one place). The barplot quickly shows the conclusion made from the numerical summary, which was

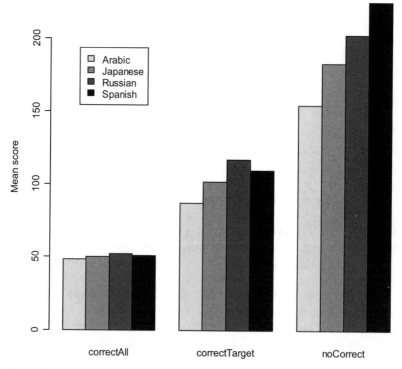

Figure 11.15 Barplot of Writing data set.

that those who were not told anything about correction got the highest overall scores and those who were told everything would be corrected got the most depressed scores. Within the condition of "correctAll," there doesn't seem to be much difference depending on L1, but within the "noCorrect" condition the L1 Spanish writers scored the highest and the L1 Arabic speakers scored the worst. The barplot doesn't tell us anything about the distribution of data as a boxplot would, though.

Going through the steps for a factorial ANOVA, I used the ANALYZE > GENERAL LINEAR MODEL > UNIVARIATE menu. I put SCORE in the Dependent variable box, and L1 and CONDITION in the "Fixed factor(s)" box. In the MODEL button I changed the SS to Type II; in the PLOTS button I called for two plots, one with L1 on the horizontal axis and one with L1 as separate lines. Both L1 and CONDITION have more than two levels, so in the POSTHOC button I moved both to the right and ticked the Tukey box for comparisons as well as the Games-Howell box for "Equal Variances Not Assumed." I ticked the boxes "Descriptive statistics," "Estimates of effect size," "Observed Power," "Homogeneity tests," and "Residual plot" in the OPTIONS button.

In the output, Levene's test is statistical, with $p = .000$ listed in the output. This means the assumption of equal variances is violated, which we pretty much assumed by looking at the numerical summaries with the widely varying standard deviations (the variance is the square of the standard deviation).

Now going to the test of between-subject effects (Table 11.8), we see that there are statistical results in all three parts of the ANOVA model: L1, CONDITION, and the interaction between L1 and CONDITION (because the p-value located in the "Sig." column is smaller than $p = .05$). The power is a perfect 1 in all cases as well, but the partial eta-squared effect size is largest for CONDITION. The total R^2 for this model is shown at the bottom of the table, and it is $R^2 = .69$, meaning that the combination of these variables accounts for 69% of the variance (or 68% if adjusted for bias).

Tip: Remember that, when you report the results of main effects from an ANOVA, you need to report two numbers for degrees of freedom, one for the levels of the independent variable and the other the overall error (within-groups variance). For example, from the data in Table 11.8, you want to report that the effect of first language was statistical. You would say: "The main effect of L1 is statistical, $F_{3,566} = 27.19, p < .0005$."

Table 11.8 Univariate ANOVA Output for Writing: Between-Subjects Effects

Tests of Between-Subjects Effects

Dependent Variable score

Source	Type II Sum of Squares	df	Mean Square	F	Sig.	Partial Eta Squared	Noncent Parameter	Observed Power[b]
Corrected Model	2.004E6[a]	11	182165.095	113.211	.000	.688	1245.317	1.000
Intercept	8577351.074	1	8577351.074	5330.590	.000	.904	5330.590	1.000
L1	131252.065	3	43750.688	27.190	.000	.126	81.570	1.000
condition	1777365.323	2	888682.662	552.292	.000	.661	1104.584	1.000
L1 * condition	70588.062	6	11764.677	7.311	.000	.072	43.869	1.000
Error	910739.882	566	1609.081					
Total	1.149E7	578						
Corrected Total	2914555.926	577						

a. R squared = .688 (Adjusted R Squared = .681)
b. Computed using alpha = .05

Now we know that participants performed differently based on their L1, and the barplot in Figure 11.15 showed that the Arabic L1 speakers always performed the worst in every condition and that the Spanish and Russian L1 speakers usually performed the highest, but we want to know whether there are any statistical differences among the speakers. We also see from the barplot that the conditions seem to be highly different from one another, but we should check this statistically as well. The post-hocs that we called for when running the ANOVA can answer these questions.

However, the interaction between L1 and Condition is statistical, and I have previously stated that simple (or main) effects may not be of interest when interactions are taking place. So we really want to know whether the combinations of L1 and CONDITION are statistically different from each other. The problem is that SPSS gives us no way to perform post-hoc tests for the interaction using drop-down menus (Landau & Everitt, 2002). Weinberg and Abramowitz (2002) provide information on how post-hocs that investigate interactions can be called for SPSS syntax. Here is how we can do this.

First, return to your factorial ANOVA command, and open the OPTIONS button. In the box under "Estimated Marginal Means: Factor(s) and Factor Interactions," highlight OVERALL and all of your parameters (in our case, L1, CONDITION, and L1*CONDITION) and move them to the right-hand box. We do this not because we actually want the means but because it will produce the syntax we want to copy. Press CONTINUE to return to the Univariate box. Now open the PASTE button on the Univariate dialogue box. This will bring up the **Syntax Editor**. The first line will read "UNIANOVA," and you are looking for a line that says:

/EMMEANS = TABLES(L1*CONDITION)

This line tells SPSS to create a table of means for the interaction. To create post-hocs for the interaction, copy the line, and add the command COMPARE(L1) to it. Copy it again and add COMPARE(CONDITION) to it as well, in order to get both types of comparisons. The first (with L1) will divide the data up into the three conditions and within each condition compare each of the L1s. The second (with CONDITION) will divide the data up into four groups of L1, and then compare the three conditions within each L1. In other words, for Arabic you will be able to see if there is a statistical difference between "CorrectAll" and "CorrectTarget." You will see omnibus tests for male and female. Here is the syntax I would use in this case:

/EMMEANS = TABLES(L1*CONDITION)COMPARE(L1)

/EMMEANS = TABLES(L1*CONDITION)COMPARE(CONDITION)

Paste both of these lines anywhere (but, if you do put them at the end, put a period to show that it is the end of the commands). Now choose the RUN menu, and either choose RUN ALL or highlight the part you want and choose RUN SELECTION (see Figure 11.16).

You'll then be looking for a title in the output that says L1*Condition (actually, if you run both, you'll have two of these!). First it will have mean scores and confidence intervals in the "Estimates" table (see Table 11.9), but keep scanning and you will see the table labeled "Pairwise Comparisons" that has statistical comparisons (Table 11.10 shows this output with a box around the title).

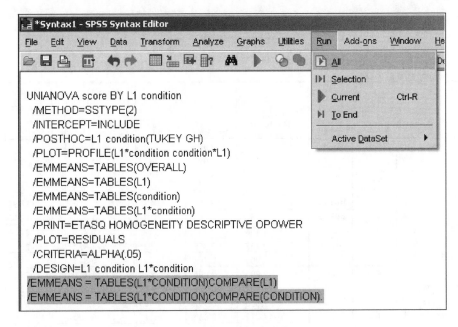

Figure 11.16 Syntax to obtain post-hocs for interaction effects.

Table 11.9 Beginning of Output for Testing Interaction Comparisons

5. L1 * condition

Estimates

Dependent Variable:score

L1	condition	Mean	Std. Error	95% Confidence Interval	
				Lower Bound	Upper Bound
Arabic	correctAll	48.237	5.222	37.980	58.495
	correctTarget	87.013	4.601	77.975	96.051
	noCorrect	154.388	4.351	145.842	162.934
Japane	correctAll	49.967	7.324	35.582	64.352

The output in Table 11.10 shows 36 comparisons. Remember that these pairwise comparisons are unadjusted p-values, and you have just run a lot of tests, so you might want to be careful in your interpretations. You can call for p-value adjustments by adding either "adj(Bonferroni)" or "adj(Sidak)" to the end of the syntax above, like this:

/EMMEANS = TABLES(L1*CONDITION)COMPARE(CONDITION) adj (Bonferroni)

but you might also want to just gather unadjusted p-values and use the FDR calculation for adjusted p-values, which will give you more power (see the Appendix for the code for FDR in R and Section 9.3.1 for more information about types of adjustments

Table 11.10 Main Output for Testing Interaction Comparisons

Pairwise Comparisons

Dependent Variable:score

condition	(I) L1	(J) L1	Mean Difference (I-J)	Std. Error	Sig.[a]	95% Confidence Interval for Difference[a]	
						Lower Bound	Upper Bound
correctAll	Arabic	Japane	-1.729	8.995	.848	-19.397	15.938
		Russia	-4.196	8.995	.641	-21.864	13.471
		Spanis	-2.896	8.995	.748	-20.564	14.771
	Japane	Arabic	1.729	8.995	.848	-15.938	19.397
		Russia	-2.467	10.357	.812	-22.810	17.877
		Spanis	-1.167	10.357	.910	-21.510	19.177
	Russia	Arabic	4.196	8.995	.641	-13.471	21.864
		Japane	2.467	10.357	.812	-17.877	22.810
		Spanis	1.300	10.357	.900	-19.043	21.643
	Spanis	Arabic	2.896	8.995	.748	-14.771	20.564
		Japane	1.167	10.357	.910	-19.177	21.510
		Russia	-1.300	10.357	.900	-21.643	19.043
correctTarget	Arabic	Japane	-14.712	7.836	.061	-30.103	.679
		Russia	-29.712*	7.836	.000	-45.103	-14.321
		Spanis	-22.437*	7.836	.004	-37.828	-7.046
	Japane	Arabic	14.712	7.836	.061	-.679	30.103
		Russia	-15.000	8.970	.095	-32.618	2.618
		Spanis	-7.725	8.970	.389	-25.343	9.893
	Russia	Arabic	29.712*	7.836	.000	14.321	45.103
		Japane	15.000	8.970	.095	-2.618	32.618
		Spanis	7.275	8.970	.418	-10.343	24.893
	Spanis	Arabic	22.437*	7.836	.004	7.046	37.828
		Japane	7.725	8.970	.389	-9.893	25.343
		Russia	-7.275	8.970	.418	-24.893	10.343
noCorrect	Arabic	Japane	-28.532*	7.149	.000	-42.574	-14.489
		Russia	-48.091*	7.242	.000	-62.316	-33.866
		Spanis	-70.452*	7.149	.000	-84.494	-56.409
	Japane	Arabic	28.532*	7.149	.000	14.489	42.574
		Russia	-19.559*	8.106	.016	-35.480	-3.638
		Spanis	-41.920*	8.023	.000	-57.678	-26.162
	Russia	Arabic	48.091*	7.242	.000	33.866	62.316
		Japane	19.559*	8.106	.016	3.638	35.480
		Spanis	-22.361*	8.106	.006	-38.282	-6.440
	Spanis	Arabic	70.452*	7.149	.000	56.409	84.494
		Japane	41.920*	8.023	.000	26.162	57.678
		Russia	22.361*	8.106	.006	6.440	38.282

Based on estimated marginal means

a. Adjustment for multiple comparisons: Least Significant Difference (equivalent to no adjustments).

*. The mean difference is significant at the .05 level.

for multiple tests). There are 36 comparisons, but only 6 are unique for each comparison (Arabic–Japanese, Arabic–Russian, Arabic–Spanish, Japanese–Russian, Japanese–Spanish, and Russian–Spanish). Using the FDR with the 18 unique comparisons I find a cut-off point of $p = .016$, meaning that anything that is 0.016 or lower would be considered statistical (this is considerably more powerful than a Bonferroni correction, which will basically say that the cut-off value is $.05/6 = .008$). Therefore, all of the comparisons in the "noCorrect" condition are statistical plus two more in the "correctTarget" condition (Arabic–Russian and Arabic–Spanish).

The final conclusion we can make is that in the "noCorrect" condition L1 was very important. Every L1 group scored differently in this condition, with the mean scores showing that, from the best performers to the worst, we have Spanish L1 > Russian L1 > Japanese L1 > Arabic L1. In the "correctTarget" condition the Russian L1 and Spanish L1 speakers performed better than the Arabic L1 speakers, and the Japanese were somewhere in the middle, neither statistically different from the Arabic speakers nor from the Russian and Spanish speakers. For the "correctAll" condition L1 made absolutely no difference. Everyone performed very poorly when they thought all of their mistakes were going to be graded. This is the story that I would tell if reporting on this study.

Tip: Sometimes logic doesn't work with multiple comparisons! For example, you may at times find that statistically Group A is different from Group B, and Group B is different from Group C, but statistically Group A is not different from Group C. As Howell (2002) points out, logically this seems impossible. If $A \neq B$ and $B \neq C$, then logically $A \neq C$. However, logic is not statistics and sometimes there is not enough power to find a difference which logically should be there. Howell says sometimes we just have to live with uncertainty!

Doing Multiple Comparisons on a Factorial (Two-Way and Higher) ANOVA

1 ANALYZE > GENERAL LINEAR MODEL > UNIVARIATE.
2 Open the OPTIONS button. In the box under "Estimated Marginal Means: Factor(s) and Factor Interactions," move everything on the left to the right-hand box. Press CONTINUE. In the Univariate dialogue box open the PASTE button, which brings up the Syntax Editor. Insert syntax that calls for a comparison of the interaction, like this:

   /EMMEANS = TABLES(L1*CONDITION)COMPARE(L1)

   Repeat the syntax line with the other parts of the interaction at the end (this will just change the order that the pairwise comparisons are done in, so in the output just choose the one you like best and ignore the other):

   /EMMEANS = TABLES(L1*CONDITION)COMPARE(CONDITION)

   In the Syntax Editor, choose RUN > RUN ALL; then look for the part of the output that shows the interaction (like L1*Condition) and find the box that says "Pairwise Comparisons."
   Consider whether you will adjust the p-value for multiple comparisons (I recommend the FDR algorithm for maximum power).

11.4.5 Application Activity with Factorial ANOVA

1　Obarow (2004) data. In the text I performed a factorial ANOVA on the gain score for Obarow's Treatment 1. Using the file Obarow.Story2.sav, first rearrange the data correctly as outlined in Section 11.4.1. You will need to decide whether to select cases. You will need to change the Trtmnt2 variable into two different IVs, music and pictures (use the values for Trtmnt2 to help guide what you do). Then calculate a gain score. Once you have configured the data to a form ready to perform an ANOVA, visually and numerically examine the data with boxplots and comment on assumptions. Last, perform a factorial ANOVA to find out what effect gender, music, and pictures had on the gain score for the second treatment (story).

2　Larson-Hall and Connell (2005). Use the LarsonHall.Forgotten.sav data. Use the SENTENCEACCENT variable to investigate whether the independent variables of gender and (immersion) status could help explain variance in what kind of accent rating participants received. Be sure to examine boxplots and comment on assumptions.

3　Dewaele and Pavlenko (2001–2003) data. Use the BEQ.Swear.sav file. Dewaele (2004a, 2004b, 2004c) explored the question of whether multilinguals' perceptions of the emotional force and frequency of swear words depended on a variety of other variables that were measured in the web questionnaire. The question that asked about the emotional force of swear words was a five-item Likert scale that asked "Do swear and taboo words in your different languages have the same emotional weight for you?" Use a factorial ANOVA to examine the effect of context of acquisition of the L2 (CONTEXTACQUISITIONSEC) and L1 dominance (whether L1 is dominant or not) on the emotional force of swear words in the L2 (WEIGHT2). Be sure to examine boxplots and comment on assumptions.

4　Open the Eysenck.Howell13.sav data set. This data comes from a study by Eysenck (1974) but the data are given in Howell (2002), Chapter 13. Eysenck wanted to see whether age group (young=18–30 years, old=55–60 years) would interact with task condition in how well the participants could recall words from a word list. There were five conditions, four of which ascertained whether the participants would learn the words incidentally, but some tasks required more semantic processing than others. The tasks were letter counting, rhyming the words in the list, finding an adjective to modify the noun in the list, forming an image of the word, and control (intentionally trying to learn the word). Perform a 2 (AgeGroup) × 5 (Condition) factorial ANOVA on the data.

11.4.6 Calculating Effect Sizes for Factorial ANOVAs

As with one-way ANOVAs, one issue in reporting effect sizes for factorial ANOVAs is what exactly to report effect sizes on! When doing regression (in the form of ANOVA), one effect size to always report is the overall R^2 of the regression equation. Then one may decide whether to report on effect sizes for main effects (and interactions) or whether to report effect sizes for post-hoc tests or planned comparisons.

R^2 effect sizes are automatically reported in SPSS output. Effect sizes for main effects and interactions are also printed in the SPSS output if you call for them. They are the partial eta-squared values, which are a percentage variance (PV) effect size for the omnibus F-test. This effect size can also easily be calculated using sums of squares:

$$_{partial}\hat{\eta}^2 = \frac{SS_{effect}}{SS_{effect} + SS_{error}}$$

or degrees of freedom and F-values:

$$_{partial}\hat{\eta}^2 = \frac{df_{hyp}F}{df_{hyp}F + df_{error}}$$

I do want to note here that calculating effect sizes for factorial designs is a complicated subject (Olejnik & Algina, 2000). Grissom and Kim (2005) note that one should be quite careful in comparing the relative effect sizes of different variables in their study. It often happens that one F-test might have more power, giving a higher PV than another factor. Also, if one level of a factor represents one kind of treatment and another level represents a totally different type of treatment, it may be like apples and oranges to try to compare their effect sizes.

To calculate effect sizes for post-hoc tests or planned comparisons, use the same approach as was given for one-way ANOVAs in Section 9.4.2 to calculate Cohen's d.

11.4.7 Reporting the Results of a Factorial ANOVA

The results of a factorial ANOVA should include information about the type of ANOVA you used. It should also include information about how you checked regression assumptions of the data, along with descriptive statistics such as the N, means, and standard deviations. Besides F-values and p-values for statistical terms in the regression equation, you should provide effect sizes. For post-hoc tests or planned comparisons, report p-values and confidence intervals.

Here is an example of a report you might write for the Obarow (2004) data:

A 2 × 2 × 2 full-factorial ANOVA examining the effects of music, pictures, and gender on the increase in participants' vocabulary size found a statistical effect for the main effect of gender only ($F_{1,56}$ = 4.486, p = .039, partial eta-squared=.07). Females overall learned more vocabulary after hearing the story three times (M = 1.53, sd = 1.76, n = 33) than males did (M = .67, sd = 1.12, n = 11). The effect size shows that this factor accounted for R^2 = 7% of the variance in the data, which is a small effect. None of the other main effects or interactions were found to be statistical. I did not check any of the assumptions of ANOVA.

Here is an example of a report you might write for the Writing data set:

A 4 (L1) × 3 (Condition) full-factorial ANOVA examined the effects of L1 (Arabic, Japanese, Spanish, and Russian) and experimental conditions (correctAll, correctTarget, and noCorrect) to explain writing scores as evaluated by four judges on a 100-point scale. The main effect of L1 was statistical ($F_{3,566}$ = 27.2, p < .0005, partial eta-squared=.13), as were the main effect of Condition ($F_{2,566}$ = 552.3, p < .0005, partial eta-squared=.66) and the interaction between L1 and Condition

($F_{6,566} = 7.31$, $p < .0005$, partial eta-squared=.07). This model explained $R^2 = 69\%$ of the variance in writing scores. Mean scores showed that all participants performed most poorly in the "correctAll" condition (M = 50, sd = 8), best in the "noCorrect" condition (M = 186, sd = 63), and somewhere in the middle in the "correctTarget condition" (M = 101, sd = 30). The interaction meant that there were differences in how some L1 groups performed in the conditions. Post-hoc Tukey HSD tests found that there were no differences ($p < .05$) between the L1 groups on the "noCorrect" condition, while, in the "correctTarget" condition, Russian speakers scored the highest (M = 117) and were statistically different only from the lowest-scoring group, the Arabic speakers (M = 87). In the "noCorrect" condition, all groups performed statistically differently from one another, with the Spanish speakers scoring highest (M = 225), followed by the Russians (M = 202), the Japanese (M = 183), and the Arabs (M = 154). I did not check any of the assumptions of ANOVA.

11.5 Summary

In this chapter we extended the analysis of variance concept to the situation when there were two independent variables. This is the beginning of multivariate analysis, because having two independent variables means we were able to look not only for main effects of the variables but also for interaction between the independent variables. With a factorial ANOVA we can begin to model more complex research designs that better mirror reality. However, I gave a warning that our brains can probably not understand more than a three-way interaction, so it is not a good idea to throw too many separate independent variables into the mix.

Just as with one-way ANOVA, a statistical omnibus effect from an ANOVA is often not going to tell us everything we want to know about the levels of the independent variable, so it is necessary to conduct further post-hocs or pairwise tests to do this.

Chapter 12

Looking for Group Differences when the Same People Are Tested More than Once Using Repeated-Measures ANOVA: Wug Tests and Instruction on French Gender

> Although complex designs and state-of-the-art methods are sometimes necessary to address research questions effectively, simpler classical approaches often can provide elegant and sufficient answers to important questions. Do not choose an analytic method to impress your readers or deflect criticism. If the assumptions and strength of a simpler method are reasonable for your data and research problem, use it. Occam's razor applies to methods as well as to theories.
>
> Leland Wilkinson and the Task Force on Statistical Inference (1999, p. 598)

In this chapter we will examine a statistical design called "repeated measures." This design is used when the same participants are measured more than once. The repeated measurement may be separated by time, as these situations are:

- pre-test, post-test, and delayed post-test scores
- proficiency levels measured after one month, six months, and one year living in the US
- past tense forms provided in conversation after five years and ten years of using the language

All of these situations would require a repeated-measures design, because they test the same people more than once. Repeated-measures designs are also often found in our field when there is only one testing point in time, but you have related tests that you view as an independent variable, such as:

- scores separated by categories, as when you divide the scores of a test instrument into:
  - noun and verb parts
  - phonemic distinctions
  - syntax and morphology components

In general, research designs which incorporate repeated measures are quite desirable, as they increase the statistical power of a test. In fact, the more closely correlated the measures are, the higher the statistical power will be with fewer participants (Murphy & Myors, 2004). This is an important factor to consider in our field, where sample sizes are generally small.

Two studies will be considered in this chapter. The first is a study by Murphy (2004) in which second language users of English were tested to see whether they would perform differently in creating past-tense regular and irregular verb morphology on nonce verbs. The second study was done by Lyster (2004), who wanted to see whether there would be positive benefits to form-focused instruction on grammatical gender in French, and he tested his participants at three different time periods.

12.1 Understanding Repeated-Measures ANOVA Designs

The main reason why repeated measures is a more powerful test than a factorial ANOVA is because it can take individual variation into account. Remember that, in factorial ANOVA, we have an error term into which we sweep all of the variance that we can't explain. A lot of this variance is due to the fact that people are just different, and so may respond differently. A repeated-measures design is able to factor out some of the variation that occurs within individuals because it looks at the same individuals with at least two different measures.

Figure 12.1 shows that the variation in any ANOVA can be divided into variation between groups, such as teaching method, and variation within groups, such as individual variation. With factorial ANOVA, we account only for between-group variation. However, with repeated-measures ANOVA, we can account for some of the within-group variation as well. This reduces the amount of error, and thus increases power. Notice that we still have an error term, but it should be reduced because we can factor out some of the individual variation.

Howell (2002, p. 480) reinforces this idea when he says, "Subjects differ. When subjects are observed only once, these subject differences contribute to the error term. When subjects are observed repeatedly, we can obtain an estimate of the degree of subject differences and partial these differences out of the error term."

Like an ANOVA design, a repeated-measures design has one dependent variable and at least one categorical independent variable. The difference with RM ANOVA is that one or more of the independent variables must be a within-groups factor. A

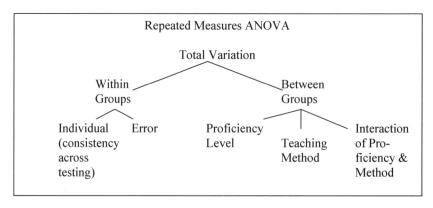

Figure 12.1 Visualizing how variance is partitioned in an ANOVA.

within-groups independent variable must make a division that includes at least two scores for each participant, because:

- the person took a pre-test and a post-test
- the same individual took one test that was divided into parts, such as semantic and syntactic categories of sentence types, phonemic categories, or pragmatic conditions
- the person took the same test after receiving three different teaching treatments (that is, the person participated in every condition of an experiment that involved multiple conditions), such as a person who might take a test after an implicit treatment and then again after an explicit treatment

> Tip: If it is a within-groups variable, then each participant will be included in *all* of the levels of the variable! For example, in a pre-test/post-test design the same person will have both a pre-test and a post-test score. In a design where the data are split into groups such as phonemic contrasts, the same person would have data for all of the phonemic contrasts.

In language acquisition data, it is very common that there will also be a **between-groups independent variable**. This variable will differentiate between groups, measuring things like:

- experimental group assignment
- teaching method received
- condition performed under
- proficiency level
- gender

> Tip: If it is a between-groups variable, then each participant can be in only *one* of the levels of the variable! For example, if a person receives instruction in only one teaching method, this is a between-groups IV because their scores are only found in one level of the Teaching Method variable. However, if the person received instruction in the three different teaching methods and scores were recorded after each type of instruction, this would be a within-groups variable since the same person's scores were in all levels of the variable.

Repeated-measures ANOVAs (RM ANOVAs) which measure *both* a between-groups and within-groups score are sometimes called **"mixed between–within" ANOVAs**. This is because they have both a **between-subjects variable** and a **within-subjects variable**. These are the types of RM ANOVAs that will be highlighted in this chapter. RM ANOVAs may, like factorial ANOVAs, be called one-way, two-way, or higher depending on how many independent variables are included.

12.1.1 RM ANOVA Design of the Murphy (2004) Study

Murphy (2004) is an example of a repeated-measures study that results from splitting the items in one testing instrument into different categories. This is a $2 \times 2 \times 3$ repeated-measures design. These numbers refer to the number of levels in each of the three independent variables, which are Status, Verb Type, and Similarity.

Murphy administered a 30-item "wug" test to participants, meaning that each of the words was a nonce word (cf. the test first used by Jean Berko Gleason in 1958). Each participant had to provide an ending for each unknown verb they heard. There was only one testing instrument, but Murphy hypothesized that non-native English speakers would perform like adult native speakers and treat the regular verbs differently from the irregular verbs. In fact, not only was Murphy interested in splitting the data into regular/irregular categories, but she had also engineered the verb sets so that the verbs showed three differing levels of similarity to real English verbs. This means that Murphy essentially divided the 30 points from the test into six categories. Note that Murphy, had she wanted to, could have said she had one within-groups independent variable with six levels (regular-prototypical, regular-intermediate, etc.), instead of looking at two independent variables. If she had done this, however, she would not be able to see whether similarity interacted with verb type (regular/irregular). The design of Murphy's study is seen in Figure 12.2.

12.1.2 RM ANOVA Design of the Lyster (2004) Study

The second study we will examine in this chapter, done by Lyster (2004), is an example of a study that gets its repeated measures from testing done over different time periods. This is a 3×4 repeated-measures design. These numbers refer to the number of levels in each of the two independent variables, which are Time of Testing and Treatment Group.

Lyster gave the French learners in the study a pre-test and then an experimental treatment followed by an immediate and delayed (eight weeks later) post-test. Lyster also administered four different tests designed to measure learners' ability to manipulate French grammar correctly. Two tests were written, and these were a binary-choice test (circle the correct article) and a completion test (assign gender to nouns in text and also write a recipe). The other two tests were oral, and these were an object identification task (student says, "It's a raft") and a picture description task. Lyster conducted four separate repeated-measures ANOVAs, one on each task, and we will mainly consider his written completion task in the chapter. The design of Lyster's study is seen in Figure 12.3.

Note that, instead of a repeated-measures ANOVA, Lyster could have performed two separate one-way ANOVAs (with Treatment as the only IV) on the gain scores from the pre-test to immediate post-test and from pre-test to delayed post-test. This might make sense if there had been only one post-test, but even in that case, since repeated measures increase the power of a study, it is a good idea to choose a repeated-measures design.

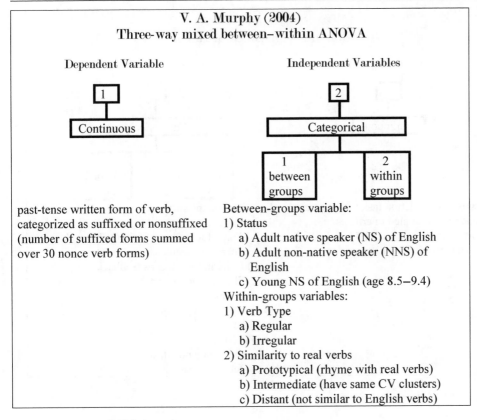

V. A. Murphy (2004)
Three-way mixed between–within ANOVA

Dependent Variable

1

Continuous

Independent Variables

2

Categorical

1
between
groups

2
within
groups

past-tense written form of verb,
categorized as suffixed or nonsuffixed
(number of suffixed forms summed
over 30 nonce verb forms)

Between-groups variable:
1) Status
   a) Adult native speaker (NS) of English
   b) Adult non-native speaker (NNS) of
     English
   c) Young NS of English (age 8.5–9.4)
Within-groups variables:
1) Verb Type
   a) Regular
   b) Irregular
2) Similarity to real verbs
   a) Prototypical (rhyme with real verbs)
   b) Intermediate (have same CV clusters)
   c) Distant (not similar to English verbs)

Figure 12.2 Murphy (2004) design box.

12.1.3 Application Activity: Identifying Between-Groups and Within-Groups Variables to Decide between RM ANOVA and Factorial ANOVA Designs

In deciding whether you need a repeated-measures ANOVA or just a factorial ANOVA, you need to be able to identify variables as between-groups or within-groups. This activity will give you practice doing this. Read the following descriptions of actual linguistic experiments. Assume that all of the information given will be analyzed with one statistical test (although this may not have been the case in the real study). Label the dependent and independent variables. Decide if each independent variable is between-groups or within-groups. Decide if you would use a repeated-measures ANOVA or a factorial ANOVA to analyze the experiment (you will have to use an RM ANOVA if any variables are within-groups).

1   Schön, Boyer, Moreno, Besson, Peretz, and Kolinsky (2008) (this study description has been altered slightly for this exercise). This study wanted to see whether singing may contribute to language acquisition. Eleven syllables were associated with a tone. There were three conditions, and participants in condition 1 heard

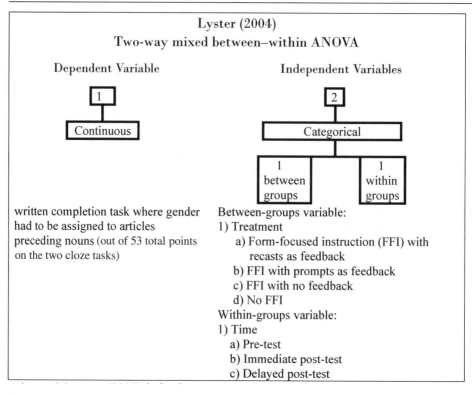

Figure 12.3 Lyster (2004) design box.

the syllables spoken, condition 2 heard the syllables sung but matched to the same tone for each syllable (so a C=gy, D=my, etc.), and condition 3 heard the syllables sung but each syllable could be used on any tone. Participants from two language backgrounds (English, French) were also tested. The participants were tested after hearing the continuous stream of syllables for seven minutes. The test presented them with two strings and asked which one was a "word" from the nonsense language, and scores were calculated from their correct answers.

				Status of IV
Dependent variable:				
Independent variable(s):	1	No. of levels:	Within-group	Between-group
	2	No. of levels:	Within-group	Between-group
	3	No. of levels:	Within-group	Between-group
For this research design, use:	RM ANOVA		Factorial ANOVA	

2   Erdener and Burnham (2005). This study examined the effects of first and second language orthography as well as audiovisual stimuli on how accurately participants

could produce nonwords orally. The first language of the participants was either Australian English or Turkish. The participants heard and/or saw nonwords in both Spanish and Irish in each of four conditions: 1) they heard the word pronounced (Aud-only); 2) they saw a video clip of the lower part of a face producing the word and simultaneously heard the word (AV); 3) along with the video clip, an orthographic representation of the nonword appeared on the video screen (AV-orth); 4) they heard the word pronounced and saw the orthographic representation (Aud-orth). The participants had to repeat the nonwords, and their responses were audiotaped and analyzed for accuracy. The authors predicted that orthographic information would enhance accuracy. They also expected there to be an interaction between first and target languages. Specifically, speakers of a transparent orthography (Turkish) should perform more accurately with a similarly transparent orthography (Spanish) than with a more opaque orthography (Irish), but the English speakers would not differ in their responses to the two orthographies as much.

Dependent variable: Independent variable(s):			Status of IV
	1	No. of Levels:	Within-group Between-group
	2	No. of Levels:	Within-group Between-group
	3	No. of Levels:	Within-group Between-group
For this research design, use:	RM ANOVA		Factorial ANOVA

3   Larson-Hall (2004). In this study I examined how accurately Japanese learners of Russian could perceive differences on 16 phonemic contrasts such as [s] vs. [ʃ]. The students were from 3 proficiency levels. There were 5 items in each category of phonemic contrast, and students were scored on whether they perceived the contrast correctly or not.

Dependent variable: Independent variable(s):			Status of IV
	1	No. of levels:	Within-group Between-group
	2	No. of levels:	Within-group Between-group
	3	No. of levels:	Within-group Between-group
For this research design, use:	RM ANOVA	Factorial ANOVA	

4   Bitchener, Young, and Cameron (2005). ESOL learners from a variety of L1 backgrounds living in New Zealand produced four writing assignments, each two weeks apart. Students then received one of three treatments with corrective feedback on their work. Students' errors were calculated as a percentage of correct use for three areas: prepositions, past simple tense, and definite article. The question investigated was how type of corrective feedback would affect accuracy over time, and whether different types of errors would be affected in different ways.

Dependent variable:			Status of IV
Independent variable(s):	1	No. of levels:	Within-group Between-group
	2	No. of levels:	Within-group Between-group
	3	No. of levels:	Within-group Between-group
For this research design, use:	RM ANOVA		Factorial ANOVA

5   Ellis, Loewen, and Erlam (2006). Students learning English in New Zealand were placed into three groups which differed according to whether they would receive explicit or implicit error correction, or no error correction at all (a control group). Students' ability to form the past tense correctly was elicited on three types of tasks, including an oral imitation task, grammaticality judgment task, and test of metalinguistic knowledge. Students took a pre-test and then were given an immediate and delayed post-test. Accuracy scores on the three tasks were examined to see whether teaching method and type of task affected how well participants could score at the different testing times.

Dependent variable:			Status of IV
Independent variable(s):	1	No. of levels:	Within-group Between-group
	2	No. of levels:	Within-group Between-group
	3	No. of levels:	Within-group Between-group
For this research design, use:	RM ANOVA		Factorial ANOVA

6   Flege, Schirru, and MacKay (2003). This study examined four groups of Italian–English bilinguals depending on the age they began using English (young or old) and their amount of Italian use (high or low). These two ideas (age and use of language) were considered separate variables. The participants produced words, and native speakers of English judged the accuracy of the Italian–English bilinguals' vowel production.

Dependent variable:			Status of IV
Independent variable(s):	1	No. of levels:	Within-group Between-group
	2	No. of levels:	Within-group Between-group
	3	No. of levels:	Within-group Between-group
For this research design, use:	RM ANOVA		Factorial ANOVA

12.2 Visualizing Repeated Measures

As with any kind of ANOVA, boxplots can be very effective and informative means of summarizing group data. A means plot, discussed in Chapter 11, can also be useful for visualizing interactions. Figure 12.4 shows a means plot for the Murphy (2004) data.

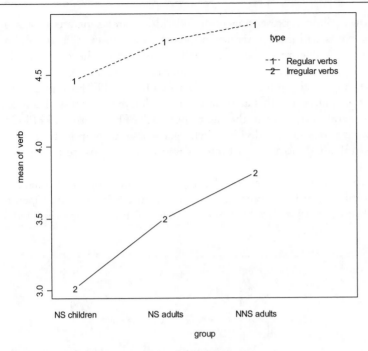

Figure 12.4 Means plot with Murphy (2004) data.

You would not be able to recreate Figure 12.4 with the Murphy.RepeatedMeasures.sav file as it is. This data is currently in the "wide" format (ready to be used in an RM ANOVA analysis) but it needs to be in the "long" format in order to create a compact means plot (see Section 11.2.2).

The means plot shows that all groups treated regular and irregular verbs differently, although there do not appear to be any interactions (the lines are parallel). NNS adults scored the highest, while NS children scored the lowest. Keep in mind that the measurement is of the number of –ed suffixed forms, so a score toward minimum means fewer of the forms were suffixed while a score toward maximum means most of the forms were suffixed.

While the means plot can be helpful in spotting patterns, this chapter will present another type of plot that can be quite useful in understanding how individuals contribute to the group scores, and that is the parallel coordinate plot.

12.2.1 Parallel Coordinate Plots

A very nice graphic that takes the place of the means plot and contains many more points of data is the parallel coordinate plot (sometimes called a profile plot). Adamson and Bunting (2005) say that a profile plot can help viewers get a general impression of the trends of individuals that go into a means plot. An example of a profile plot for the Lyster (2004) data is seen in Figure 12.5. This shows the performance of individuals in the four different conditions over the three times participants were tested (pre-test, immediate post-test, and delayed post-test) on the written completion task.

The graphic shows a line representing each individual, and separate panels are given for the participants within each treatment group. Considering that the further to the right in the panel a score is the higher it is, a leaning to the right in a line indicates that the learner has improved on their ability to use French gender correctly for this task. We see a very strong trend toward learning for the FFI Prompt group in the immediate post-test, although this attenuates in the delayed post-test. There also seems to be some general movement to the right in both the FFI Recast and FFI Only groups, although we can see some individuals who get worse in the post-tests. In the Control group the individual movement of lines from pre-test to post-test seems very random.

This plot was created in SPSS but cannot be done using the drop-down menus. In order to create a parallel coordinate plot you will have to use SPSS syntax. Open the Syntax Editor by choosing FILE > NEW > SYNTAX. A new window will open and will be

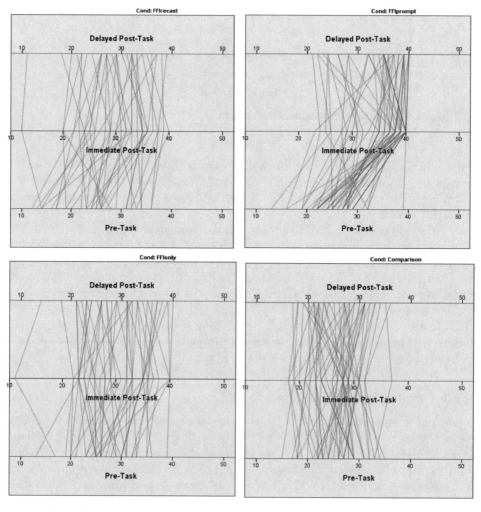

Figure 12.5 Parallel coordinate plot for Lyster (2004).

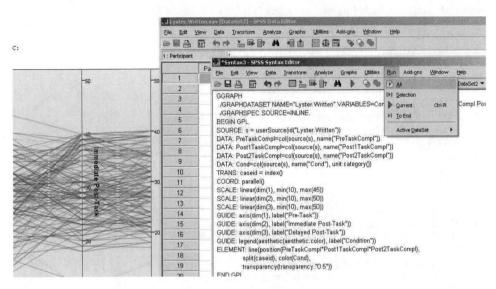

Figure 12.6 Running syntax for a parallel coordinate plot.

called the SPSS Syntax Editor (see Figure 12.6). You will then enter some code that SPSS labels Graphic Production Language (GPL). With this code entered, in the SPSS Syntax Editor choose the RUN > ALL menu choice. If you actually try this with the Lyster.Written.sav file, you will not get the same results (you'll see a plot like the one shown to the left of the SPSS Data Editor that has all of the different groups distinguished by different color lines). In order to get a separate plot for each condition I also split the file (DATA > SPLIT FILE; then "Organize Output by groups" and I put the COND variable into the "Groups based on" box).

Now all you need to know is what code to use! The code should be typed in exactly as I show in Table 12.1, except for line numbers; differences in lowercase and uppercase letters will cause the code not to run, as will differences in whether double or single quotation marks are used. More information about the GPL system can be obtained by searching the SPSS online help (HELP > TOPICS) and typing in "GPL" (and, for this graph specifically, try "GPL parallel"). Hopefully, however, given my explanation that follows you will be able to alter this code to fit your own file.

The parts in the code that are underlined are the parts you would fill in with your own data if you had three measurements to compare, as I did for the Lyster (2004) data (the pre-test, immediate post-test, and delayed post-test). The first place you would fill in is line 2, where you put the name of the file after NAME. Then put in all of the names of the variables that you will use in the graph (mine spill over to line 3). For Figure 12.5 I needed the names of the measurements at different times and the name of the categorical between-group variable (COND). Put one space between all of the names of the variables.

In line 6, fill in the name of the file again as the source for the graph. In lines 7–9, fill in the names of the variables that will form the different measurement lines in your graph. I had three: pre-test (PRETASKCOMPL), immediate post-test (POST1TASKCOMPL),

Table 12.1 Code to Obtain Parallel Coordinate Plot Shown in Figure 12.4

```
 1   GGRAPH
 2   /GRAPHDATASET NAME="Lyster.Written" VARIABLES=Cond PreTaskCompl
 3   Post1TaskCompl Post2TaskCompl
 4   /GRAPHSPEC SOURCE=INLINE.
 5   BEGIN GPL
 6   SOURCE: s = userSource(id("Lyster.Written"))
 7   DATA: PreTaskCompl=col(source(s), name("PreTaskCompl"))
 8   DATA: Post1TaskCompl=col(source(s), name("Post1TaskCompl"))
 9   DATA: Post2TaskCompl=col(source(s), name("Post2TaskCompl"))
10   DATA: Cond=col(source(s), name("Cond"), unit.category())
11   TRANS: caseid = index()
12   COORD: parallel()
13   SCALE: linear(dim(1), min(10), max(50))
14   SCALE: linear(dim(2), min(10), max(50))
15   SCALE: linear(dim(3), min(10), max(50))
16   GUIDE: axis(dim(1), label("Pre-Task"))
17   GUIDE: axis(dim(2), label("Immediate Post-Task"))
18   GUIDE: axis(dim(3), label("Delayed Post-Task"))
19   GUIDE: legend(aesthetic(aesthetic.color), label("Condition"))
20   ELEMENT: line(position(PreTaskCompl*Post1TaskCompl*Post2TaskCompl),
21   split(caseid), color(Cond), transparency(transparency."0.5"))
22   END GPL.
```

and delayed post-test (Post2TaskCompl). If you only have two, take out one of the lines. If you have four, add another line that is the same except for the name that is filled in.

Lines 13–15 are not strictly necessary. I added these in order to have the same scale range for every one of my four graphs. If you only had one graph you could just delete these lines. In line 13, dim(1) refers to the first dimension, or the first variable I have told it to plot, which is PreTaskCompl. I tell SPSS to plot it from 10 to 50 so that I can compare each of the four conditions to the others visually. I kept the same scale for the other two variables which measured scores at different times.

Lines 16–19 give you a chance to add your own labels to the graph. Fill in whatever label you think is descriptive and useful. Again, as for lines 13–15, the dim() indexes the variable that will be plotted, so that dim(3) refers to the third variable we've asked it to plot, which is Post2TaskCompl. Last of all, in lines 20–21, the ELEMENT part of the syntax tells SPSS what element to use (in this case, a line graph) and which variables to graph in those lines (PreTaskCompl, Post1TaskCompl and Post2TaskCompl). The categorical variable which splits up the groups (Cond) is called for in different colors for each group. If you had only two variables to graph (say, a pre-test and a post-test), you'd only put in those two after "position," like this:

ELEMENT: line(position(PreTaskCompl*Post1TaskCompl),

Likewise, if you had four times (or tests) to plot, you'd just add one more name after an asterisk ("*").

Tip: In order to get the code to work correctly you'll need to be very precise and careful. I had the following problems when using the syntax:

1   I got a warning that SPSS could not **resolve identifier** for a variable in the set. I found that I had forgotten to substitute that value in the DATA line. For example, I had DelayObjectID in the list of variables in the second line, but then I had
DATA: Post2TaskID =col(source(s), name("DelayObjectID"))
I solved the problem by changing the old value to the new one, like this:
DATA: DelayObjectID =col(source(s), name("DelayObjectID"))

2   When I substituted in new values I accidentally **left spaces** in commands, like this:
ELEMENT: line(position(PreObjectID * PostObjectID * DelayObjectID))
This resulted in the graphs being put down with no warnings given, but no lines were drawn on the graphs. I solved the problem by taking out the extra spaces before and after the asterisks.

In order to avoid having to type in most of the syntax in Table 12.1, simply go to the Online help and search for "GPL parallel"; then choose the result that's called "Line Chart in Parallel Coordinates." This has an example with syntax for a four-variable parallel coordinate plot, and you can just modify this syntax as explained here. However, be sure to add lines 1–5 to the beginning and line 22 at the end of your syntax code.

Tip: To obtain the graphs shown in Figure 12.5 I opened each graph in the output and changed the coordinate axis. You can open the Chart Editor by double-clicking on the graph in the output. In the Chart Editor, push the button that

looks like this: ![button]   or use the menu system to choose OPTIONS > TRANSPOSE

CHART. I then used the Ctrl + C key sequence to copy the graphs from the SPSS output to the Paint program (a Windows accessory). I used the Paint program to be able to put two graphs together on a line.

12.2.2 Application Activity with Parallel Coordinate Plots

1   Create a parallel coordinate plot for the Murphy.RepeatedMeasures.sav file, but just for the three variables for regular verbs. Use SPSS syntax to do this and describe the trends you can see in the parallel coordinate plot. Why are there only a couple of lines for each group? Try splitting the file as well.

2   Lyster (2004) data. Create a parallel coordinate plot for a different task in the Lyster data set (Lyster.Written), that of the written binary task. Use the variables PreBinary, Post1Binary and Post2Binary. Make sure you split the file before you run the syntax. Describe what the plots show for each of the four groups.

12.3 Repeated-Measures ANOVA Assumptions

12.3.1 Assumptions of Repeated-Measures ANOVAs

For the RM ANOVA, besides the two familiar assumptions of normality of data and homogeneity of variances for both data and residuals, there is an additional assumption for repeated-measures ANOVAs called **sphericity**. Sphericity is not a simple concept, but very basically it measures whether differences between the variances of a single participant's data are equal, so it's like our homogeneity of variances assumptions for the same person when we have repeated measures. Your SPSS output will have a place to do a formal check of this assumption, and we can also eyeball the assumption by looking for **compound symmetry** in the covariance matrix (I'll show you what that looks like later). Explanations of how to test the assumptions and what to do if assumptions are not met are found in Table 12.2.

12.3.2 Exploring Model Assumptions

Let's examine both of our featured data sets to see if they adhere to the assumptions of normality and homogeneity of variances. For the Murphy (2004) data we want to look at each variable (such as "Regular Intermediate," "Irregular Similar") with the data separated by the between-subjects variable (GROUP). To do this choose GRAPHS > LEGACY DIALOGS > BOXPLOTS; then choose SIMPLE plus "Summaries for groups of cases." Put each of the six variables one at a time in the "Variable" box, and put the GROUP factor in the "Category Axis" box. Figure 12.7 shows only two of the six boxplots, one for the "Regular Prototypical" variable and another for the "Irregular Distant" variable.

The boxplots in Figure 12.7 show that the data are not normally distributed (the median is not centered in the boxes and there are not equal-length tails on both ends of the boxes). For the "Regular Prototypical" data, all participants are heavily skewed toward 5, meaning most participants suffixed all of the verbs in that category with the regular (–ed) category. The boxplots also show that the three groups do not have equal variances. For the "Regular Prototypical" data, for both the children and NNS adults, there is basically no variance at all, but there is variance for the NS adults.

We could try to transform the data and see whether this changed things for the better. The log transformation is often recommended when variances are heterogeneous. Use the TRANSFORM > COMPUTE variable menu and then append "log" to the new variable we create. Choose ARITHMETIC from the Function group and then LG10. A look at the new boxplots, however, shows that they do not differ from Figure 12.7. Transforming the data has not fixed the problem of non-normality or of homogeneity of variances. We will proceed with this analysis, noting that our data do not meet the requirements for normality or homogeneity of variances. We will examine the assumption of sphericity in the main output of the RM ANOVA.

Looking at the data numerically in Table 12.3 there is fairly wide variation in each variable (in the columns) as to its standard deviation (which, squared, equals the variance). For example, for the regular intermediate verbs, there are only five points possible but the standard deviations vary from 0.2 to 0.9. This confirms what we saw visually, which is that the groups are quite different from each other in how much variance they had.

Table 12.2 Assumptions for RM ANOVA

Meeting repeated-measures ANOVA assumptions

1 Normal distribution of data (looking at the data according to groups)	Required?	Yes
	How to test assumption?	Examine boxplots; plot normal curve over histogram; use Q-Q plots (see Chapter 3)
	What if assumption not met?	Transform data and reexamine
2 Equal variances (looking at the data according to groups)	Required?	Yes
	How to test assumption?	Examine side-by-side boxplots; look at summary statistics for variance (see Chapter 3); examine spread versus level plot (called for in ANOVA)
	What if assumption not met?	Try transformation with a log function and reexamine
3 Sphericity	Required?	Yes
	How to test assumption?	1) Use Mauchly's test of sphericity, given in SPSS output, to formally measure sphericity (Box is too conservative, according to Howell, 2002, but Mauchly's test is not very robust); 2) Howell (2002) also asserts that sphericity is not a big concern for between-subject terms if there is homogeneity of variance
	What if assumption not met?	1) Use the multivariate procedure if sphericity does not hold (Howell, 2002; Landau & Everitt, 2002); 2) Use a correction (either the Greenhouse–Geisser or Huynh–Feldt) for the test of overall main effects and the interactions (Howell, 2002) (Howell actually recommends using these corrections even if sphericity is met according to Mauchly's test); 3) test within-subject effects by using separate RM ANOVA for each level of a group (Howell, 2002), but to control for increased Type I errors (increasing the effective alpha level) decide beforehand the important questions to look for and use the separate RM ANOVAs to answer those questions only (remember, you don't have to report everything you discover!)
4 Normal distribution of residuals	Required?	Yes
	How to test assumption?	Call for residuals and examine a histogram of their distribution
	What if assumption not met?	Transform data and reexamine
5 Equal variances of residuals	Required?	Yes
	How to test assumption?	Examine scatterplot of predicted values versus studentized residuals. Should see random horizontal scatter and no patterns of data
	What if assumption not met?	Transform data and reexamine

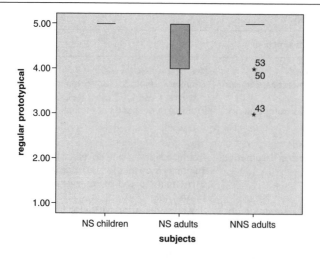

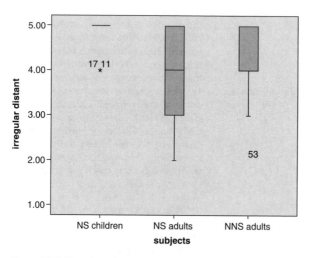

Figure 12.7 Boxplot of variables in Murphy (2004) data set.

Table 12.3 Numerical Summary of the Murphy (2004) Data

Group	N	Regular Prototypical	Regular Intermediate	Regular Distant	Irregular Prototypical	Irregular Intermediate	Irregular Distant
NS children	20	5.0 (.0)	5.0 (.2)	4.6 (.6)	2.9 (1.2)	3.8 (.9)	4.9 (.4)
NS adults	20	4.5 (.7)	4.6 (.9)	4.3 (.9)	2.3 (.9)	2.7 (1.1)	4.1 (1.0)
NNS adults	20	4.8 (.5)	4.8 (.4)	4.7 (.5)	3.4 (1.1)	2.7 (1.6)	4.5 (.8)

For the Lyster (2004) data we should look at the pre-test, immediate post-test, and delayed post-test divided by the four conditions. Figure 12.8 shows a clustered boxplot for all three of the completion test variables. Except for the Comparison group, all of the groups display some non-normality because outliers are shown or boxes are not

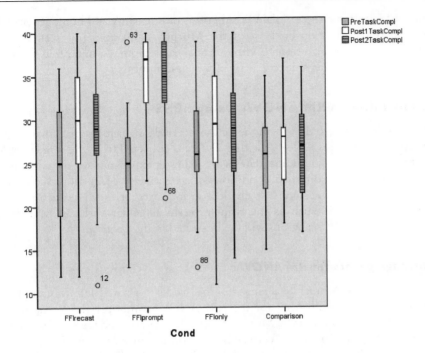

Figure 12.8 Boxplot of task completion variable in Lyster (2004) data set.

Table 12.4 Numerical Summary of the Lyster (2004) Data

Group	Pre-test			Immediate post-test			Delayed post-test		
	N	Mean	sd	N	Mean	sd	N	Mean	sd
FFI Recast	38	24.6	6.8	38	29.7	6.4	38	28.8	6.0
FFI Prompt	49	25.0	4.7	49	35.3	5.0	49	33.8	5.8
FFI only	42	26.9	5.4	42	29.8	6.3	42	29.1	6.2
Comparison	51	25.5	4.9	51	26.3	4.3	51	25.9	5.1

symmetrical around their medians. We see some clear skewness in the FFI Prompt group, which we saw earlier (Figure 12.5) and again see that the Prompt group performed better than other groups in the post-tests. Visually, for variances we want to compare the length of boxes with same colors across the four groups. They do not seem too different, except possibly for the pre-task variable where the FFI Recast group has a larger variance than the other groups.

Table 12.4 shows the sample size, mean scores, and standard deviations for the task completion (cloze) test from the Lyster (2004) study. In studying these with respect to the homogeneity of variances assumption, there is some variation especially in the pre-test, where the smallest standard deviation is 4.7 and the largest is 6.8, almost 2 points of difference.

To summarize, both data sets violate assumptions of normality and homogeneity of variances, and transformation (at least of the Murphy data) does not seem to fix anything. We will proceed cautiously with our analysis, keeping in mind that we may be losing power by not being able to exactly satisfy assumptions.

12.4 Performing an RM ANOVA Using SPSS

There are two basic research designs in the field of second language research that might call for a repeated-measures ANOVA: either 1) data is collected from the same people at different time periods (longitudinal data as in the Lyster experiment or data obtained after participants undergo different conditions of a treatment) or 2) data is collected from the same people at one time but divided up into categories where each person has more than one score (such as the regular versus irregular verbs in Murphy's experiment). Both of these situations will be illustrated in this section.

12.4.1 Arranging Data for RM ANOVA

Data for an RM ANOVA must be arranged in the "wide" format. To understand how many columns of data you'll need for the RM ANOVA, multiply the levels of the within-groups IVs together. For the Murphy (2004) data set, the independent variables are verb type (regular or irregular), verb similarity (prototypical, intermediate, or distant), and group affiliation (NS child, NS adult, or NNS adult). The first two independent variables are within-groups. Multiplying the levels of the within-group IVs together, we get: $2 \times 3 = 6$. This means the *dependent* variable should be split into six groups. There will also have to be a separate column for every *independent* variable, so for Murphy's (2004) data there should be one column for group affiliation. Murphy's data, as seen in Figure 12.9, is already in the correct form for using RM ANOVA in SPSS and contains seven columns.

Lyster (2004) wanted to investigate how well learners of French could learn to use the correct gender of the article depending upon whether form-focused instruction and different types of error correction were provided. Lyster did not view type of instruction and type of error correction as separate variables, but simply as one between-groups variable of treatment condition. This means Lyster needed one column containing indications of which condition people belonged to. The other

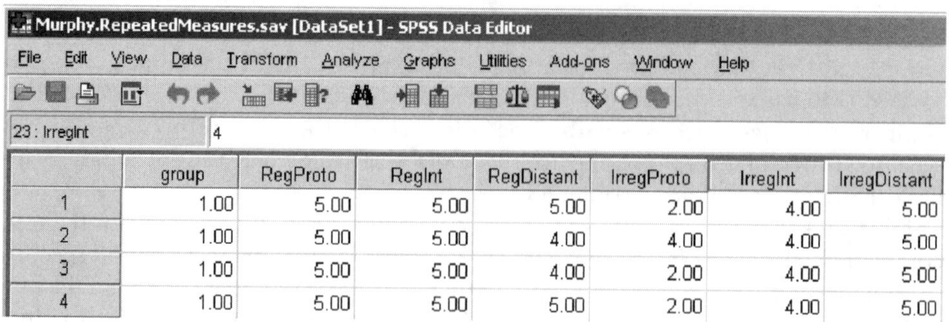

Murphy.RepeatedMeasures.sav [DataSet1] – SPSS Data Editor

File   Edit   View   Data   Transform   Analyze   Graphs   Utilities   Add-ons   Window   Help

23 : IrregInt   4

	group	RegProto	RegInt	RegDistant	IrregProto	IrregInt	IrregDistant
1	1.00	5.00	5.00	5.00	2.00	4.00	5.00
2	1.00	5.00	5.00	4.00	4.00	4.00	5.00
3	1.00	5.00	5.00	4.00	2.00	4.00	5.00
4	1.00	5.00	5.00	5.00	2.00	4.00	5.00

Figure 12.9 Murphy's (2004) data in the "wide" format.

independent variable was time, for the participants were tested at three different time periods. This is a within-groups IV with three levels, but it is the only IV, so the dependent data should be divided into three separate columns. Figure 12.10 shows that, for each of his tests, such as the binary choice test, there are indeed three columns with the dependent data measure divided into the time it was collected: PreBinary, Post1Binary, and Post2Binary. Therefore, Lyster's (2004) data is already in the correct form to use in SPSS.

Arranging Data for RM ANOVA Analysis

The data need to be in the "wide" form, where the number of rows equals the number of participants. There should be more than one column of response variable data. The number of columns should be the product of the number of levels of the within-subject variables. For example, in the Murphy (2004) data the within-subject variables are verb type (two levels) and similarity (three levels). There should thus be six columns of response variable data.

12.4.2 Performing the Repeated-Measures ANOVA

To get started with RM ANOVA, I'll use the Murphy.RepeatedMeasures.sav file. From the SPSS menu bar, choose ANALYZE > GENERAL LINEAR MODEL > REPEATED MEASURES. The first box to appear is shown on the left panel in Figure 12.11. This box asks you to define your within-subject independent variables. For the Murphy (2004) analysis there are two within-subject IVs, which I'll call VERBTYPE (with two levels) and SIMILARITY (with three levels). In the line labeled "Within-Subject Factor Name" type your first within-subject IV and the number of levels it has; then press the ADD button. The right panel of Figure 12.11 shows what the dialogue box looks like after pressing the ADD button. I go ahead and define the second IV and, when I'm done and both IVs are in the box, I press DEFINE.

	Cond	PreBinary	Post1Binary	Post2Binary	PreTaskCompl	Post1TaskCompl	Post2TaskCompl
1	1	42	41	43	34	34	33
2	1	36	38	43	25	28	27
3	1	35	41	44	25	33	32
4	1	39	41	48	27	37	36
5	1	38	40	40	31	35	31
6	1	36	36	33	26	29	27
7	1	32	42	36	29	31	29
8	1	27	45	40	26	36	32
9	1	37	48	46	31	35	32
10	1	39	41	42	33	40	35

Figure 12.10 Lyster's (2004) data in the "wide" format.

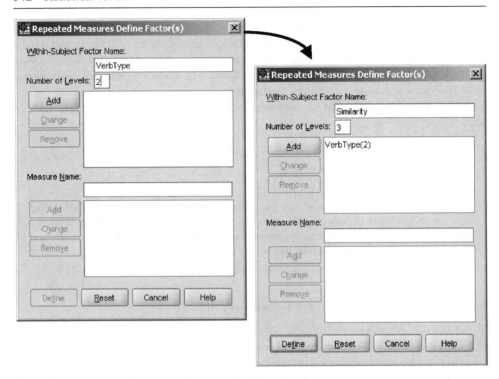

Figure 12.11 Defining within-subject factors in RM ANOVA.

Again, notice that you are only defining *within-subject* variables in the first dialogue box. After you press DEFINE, the Repeated Measures box in Figure 12.12 appears. At first you will see question marks asking to define your variables. For example, (1,1) asks for the data which corresponds to level 1 of VERBTYPE and level 1 of SIMILARITY (notice that these variables are listed in this order above the box). Since the data are already in the correct format, it is an easy step to move all six variables over to the "Within-Subjects Variables" box. Move the between-subjects variable (SUBJECTS for this data set) to the correct box too.

As with every other SPSS procedure, we will also be interested in changing a few settings before continuing with the analysis. Along the side of the Repeated Measures box we will open up the MODEL, PLOTS, POST HOC, SAVE, and OPTIONS buttons.

In the MODEL button you can change to a Type II sum of squares analysis if you agree with me that it makes more sense than Type III (see Section 11.4.3 for an explanation). In the PLOTS button you can call for some interaction plots (choose a few configurations to see which works the best). The POST HOC button can only be used to test for differences in the between-subjects variable, so if that variable has more than two levels choose a post-hoc test. Howell (2002) recommends the Games–Howell procedure, which has separate covariance matrices. This post-hoc is used when equal variances are not assumed. Also open the Save button and tick "Unstandardized" under Residuals and "Cook's Distance" under Diagnostics. Lastly, open the OPTIONS button and tick the boxes for "Descriptive statistics," "Estimates of effect size," "Observed

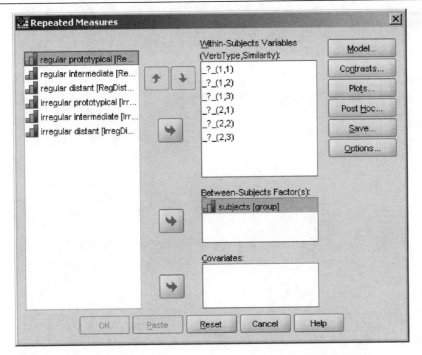

Figure 12.12 The Repeated Measures dialogue box for the Murphy (2004) data.

Power," "Residual SSCP matrix," "Spread vs. Level plot," and "Residual plot." Then press the OK button on your Repeated Measures dialogue box.

For the Lyster (2004) data, when we open the Repeated Measures dialogue box we are confronted with the question of what our within-subject variable should be called. We know that we have measurements on the task completion test at three different times, so we will call the variable TIME, and it has three levels. Then when we need to define the RM ANOVA we will just put the three measurements in the "Within-Subjects Variables" box as shown in Figure 12.13.

12.4.3 RM ANOVA Output

The first two pieces of output outline how your within-subject and between-subject variables are set up and are shown for the Murphy (2004) data in Table 12.5.

We see that the first verb type is regular verbs, with the three levels of similarity, and the second verb type is irregular verbs. We also see there are 20 participants in each (between-subjects) group. The next piece of output is descriptive statistics for each group within the six verb factor levels. Remember that, the closer the score is to 5, the more often the group put an –ed ending on the verb. You should find some way to give your reader your descriptive statistics, whether in a table or in prose, as you report your results. Note that it is not a good idea to simply cut and paste the output table into your report, as the results can be consolidated much better in a different kind of table. Table 12.6 shows just the beginning of this very long table.

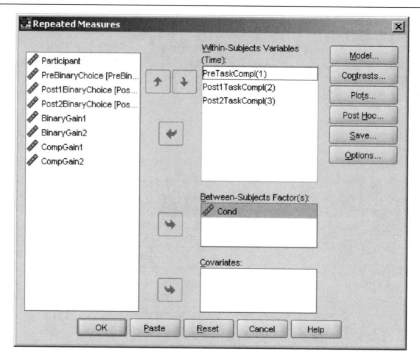

Figure 12.13 The Repeated Measures dialogue box for the Lyster (2004) data.

Table 12.5 The First Two Boxes of Output from the RM ANOVA

Within-Subjects Factors

Measure: MEASURE_1

verbtype	similarity	Dependent Variable
1	1	Reg_Proto
	2	Reg_Int
	3	Reg_Distant
2	1	Irreg_Proto
	2	Irreg_Int
	3	Irreg_Distant

Between-Subjects Factors

		Value Label	N
subjects	1.00	NS children	20
	2.00	NS adults	20
	3.00	NNS adults	20

The next part of the output is labeled "Multivariate Tests" and is shown in Table 12.7. This output is actually a multivariate ANOVA (**MANOVA**) procedure, which is used when you have more than one dependent variable. SPSS gives these results because a MANOVA test does not require sphericity. Some researchers note that you can use the MANOVA results whenever sphericity does not hold (Landau & Everitt, 2002), and Tabachnick and Fidell (2001) give detailed advice about how to do so for those who want more information. However, Howell (2002) says that MANOVA is considerably more complicated than ANOVA and does not have as much power, especially for small sample sizes. Since it is possible to use correction factors for the RM ANOVA or perform separate RM ANOVAs for within-subjects simple effects, we

Table 12.6 Descriptive Statistics from the RM ANOVA Output

Descriptive Statistics

	subjects	Mean	Std. Deviation	N
regular prototypical	NS children	5.0000	.00000	20
	NS adults	4.5000	.68825	20
	NNS adults	4.8000	.52315	20
	Total	4.7667	.53256	60
regular intermediate	NS children	4.9500	.22361	20
	NS adults	4.6000	.88258	20
	NNS adults	4.7500	.44426	20
	Total	4.7667	.59280	60

Table 12.7 Multivariate Tests Output from the RM ANOVA—Warning, Do Not Use!

Multivariate Tests[d]

Effect		Value	F	Hypothesis df	Error df	Sig.	Partial Eta Squared	Noncent. Parameter	Observed Power[a]
verbtype	Pillai's Trace	.804	233.239[b]	1.000	57.000	.000	.804	233.239	1.000
	Wilks' Lambda	.196	233.239[b]	1.000	57.000	.000	.804	233.239	1.000
	Hotelling's Trace	4.092	233.239[b]	1.000	57.000	.000	.804	233.239	1.000
	Roy's Largest Root	4.092	233.239[b]	1.000	57.000	.000	.804	233.239	1.000
verbtype * group	Pillai's Trace	.072	2.200[b]	2.000	57.000	.120	.072	4.399	.431
	Wilks' Lambda	.928	2.200[b]	2.000	57.000	.120	.072	4.399	.431
	Hotelling's Trace	.077	2.200[b]	2.000	57.000	.120	.072	4.399	.431
	Roy's Largest Root	.077	2.200[b]	2.000	57.000	.120	.072	4.399	.431
similarity	Pillai's Trace	.561	35.775[b]	2.000	56.000	.000	.561	71.551	1.000
	Wilks' Lambda	.439	35.775[b]	2.000	56.000	.000	.561	71.551	1.000
	Hotelling's Trace	1.278	35.775[b]	2.000	56.000	.000	.561	71.551	1.000
	Roy's Largest Root	1.278	35.775[b]	2.000	56.000	.000	.561	71.551	1.000
similarity * group	Pillai's Trace	.227	3.640	4.000	114.000	.008	.113	14.562	.866
	Wilks' Lambda	.774	3.830[b]	4.000	112.000	.006	.120	15.322	.884
	Hotelling's Trace	.292	4.013	4.000	110.000	.004	.127	16.054	.899
	Roy's Largest Root	.290	8.276[c]	2.000	57.000	.001	.225	16.552	.953
verbtype * similarity	Pillai's Trace	.708	67.920[b]	2.000	56.000	.000	.708	135.840	1.000
	Wilks' Lambda	.292	67.920[b]	2.000	56.000	.000	.708	135.840	1.000
	Hotelling's Trace	2.426	67.920[b]	2.000	56.000	.000	.708	135.840	1.000
	Roy's Largest Root	2.426	67.920[b]	2.000	56.000	.000	.708	135.840	1.000
verbtype * similarity * group	Pillai's Trace	.179	2.808	4.000	114.000	.029	.090	11.232	.752
	Wilks' Lambda	.821	2.909[b]	4.000	112.000	.025	.094	11.635	.769
	Hotelling's Trace	.219	3.005	4.000	110.000	.021	.098	12.019	.784
	Roy's Largest Root	.218	6.223[c]	2.000	57.000	.004	.179	12.447	.878

a. Computed using alpha = .05

b. Exact statistic

c. The statistic is an upper bound on F that yields a lower bound on the significance level.

d.

Design: Intercept+group

Within Subjects Design: verbtype+similarity+verbtype*similarity

will skip the multivariate (MANOVA) tests section of the print-out. Thus you should be aware that *the "Multivariate Tests" table does not contain the results you are looking for!* I have actually not included any information about conducting MANOVA in this book because it is so rarely used in our field. Those who claim to have used it have almost always actually used MANOVA results from an RM ANOVA printout (I can tell because they have only one dependent variable, and MANOVA is used where there are multiple dependent variables).

The next section of the printout is Mauchly's test of sphericity. Just as with most formal tests of statistical assumptions, this one suffers from not being very robust or powerful (Howell, 2002). In Table 12.8 you can notice that, for Murphy's data, the within-subject VERBTYPE variable has only two levels, so the test for sphericity cannot

Table 12.8 Mauchly's Test of Sphericity Output from the RM ANOVA

Mauchly's Test of Sphericity

Measure: MEASURE_1

Within Subjects Effect	Mauchly's W	Approx. Chi-Square	df	Sig.	Greenhouse-Geisser	Huynh-Feldt	Lower-bound
					Epsilon[a]		
verbtype	1.000	.000	0		1.000	1.000	1.000
similarity	.988	.661	2	.719	.988	1.000	.500
verbtype * similarity	.991	.506	2	.776	.991	1.000	.500

be applied. According to Mauchly's test for Murphy's data, there is no problem with sphericity for SIMILARITY (the Sig. column shows that the *p*-value is *greater* than $p = .05$, meaning the assumption that sphericity holds should not be rejected), nor for the interaction of VERBTYPE and SIMILARITY (again, because $p > .05$).

We come now to the main table that we want to look at, which is titled "Tests of Within-Subjects Effects," shown in Tables 12.9, 12.10, and 12.11. Notice that the table is conceptually ordered by rows of three, and I will display these groups separately.

The first three rows, shown in Table 12.9, deal with the within-subjects variable of VERBTYPE. The first row shows simple main effects for verb type; the second row shows the interaction between VERBTYPE and GROUP; the third row shows the error for VERB-TYPE. Remember, one of the features of repeated measures is that, instead of using the same error term as the denominator for every entry in the ANOVA table, an RM ANOVA is able to use different (appropriate) error terms as denominators and thus factor out subject differences.

Rows 4–6, shown in Table 12.10, deal with the within-subjects variable of SIMILARITY. The first row shows simple main effects for similarity of verbs; the second row shows the interaction between SIMILARITY and GROUP; the third row shows the error for SIMILARITY.

The last three rows, shown in Table 12.11, deal with the interaction between the two within-subjects variables. The first row shows the interaction between VERBTYPE and SIMILARITY. The second row shows the three-way interaction between VERBTYPE, SIMILARITY, and GROUP. The third row shows the error term for the interaction.

In trying to interpret this table, I advise researchers to look first at the largest interactions and then work backwards, since main effects for single variables may not retain

Table 12.9 Tests of Within-Subjects Effects from the RM ANOVA, Rows 1–3

Tests of Within-Subjects Effects

Measure: MEASURE_1

Source		Type II Sum of Squares	df	Mean Square	F	Sig.	Partial Eta Squared	Noncent. Parameter	Observed Power[a]
VerbType	Sphericity Assumed	138.136	1	138.136	233.239	.000	.804	233.239	1.000
	Greenhouse-Geisser	138.136	1.000	138.136	233.239	.000	.804	233.239	1.000
	Huynh-Feldt	138.136	1.000	138.136	233.239	.000	.804	233.239	1.000
	Lower-bound	138.136	1.000	138.136	233.239	.000	.804	233.239	1.000
VerbType * group	Sphericity Assumed	2.606	2	1.303	2.200	.120	.072	4.399	.431
	Greenhouse-Geisser	2.606	2.000	1.303	2.200	.120	.072	4.399	.431
	Huynh-Feldt	2.606	2.000	1.303	2.200	.120	.072	4.399	.431
	Lower-bound	2.606	2.000	1.303	2.200	.120	.072	4.399	.431
Error(VerbType)	Sphericity Assumed	33.758	57	.592					
	Greenhouse-Geisser	33.758	57.000	.592					
	Huynh-Feldt	33.758	57.000	.592					
	Lower-bound	33.758	57.000	.592					

Table 12.10 Tests of Within-Subjects Effects from the RM ANOVA, Rows 4–6

Tests of Within-Subjects Effects

Measure:MEASURE_1

Source		Type II Sum of Squares	df	Mean Square	F	Sig.	Partial Eta Squared	Noncent. Parameter	Observed Power[a]
Similarity	Sphericity Assumed	32.372	2	16.186	38.216	.000	.401	76.433	1.000
	Greenhouse-Geisser	32.372	1.977	16.376	38.216	.000	.401	75.546	1.000
	Huynh-Feldt	32.372	2.000	16.186	38.216	.000	.401	76.433	1.000
	Lower-bound	32.372	1.000	32.372	38.216	.000	.401	38.216	1.000
Similarity * group	Sphericity Assumed	6.678	4	1.669	3.942	.005	.122	15.767	.894
	Greenhouse-Geisser	6.678	3.954	1.689	3.942	.005	.122	15.584	.891
	Huynh-Feldt	6.678	4.000	1.669	3.942	.005	.122	15.767	.894
	Lower-bound	6.678	2.000	3.339	3.942	.025	.122	7.883	.686
Error(Similarity)	Sphericity Assumed	48.283	114	.424					
	Greenhouse-Geisser	48.283	112.678	.429					
	Huynh-Feldt	48.283	114.000	.424					
	Lower-bound	48.283	57.000	.847					

Table 12.11 Tests of Within-Subjects Effects from the RM ANOVA, Rows 7–9

Tests of Within-Subjects Effects

Measure:MEASURE_1

Source		Type II Sum of Squares	df	Mean Square	F	Sig.	Partial Eta Squared	Noncent. Parameter	Observed Power[a]
VerbType * Similarity	Sphericity Assumed	62.539	2	31.269	62.630	.000	.524	125.261	1.000
	Greenhouse-Geisser	62.539	1.982	31.551	62.630	.000	.524	124.143	1.000
	Huynh-Feldt	62.539	2.000	31.269	62.630	.000	.524	125.261	1.000
	Lower-bound	62.539	1.000	62.539	62.630	.000	.524	62.630	1.000
VerbType * Similarity * group	Sphericity Assumed	6.544	4	1.636	3.277	.014	.103	13.108	.823
	Greenhouse-Geisser	6.544	3.964	1.651	3.277	.014	.103	12.991	.820
	Huynh-Feldt	6.544	4.000	1.636	3.277	.014	.103	13.108	.823
	Lower-bound	6.544	2.000	3.272	3.277	.045	.103	6.554	.600
Error(VerbType*Similarity)	Sphericity Assumed	56.917	114	.499					
	Greenhouse-Geisser	56.917	112.983	.504					
	Huynh-Feldt	56.917	114.000	.499					
	Lower-bound	56.917	57.000	.999					

their importance in the face of the interactions. The largest interaction is the three-way interaction between type of verb, similarity of verb, and participants. The *p*-value, found in the column labeled "Sig.," shows that this interaction is statistical ($p = .014$). What this means is that participants from the different groups performed differently on regular and irregular verbs, and they also performed differently on at least one of the types of similarities of verbs. In other words, the groups did not all perform in a parallel manner on both types of verbs and all three types of verb similarities. The partial eta-squared effect size (which we have seen previously in conjunction with ANOVAs) shows that the three-way interaction accounts for about 10% of the variance in scores on this test. This is a medium effect size. Additionally, the power analysis shows that this interaction had sufficient power (over 80%) to find statistical differences in the interaction. We will want to note a couple more pieces of information about this interaction, which are the F-value and the degrees of freedom.

The value of the F-statistic and the degrees of freedom will often depend on which of the four correction factors we use (Sphericity assumed, Greenhouse–Geisser, Huynh–Feldt, or Lower-bound). The **Greenhouse–Geisser correction** is more conservative than the **Huynh–Feldt correction**. In the case of Murphy's (2004) data, there are basically no differences in the F-value for any of these choices, but there are differences in degrees of freedom. Because Mauchly's test for sphericity was not statistical, we might use the "Sphericity assumed" line, but Howell (2002) advocates always using a correction to degrees of freedom whatever the results of Mauchly's test. I would therefore report, say for the three-way interaction, that it was statistical using the Greenhouse–Geisser correction ($F_{3.96,112.98}$ = 3.28, p = .014, partial eta-squared = .10, power = .82).

The process of understanding the output is the same for other interactions and main effects, although, as we will see in Section 12.4.4 where we analyze this data further, you may not want to report every statistical effect. Sometimes there may even be some non-statistical effects you will want to report.

Turning to the Lyster output, Mauchly's test of sphericity was statistical (Sig. = .000), so there is an additional reason to look at the results with corrections applied. Table 12.12 shows the test of between-subject effects for the Lyster data, which only had two independent variables (so the three rows shown in Table 12.12 are all of the output). Here again the interaction between the two independent variables of time and condition is statistical using the Huynh–Feldt correction ($F_{5.5,323.7}$ = 21.1, $p < .0005$, partial eta-squared = .3, power = 1.0). The power to find differences is high and the effect size is quite large.

Returning to Murphy's output, the next table is "Tests of Within-Subjects Con-trasts," and we will ignore this table. The following table is the "Tests of Between-Subjects Effects" and is shown in Table 12.13. The output shows that there was a statistical effect for group (p = .006, partial eta-squared = .17), but, since we already know that the three-way interaction that involved group is statistical, we may not really care too much about this particular result.

The next part of the output is called the "Residual SSCP Matrix," shown in Table 12.14. I called for this piece of output to show you the matrix which can be examined for the requirements of sphericity. This matrix is called the **sum of squares and cross-**

Table 12.12 Tests of Within-Subjects Effects from the RM ANOVA for Lyster (2004)

Tests of Within-Subjects Effects

Measure:MEASURE_1

Source		Type II Sum of Squares	df	Mean Square	F	Sig.	Partial Eta Squared	Noncent. Parameter	Observed Power[a]
Time	Sphericity Assumed	2338.026	2	1169.013	100.759	.000	.364	201.517	1.000
	Greenhouse-Geisser	2338.026	1.791	1305.233	100.759	.000	.364	180.486	1.000
	Huynh-Feldt	2338.026	1.839	1271.123	100.759	.000	.364	185.329	1.000
	Lower-bound	2338.026	1.000	2338.026	100.759	.000	.364	100.759	1.000
Time * Cond	Sphericity Assumed	1466.697	6	244.449	21.069	.000	.264	126.416	1.000
	Greenhouse-Geisser	1466.697	5.374	272.934	21.069	.000	.264	113.223	1.000
	Huynh-Feldt	1466.697	5.518	265.801	21.069	.000	.264	116.261	1.000
	Lower-bound	1466.697	3.000	488.899	21.069	.000	.264	63.208	1.000
Error(Time)	Sphericity Assumed	4083.944	352	11.602					
	Greenhouse-Geisser	4083.944	315.264	12.954					
	Huynh-Feldt	4083.944	323.724	12.616					
	Lower-bound	4083.944	176.000	23.204					

a. Computed using alpha = .05

Table 12.13 Tests of Between-Subjects Effects from the RM ANOVA Output

Tests of Between-Subjects Effects

Measure: MEASURE_1
Transformed Variable: Average

Source	Type III Sum of Squares	df	Mean Square	F	Sig.	Partial Eta Squared	Noncent. Parameter	Observed Power[a]
Intercept	5945.469	1	5945.469	3132.328	.000	.982	3132.328	1.000
group	21.506	2	10.753	5.665	.006	.166	11.330	.844
Error	108.192	57	1.898					

a. Computed using alpha = .05

Table 12.14 Residual SSCP Matrix to Test Sphericity from the RM ANOVA Output

		regular prototypical	regular intermediate	regular distant	irregular prototypical	irregular intermediate	irregular distant
Covariance	regular prototypical	.249	.035	.168	.112	.225	.216
	regular intermediate	.035	.342	.075	.193	.173	.219
	regular distant	.168	.075	.448	.183	.346	.292
	irregular prototypical	.112	.193	.183	1.216	.652	.160
	irregular intermediate	.225	.173	.346	.652	1.476	.478
	irregular distant	.216	.219	.292	.160	.478	.604

products (SSCP) matrix. This table contains three rows, but I am examining only the middle row that says "Covariance."

The numbers above the diagonal line in Table 12.14 are the variances within each treatment (the sum of squares of the intersection of each treatment with itself). To show **compound symmetry** and satisfy the sphericity condition, these numbers should all be rather similar. However, the largest number (1.476) is almost six times as large as the smallest number (.249), meaning these variances are not similar. The other part of the matrix involves the off-diagonal elements, which are the covariances or cross-products of two variables (and are mirrored in the table, so that you only need to look at either the top or the bottom half). These covariances should also be more or less equal, although they do not need to be of the same magnitude as the variances. Here there is even more disparity, as the largest number (.652) is 18 times as large as the smallest (.035). Thus, even though the formal sphericity test (Mauchly's) did not show any problems with sphericity, examination of the covariance matrix shows that there is disparity. We would be well advised to use one of the correction factors.

After this part of the output the spread versus level plots are shown. Remember that these test for the assumption of homogeneity of variances in the data. For this data set there are so few points (just three in each plot) that it is hard to tell whether there are any patterns at all. The residual plots are also divided up according to the six categories of verbs. Here we will examine the Std. Residual vs. Predicted table. These look fairly random. To examine the assumption of normality of residuals, look to the columns appended to the end of your data set called RES_1 through RES_6 (one for each of the verb types). These can be examined for normality by looking at histograms. One wonders whether anyone ever goes through all of the work to do this though! The assumptions become very complicated once we move to repeated-measures ANOVA, and there is not much recourse if we violate the assumptions. So we soldier on.

The next part of the output is labeled "Post Hoc Tests." From this table labeled "Multiple Comparisons" and using the Games–Howell post-hoc test, we see that NNS adults perform more like NS children than NS adults (since there is a statistical difference between NS children and NS adults, but not between NS children and NNS children). Again, however, we may not be particularly interested in this in light of the interaction. Keep in mind that the post-hocs are only done for between-group variables. If, for the Murphy (2004) data, you had found no interaction and one statistical simple main effect, such as similarity, you would still not know whether the comparisons among the three levels of similarity were all statistical, because the post-hoc would not address that comparison.

I will explore the specific conclusions that we can make from the output for the Murphy (2004) data, how to understand interactions, and how to get further comparisons for the within-group variables if you need them in the following sections.

Finally, the last part of the output will be means plots if you called for them, and studying these can help you understand the trends in your data. If possible, I would rather include a parallel coordinate plot than a means plot, as it lets the reader see all of the data visually but is still able to capture patterns within groups. On the other hand, for the Murphy (2004) data the parallel coordinate plot is not very informative and the means plot may be much more helpful for understanding interactions.

Performing an RM ANOVA

1   Make sure data are in the correct "wide" format, with as many columns as needed (the number of columns will be equal to the product of the number of levels of the within-group variables).
2   Analyze > General Linear Model > Repeated Measures.
3   With first box open, enter your own descriptive names of within-subject variables into factor name box, and put in number of levels. Press Add after each variable, and Define when done.
4   Move within-subject variable(s) to large box labeled "Within-Subjects Variables" and move between-subject variable to "Between-Subjects Factors" box.
5   Change the sum of squares to Type II in the Model button. Open the Plots button and create some interaction plots, useful for discerning trends. Open the Post hoc button if your between-subjects variable has more than two levels, and call for post-hocs using the Games–Howell method. Open the Save button and tick "Cook's Distance" and "Unstandardized." Open the Options button and tick "Descriptive statistics," "Estimates of Effect Size," "Observed Power," "Residual SSCP Matrix," "Spread vs. Level Plot," and "Residual plot."

12.4.4 Exploring Interactions and Main Effects

This section will examine what to do with the main output you are interested in. Specifically, I stated previously that you should first examine the statistical interactions in your model and only then think about whether you want to look at simple main effects. So we will first look at the interactions in the Murphy (2004) data sets as we think about what data we want to report.

At first it can be very confusing to think about what an interaction between three variables means (and this is why many authors recommend not using *more* than three variables, because you could end up with mind-blowing four-way or five-way interactions!). This is where the means plot can conceptually make understanding easier.

The means plots (also called profile plots) in Figure 12.14 were created when I called for the RM ANOVA in the Plots button by putting Group in the "Horizontal Axis" box, Similarity in the "Separate Lines" box, and VerbType in the "Separate Plots" box (although I have edited the plots and changed the look of the line using the Graph Editor that appears when you click twice on the plot in the output). The plots will help us understand the nature of the three-way interaction.

The plot for regular verbs on the left panel of Figure 12.14 shows that the number of suffixed forms for type of verb similarity depends on both group membership and verb similarity. NS adults suffix regular verbs less than NS children and NNS adults, but verbs that are distant (very non-prototypical) receive less suffixing than the inter-

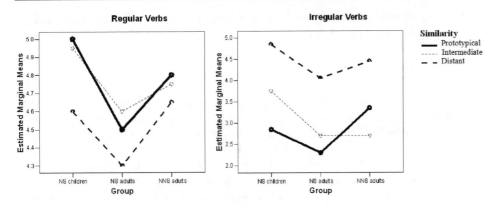

Figure 12.14 Interaction plots for the Murphy (2004) data.

mediate or prototypical verbs. For the irregular verbs on the right panel of Figure 12.14 we see even more striking differences between group membership and verb similarity. Here the NNS adults clearly suffix more prototypical irregular verbs than intermediate verbs, while it is the opposite for NS adults and children. This shows the interaction between group and similarity. Comparing across the regular and irregular verb plots in Figure 12.14, we also see the interaction between verb type. For regular verbs, distant verbs are suffixed the least by all groups, but, for irregular verbs, distant verbs are suffixed the most by all groups.

What we would like to know now is which comparisons are statistical. For example, is the difference between verb similarities statistical for all three groups of participants? Is the difference between verb regularity statistical across all three similarities of verbs? Some of these questions we can answer based on data already contained in the output, but some we will have to do some extra work to request.

Howell (2002) notes that researchers should not feel compelled to report every statistical effect that they find, feeling they must do so for the sake of completeness. In addition, Kline (2004) observes that non-statistical effects may be at least as interesting as, if not more interesting than, statistical effects. One important point to consider is the effect size. If a certain comparison has an effect size that is noteworthy but the comparison is not statistical, this may be due to insufficient power (probably owing to a small group size), and further testing with larger groups would probably uncover a statistical relationship. If this information could further hypotheses, then it should probably be reported.

What should get reported? Results that are pertinent to the theoretical hypotheses and address the issues the researcher wants to illuminate are the right choice. A report full of statistics can be mind-numbing for readers (I confess to a few of these kinds of articles myself! Please forgive me), so choose only the information that is vital.

For the Murphy (2004) data, let us look at the hypotheses Murphy formulated and, knowing that there is a statistical three-way interaction, decide which further comparisons to look at. Murphy's (2004) hypotheses were:

1   All groups will add more –ed forms to regular verbs than irregular verbs.
2   Similarity should play a role on irregular verbs but not regular verbs.

3   Group differences in amount of suffixed forms should only be seen in the irregular verbs, not the regular ones.

4   No previous research looked at these three groups, so it is unclear which groups will pattern together.

For hypothesis 1 we could first look at descriptive statistics. Table 12.3 gave descriptive statistics for the Murphy (2004) data, but the data are not in the right form to answer the question of how regular and irregular verbs pattern together. To get our answer we need to manipulate our data so all of the regular verbs are in one column and all of the irregular verbs are in another column (so each of these columns will have a maximum score of 15 points). This can be done by using TRANSFORM > COMPUTE VARIABLE and creating two new variables, one adding together all three regular verb columns and one adding all three irregular verb columns. Then we separate these new variables by group membership using the DATA > SPLIT FILE command and call for descriptive statistics. The descriptive statistics show in every case that regulars were suffixed more than irregulars (mean scores—NS children: reg.V = 14.6, irreg.V = 11.5; NS adults: reg.V = 13.4, irreg.V = 9.1; NNS adults: reg.V = 14.2, irreg.V = 10.5). We also know there is a statistical difference with a very strong effect size for "verb type" using the Greenhouse–Geisser correction ($F_{1,57} = 233.2$, $p < .0005$, partial eta-squared = .80), but no interaction between verb type and participant ($F_{2,57} = 2.2$, $p = .12$, partial eta-squared = .07, but power is low at .43). Since there were only two levels for verb type and we know that verb type is statistical, no further analysis is necessary to state that regular verbs received statistically more –ed forms than irregulars, and that all of the participant groups followed this pattern.

For hypothesis 2 we would want to see an interaction between similarity and verb type. This interaction was indeed statistical, again with a large effect size and power of 100% ($F_{1.98,113.0} = 62.6$, $p < .0005$, partial eta-squared = .52). We need to know more about this interaction, but the only post-hocs that are available in the output are for differences between GROUP. To look at the comparisons we really want, we can use the technique mentioned in Section 11.4.4, where we go back to the Repeated Measures box and find out what the syntax is for the marginal means of verbtype*similarity. We then modify this syntax in the Syntax Editor to ask for comparisons, like this:

/EMMEANS = TABLES(verbtype*similarity)COMPARE(verbtype)

/EMMEANS = TABLES(verbtype*similarity)COMPARE(similarity)

Pasting these lines into the syntax and running this analysis, we're interested in the output shown in Table 12.15.

To know what the numbers in the output in Table 12.15 refer to, we'll need to look back at our first pieces of output. Verbtype 1 is regular verbs, and 2 is irregular. Similarity 1 is prototypical, 2 is intermediate, and 3 is distant. The pairwise comparisons show that, for regular verbs, prototypical and intermediate verbs are statistically different from distant verbs (a look at the summary statistics in Table 12.3 shows us they are more suffixed than distant verbs; in fact, prototypical and intermediate verbs that are regular have exactly the same mean). This contradicts the hypothesis that similarity plays no role for regular verbs. For irregular verbs (verbtype 2), there are

Table 12.15 Output Obtained through the Syntax Editor for Murphy (2004)

Pairwise Comparisons

Measure: MEASURE_1

verbtype	(I) similarity	(J) similarity	Mean Difference (I-J)	Std. Error	Sig.[a]	95% Confidence Interval for Difference[a]	
						Lower Bound	Upper Bound
1	1	2	.000	.093	1.000	-.187	.187
		3	.250*	.078	.002	.095	.405
	2	1	.000	.093	1.000	-.187	.187
		3	.250*	.103	.019	.043	.457
	3	1	-.250*	.078	.002	-.405	-.095
		2	-.250*	.103	.019	-.457	-.043
2	1	2	-.217	.152	.160	-.521	.088
		3	-1.617*	.158	.000	-1.933	-1.300
	2	1	.217	.152	.160	-.088	.521
		3	-1.400*	.137	.000	-1.674	-1.126
	3	1	1.617*	.158	.000	1.300	1.933
		2	1.400*	.137	.000	1.126	1.674

statistical differences between prototypical and distant verbs (1 and 3) and also between intermediate and distant verbs (2 and 3).

Thus hypothesis 2 is not upheld, because similarity interacts with both types of verbs. Murphy (2004) points out that these effects run in opposite directions; participants suffix least for distant similarity when verbs are regular, but suffix most for distant similarity when verbs are irregular (look back to the means plot in Figure 12.14 to confirm this visually).

Hypothesis 3 posited that the groups would suffix differently on the irregular verbs but not on the regular verbs. In other words, there should be an interaction between verb type and participants, but there is none ($F_{2,57} = 2.2$, $p = .12$, partial eta-squared = .07, power = .43). The means plots indicate that group differences in the amount of suffixed verbs are present for both regular and irregular verbs.

To look in more detail at how the groups performed on both types of verbs, we can run the RM ANOVA analysis again but only put in regular verbs (so there would only be one IV of similarity). We would run it again with just the irregular verbs too.[1] Post-hocs will then tell us whether the groups performed differently on the regular verbs (in the first run) and on the irregular verbs (in the second run). In the case of Murphy's data, where there were two IVs, the RM ANOVA is appropriate, but, in other cases where there is only one IV, further testing would need to be done with a one-way ANOVA (you'll see this in Activity 1 in the application activities in Section 12.4.5).

Doing this for the regular verbs, I found that the variable of GROUP was statistical. Games–Howell post-hocs showed that children are statistically different from NS adults ($p = .03$) but not NNS adults, and that NS and NNS adults are not statistically different from one another. For irregular verbs, post-hocs showed exactly the same situation as with regular verbs. Hypothesis 3 is therefore discredited, as there are group differences for both irregular and regular verbs.

---

1 Howell (2002) actually recommends this procedure for testing the levels of the within-subjects effects. He worries that sphericity adjustments may not be adequate with the original RM ANOVA so running the RM ANOVA again with within-groups variables separated will result in a more appropriate error term.

Note that running a couple more tests beyond the original RM ANOVA to answer a hypothesis (such as I just did for hypothesis 3) does not mean that you need to adjust p-values for everything because you have run too many tests. Howell (2002) has only two cautions in such cases. One is that you not try to include every result from the tests. Just get the results you need and don't look at the rest. The second caution is that, if you are going to use *many* more results from such additional testing, then you should adjust the familywise error rate. However, in this case where only a couple of results were investigated, and in fact we did not look at the results of every single comparison included in the "Tests of Within-Subjects Effects," there is no need to adjust the error rate.

Hypothesis 4 was concerned about which groups would pattern together. To answer this question we can report there was an overall statistical main effect for group ($F_{2,57} = 5.7$, $p = .006$, PV = .17). Games–Howell post-hoc tests for GROUP showed that NS children were statistically different from NS adults (mean difference = .59, $p = .002$, 95% CI .24, .95), and NNS adults were statistically different from the NS adults (mean difference = .38, $p = .04$, 95% CI .02, .73) but not children (95% CI of mean difference: $-.57$, .14). Wide confidence intervals here show that estimates are not very precise.

12.4.5 Application Activities with RM ANOVA

1   Section 12.4.4 explored the results of the RM ANOVA with Murphy's (2004) data. Conduct an RM ANOVA with Lyster's (2004) data on the task completion test (as shown partially in Section 12.4.2; use Lyster.Written.sav) and decide what parts of the output you need to answer Lyster's research questions. Lyster's questions all concerned the performance of the groups:

   1) Will form-focused instruction (FFI) help students to perform better with gender assignment?
   2) In groups that get FFI, will feedback (in the form of recasts or prompts) help students to perform better with gender assignment than when they get no feedback?
   3) Which type of feedback is better—prompts or recasts?

2   Using Lyster's (2004) written data (Lyster.Written.sav), perform an RM ANOVA on the binary-choice test results (PREBINARY, POST1BINARY, POST2BINARY). First, examine the data as to normality and constancy of variances between groups (use boxplots). Then run an RM ANOVA (also check the covariance matrix for the sphericity assumption). Report results and describe interaction plot. If the interaction is statistical, investigate further by running three one-way ANOVAs for each of the time periods the test was taken in. Focus on post-hoc tests, especially the question of which group did best, and whether all of the FFI groups were different from the Comparison group.

3   Larson-Hall (2004). I examined how well Japanese students of Russian perceived 16 contrasts, with five items in each contrast. My between-subjects variable was proficiency in Russian, with three levels for Japanese users of Russian and one level for native Russians (NR). Using the LarsonHall2004.sav file, investigate whether there were differences between the groups and between the sound contrasts, and

whether there was an interaction between the two. First examine the data as to normality and constancy of variances (focus just on R_L, SH_SHCH, and PJ_P here, because there are a lot of variables!). If necessary, drop the NR from the analysis. Run the RM ANOVA with all 16 contrasts and report results. If the interaction is statistical, run one-way ANOVAs on those contrasts which, from the profile plots, look most as though they show differences between groups.

4   Erdener and Burnham (2005). Use the Erdener&Burnham2005.sav file. These authors constructed a research design that took into effect L1 (two levels, either English or Turkish) and target language (Spanish or Irish), and had four conditions with various levels of auditory and visual information (this is described in more detail in the application activity in Section 12.1.3, Activity 2). Both TARGET-LANGUAGE and CONDITION are within-group measures, while L1 is a between-group measure. The authors hypothesized that speakers of a transparent orthography (Turkish) should perform more accurately with a similarly transparent orthography (Spanish) than with a more opaque orthography (Irish), but the English speakers would not differ in their responses to the two orthographies as much. The scores in the data files are error scores, so a higher number means more errors. First, examine the data as to normality and homogeneity of variances of the groups. Run the RM ANOVA and report results. If there is an interaction, use SPSS syntax and look at pairwise comparisons to answer the question of whether L1 interacted with target language and how this affected conditions with orthography.

12.4.6 Reporting the Results of an RM ANOVA

When you do an RM ANOVA you will get a lot of results! As noted in Section 12.4.4, please do not feel obligated to report *all* the statistics which are returned to you by any procedure. What it will be important to report is results which address the questions you have asked. You should definitely report that you have run an RM ANOVA, because this is only one of a number of possible analyses that could be run on the data. You may have run additional analyses, such as one-way RM ANOVAs or one-way ANOVAs to try to ascertain the effects of an interaction, and the fact that you did these should be reported as well.

You should report on the results of preliminary examination of the data for satisfying the assumptions of an RM ANOVA, and also include the results of tests for sphericity. If your data do not meet the assumptions of homoscedasticity and normality of distribution, this fact should definitely be reported, but does not mean your results are invalid. It is not true that ANOVA is necessarily robust to these deviations from assumptions (in fact, it most likely is not, given what Wilcox, 2001, reports), but any statistical results you report are likely to be accurate. It is just that deviations away from normality and homoscedasticity are likely to result in a loss of power to find statistical results (Larson-Hall & Herrington, forthcoming; Wilcox, 2001).

Since Section 12.4.4 essentially went through the statistical reporting that I would do for Murphy's data, I will not repeat that information here.

12.5 Summary

The repeated-measures ANOVA test is the one you'll want to use when you test the same people more than once (and have more than just two mean scores, in which case you'd just use a paired-samples t-test). There are two distinct types of situations in the field of second language research when RM ANOVAs are necessary. One situation is when you test the same people more than once, as happened in the Lyster (2004) study when participants were tested at three different times. The other situation is when you test the same people just once, but you divide your test up into different parts that you see as an independent variable, such as phonemic contrast distinctions or types of verbs, as we saw for the Murphy (2004) data.

One thing that makes RM ANOVA somewhat confusing is that your data must be arranged differently than the way they would be for a factorial ANOVA. The RM ANOVA analysis in SPSS needs data to be arranged in the "wide" format, where the number of rows is equal to the total number of participants, and scores for independent variables are split into different columns. In contrast, for the factorial ANOVA the data needed to be arranged in the "long" format where all of the data for the independent variable had to be found in just one column. This difference can cause confusion for novices who encounter the RM ANOVA dialogue box in SPSS for the first time.

The assumptions for an RM ANOVA test are similar to those of other parametric tests we've seen (normality, homogeneity of variances), but also include the assumption of sphericity. We've seen in the chapter that most real data sets will violate one or all of these assumptions! Correction factors are available in the output if sphericity is violated, and I advised readers to always use the correction factor whether or not the formal test for sphericity is violated. I also advised readers to use the Games–Howell post-hoc in case the heterogeneity of variances requirement is violated, but this only applies to the between-subjects variable, not the within-subjects variables. In short, there is a lot of room for, and a high likelihood of, your data violating the assumptions of parametric tests. What this means for you is that you may not have the power to find differences that may actually exist.

RM ANOVA output is voluminous and returns a large number of tests. I have emphasized in this chapter that you do not need to report all of the statistics that are found in the output; be selective and report only on the tests that will answer your research questions. In some cases additional analyses, such as one-way ANOVAs or pairwise comparisons called for through SPSS syntax, may have to be used to answer all your questions.

Chapter 13

Factoring out Differences with Analysis of Covariance: The Effect of Feedback on French Gender

> A covariate is, after all, nothing but an independent variable which, because of the logic dictated by the . . . issues of the research, assumes priority among the set of independent variables as a basis for accounting for . . . variance.
>
> Jacob Cohen (1968, p. 439)

Analysis of covariance (ANCOVA) is a statistical technique you can use when you want to focus on the effects of a main response variable with the effects of other interval-level variables factored out. Such a technique may be useful when:

- you assume that there is some external factor, such as pre-test or TESOL score, which will affect how your students will perform on the response variable
- previous studies have shown that another variable, such as aptitude or writing scores, affects how your participants will perform on the variable of interest
- you find after the fact that an unplanned variable, such as age, affected the performance of participants on the response variable

In essence, ANCOVA works by simply including the additional variable (the **covariate**) in the regression, but, by doing so, it allows the effects of that variable (such as age, or aptitude scores) to be separated out from the response variable. In this way, ANCOVA is like partial correlation, which we saw in Sections 6.5.1 and 6.5.2, because it includes the variable whose effects we want to "partial out" in the analysis in order to separate them from the other effects. ANCOVA works like the repeated-measures or mixed-effect designs that we saw previously in Chapter 12 as well to reduce the amount of variability in the model that is unexplained. If we think that scores on an aptitude test help account for the variability on the response variable, then by including the aptitude test in the design we help reduce the amount of variability that is unexplained.

The ANCOVA design, then, is quite similar to the ANOVA design but includes one or more variables as explanatory variables. The example we will look at in this section involves the Lyster (2004) data set we examined previously in Chapter 12. Lyster was examining the effects of instruction on the accuracy of French gender. However, he found a statistical difference between his two groups in their performance on the pre-test for the oral object identification task. This is problematic, as it means the two groups were not starting on equal footing. Lyster (2004) therefore used an ANCOVA with the pre-test scores as the covariate and the immediate post-test scores as the response variable of interest.

13.1 Visually and Numerically Examining the Data

Because we haven't looked specifically at scores from Lyster's object identification test, which was an oral test, I will provide several measures here including a parallel coordinate plot, boxplots, and a scatterplot to examine the data.

The parallel coordinate plots in Figure 13.1 show that, for this task, the FFI Prompt group had the largest number of participants whose scores improved sharply from pre-test to post-test. The FFI Recast group also had a number of participants who improved sharply from pre-test to post-test, just not as many as the FFI Prompt group.

The numerical summary of the scores is shown in Table 13.1. These numbers show that the Comparison group had the lowest average scores on the pre-task measure-

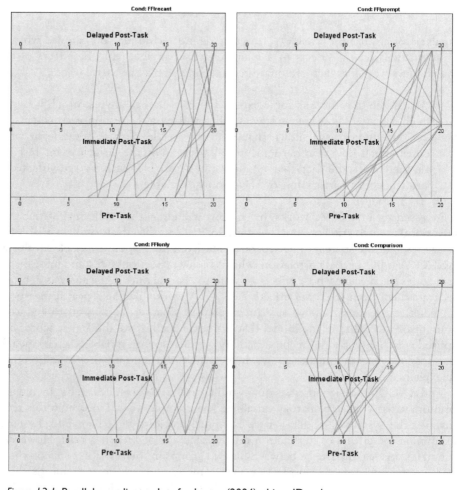

Figure 13.1 Parallel coordinate plots for Lyster (2004) object ID task.

Table 13.1 Mean Scores and Standard Deviations for the Object Identification Task in the Lyster (2004) Data Set

Object identification	Pre-task	Immediate post-task	Delayed post-task
FFI Recast (N = 15)	12.9 (4.0)	16.1 (3.8)	16.5 (3.9)
FFI Prompt (N = 15)	12.0 (3.4)	16.0 (4.3)	16.8 (3.3)
FFI Only (N = 15)	14.3 (3.3)	15.9 (3.9)	16.6 (3.5)
Comparison (N = 15)	10.6 (3.0)	12.3 (3.4)	11.4 (3.7)

ment, whereas the FFI Only group had scores more than one standard deviation above them. This creates problems for trying to interpret any gains and for assuming that the groups were equal before testing time.

Figure 13.2 shows boxplots of the distributions of the pre-test and immediate post-test measurements. Data are slightly skewed and in a few instances there are outliers

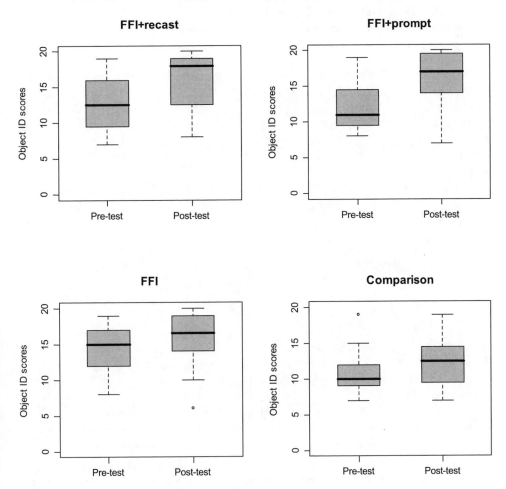

Figure 13.2 Boxplots of Lyster (2004) object ID task.

(for the FFI only post-test and the Comparison group pre-test). The boxplots show that the FFI Only group had rather high pre-test scores compared to the three other groups. Both the FFI Recast and the FFI Prompt group showed quite a bit of improvement from pre-test to post-test. From the length of the boxes, variances look fairly equal for all groups except for the Comparison group in the pre-test.

One more graph which can be helpful in assessing what is happening in a situation with covariates is to look at a scatterplot of the continuous variables with data divided by groups. The scatterplot should have regression lines drawn for the groups because the hypothesis that is being tested in a standard ANCOVA is that the regression lines for the groups are parallel. Figure 13.3 shows scatterplots between the post-test measurement and the pre-test measurement, which is the covariate. Straight regression lines are drawn in on the graphs as well as the fitted Loess lines which follow the trend of the data. I made this graph by first splitting the data in SPSS (DATA > SPLIT FILE; then choose "Organize output by groups" and put the COND variable into the box) and then calling for a scatterplot of the pre-test versus the post-test (GRAPHS > LEGACY DIALOGS > SCATTER/DOT, choose SIMPLE SCATTER and DEFINE, and then put PREOBJECTID in the "Y-Axis" box and POSTOBJECTID in the "X-Axis" box).

What can be seen from Figure 13.3 is that, while all of the FFI groups had Loess lines

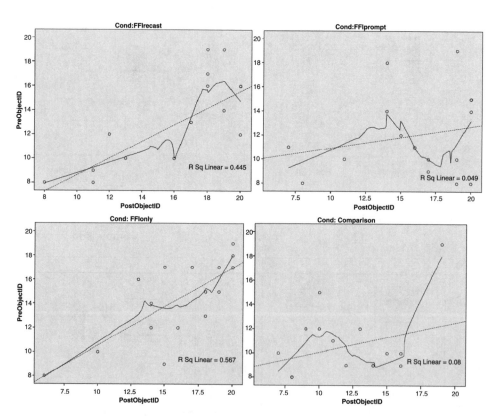

Figure 13.3 Scatterplots of pre-test scores versus immediate post-test scores by group for the object identification task in the Lyster (2004) data (regression lines are dotted and Loess lines are straight).

that basically followed the upward trend of the dotted regression line, the Comparison group seems different. In fact, if the point at the farthest right of the graph is considered an outlier, the Loess line would actually have a slight negative slope. It does appear from the graphs that something is different about the Comparison group for this particular task.

13.2 ANCOVA Design

While an ANOVA design includes one continuous dependent variable and one or more categorical independent variables, an ANCOVA design differs by being able to have continuous independent variables. Covariates can be either categorical or continuous (Howell, 2002), although in the field of second language research they are by and large continuous. Covariates are considered independent variables.

Covariates can be entered into any of the ANOVA designs—one-way ANOVAs, factorial ANOVAs, and even repeated-measures ANOVAs. Therefore, an analysis of covariance does not so much tell you about the design of the study as much as the fact that covariates will be included in it.

Any number of covariates may be entered into the research design, although Howell (2002) cautions that interpreting an analysis of covariance may be difficult enough with just one covariate, let alone more. The research design used in SPSS will not enter the covariates into any interactions with the other independent variables. What you will see by including a covariate is whether that variable is statistical or not. If a covariate is found to be statistical then it has an independent effect on the variance of the dependent variable. Basically, a statistical covariate means that the covariate does affect scores on the dependent variable. In fact, this would be the same interpretation you would make if any simple main effect of an independent variable were statistical.

Figure 13.4 shows the research design for the Lyster (2004) analysis I will be showing in this chapter with the oral object identification task. The research design will depend upon the number and type of variables involved in the test if the covariate is ignored. Figure 13.4 shows that, without the covariate, the design includes one categorical independent variable and one continuous dependent variable. This is a one-way ANOVA design, so with the covariate we would call it a one-way ANCOVA design.

13.2.1 Application Activity: Identifying Covariate Designs

Look at the following descriptions of experimental studies in the second language research field. Decide whether the design is one-way ANCOVA, factorial ANCOVA, or RM ANCOVA. Remember that the design depends on what test you would use if the covariates were not included in the design. Just to remind the reader I will list the requirements for each of these research designs in Table 13.2.

1   Fraser (2007). The author wanted to compare the performance of two groups of Mandarin Chinese users of English (one living abroad, one not) on five reading tasks. The same tasks were given to the participants in both their L1 (Mandarin) and their L2 (English). There was also a covariate, which was scores on the listening portion of a measure of English language proficiency called the CELT. Using this study as a covariate would factor out differences between participants due to their

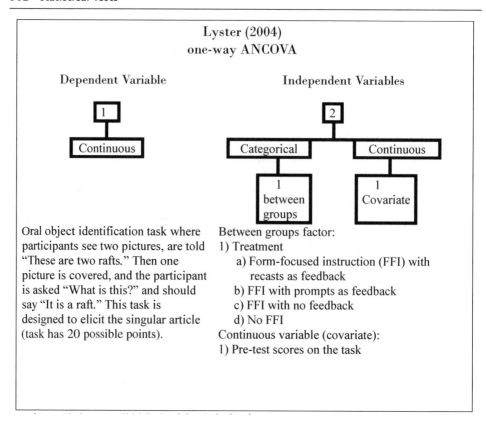

Figure 13.4 Lyster (2004) ANCOVA design box.

Table 13.2 ANOVA Design Requirements

	Dependent	*Independent*
one-way ANOVA	one, continuous	one, categorical
factorial ANOVA	one, continuous	two or more, all categorical, all between-groups
RM ANOVA	one, continuous	one or more, all categorical, at least one within-groups (repeated)

English listening proficiency. Fraser specified her research design (2007, p. 380): "Thus, there was one between-subject factor (group with two levels: Canada group and China group), and two within-subject factors (language condition with two levels: L1 and L2; and Task with five levels: rauding [normal, ordinary reading], scanning, skimming, learning, memorizing). . . . In addition, to examine the impact of L2 proficiency on L2 reading rate and task performance, the CELT scores were used as a covariate in the analyses of the L2 data."

Research design:	One-way ANCOVA	Factorial ANCOVA	RM ANCOVA

2   Lim and Hui Zhong (2006). The authors wanted to see how computer-assisted learning (CALL) compared to traditional reading classes in promoting reading comprehension in Korean college students learning English. There were two groups of students whose reading comprehension was measured at the beginning and end of the semester. The authors found that scores on the comprehension task were higher for the traditional learners ($X = 54$) than for the CALL class ($X = 49$) on the 100-point test, and thus decided to use the pre-test comprehension task as a covariate. In this way the authors could compare the scores of the two groups, adjusted by subtracting out variation due to the pre-test scores.

Research design:	One-way ANCOVA	Factorial ANCOVA	RM ANCOVA

3   Beech and Beauvois (2005). These researchers begin their study with the assumption that in-utero influence of sex hormones can affect auditory development, which in turn can affect phonology. Problems with phonology have in turn been linked to reading disorders. The authors assert that the influence of sex hormones can be measured by a ratio between the length of the index and ring fingers. Thus, one of the variables in their study is digit ratio, and participants were split into three groups: top, middle, or bottom. The authors wanted to control (or even out) the effects of intelligence on their participants, so they used the Baddeley reasoning task. One of the statistical tests they performed looked at the effects on a silent reading task (the dependent variable) of the covariate reasoning task and the digit ratio as a categorical independent variable.

Research design:	One-way ANCOVA	Factorial ANCOVA	RM ANCOVA

4   Larson-Hall (2008). I examined Japanese college users of English in order to see whether an earlier start in learning English would result in any advantages on an English grammaticality judgment test (GJT). Thus my dependent variable was scores on the GJT, while my independent variables were a categorical division into earlier and later starters (those who began learning English before age 12 or 13, when it is a required subject in public schools), a continuous variable of language aptitude, and a continuous variable of the amount of total input the participants reported in English before they reached college (this was, of course, estimated!). Both language aptitude and amount of input were covariates.

Research design:	One-way ANCOVA	Factorial ANCOVA	RM ANCOVA

5   Culatta, Reese, and Setzer (2006) (slightly adjusted from the original). The authors examined the effects on several different reading tasks of presenting skills in the first six weeks or second six weeks of instruction in a dual-language

immersion kindergarten. A pre-test and post-test were also given, so that time was a categorical independent variable. Whether the skill of alliteration or rhyme was presented first was categorized as the class independent variable. The dependent variable was word recognition. In order to control for differences in reading ability, scores from a standardized test of reading were used as a covariate.

Research design:	One-way ANCOVA	Factorial ANCOVA	RM ANCOVA

13.3 Assumptions of ANCOVA

ANCOVA carries with it the normal assumptions of any ANOVA test, including normal distribution of data and homogeneity of variances. However, ANCOVA also carries a couple more requirements that are special to the covariate situation. I won't specifically list the assumptions of ANOVA here (they can be found in Section 10.3 for one-way ANOVA, Section 11.3 for factorial ANOVA, and Section 13.3.1 for RM ANOVA), just the additional requirements in Table 13.3.

Table 13.3 Additional Assumptions for Covariates

Meeting assumptions		*Factorial ANOVA*
1 No strong correlations among the covariates themselves	Required? How to test assumption?	Yes If you have more than one covariate, perform a correlation test on your covariates; Tabachnick and Fidell (2001) say that any covariate which correlates with another covariate at $R^2=.5$ or higher should be eliminated, as it is not adding much additional information independent of the other variable
	What if assumption not met?	Eliminate one of the covariates
2 The relationship between the covariate and response variable should be linear	Required? How to test assumption?	Yes Look at correlation statistics or scatterplots between the covariate and the response variable; impose a regression line and a Loess line to see if the relationship is linear "enough"; this should be done with data divided into the separate groups used in your analysis, as shown in Figure 13.3
	What if assumption not met?	1) Try transformation of one or both variables; 2) do not use ANCOVA; 3) use robust ANCOVA analysis which does not require linearity
3 The slopes for each group of the regression should be the same (homogeneity of regression slopes)	Required? How to test assumption?	Yes 1) Check scatterplot to see if all groups are similar in their slopes; 2) include an interaction term between the covariate and the treatment—if it is statistical (p<.05) then you have a problem (I will demonstrate how to check this assumption in Section 13.3.1)
	What if assumption not met?	1) Do not use ANCOVA; 2) use robust ANCOVA analysis which does not require homogeneity of regression

13.3.1 Checking the Assumptions for the Lyster (2004) Data

For the first assumption that there may be a strong correlation between covariates, for Lyster's data, since there is only one covariate, I do not need to worry about correlation between covariates. However, for my own study (Larson-Hall, 2008), I used two covariates, and we can check the correlation between the two variables of language aptitude and total amount of input in English. Using the LarsonHall2008.sav file, I choose ANALYZE > CORRELATE > BIVARIATE. I put the variables of TOTALHRS and APTSCORE in the "Variables" box and ran the correlation. The correlation between these two variables is $r = 0.08$. This is not cause for worry at all.

For the second assumption of linearity between the covariate and the dependent variable, the scatterplots shown in Figure 13.3 are a good way to test this. The Loess line imposed on each of the scatterplots, separated out by experimental group, shows that a line may not be the best descriptor for any of the situations except that of the FFI Only group. For the FFI Recast and FFI Prompt groups the data seem to be scattered somewhat randomly, and for the Comparison group there is clearly an outlier. If you get rid of this one point and rerun the analysis then you are going to find that the slopes of the lines for the groups are not parallel, which will violate the third assumption of homogeneity of regression. This data set seems to be a good candidate for a robust analysis, but since that is not available to us in SPSS we will continue with the linear (parametric) analysis. Remember, what we risk losing is the power to find differences that do exist.

For the third assumption we can again go to Figure 13.3 to see if slopes are parallel for the four experimental groups. They are not exactly parallel but they are probably not so deviant that we will call them unparallel. Another way to test whether there is **homogeneity of regression slopes** is to test for the presence of an interaction between the covariate and the treatment or grouping variable. If the interaction is not statistical, I can proceed with the normal model, according to Tabachnick and Fidell (2001, p. 292).

In order to test the homogeneity of regression slopes assumption in SPSS, we will request the interaction between the covariate and the grouping variable in our initial model. To do this, open ANALYZE > GENERAL LINEAR MODEL > UNIVARIATE. In the Univariate dialogue box, move the variables you want to analyze to the right. For Lyster's (2004) data, move POSTOBJECTID to the "Dependent variable" box, COND to the "Fixed Factor(s)" box, and PREOBJECTID to the "Covariate(s)" box. Now open the MODEL button.

Figure 13.5 shows a box where you can build a custom ANOVA model. Click on the button that says "Custom." Click on COND, and in the "Build Term(s)" area use the arrow to move it to the right under "Model." Do the same for PREOBJECTID. Then use the Ctrl button to click on both variables at the same time. In the "Build Term(s)" area the "Type" button should say INTERACTION. This will let you set up the third term in the "Model" area as I have. Notice also that I have changed the sum of squares to Type II. Press CONTINUE and then OK to run the analysis.

The main output table, the "Tests of Between-Subjects Effects," shows that the interaction (Cond*PreObjectID) is not statistical ($p = .09$). This is one of those times when we are hoping the p-value will be *larger* than $p = 0.05$. If it is, we can conclude that the slopes of the groups on the covariate are parallel enough and that there is

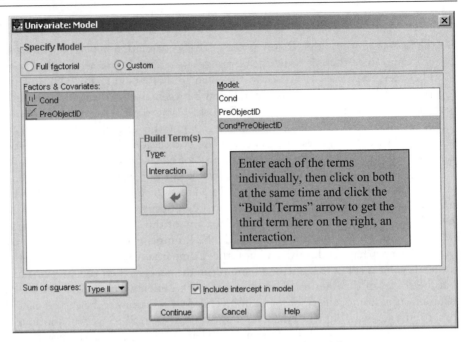

Figure 13.5 Creating an interaction term in a custom ANCOVA model.

Table 13.4 Output for an Interaction between the Covariate and the Group Variable

Tests of Between-Subjects Effects

Dependent Variable:PostObjectID

Source	Type II Sum of Squares	df	Mean Square	F	Sig.
Corrected Model	449.021[a]	7	64.146	5.832	.000
Intercept	338.874	1	338.874	30.808	.000
Cond	61.459	3	20.486	1.862	.147
PreObjectID	171.700	1	171.700	15.610	.000
Cond * PreObjectID	75.221	3	25.074	2.280	.090
Error	604.979	55	11.000		
Total	15229.000	63			
Corrected Total	1054.000	62			

a. R Squared = .426 (Adjusted R Squared = .353)

homogeneity of regression. If there were a statistical interaction, then you can see that that would mean that the groups performed differently on the covariate. In the output, shown in Table 13.4, the interaction (Cond*PreObjectID) is the only thing that you need to look at; you can ignore the other parts of the output.

13.4 Performing an ANCOVA

Performing an ANCOVA involves using SPSS's GENERAL LINEAR MODEL choices in the ANALYZE menu. The three pertinent choices in that menu are: UNIVARIATE, MULTIVARIATE, and REPEATED MEASURES (the Variance Components choice is for mixed-effects models, which are not discussed in this book; for more information see Baayen, 2008; Johnson, 2008; Pinheiro & Bates, 2000). Use the UNIVARIATE command for one-way or factorial ANOVA. Use the MULTIVARIATE command for MANOVA. I don't discuss MANOVA in this book, but it would involve analyzing more than one dependent variable in the same test. Use the REPEATED MEASURES command when you have any independent variable which measures the same people more than once.

Because the Lyster (2004) research design is a one-way ANCOVA, I'll use the UNIVARIATE choice. So I choose ANALYZE > GENERAL LINEAR MODEL > UNIVARIATE and move POSTOBJECTID to the "Dependent variable" box, COND to the "Fixed Factor(s)" box, and PREOBJECTID to the "Covariate(s)" box.

You should now open some of the buttons that are found on the right side of the Univariate dialogue box. First, open the MODEL button and choose a Type II sum of squares analysis. If you previously explored a "Custom" model to check for interactions between the covariate and the IV, change this back to the "Full Factorial" model. Because there's only one non-covariate independent variable for the Lyster (2004) data, a means plot would not be possible, so there's no reason to open the PLOT button. However, if you had two or more non-covariate independent variables you might like to call for some means plots using this button.

If your independent variable has more than two levels, Tabachnick and Fidell (2001, p. 313) state that one should be able to run post-hoc tests after an ANCOVA run, but in SPSS the POST HOC button will become unavailable if a covariate is entered, as shown in Figure 13.6. To obtain post-hoc tests on the independent variable you can instead open the OPTIONS button and move the independent variables to the "Display Means for" box, as shown for COND in Figure 13.6. If you tick the box that says "Compare main effects," pairwise comparisons will be done for all of the levels of the IV. The SPSS Options dialogue box gives only three choices for ways to adjust the p-values of the pairwise comparisons—LSD, which means no adjustments are made, Bonferroni, which means 0.05 is divided by the total number of comparisons that are made, and Sidak, which is a conservative familywise error rate adjustment, but slightly less conservative than the Bonferroni. As I am an advocate for higher power, I recommend using the LSD choice. If you are nervous about having too many comparisons, I would recommend still using LSD and then using the algorithm for the FDR (in the Appendix) to adjust p-values.

While the OPTIONS button is open, also check the "Descriptive statistics," "Estimates of effect size," and "Observed Power" boxes. If you want a Levene's test of homogeneity of variances, tick "Homogeneity Tests." Press CONTINUE and then OK in the main dialogue box.

13.4.1 ANCOVA Output

For the Lyster (2004) oral object identification task, the first thing you will see in the

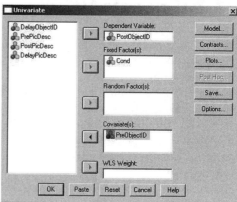

Figure 13.6 Performing an ANCOVA in SPSS.

output is the list of groups and descriptive statistics for the immediate post-test score. We have already noted these in Table 13.1. They show that for the post-test there is not much difference between any of the three FFI groups.

The output with the main results we are looking for is shown in Table 13.5. We see that the effect of condition is above $p = .05$ when the pre-test scores are adjusted for ($F_{3,58} = 2.57$, $p = .063$, partial eta-squared = .11, power = .58). This p-value is above 0.05 but not by very much. As for the effect size, according to Cohen (1962) this a medium to large effect size.

If we decide that we cannot reject the null hypothesis, this means that, when post-test scores are adjusted for pre-test scores, condition is not a factor in explaining variance in the model. If, on the other hand, we decide that the effect size is fairly large and that low power might explain the non-statistical result, we might argue that condition did indeed explain variance in the post-test scores when adjusted for pre-test scores.

The line that lists our covariate, PREOBJECTID, shows that pre-test scores *are* a statistical covariate with a fairly strong effect size ($F_{1,58} = 14.6$, $p < .0005$, partial eta-squared = .20, power = .96). This means that pre-test scores did have a strong effect on how the participants performed on the post-test. We can say more about this effect

Table 13.5 Tests of Between-Subjects Effects in the ANCOVA Output

Tests of Between-Subjects Effects

Dependent Variable:PostObjectID

Source	Type II Sum of Squares	df	Mean Square	F	Sig.	Partial Eta Squared	Noncent. Parameter	Observed Power[b]
Corrected Model	373.800[a]	4	93.450	7.968	.000	.355	31.874	.997
Intercept	278.113	1	278.113	23.714	.000	.290	23.714	.998
PreObjectID	171.700	1	171.700	14.641	.000	.202	14.641	.964
Cond	90.232	3	30.077	2.565	.063	.117	7.694	.603
Error	680.200	58	11.728					
Total	15229.000	63						
Corrected Total	1054.000	62						

a. R Squared = .355 (Adjusted R Squared = .310)

b. Computed using alpha = .05

by looking at the output found under the title "Estimated Marginal Means." These results are shown in Table 13.6.

The estimates for the means shown in Table 13.6 are the post-test means for the object identification task, but adjusted for the pre-test, so these means are different from those seen in the descriptive statistics at the beginning of the output. The **adjusted mean** is the mean score with the influence of the covariate factored out, and in this data set there is more difference between scores of the FFI groups in these adjusted means than in the original means.

The Pairwise Comparisons table shows comparisons between the different groups. The comparisons which are statistical are all with the Comparison group, so I have only shown that row. These pairwise comparisons can be interpreted as for any other post-hoc tests, but remember that we asked for no adjustment on our p-values. If you decided to count the results of the Cond main effects as statistical, you could then report that the differences between groups lie in statistical differences between the Comparison and FFI Recast groups (95% CI in mean difference: $-5.1, -.2$) and the Comparison and FFI Prompt groups (95% CI in mean difference: $-5.4, -.6$) (mean scores show the FFI groups did better than the Comparison group). None of the other groups are statistically different from each other. Effect sizes cannot be calculated with standard error; they will need to be calculated with standard deviations. The standard error is equal to the standard deviation divided by the square root of the number of participants, and in this way we can work back to calculate the standard deviation for each group. So, for example, the standard error for the FFI Recast group is .854, so the sd = $.854*\sqrt{15}$ = 3.3. Working the same way, sd(FFI prompt) = 3.3, sd(FFI Only) = 3.4, and sd(Comparison) = 3.4. Then, using an online calculator for effect sizes that uses mean scores and standard deviation, d = .81 for the FFI Recast versus Comparison group, d = .9 for the FFI Prompt versus Comparison group, and d = .5 for the FFI Only versus Comparison group.

Table 13.6 Estimated Marginal Means Output from an ANCOVA

Estimates

Dependent Variable:PostObjectID

Cond	Mean	Std. Error	95% Confidence Interval	
			Lower Bound	Upper Bound
FFIrecast	15.895[a]	.854	14.186	17.604
FFIprompt	16.247[a]	.854	14.538	17.957
FFIonly	14.860[a]	.884	13.091	16.630
Comparison	13.248[a]	.883	11.480	15.015

a. Covariates appearing in the model are evaluated at the following values: PreObjectID = 12.45.

Pairwise Comparisons

Dependent Variable:PostObjectID

(I) Cond	(J) Cond	Mean Difference (I-J)	Std. Error	Sig.[a]	95% Confidence Interval for Difference[a]	
					Lower Bound	Upper Bound
Comparison	FFIrecast	-2.647*	1.239	.037	-5.126	-.168
	FFIprompt	-3.000*	1.218	.017	-5.437	-.562
	FFIonly	-1.613	1.293	.217	-4.201	.975

Performing an ANCOVA in SPSS

1   If one-way or factorial ANOVA: Analyze > General Linear Model > Univariate. If RM ANOVA: Analyze > General Linear Model > Repeated Measures.

2   Put dependent variable in "Dependent Variable," independent variables in "Fixed Factor(s)," and covariate in "Covariate(s)."

3   Open the Model button and create a custom model that includes an interaction between the covariate and your fixed factor(s). If this is statistical, stop and do not continue with your ANOVA. If this is not statistical, go back and click the "Full Factorial" button, which removes the interaction, and also change to a Type II sum of squares.

4   Open the Options button and tick "Descriptive statistics," "Estimates of effect size," and "Observed power." Move between-group variables over to "Display Means for" in order to get post-hoc comparisons.

5   Open the Plots button and call for an interaction plot if you have more than one independent variable. Now run the ANCOVA.

13.4.2 Application Activities for ANCOVA

1   Larson-Hall (2008). The design of my study is described in Activity 4 in Section 13.2.1. Using the LarsonHall2008.sav file, perform an ANCOVA with grammaticality judgment test (GJTSCORE) as the dependent variable, status as an earlier or later starter as a factor (ERLYEXP), and total hours of input (TOTALHRS) and language aptitude (APTSCORE) as covariates. Use the LarsonHall2008.sav file and first check the special assumptions for ANCOVA outlined in Section 13.3. Even if the data violates the assumptions, go ahead and perform the ANCOVA. What are the results of the parametric ANCOVA?

2   Class Time. Use the data set I have called ClassTime.sav (this data set was taken from Howell, 2002, p. 629, but I adapted it to reflect a design that will be associated with the second language research field). Let's pretend that a researcher who is in charge of teaching Arabic at the university level notices that there seems to be a difference in how students in her 8 a.m. class respond to her teaching versus how students in the later classes respond. At the start of a new school year she gives them an initial test of their enthusiasm and motivation for learning Arabic. There are 30 items which contain a ten-point Likert scale, where a higher score is more positive about the class. The researcher averages their answers together for a score out of 10. She then administers the same test at the end of the semester. The researcher has five classes, one at 8 a.m., one at 10 a.m., one at 11 a.m., one at 1 p.m., and one at 2 p.m. This study could be analyzed with an RM ANOVA (if the data were arranged in the "wide" format) but the researcher decides to analyze it with an ANCOVA using the pre-test scores as a covariate so that any differences among the post-test scores due to variability in pre-test scores will be controlled. Use PreTestScores as the covariate, PostTestScores as the dependent variable, and TimeOfClass as the independent variable. First check the special assumptions for ANCOVA. Even if the data violates the assumptions, go ahead and perform the ANCOVA. What are the results of the parametric ANCOVA?

13.4.3 Reporting the Results of an ANCOVA

In an ANCOVA you'll want to report specifically about whether the assumptions of ANCOVA were satisfied. You should then report the results of the test and be sure to include the F-value, the p-value, the degrees of freedom, the effect size, and the power. If post-hoc comparisons are made it would be good to include confidence intervals. Whether you report about the covariate depends on whether you are just trying to factor its influence out or whether you are still interested in its effect on the dependent variable. I will report the results of the ANCOVA on Lyster's (2004) object identification task. Lyster was just interested in factoring out the effect of the covariate so I will not report on it here.

> Lyster (2004) investigated the question of whether conditions involving the provision of form-focused instruction had differing effects on the post-task results of participants taking an object identification task. Because groups were found to differ statistically on the pre-test, the pre-test was used as a covariate in an ANCOVA analysis. An examination of the linearity of the pre-test and post-test scores by group showed some deviation away from linearity, but slopes were sufficiently parallel to satisfy the assumption of homogeneity of regression. The between-groups independent variable of condition was not found to be statistical ($F_{3,58}$ = 2.57, p = .063, partial eta-squared = .11, power = .58), but with such a large effect size (Cohen, 1962) this IV should be considered a factor which explains much of the variance in the scores. Pairwise comparisons between the Comparison group and the FFI groups found differences at p < .05 for two of the groups (95% confidence intervals and effect sizes are shown below).

> FFI Prompt versus Comparison   −5.4, −0.56 d = .81
> FFI Recast versus Comparison   −5.1, −0.17 d = .90
> FFI Only vesus Comparison   −4.2, 0.98 d = .50

> The wide confidence intervals show that estimates are not very precise but effect sizes are medium to large.

13.5 Summary

Use an analysis of covariance when you want to control for the effect of some variable. Your covariate will most likely be a continuous variable. Ones we saw in this chapter used in second language research designs were pre-test scores, language proficiency, intelligence, amount of input in the L2, and reading ability. When you factor the effects of these variables out you will then be able to test for the effect of other independent variables, disregarding the effects of the covariate. Remember that basically the covariate is just another independent variable. In some cases it may be of interest to report whether the covariate was statistical, meaning that it had a statistical effect on the dependent variable. In other cases, the goal may just be to factor the effects of that variable out of the equation. ANCOVA can be used with any of the ANOVA research designs, including one-way, factorial, and RM ANOVA. ANCOVA should be used with caution, however, as it contains even more assumptions than a regular ANOVA, and these assumptions may not accurately describe the data.

Howell (2002) also warns against a use of the ANCOVA when it would result in a situation that would go against logic or common sense. If controlling for your covariate results in a design that does not exist in reality, then it doesn't make much sense to test for it statistically. For example, you probably wouldn't want to factor age of acquisition out of a research design involving early and late bilinguals. Would you really want to examine, say, context of acquisition (naturalistic, instructed, or both) while ignoring the effects of age? Age is an important factor and it would be silly to ignore it while examining the effects of a different variable.

Chapter 14

Statistics when Your Data Do Not Satisfy Parametric Assumptions: Non-Parametric Statistics

> [I]t is easy to . . . throw out an interesting baby with the nonsignificant bath water. Lack of statistical significance at a conventional level does not mean that no real effect is present; it means only that no real effect is clearly seen from the data. That is why it is of the highest importance to look at power and to compute confidence intervals.
>
> William Kruskal (1978, p. 946)

Well, you've arrived at the final chapter! Why do statistics books often end with a chapter on non-parametric statistics? Is it because the chapter on non-parametric statistics is one that can be skipped or left out if there's not enough time to cover everything in the book? Well, my reason to put the non-parametric statistics at the end is that the regular chapters were long and confusing enough without adding an alternate statistical test that you could use. So this chapter will be a collection of non-parametric techniques available in SPSS.

14.1 Why Use Non-Parametric Statistics?

The first question I want to answer at the outset of this chapter is why you would use non-parametric statistics. Non-parametric statistics are also called distribution-free statistics (Howell, 2002) because they do not require that the data be normally distributed. Maxwell and Delaney (2004) note that it is not accurate to say that non-parametric tests do not assume homogeneity of variances, however. They point out that non-parametric tests like the Kruskal-Wallis assume that population distributions are equal, which would clearly imply that variances are equal as well. Other requirements of non-parametric tests are that sampling is random and observations are independent.

But wait a minute, you might say. Did we see that most of the data sets used in this book didn't satisfy the assumptions of parametric statistics? They weren't perfectly normal, because they weren't perfectly symmetrically distributed and/or they contained outliers. They often violated the assumption that the variances of the groups would be equal. And yet the authors of these studies continued to use parametric tests. So is it or isn't it OK to just use parametric statistics even when your data do not satisfy the assumptions of parametric statistics? It's hard to get a straight answer to this question when you consult the statistical experts. Some authors claim that parametric statistics are robust to violations of the assumptions, while others claim that even small violations can spell certain doom (OK, not certain doom, but cause you to conclude that there are no differences between groups or no relationship between variables when they do in fact exist). Statistical simulation studies have shown that problems with skewness, unequal variances, and outliers can have large effects on the conclusions you draw from statistical tests (Wilcox, 1998).

You already know that I'd rather be using robust statistical methods, which were thought up early in the twentieth century but have only become possible since the advent of strong computing power (Larson-Hall & Herrington, forthcoming). Howell (2002) also believes that robust methods will shortly "overtake what are now the most common nonparametric tests, and may eventually overtake the traditional parametric tests" (p. 692). The reason parametric and so-called non-parametric statistics (the ones I will show you in this chapter) were the ones that became well known was because their computing requirements were small enough that people could compute them by hand. The usually unreasonable assumptions of the parametric statistics were put in place so that the statistical test would be much easier to compute by hand. Maronna, Martin, and Yohai (2006) recommend that those who are interested in using robust statistics use the computer program S-PLUS, or its free version, R (available at www.r-project.org). Wilcox's various books (2001, 2003, 2005) are also useful for learning how to do robust statistics.

But since SPSS hasn't incorporated robust methods yet, our best alternative to parametric statistics will be the non-parametric ones. Some authors assert that non-parametric statistics are less powerful than parametric statistics, but that is not always true. It really depends upon the problems that are found in the distribution of the data. If there are outliers, then a non-parametric test, which uses the median which is insensitive to outliers, might result in more power to find a statistical result than a parametric test. It would probably be a good idea to use both a parametric and a non-parametric test and compare the results if you are worried about satisfying the distributional assumptions of a parametric test. I would then pick the test that had the most power.

14.2 Non-Parametric Statistics in SPSS

The place to go to find ways to analyze statistics with non-parametric methods in SPSS is the ANALYZE > NONPARAMETRIC TESTS menu, shown in Figure 14.1. You will see eight different non-parametric tests but I will only discuss the last four in this chapter. Table 14.1 lists the parametric counterpart to each non-parametric test. The Spearman rank order correlation is also a non-parametric alternative to the parametric Pearson correlation, but this test has already been demonstrated in Chapter 6 on correlation so I won't discuss it further in this chapter.

This section will explain the first four non-parametric tests available in SPSS. The **chi-square test** is a non-parametric test, and we have already examined that test in Chapter 8. There is no parametric alternative to the test.

The **binomial test** examines the proposition that the proportion of counts that you have fits a binomial distribution. It starts with the assumption that either of two choices is equally likely. In Section 8.1.3 we examined some aggregate binary choice data to see the probability of getting counts of 339 versus 111 if both choices were equally likely. The probability was less than 0.0005, so we concluded that the distribution of answers was not random.

The **runs test** is designed to test whether a categorical level of your variable (with

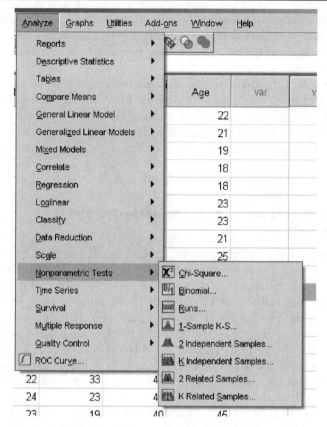

Figure 14.1 Non-parametric tests available in SPSS.

Table 14.1 Non-Parametric Tests in SPSS and their Parametric Counterparts

Non-parametric test	Parametric counterpart	Statistic used
Chi-square	–	χ^2
Binomial	–	p-value returned
Runs	–	p-value returned
1-sample K–S	–	p-value returned
2 independent samples	Independent-samples t-test (Chapter 9)	Mann–Whitney U or Wilcoxon rank-sum test W
K independent samples	One-way ANOVA (Chapter 10)	Kruskal–Wallis, χ^2
2 related samples	Paired-samples t-test (Chapter 9)	Wilcoxon signed ranks test, Z
K related samples	RM ANOVA with only one within-subject independent variable (Chapter 12)	Friedman, χ^2

only two levels) is randomly distributed in your data. For example, you could use the runs test to see whether males and females were randomly distributed in your sample. This test is not frequently used in the second language research field so I will not demonstrate how to use it in this chapter.

The one-sample **Kolmogorov–Smirnov** test is sometimes used to test whether a variable has a normal distribution. This test can also be used to compare the distribution of a variable with other distributions besides the normal distribution, such as the Poisson distribution. As I have discouraged the use of such tests throughout this book because they are usually not sensitive enough to detect deviances from the normal distribution with small sample sizes and too sensitive to deviances for large sample sizes, I also will not demonstrate how to use this test in this chapter.

14.2.1 Non-Parametric Alternative to the Independent-Samples T-Test (Mann–Whitney Test)

Use an independent-samples t-test when you have two mean scores from two different groups or, in other words, two levels in your independent variable. In Chapter 9 I illustrated the use of the independent-samples t-test with Leow and Morgan-Short's (2004) study of comprehension ability when participants had to engage in a think-aloud task. I used a parametric test for the recognition post-score test and found a non-statistical difference between the think-aloud and non-think-aloud groups with a $p = .105$. Actually, Leow and Morgan-Short analyzed this variable with a **Mann–Whitney U test** because their data did not fit the assumptions of a parametric test. Let's take the same variable and see what results we get with the non-parametric alternative (use the LeowMorganShort.sav file).

Go to ANALYZE > NONPARAMETRIC TESTS > 2 INDEPENDENT SAMPLES. Move RECPOST-SCORE to the "Test Variable List" and GROUP to the "Grouping Variable" box. Just as with the independent-samples t-test, you'll need to define the groups with numbers before moving on. I just called them 1 and 2, as shown in Figure 14.2. Notice that you

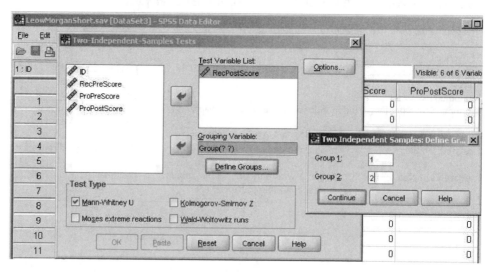

Figure 14.2 The non-parametric alternative to the independent-samples t-test.

have several choices for the type of test that you will use, but just keep the tick on the default box, the "Mann–Whitney U." This test is exactly the same as the Wilcoxon Rank Sum Test that returns a statistic of W (Howell, 2002), in case you ever see that result and wonder what test it is. The descriptive statistics returned by the choice of "Descriptive Statistics" in the OPTIONS button are not divided by group, so there is no need to open that button.

Your output will not show mean scores (as it does not use mean scores), but instead mean ranks. The non-parametric test will rank the data for the whole data set and then compare whether the ranks divided up by groups are different from the rank for the whole set. In this case, the mean rank of the non-think-aloud group is lower than the mean rank of the think-aloud group, but they are fairly similar (as shown in Table 14.2). The Test Statistics table in Table 14.2 shows the U-value (663.5) and the associated p-value ($p = .424$). The result is the same as with the parametric test—there is no difference between the groups.

> Tip: If you have 20 or fewer cases in your data set, besides the normal p-value under "Asymp. Sig. (2-tailed)" you will receive another p-value after the line "Exact Sig." SPSS uses a method of calculating the p-value associated with each test that is good for large samples, but Field (2005) says that with small samples the exact method is more accurate.

You can calculate an effect size for any non-parametric test which returns a z-score (the capital "Z" in the output in Table 14.2) by using the following equation to turn it into a percentage variance measure of r:

Table 14.2 Results from Mann–Whitney U Test (Alternative to Independent-Samples T-Test)

Mann-Whitney Test

Ranks

	Group	N	Mean Rank	Sum of Ranks
RecPostScore	Non Think Aloud	39	37.01	1443.50
	Think Aloud	38	41.04	1559.50
	Total	77		

Test Statistics[a]

	RecPost Score
Mann-Whitney U	663.500
Wilcoxon W	1443.500
Z	-.799
Asymp. Sig. (2-tailed)	.424

a. Grouping Variable: Group

$$r = \frac{z}{\sqrt{N}}$$

where N=the total number of observations (Rosenthal, 1991, p. 19). For the Mann–Whitney U test we did for the Leow and Morgan-Short variable of recognition post-test, $r = \frac{.8}{\sqrt{77}} = .09$, a small effect size.

14.2.2 Non-Parametric Alternative to the One-Way ANOVA (Kruskal–Wallis)

Use a one-way ANOVA when you have three or more levels of your independent variable or, in other words, you want to compare three or more mean scores on one dependent variable. In Chapter 10 I illustrated the use of the one-way ANOVA with the Ellis and Yuan (2004) data set, which looked for differences in groups that received differing amounts of planning and writing time (EllisYuan.sav). We examined group differences with the dependent variable of how much syntactical variety was found in each participant's writing sample. With the one-way ANOVA we found a statistical result ($F_{2,39} = 9.05$, $p = .001$), and further post-hoc tests showed that the pre-task planning (PTP) group was better than both the online planning (OLP) and no-planning (NP) groups. Let's see what happens when we use the non-parametric alternative, the **Kruskal–Wallis test**.

To call for the test, go to ANALYZE > NONPARAMETRIC TESTS > K INDEPENDENT SAMPLES. Move the SYNTAXVARIETY variable to the "Test Variable List" and GROUP to the "Grouping Variable" box. Figure 14.3 shows that you can't continue until you define your groups. Click the box under "Grouping Variable" that says DEFINE RANGE. For "Minimum," enter the number of the lowest level of your group (I put 1), and in "Maximum" put the number of the highest level of your group (I put 3). Press CONTINUE. Leave the "Kruskal-Wallis H" test box ticked. Use the Jonckheere–Terpstra test to get more power if there is some a priori ordering to your groups (this is only available if you have the Exact Tests add-on module for SPSS). The descriptive statistics do not split the data up between groups so I do not see any use calling for them in the OPTIONS button.

The Kruskal–Wallis test is an extension of the Mann–Whitney to the case of more than two levels, so the same type of ranking is taking place in this test and the first table of the output will show the rankings of the groups. The highest ranking is for the PTP group at 30.3; then there is 20.9 for the OLP group, and 13.3 for the NP group. The output, shown in Table 14.3, returns a chi-square statistic that has a probability of $p = .001$ at 2 degrees of freedom. We conclude that there are statistical differences between the three groups. This is the same conclusion we drew from the parametric tests.

There's just one problem, which is that the Kruskal–Wallis test does not provide post-hoc tests in the same way as the one-way ANOVA did not, so we can't be sure which groups are statistically different from one another. Field (2005) suggests using

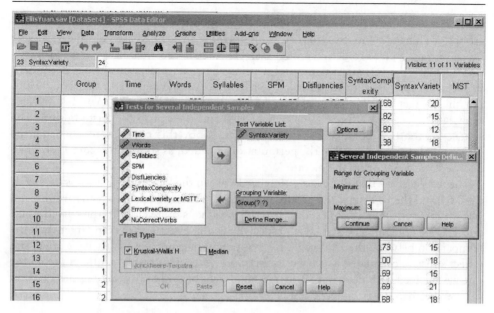

Figure 14.3 The non-parametric alternative to the one-way ANOVA.

Table 14.3 Results from Kruskal–Wallis Test (Alternative to the One-Way ANOVA)

Kruskal-Wallis Test

Ranks

	Group	N	Mean Rank
SyntaxVariety	NP_No planning	14	13.32
	PTP_PretaskPlanning	14	30.32
	OLP_OnlinePlanning	14	20.86
	Total	42	

Test Statistics[a,b]

	SyntaxVariety
Chi-Square	13.635
df	2
Asymp. Sig.	.001

a. Kruskal Wallis Test

b. Grouping Variable: Group

separate Mann–Whitney U tests in place of the post-hoc tests.[1] Since there are three groups, we'll need to do three more tests. Remember that the Mann–Whitney dialogue box gives you a place to define groups (see Figure 14.2), so we'll first put in Groups 1 and 2, then 1 and 3, and then 2 and 3 using the same independent and dependent variables that we used for the Kruskal–Wallis test. A faster way to do this would be to put the correct variable in the boxes for the Kruskal–Wallis test (ANALYZE > NON-PARAMETRIC TESTS > 2 INDEPENDENT SAMPLES) and then push the Paste button. The syntax for the first comparison will be shown. Copy this twice more, changing the group numbers to cover all of the permutations needed, as shown in Figure 14.4. Then choose RUN > ALL from the menu.

The results show that there is a difference between the PTP and NP groups ($p = .001$, $r = 0.64$) and the PTP and OLP groups ($p = .02$, $r = 0.36$), but not between the OLP and NP groups ($p = .054$, $r = 0.44$), although this p-value is quite close to the cut-off point and may be argued to be statistical, especially as the effect size is even larger than the comparison between the PTP and OLP groups and in general is a fairly large effect size (effect sizes are calculated as shown in Section 14.2.1). This result is different from the one we received with the parametric test, and might be said to have more power to find differences than the parametric test.

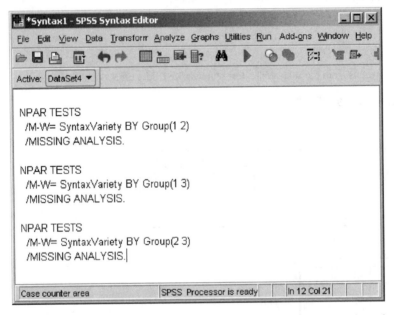

Figure 14.4 Pasting in syntax to run three Mann–Whitney tests as post-hocs for the Kruskal–Wallis test.

---

1 If you run a large number of tests you might consider doing something to minimize the familywise error rate, such as using the FDR adjustment. The Bonferroni, although conservative, is quick to calculate— simply divide 0.05 by the number of tests that you are using and that is your critical value.

14.2.3 Non-Parametric Alternative to the Paired-Samples T-Test (Wilcoxon Signed Ranks Test or McNemar Test)

Use a paired-samples t-test when you have two mean scores you want to compare and these scores come from the same group of people. In other words, use a paired-samples t-test when your independent variable has only two levels and those levels are repeated measures. I illustrated the use of the paired-samples t-test with data from French and O'Brien (2008) which asked whether children learning English improved on two measures of working memory over time (French & O'Brien Grammar.sav). One measure used English non-words (ENWR) and the other used Arabic non-words (ANWR). The parametric paired-samples t-test showed that there was a statistical difference over the two testing times for the English test (t_{103} = 14.3, p < .0005) but not for the Arabic test (t_{103} = 1.8, p = .07). Let's see what happens when we use the non-parametric **Wilcoxon signed ranks test** to compare the two times the tests were taken.

To call for the test, go to ANALYZE > NONPARAMETRIC TESTS > 2 RELATED SAMPLES. Move the variables ANWR_1 and ANWR_2 to the right to form Pair 1 and then move ENWR_1 and ENWR_2 over to form Pair 2, as shown in Figure 14.5. Leave the box ticked for test type as "Wilcoxon." Use the **McNemar test** when you have nominal data and want to see how many people changed their categories over time and you only have two categories. Unlike the case with the non-parametric tests we've seen up until now, the descriptive statistics will be useful, so also open the OPTIONS button and tick "Descriptive statistics."

Just like the Mann–Whitney and Kruskal–Wallis tests, the Wilcoxon signed ranks test ranks data. This is why we see mean ranks for the two groups in the output shown in Table 14.4. Positive ranks mean that an individual scored more highly at Time 2; negative ranks mean they scored lower at Time 2. For those instances where an individual's score did not change, these ties are dropped out of the analysis. From Table

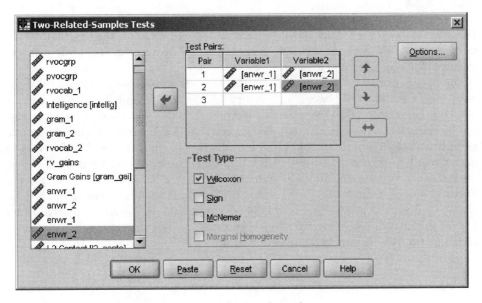

Figure 14.5 The non-parametric alternative to the paired-samples t-test.

Table 14.4 Results from Wilcoxon Signed Ranks Test (Alternative to the Paired-Samples T-Test)

Wilcoxon Signed Ranks Test

Ranks

		N	Mean Rank	Sum of Ranks
anwr_2 - anwr_1	Negative Ranks	30[a]	50.13	1504.00
	Positive Ranks	58[b]	41.59	2412.00
	Ties	16[c]		
	Total	104		
enwr_2 - enwr_1	Negative Ranks	3[d]	6.00	18.00
	Positive Ranks	92[e]	49.37	4542.00
	Ties	9[f]		
	Total	104		

a. anwr_2 < anwr_1
b. anwr_2 > anwr_1
c. anwr_2 = anwr_1
d. enwr_2 < enwr_1
e. enwr_2 > enwr_1
f. enwr_2 = enwr_1

Test Statistics[b]

	anwr_2 - anwr_1	enwr_2 - enwr_1
Z	-1.973[a]	-8.446[a]
Asymp. Sig. (2-tailed)	.049	.000

a. Based on negative ranks.
b. Wilcoxon Signed Ranks Test

14.4 you see that there's quite a lot of difference between ranks for the English working memory test, with many more people gaining in scores than losing. For the English test the proportion of gains and losses is more even.

The z-score calculated as a statistic for this test has a probability below $p = .05$ for both tests. For the English working memory test $p < .0005$, while for the Arabic test $p = .049$. This result differs from the parametric alternative. The effect size for the tests can be calculated the same way as stated in Section 14.2.1, where N will be the total number of negative and positive ranks, with the ties dropped out (and it also doesn't matter that we tested people more than once; the N is supposed to be the number of observations used in calculating the statistic, not the number of participants). For the English working memory test $r = 1.973/sqrt(88) = 0.21$; for the Arabic test $r = 8.45/sqrt(95) = 0.87$. The effect size is very large for the Arabic class, but a small to medium size for the English test (remember, this is an r-family effect size, which is a percentage variance effect size, not the d-family effect size).

14.2.4 Non-Parametric Alternative to the One-Way RM ANOVA Test (Friedman Test)

Use an RM ANOVA test when you have tested the same people more than once. You would need to use a one-way RM ANOVA when the one independent variable that you have has more than two levels (if you only had two levels that were repeated measures you could use a paired-samples t-test). The parametric RM ANOVA can be used with any number of independent variables, but for the non-parametric alternative you can only use the **Friedman** test when there is just one independent variable. We saw an RM ANOVA illustrated through the data of Murphy (2004) and Lyster (2004). However, both of these ANOVAs used more than one independent variable, so we would not be able to apply a non-parametric test to either design as a whole. However, to illustrate the non-parametric test we could ask if there were differences between verb similarity for the Murphy (2004) data for just regular verbs for the NNS adults. This would give us just one independent variable of verb similarity, with three levels (prototypical, intermediate, distant).

In the parametric RM ANOVA that was conducted in Chapter 12 there was a statistical difference for the simple main effect of similarity, but we didn't care too much about that since there was a statistical three-way interaction between verb type, similarity, and group. In the analysis in Chapter 12 I didn't specifically test whether the levels of similarity were statistically different for the regular verbs for the NNS adults. We can look at a means plot with the data, given in Figure 12.14 and reprinted here as Figure 14.6, and see that, as far as the mean score goes, there is not that much difference in the scores on similarity for the NNS adults for the regular verbs.

The data for a Friedman's test will need to be arranged in the "wide" format, the same as was necessary to run the RM ANOVA. In other words, there needs to be one column with the data for the regular verbs that are prototypical, one column for regular verbs that are intermediate, and one column for regular verbs that are distant if I want to test those three levels of similarity. In order to test just the NNS adults, however, I need to select only specific cases of the Murphy (2004) data set (Murphy.RepeatedMeasures.sav). I go to DATA > SELECT CASES, hit the "If condition is satisfied" radio button, and push the IF button. I want to select only cases where

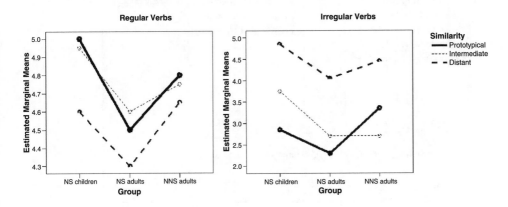

Figure 14.6 Means plots for the Murphy (2004) data.

the group=NNS adults, so I move the group variable to the right. I can't actually remember what number the NNS adults are, but looking back I see they are Group 3. So inside the IF button I say "GROUP = 3" and press CONTINUE (remember, I want to choose who I want to *keep*, not throw away!). I'll leave the "Output" button alone to simply filter out the cases I don't want, and press OK. Checking, there are lines over all cases except those where the group is 3. Now I can run the non-parametric test.

To call for the Friedman test, go to ANALYZE > NONPARAMETRIC TESTS > K RELATED SAMPLES. Move the variables that represent your levels to the box labeled "Test Variables." In my case I am testing the three levels of similarity within the regular verbs, so I move REGPROTO, REGINT, and REGDISTANT to the right as shown in Figure 14.7. It's worth choosing the descriptive statistics for this box, so open the STATISTICS button and tick "Descriptive." Leave the test type box at "Friedman." Kendall's W is used for looking at the agreement between raters, and in that case each separate variable would be one judge's ratings for all of the people they rated. Cochran's Q is used when your data are dichotomous, and in that sense is like an extension to any number of levels of the McNemar test (for more information about these tests, open the Help button when you are looking at the dialogue box that is shown in Figure 14.7).

The mean scores in the descriptive statistics (not shown) are not very different from one another. They are Regular Prototypical, X = 4.8 (sd = 0.5), Regular Intermediate, X = 4.75 (sd = 0.4), and Regular Distant, X = 4.65 (sd = 0.5). The mean ranks are not very different either, as shown in the output in Table 14.5. A chi-square statistic is returned, and the associated probability of this chi-square value given the degrees of freedom is $p = .42$. We cannot reject the hypothesis that there is no difference between verb similarities for regular verbs among the NNS adults.

If we had found a statistical difference, we would be left in the situation of not having post-hocs to ascertain where the difference lay, and we would need to do what I suggested in Section 14.2.2 for the Kruskal–Wallis test, which is to go back to the test

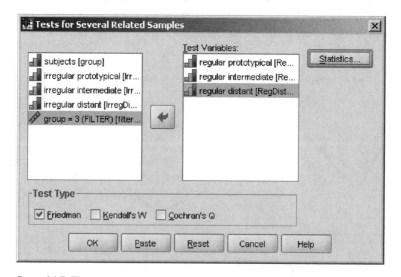

Figure 14.7 The non-parametric alternative to the one-way RM ANOVA test.

Table 14.5 Results from Friedman test (alternative to the one-way RM ANOVA test)

Friedman Test

Ranks

	Mean Rank
regular prototypical	2.10
regular intermediate	2.02
regular distant	1.88

Test Statistics[a]

N	20.000
Chi-Square	1.750
df	2.000
Asymp. Sig.	.417

a. Friedman Test

with only two levels, in this case the Wilcoxon signed ranks test, and test only two levels at a time.

As for effect sizes, I wouldn't recommend giving an effect size for the Friedman test, as it is a kind of omnibus test. It would be better to give an effect size for the individual pairings of groups, and this is easily done from the Kruskal–Wallis output with the equation that involves the z-score statistic and the total N that has been used throughout this chapter.

14.3 Summary

In this chapter I have shown how to perform the non-parametric tests which are available in SPSS as counterparts to the parametric tests demonstrated in this book. Although you may sometimes feel that you would rather use a parametric test instead of a non-parametric one, I think the comparison in this chapter of the parametric results with the non-parametric ones has shown that at times the non-parametric test may have more power than the parametric test to find results. If your data do not satisfy the assumptions of parametric tests, then non-parametric tests can be a better choice and I would recommend using them.

Appendix

Calculating Benjamini and Hochberg's (1995) FDR using R

pvalue<-c(.03,.002,.002,.93)	Insert all of your *p*-values for your multiple tests into the parentheses after "c"
sorted.pvalue<-sort(pvalue)	
j.alpha<-(1:4)*(.05/4)	Here I used 4 because I had four *p*-values; insert your own number of comparisons wherever there is a 4
dif<-sorted.pvalue-j.alpha neg.dif<-dif[dif<0] pos.dif<-neg.dif[length(neg.dif)] index<-dif==pos.dif p.cutoff<-sorted.pvalue[index]	
p.cutoff	This line will return the cut-off value
p.sig<-pvalue[pvalue<=p.cutoff]	
p.sig	This line will return the *p*-values which are significant

Glossary

95% confidence interval   A range for any parameter that specifies where the true parameter will be found in 95 cases out of 100 if the test were repeated that many times.

Adjusted mean   In an ANCOVA an adjusted mean refers to the value of your group mean with the covariate or covariates factored out. This will probably differ from the original mean.

Alpha (a)   In a regression equation, the alpha is the intercept. It is a constant number that is generated from doing the regression and which is the same for all individuals.

Alpha level (a-level)   The point we choose for deciding whether a p-value is extreme or not. In the field of second language research, the alpha level is generally set at $a = .05$.

Alternative hypothesis (H_a)   A hypothesis that posits that there is a relationship between variables or that there is a difference between groups. It can be accepted if you can reject the null hypothesis.

Analysis of covariance (ANCOVA)   A technique that involves adding a variable to the ANOVA model in order to factor its effects out of the other variables. The covariate added is essentially another independent variable, but it does not enter into any interactions with other variables. Because this is an ANOVA model we are basically interested in seeing whether groups defined by the independent variables performed differently on the dependent variable after the influence of the covariate or covariates has been removed. The statistic returned by the ANCOVA is an F-ratio.

Analysis of variance (ANOVA)   A model that includes at least one categorical independent variable. We are basically interested in seeing whether groups defined by the independent variable or variables performed differently on the dependent measure. The statistic returned by the ANOVA is an F-ratio.

Assumptions   When you use a statistical test there are certain assumptions that are made about your data. For parametric statistics these assumptions are that your data are normally distributed and if there are groups that they have equal variances (homogeneity). Data should also be independent, that is, one person's score does not affect another person's score. For a correlation, there is an assumption that the relationship between the variables is linear. Checking your data numerically and graphically can help you determine if your data meet the assumptions of the test. If your data do not meet the assumptions of the test, then you will have less power to find the true results.

B   In multiple regression output, the B is the unstandardized regression coefficient. This coefficient gives the strength of the change in outcomes associated with a change of 1 in the predictor variable.

β **(Beta)**   In multiple regression output, the *β* (beta) is the standardized regression coefficient. Some people use standardized coefficients to compare the strength of the predictor variables, but I have instead recommended using the change in R^2. In addition, in a regression equation, the beta is the slope. It is a number that is multiplied by the data (*x*) for each person. In a regression with more than one variable, there will be several betas, and these are called partial coefficients (because they only partially give the slope if considered singly).

Barplot   A graphic that divides data into scores obtained by different groups and then shows their mean score by the height of the bar.

Between-groups design   A name for a research design where people are members of one and only one level of a group.

Between-groups independent variable   See *Between-groups variable*.

Between-groups variable   A variable which divides people into groups and each person is a member of one and only one level of a group. In other words, people participate in only one condition of the experiment for that variable.

Between-subjects variable   See *Between-groups variable*.

Bimodal   A distribution that has two or more highest points.

Binomial test   A non-parametric test which asks whether a summary count from a question with only two answers is likely given the probability of each answer (usually 50%).

Bivariate correlation   See *Correlation*.

Bonferroni adjustment   An adjustment made to the alpha level whereby the alpha level is divided by the number of tests. This results in a new alpha level, and to be statistical a test must be below this level. This test is very conservative, especially when adjusting for a large number of tests.

Boxplot   A graph that was designed by Tukey which uses a box to enclose the middle part of the data (the 25th to 75th percentile of the data). The boxplot shows a median line and then whiskers drawn out from the box to the minimum and maximum points, unless those points lie beyond one and a half times the length of the box, in which case they are labeled as outliers. The boxplot is the best graphic for examining the distribution of the data when there are groups involved (much better than a barplot).

Categorical variable   A variable which is divided up into categories that have no inherent numerical value but are just named. An example would be first language background. This is also called a nominal variable.

Chi-square test   A non-parametric test which uses only nominal data for both the dependent and the independent variable. It tests whether there is a relationship between two variables. This test is not the only one which is based on the chi-square distribution (some of the non-parametric tests in Chapter 14 are as well), but this test has become known as the chi-square test.

Cohen's *d*   An effect size that measures the difference between two independent sample means. This is a group difference index of effect size. Cohen's *d* can start from zero and range as high as it needs to, although a $d = 1$, meaning the differences between groups are as large as one standard deviation, would generally be considered a large effect size.

Cohen's f^2   An effect size that measures differences between groups and is generally appropriate for multiple regression or ANOVA. This is a group index of effect size, but it is not used as frequently as Cohen's d. Cohen's f^2 can start from zero and range as high as it needs to. It measures differences between groups in terms of the number of standard deviations they differ by.

Compound symmetry   An SSCP matrix has compound symmetry if the numbers on the diagonal (which are the sums of squares of the variable) are of similar size, and the numbers off the diagonal (cross-products of pairs of variables) are also of similar size (but they need not be the same size as the numbers on the diagonal).

Confidence interval   The range of values around a statistic such as the mean that defines the range where the true population value of the statistic will be found on repeated testing of the research question, with 95% confidence.

Contingency table   A table with two or more rows and two or more columns which examines the intersection of categorical variables such that all the events that could happen can be seen (all contingencies!). The numbers inside the grid represent counts. Such tables are commonly made when using a chi-square analysis on categorical (nominal) data.

Continuous variable   A group of data measured with numbers that have a large range of possible answers. A continuous variable is opposed to a categorical variable.

Cook's distance   A diagnostic test in multiple regression that measures the influence of one case on the whole regression; values of higher than 1 are cause for concern that there are influential outliers.

Correlation   A statistical test that measures the strength of a relationship between two variables, for example between language learning aptitude and intelligence. The higher the correlation, the stronger the relationship.

Covariate   A variable that is entered into an ANOVA model and which the researcher includes not so much to examine its effect on the dependent variable but to subtract out its influence from the other independent variables. A covariate is indeed an independent variable as well, and as such its statistical influence on the dependent variable can also be considered.

Cramer's V   An effect size for a chi-square analysis that has only categorical variables. It is a variant of phi that is used when there are more than two rows and/or two columns in the contingency table.

Critical value   The number above which the test statistic will be considered statistical for a given distribution and given degrees of freedom.

Cronbach's alpha (a)   A measure of internal consistency, it is the ratio of variability attributable to subjects divided by the variability attributed to the intersection between subjects and items.

d family of effect sizes   See *Group difference index*. The term was coined by Rosenthal (1994), and this family of effect sizes measures how much groups vary in terms of standard deviations of difference.

Data   In order to conduct a statistical analysis you need information, and this is your data. You obtain data by conducting some type of experiment or analysis.

Statistical analysis can only be used with quantitative data, or data which can be measured (not all data can!). Data comes in different forms, and may be measured by different types of variables—categorical, ordinal, or interval.

Data Editor   The first window that SPSS brings up when you open the program; it is the area that looks like a spreadsheet, where the data are entered.

Data view   One of the tabs in the Data Editor of SPSS. This is where you see the data arranged with columns representing variables and rows representing individual data observations (usually participants in second language research).

Degrees of freedom   A number that is reported in conjunction with a statistic and specifies the number of components that are free to be chosen. Think of a bowl of ten marbles—how much freedom is there to choose the first marble? There are ten choices. For the second marble, there are only nine choices. By the tenth marble, there are no choices—you must pick the last marble. Therefore, there are $10 - 1 = 9$ degrees of freedom for choosing the order of the marbles in.

Dependent variable   The variable that is of direct interest in the experiment, usually thought of as the "data" that is collected, the one which shows outcomes. This variable might be scores on a proficiency test, number of errors in a writing assignment, number of vocabulary words learned, or number of words elicited in Spanish. Also called the *response variable* in a multiple regression.

Descriptive statistics   Statistics such as the mean, median, and standard deviation, which are calculated from the sample of people (or texts or test scores) who participated in the experiment.

Dichotomous variable   A variable with only two choices. This will by necessity be an ordinal or categorical variable, not a continuous variable.

Directional test   See *One-tailed test*.

Effect size   An effect size measures how much effect can be attributed to the influence of an independent variable on a dependent variable, or to the relationship between variables. Effect sizes do not depend on sample size. Basically effect sizes tell you how important your statistical result is (whether it is "statistically significant" or not). Measures include Cohen's d, partial eta-squared, Pearson's r, and R^2.

Error sum of squares (SSE)   The total of the sum of squares calculated separately for each group. This gives a measure of the variance calculated for each group separately (within each group). In SPSS, this number is found in the "Within" line of the ANOVA table.

Explanatory variables   Basically another name for independent variables, and I have used this term with multiple regression because these variables are trying to explain parts of the variance of the response variable. For example, you might measure language learning aptitude, motivation, and level of anxiety to explain students' scores on a language proficiency test, such as the TOEFL. The measurements for aptitude, motivation, and anxiety will be your explanatory variables. You will try to explain differences in TOEFL scores through the differences in scores on aptitude, motivation, and anxiety.

Factor   Another name for an independent variable.

Factorial ANOVA   A parametric test that has two or more independent variables and one dependent variable. It is used to test for interactions between the independent variables and main effects.

False detection rate (FDR) A correction applied to p-values to control the family-wise error rate, which has much more power to find differences than the too-conservative Bonferroni adjustment. The FDR was created by Benjamini and Hochberg (1995). Instructions for calculating the FDR critical value for a group of p-values can be found in the Appendix.

Familywise error rate (FWE) The amount of Type I error which you allow to enter into your statistical calculations. If you run a large number of statistical tests all concerning the same research question then you need to think about controlling the FWE by using some type of correction (Bonferroni is quite conservative, and I have recommended the FDR in this text).

Fixed effects Fixed effects are those whose parameters are fixed and are the only ones we want to consider. Fixed effects have informative labels for factor levels, and the factor levels exhaust the possibilities. For fixed effects we are interested in the levels that are in our study and we don't want to generalize further. Examples of fixed effects are treatment type, gender, status as NS, child versus adult, L1, and TL.

Frequency counts A count of how often a certain value occurs in a data set; counts of frequency data can be displayed visually in a histogram, stem and leaf plots, or barplots.

Friedman ANOVA A non-parametric version of the one-way RM ANOVA. Thus it is used when you have one independent variable with repeated measures (the same people are tested more than once) and one dependent variable.

Greenhouse–Geisser correction A correction that is used when data in an RM ANOVA do not satisfy the assumption of sphericity. Some authors (Howell, 2002) recommend always using a correction even if statistical tests indicate that your data do satisfy the assumption of sphericity. The Greenhouse–Geisser correction is more conservative than the Huynh–Feldt correction.

Group difference index A type of effect size that measures the difference between two independent sample means, and expresses how large the difference is in standard deviations. Cohen's d, for example, is a group difference index. This effect size may be larger than 1, although a $d = 1$ is generally considered a large effect. This is also called a d family effect size.

Heteroscedasticity The condition when the variances of the groups in question are different; the opposite condition is homoscedasticity, which is a general assumption for all parametric statistical tests.

Hierarchical regression See *Sequential regression*.

Histogram A graphic that divides data up into partitions and, in the usual case, gives a frequency count of the number of scores contained in each partition (called a bin).

Homogeneity of regression slopes (assumption) An assumption for an ANCOVA which says that the slopes of all of the groups on the cross between the dependent variable and the covariate should be similar. In other words, the relationship between the covariate and the dependent variable is constant across different treatment levels.

Homogeneity of variance (assumption) An assumption used by all (parametric/inferential) statistical tests that, if there are groups, their variances should be the same (or their standard deviations, because the variance is just the square of the standard deviation). In a regression, it means the error variance around the regression line is the same for all values of the explanatory variables.

Homoscedasticity   The condition of having homogeneity of variance.

Huynh–Feldt correction   A correction that is used when data in an RM ANOVA do not satisfy the assumption of sphericity. Some authors (Howell, 2002) recommend always using a correction even if statistical tests indicate that your data do satisfy the assumption of sphericity. The Huynh–Feldt correction is more liberal (and thus gives more power) than the Greenhouse–Geisser correction.

Hypothesis   A formal statement of what you expect to find when you conduct your experiment.

Independence (assumption)   An assumption in many statistical tests (except for the ones that measure the same people on more than one experimental condition) that one person's scores will not affect another person's scores, or that the behavior of one person will not affect the behavior of another. Independence is required whether a test is parametric or non-parametric.

Independent-samples t-test   A parametric test which can tell you whether scores of two separate groups on one measure are statistically different from one another.

Independent variable   The variable the researcher thinks will influence outcomes, often controlled by the researcher in experimental work. This variable might be group membership, first language background, gender, or amount of times a person attends a chat group in the language. Independent variables are also called *explanatory variables*.

Inferential statistics   Statistics that generalize to the population that a sample was randomly drawn from, meaning that the results of a statistical test may be generalized to a wider group of people (or texts or test scores) than just those who participated in the experiment.

Interaction   When there is more than one independent variable (IV) in an ANOVA we may find that the effect of the IVs is different depending on how the IVs are combined. For example, looking at the IVs of age and L1 on reading ability in Chinese L2, if we find that being older when you start learning an L2 is difficult no matter whether you have L1 English or L1 Japanese, the IVs are parallel. However, if we find that being older is only more difficult if your L1 is English but not Japanese, then there is an interaction between the two variables.

Interquartile range (IQR)   The 25th to 75th percentile of the data. This is another way of examining the central part of a distribution.

Inter-rater reliability   Measures the extent to which all of the data (which came from judges who rated something) agree.

Interval scale   A scale where all the points on the scale are equally distant from one another, for example scores on a test where we assume that the difference between receiving a 71 and a 72 is the same as the difference in receiving a 41 versus a 42.

Kendall's tao-b test   A non-parametric test of correlation that is preferred with ordinal data.

Kolmogorov–Smirnov test   A non-parametric test that examines a data set to assess its normality. I do not recommend using this test as your sole source of information about normality because when your data set is small it is not very sensitive to deviation from normality and when your data set is large it is too sensitive to deviations. I prefer visual judgment of normality, and tried to show that when data sets are small it may be impossible to accurately judge if the data come from a normal distribution or not.

Kruskal–Wallis test   A non-parametric counterpart to the one-way ANOVA. It should be used when you have one IV with three or more levels and one dependent variable.

Kurtosis   A concept that refers to the shape of a distribution curve, whether it is pointy or flat in the middle. If it is pointy with a small range of values (there is too much data in the center of the distribution), it is called leptokurtic; if it is flat with a wide range of values (it is too flat at the peak of the normal curve), it is called platykurtic.

Least squares principle   This principle says that the line which best fits a collection of points is one where the sum of squares has been applied.

Level   Used to define different groupings within a categorical (usually independent) variable. For example, if the categories are experimental groups and there are three of them, then there are three levels for the variable of group.

Levene's test   A formal statistical test of the assumption of homogeneity of variances. The hypothesis is that variances are homogeneous, so that a p-value of less than 0.05 means we must reject the null hypothesis and accept the hypothesis that variances are heterogeneous. I do not recommend using this test as your sole source of information about homogeneity, as it suffers from too much sensitivity when data sets are large and not enough sensitivity (power) when data sets are small (Dalgaard, 2002; Wilcox, 2003).

Likert scale   A scale often used in questionnaires that asks participants to rate some idea using a range of numbers, usually not more than 10. A typical Likert scale may have five points, where 1=strongly agree, 2=somewhat agree, 3=neutral, 4=somewhat disagree, and 5=strongly disagree. Most researchers treat this type of data as interval data, although strictly speaking it may not be.

Linearity   An assumption in a correlation is that the relationship between two variables can best be described by a straight line, and this is the assumption of linearity. I have suggested that the best way to assess this assumption is visual comparison of a regression line against a Loess line.

Loess line   A running smoother that follows the trend of the data. It is useful to compare a straight regression line with a Loess line to see whether the data are linear or not.

Mahalanobis distances   A diagnostic for multiple regression that investigates influential outliers. Values that would be a cause for concern here depend on the sample size.

Main effect   The effect of a variable, by itself, on the dependent variable. In an ANOVA analysis, this can be compared to an interaction effect, which is the effect that two variables together have on the dependent variable. It is also called a simple main effect.

Mann–Whitney U test   A non-parametric alternative to the independent-samples t-test. It is used when you have an independent variable with just two groups and one dependent variable. It is essentially the same as the Wilcoxon rank-sum test.

MANOVA   This stands for multivariate analysis of variance. This is used when you want to examine the effects of more than one related dependent variable at a time.

It is not a common procedure in second language research, so I have not demonstrated it in this book.

Matched-samples t-test   See *Paired-samples t-test*.

McNemar's test   A non-parametric test which can be used when all variables contain categorical (nominal) data.

Mean (X or M)   The average of a group of numbers.

Median   The point at which 50% of the scores are higher and 50% of the scores are lower.

Mixed between–within ANOVA   Another name for a *repeated-measures* ANOVA; an ANOVA which has both a between-groups independent variable (such as group membership, gender, L1) and a within-groups independent variable (such as pre-test and post-test scores, scores on both a semantic and a syntactic section of a related test, or scores from each of the experimental groups).

Mode   The most frequently occurring score in the data set.

Multicollinearity   A situation that is examined in regression and looks at the amount of correlation that exists among explanatory variables. If there is multicollinearity it means that the variables are too closely related and thus both should not be entered into a regression because they explain the same part of the variance.

Multiple regression   A test used when you have two or more continuous variables and one is the response variable (dependent variable) and one or more are explanatory variables (independent variables). The point of a multiple regression is to find out how much of the variance in scores the explanatory variables explain and/or predict future performance on the response variable.

Negatively skewed   A distribution where the majority of the cases are found in the upper end of the scale and the tail is long to the left side of the distribution.

Nominal scale   A scale which does not really measure at all but labels groups or things as belonging to one class or another, for example experimental group or L1 classification.

Non-parametric statistics   Statistics which do not depend on the data having a normal distribution, but which still impose assumptions on data distribution, such as the requirement that variances be equal across groups. Examples are the Mann–Whitney U test and the Kruskal–Wallis one-way ANOVA.

Normal distribution   A distribution of data where the probability curve follows a bell-curve-shaped distribution. Normal distributions are symmetric around their mean. The requirement for a normal distribution is exact; the data must come from this particular distribution. However, verifying this fact with small sample sizes is usually impossible.

Null hypothesis   A hypothesis that there is no relationship among variables or that there will be no difference between groups or variables. It is represented by "H_0" and can be tested statistically. Often this is not the real hypothesis that researchers want to test, but they set it up so that it will be easy to find data to refute it (for example, "There is no relationship between smoking and the incidence of lung cancer"). If the *p*-value is below 0.05, we may reject the null hypothesis.

Null hypothesis significance testing (NHST)   An approach to testing statistics that features a null hypothesis and estimation of the conditional probability of the data with statistical tests. It focuses on *p*-values as the important criterion to use to determine whether the null hypothesis can be rejected or not. It also provides an alternative hypothesis which can be accepted if the null hypothesis is rejected. For an excellent and readable critique of problems with NHST, see Kline (2004).

Odds ratio   An alternative to an effect size, an odds ratio tells you how likely one event is in comparison with another event. This type of summary number is sometimes recommended as being more intuitively understandable than an effect size. People have heard of odds ratios such as "You are ten times more likely to die by age 50 if you smoke than if you don't."

Omnibus test   In an ANOVA, an omnibus test reveals whether a given factor can be considered statistical or not. If there are more than two levels within this variable, the omnibus test cannot reveal which levels are statistically different from each other. This will need to be ascertained through a post-hoc test.

One-tailed test   Returns a probability that the sample statistic could be as extreme as or larger than only either the positive or negative value of the statistic. In other words, it uses only one side of the distribution to test the hypothesis. One-tailed tests should be used with caution and mostly if there has been previous research showing the direction of influence, but they can give you more power to find differences.

One-way ANOVA   A parametric test that has one dependent variable (such as score on a test) and one independent variable (such as experimental group). It is usually used when there are three or more levels in the independent variable, but can be used when there are only two (in which case a *t*-test could also be used). The one-way ANOVA asks whether groups differ in their performance on the dependent variable.

Operationalize   Take an abstract idea and make it measurable.

Ordinal scale   A scale which measures a property in relation to others (ranking) but where the steps between the measurements may not be equal, for example measures of language anxiety or amount of language usage.

Outlier   A point or points which do not fit with the rest of the data trends. Means can be substantially skewed (biased) by outliers, while medians are not.

Paired-samples t-test   A parametric test which can tell you whether scores of two groups where the same people were tested twice are statistically different from one another.

Pairwise comparisons   These are comparisons between only two mean scores and, as such, are really the same as post-hoc tests.

Parameter   The value of a sampling statistic (such as a mean) or a test statistic (such as an *r*) in the population, not just in the particular sample taken.

Parametric statistics   Also known as inferential statistics, parametric statistics rely on data fulfilling stringent assumptions of having a normal distribution, having equal variances between groups, having interval-scale (continuous) data, and being independent.

Partial coefficient   This is the beta (β) in a regression equation with more than one explanatory variable. The output of a regression equation will give you the value of each beta, and these are multiplied by the score of the person on each variable to obtain the slope for that particular variable.

Partial correlation   A type of correlation where three variables are involved. This type of correlation is used when you want to get rid of the influence of the third variable.

Pearson's correlation   The technical name for a correlation test that is parametric and inferential; correlation formally tests for a covariance in scores between two interval-level variables. This test asks whether there is a relationship between two variables.

Percentage variance effect size (PV)   An effect size that measures how much of the variance of the dependent variable the variable in question explains. For example, the age that a person begins learning a second language has been found to explain about 50% of their ultimate proficiency in many language areas. This 50% is a PV effect size. This number can go only from 0 to 1 (or 0 to 100 if expressed in a percentage).

Phi (φ)   An effect size that can be calculated for a chi-square (all nominal variables) statistical test where both variables have only two levels (they are dichotomous).

Planned comparisons   A planned comparison can be used instead of an omnibus test and post-hocs in an ANOVA. Planned comparisons are usually used in order to retain more power to find statistical differences. Post-hoc comparisons will test all possible pairs, but, if the researcher is not interested in all pairs, using planned comparisons will help preserve more of the 5% alpha level that gets diluted with more comparisons in post-hoc tests. For example, if a test has an IV of L1 background and you have four levels—L1 French, L1 German, L1 Turkish, and L1 Dutch—you may decide beforehand you don't want to test all of these levels against each other. Instead, what you are really interested in is the comparison between L1 Turkish and all the other L1s together. In this way, you end up doing only one comparison, and you reserve more power (more of the p-value) to find real differences rather than splitting the p-value by conducting six separate tests to see if all of the L1 groups are different from each other. Planned comparisons may also be used by researchers interested in a comparison different from simple pairs, such as A and B versus C.

Platykurtic   See *Kurtosis*.

Point-biserial correlation (r_{pb})   A correlation between one dichotomous variable (only two possible choices) and a continuous variable. This test asks whether there is a relationship between variables.

Population   The wider group of people (or texts or test scores) that you would like your experiment to say something about. Most of the time authors do not state what their particular population is, and you must infer it. In the second language research field an intended population may be all ESL learners in a particular country, but this may be overreaching if only a few ESL learners at one particular university are tested!

Positively skewed   A distribution where the majority of the cases are found in the lower end of the scale and the tail is long to the right side of the distribution.

Post-hoc test   So-called because it is performed after an omnibus test in an ANOVA finds a statistical difference between levels of a variable. The post-hoc test performs paired tests between groups or levels in order to find out which levels are statistically different from one another. The post-hoc test will perform all permutations of paired comparisons, so if there are three levels there will be three comparisons (AB, AC, BC), if there are four levels there will be six comparisons (AB, AC, AD, BC, BD, CD), and so on.

Power   The probability of detecting a statistical result when there are in fact differences between groups or relationships between variables. You may think of power in terms of looking through a microscope—if it has sufficient power to see the details, you will be able to see the true situation, but if the power is too low you will not be able to find out any useful information. It is suggested that a power of .80 is a good level to try for.

p-value   The probability that we would find a statistic as large as the one we found if the null hypothesis were true.

Quantile-quantile plot (Q-Q plot)   A graphic that plots the quantiles of the data under consideration against the quantiles of the normal distribution.

Quantitative approach   An approach to collecting and analyzing data that focuses on collecting measurements that can be represented by numbers. This approach asserts that there is one objective, verifiable truth. This type of research is often thought to be reliable because it can be replicated.

r family of effect sizes   See *Relationship index*. The term was coined by Rosenthal (1994), and this family of effect sizes measures how much the independent and dependent variables vary together.

Random effects   Random effects are those effects where we want to generalize beyond the parameters that constitute the variable. Random effects do not have informative factor levels, and the factor levels do not exhaust the possibilities. We want to generalize beyond the levels in our study if we have a random effect. A "subject" term is clearly a random effect, because we want to generalize the results of our study beyond those particular individuals who took the test. Other examples of random effects are the particular words or sentences used in a study, the classroom, or the school test. Note that the difference between fixed and random factors is *not* the same as between-subject and within-subject factors.

Randomize   The process of randomly collecting data from a sample that adequately represents the population you intend to test. Testing intact classes would not be random selection of participants for an experiment. Getting a list of all volunteers for a study and then randomly selecting a smaller number of the volunteers would be a good way to randomize data, but perhaps not a very realistic method in the field of second language research!

Random variables   See *Random effects*.

Range   A single number which shows the distance between the minimum and maximum points. For example, if the maximum score on a test was 199 and the minimum was 76, the range would be 123. Ranges can be greatly affected by outliers.

Ratio scale   A scale where all the points on the scale are equally distant from one another and there is a true zero point which signifies a lack of that quality. Weight is a good example of a ratio scale.

Regression   See *Multiple regression*.

Regression coefficient   In a multiple regression, the regression coefficient is the number that is put in front of the variable to create the regression equation, like this: TOEFL score = 29.2 + 10.1*Hours of study + 12.6*MLAT score. In this example, the 10.1 and the 12.6 are regression coefficients. Regression coefficients are reported in a standardized (beta or β) and unstandardized (B) form. I recommended not using the standardized regression coefficients to compare the strength of the variables; instead, use the change in R^2.

Regression line   A line drawn on a scatterplot that is the best fit to the data. When the regression line slopes up, this indicates a positive correlation; sloping down indicates a negative correlation. A horizontal line indicates no relationship at all between the variables.

Regression model   An equation that models the relationship between two or more variables by means of a regression equation, TOEFL score = constant + hours of study + MLAT score.

Reject the null hypothesis   If your p-value is sufficiently large, this means the probability of finding a statistic as large as or larger than was found, given that the null hypothesis is true, is over the acceptable limit (usually set at .05). In this case, you can reject the null hypothesis.

Relationship index   A type of effect size that measures how much an independent and dependent variable vary together or, in other words, the amount of covariation in the two variables. Pearson's r statistic, for example, is a relationship index. When squared, this type of effect size is also called a percentage variance (PV) effect size because it is interpreted as how much of the variance in one variable is explained by the other variable. This effect size ranges from 0 to 1 for both the non-squared and squared versions of the effect size, although how large the effect size is is interpreted differently depending on whether it is a squared or a non-squared measurement. This is also called the r *family of effect sizes*.

Reliability   DeVellis (2005) defines it as the "proportion of variability in a measure ascribed to the true score" (p. 317). Mackey and Gass (2005) define consistency in a test instrument as being a reliable test; in other words, a person would receive the same score if they took the test again. A study should report the reliability of any test instruments used in the study, but reliability is only a valid construct in the sense of the reliability of a test with a certain sample of test takers. Thus, you should not report the reliability of a test given by someone else in lieu of your own reliability statistics.

Repeated-measures ANOVA   An ANOVA which has a within-groups independent variable (such as pre-test and post-test scores, scores on both a semantic and a syntactic section of a related test, or scores from each of the experimental groups). If there is only one within-groups variable with just two levels, then this would be a paired-samples t-test.

Research question   A question that you have that has motivated you to conduct research. The research question does not need to be posed as a formal hypothesis; it can just be a common-sense formulation of the question that you hold.

Residual   In a regression equation, this is the part that can't be explained by any of the posited explanatory variables. It is also called the error. Obviously, we want to minimize this number. The smaller this number is, the larger the percentage of variance that is explained by the explanatory variables.

Response variable   In a regression, this is the variable you are trying to predict (basically another name for dependent variable). For example, you might measure language learning aptitude, motivation, and level of anxiety to explain students' scores on a language proficiency test, such as the TOEFL. The TOEFL score would be the response variable. You will try to explain differences in TOEFL scores through differences in the other variables you have measured.

Robust statistics Statistics which do not depend on the data having a normal distribution or, in fact, any certain type of distribution.

Runs test A non-parametric test which asks whether the distribution of some level of a binary categorical variable is randomly distributed.

Sample The actual people (or texts or test scores) who participate in the experiment. They will hopefully be representative of the population you would like to test.

Sample size (N) The number of participants in a study. This is often represented by the letter N, upper or lower case.

Sampling distribution The probability distribution of data obtained from repeated samples of the population. For example, if you test a large number of samples from a population and calculate their mean score on a test, their scores will form a distribution that can be examined to discover the probability of receiving that particular score. This distribution is called the sampling distribution.

Sampling error Variation in scores that cannot be attributed to any factors that we have tested. The term "error" makes it sound as though there's been a mistake, but really error is the part of the score that we can't explain.

Sampling statistic A number that measures something about the sample that has been collected. Examples are the mean and standard deviation of the scores of a sample.

Scatterplot A graphic which plots two interval-level variables against each other; this is an excellent graph for displaying a large amount of information and for showing relationships among variables.

Sequential regression A type of multiple regression where the explanatory variables (also known as independent variables) are entered into the equation in steps. The model counts all areas of overlap of the explanatory variable with the response variable (the dependent variable) so that the order in which variables are entered into the model can often make a difference as to whether they will be found to be statistical predictors. The researcher tells the computer what order variables should be entered in.

Significance level See *Alpha level*.

Skewness A concept that refers to the shape of a distribution curve, whether it is symmetric around its mean or not. If it is not symmetric it is called skewed. A distribution can be positively skewed (the bulk of the data are toward the lower end of the scale so the tail is in a positive direction) or negatively skewed (the bulk of the data are toward the upper end of the scale so the tail is in a negative direction).

Spearman's rank order correlation A non-parametric version of Pearson's correlation test. It tests for the possibility of a relationship between two interval-scale variables.

Sphericity An assumption for ANCOVA analyses. Sphericity refers to compound symmetry in the variance–covariance matrix, and measures whether the differences between the variances of an individual participant's data are equal.

SPSS Viewer The window that contains SPSS output, including graphs, tables, and statistical tests.

Standard deviation (s or sd or SD)   A measure of how tightly or how loosely data are clustered around the mean. The variance is equal to the standard deviation squared.

Standard error of the mean (SEM)   The standard deviation of the sampling distribution of the mean. The SEM is an estimate of the variability in the mean that you would get if you repeated the same experiment several times over and looked at the distribution of the mean. Thus smaller SEMs are much to be preferred over larger ones!

Standard multiple regression   A type of regression technique where only the areas of unique overlap of the explanatory with the response variable are counted. In other words, there is no order effect for the order in which variables are entered.

Statistic   A number that is reported from a statistical test and is associated with a mathematical symbol such as χ^2, r, t, or F. This number results from calculations mostly involving the mean and standard deviation of the variables involved.

Statistical result (statistically significant result)   When the outcome of a statistical test is such that the null hypothesis can be rejected, this is commonly known as a "statistically significant result." In this book I have adopted Kline's (2004) recommendation that we return the word "significant" to its common meaning of "important" and instead call such a result a "statistical" one.

Stem and leaf plots   A graphic that divides up the data like a histogram but uses the actual data itself as the way of binning the data (the last number of the score is tallied as a count).

Stepwise regression   A type of multiple regression where the explanatory variables (also known as independent variables) are entered into the equation in steps. The model counts all areas of overlap of the explanatory variable with the response variable (the dependent variable) so that the order in which variables are entered into the model can often make a difference as to whether they will be found to be statistical predictors. This type of regression, however, leaves the decision of which variables to enter first up to the computer, and for that reason is not recommended.

String variables   SPSS labels any variable that contains letters as a string variable. A string variable is counted as a categorical variable and can participate in a statistical test as one.

Sum of squares   The number obtained from the procedure of subtracting each point from the average of all the points and then squaring the number, summing over all the points treated this way, and taking the square root of the entire sum. This procedure minimizes the distance from a line to any number of points.

Sum of squares and cross-products (SSCP) matrix   A matrix that contains the sum of squares for a variable on the diagonal and the cross-products between pairs of variables in the off-diagonal places. We used the SSCP in an ANCOVA analysis to numerically examine the assumption of sphericity. If sphericity holds, all of the numbers on the diagonal will be of similar magnitude, as will all of the numbers off the diagonal.

Symmetric distribution   One in which both halves of the curve around the midpoint are mirror images of one another.

Syntax Editor   In SPSS this is a window where commands will run based on written input instead of using the menu system; we used this when we wanted to obtain post-hocs for the interaction of two variables in ANOVAs. It could also be useful (faster than the menu system) if you wanted to replicate the same procedure a number of times. In SPSS 16.0 the syntax for each procedure you do is printed to the output window.

t-distribution   A probability distribution that is used to calculate the probability of two mean scores being statistically different from one another.

Test statistic   A statistic for which we know the frequency with which different values occur. This statistic is used to test the null hypothesis. For parametric tests the statistics we have seen in this book are F for ANOVA, r for Pearson's correlation, and t for t-tests. For non-parametric tests we have seen χ^2, U, w and Z.

Total sum of squares (SST)   The sum of squares for all participants in a study, no matter what group they belonged to. This gives a measure of the variance from a mean score for all groups taken together. In SPSS, this number is found in the "Total" line of the ANOVA table.

Transform data (transformation)   A mathematical procedure performed on the distribution of a variable to try to make it more normally distributed using functions such as the square root or a logarithmic function.

t-test   A parametric test that is used when you have one independent variable with only two levels and one dependent variable. You want to know if the two groups are different from each other.

Two-tailed test   Use this when you want to know the probability that the sample statistic could be as extreme as or larger than both the positive and the negative value of the statistic. In other words, it adds together the probabilities that a statistic that extreme would be found on both the left and the right tail of the distribution.

Two-way ANOVA   A parametric test that has exactly two independent variables and one dependent variable. This is also called a factorial ANOVA.

Type I error   Occurs when the real situation is that there are no differences between groups (or no relationship between variables) but the researcher mistakenly concludes that there are differences (or a relationship). This has been called an error of being "overeager."

Type II error   Occurs when the real situation is that there are differences between groups (or relationships between variables) but the researcher mistakenly concludes that there are no differences (or no relationships). This has been called an error of being "overly cautious."

Variable   A collection of data that all belong to the same sort, such as a test score, a participant ID, or an experimental group label.

Variable view   One of the tabs in the Data Editor of SPSS. This is where you see the data arranged with rows representing the variables. Columns here let you define things like how many decimals to display and what numbers for a categorical variable refer to.

Variance   The variance is a measure of the amount of variability around a mean. Formally, it is the average squared distance from the mean to any point. The variance is the square of the standard deviation.

Wilcoxon rank-sum test A non-parametric test alternative to the independent-samples t-test that is used when you have one independent variable with two levels and one dependent variable. It is functionally the same as the Mann–Whitney U test.

Wilcoxon signed-ranks test A non-parametric test alternative to the paired-samples t-test that is used when you have two mean scores that are related, by being either from the same group at different times or from the same group taking two different tests.

Within-groups variable A variable which is repeated among the participants. If your participants have taken more than one set of scores, they have essentially repeated scores. This type of data must be treated with a repeated-measures ANOVA *unless* you have only two mean scores, in which case you use a paired-samples t-test.

z-score A standardized expression of a variable's values. The z-score expresses how many standard deviations each score is away from the mean. This new distribution has a mean of 0 and a standard deviation of 1.

References

Adamson, G., & Bunting, B. (2005). Some statistical and graphical strategies for exploring the effect of interventions in health research. In J. Miles & P. Gilbert (Eds.), *A handbook of research methods for clinical and health psychology* (pp. 279–294). New York: Oxford University Press.

Agresti, A. (2002). *Categorical data analysis* (2nd ed.). Hoboken, NJ: Wiley.

Alderson, J. C., Clapham, C., & Wall, D. (1995). *Language test construction and evaluation.* New York: Cambridge University Press.

Angier, N. (2007). *The canon: A whirligig tour of the beautiful basics of science.* Boston, MA: Houghton Mifflin.

Anscombe, F. J. (1973). Graphs in statistical analysis. *The American Statistician, 27*(1), 17–21.

Baayen, R. H. (2008). *Analyzing linguistic data: A practical introduction to statistics using R.* Cambridge: Cambridge University Press.

Baker, F. B., & Kim, S.-H. (Eds.). (2004). *Item response theory: Parameter estimation techniques.* New York: Marcel Dekker.

Baker, W., & Trofimovich, P. (2006). Perceptual paths to accurate production of L2 vowels: The role of individual differences. *International Review of Applied Linguistics, 44,* 231–250.

Beech, J. R., & Beauvois, M. W. (2005). Early experience of sex hormones as a predictor of reading, phonology and auditory perception. *Brain and Language, 96*(1), 49–58.

Benjamini, Y., & Hochberg, Y. (1995). Controlling the false discovery rate: A practical and powerful approach to multiple testing. *Journal of the Royal Statistical Society, B, 57,* 289–300.

Berko Gleason, J. (1958). The child's learning of English morphology. *Word, 14,* 150–177.

Bialystok, E., Craik, F. I. M., Klein, R., & Viswanathan, M. (2004). Bilingualism, aging, and cognitive control: Evidence from the Simon task. *Psychology and Aging, 19*(2), 290–303.

Bitchener, J., Young, S., & Cameron, D. (2005). The effect of different types of corrective feedback on ESL student writing. *Journal of Second Language Writing, 14*(3), 191–205.

Boers, F., Eyckmans, J., Kappel, J., Stengers, H., & Demecheleer, M. (2006). Formulaic sequences and perceived oral proficiency: Putting a lexical approach to the test. *Language Teaching Research, 10*(3), 245–261.

Brace, N., Kemp, R., & Snelgar, R. (2003). *SPSS for psychologists: A guide to data analysis using SPSS for Windows.* Mahwah, NJ: Erlbaum.

Breaugh, J. A. (2003). Effect size estimation: Factors to consider and mistakes to avoid. *Journal of Management, 29*(1), 79–97.

Clark-Carter, D. (2005). The importance of considering effect size and statistical power in research. In J. Miles & P. Gilbert (Eds.), *A handbook of research methods for clinical and health psychology* (pp. 185–192). New York: Oxford University Press.

Cohen, J. (1962). The statistical power of abnormal-social psychological research: A review. *Journal of Abnormal and Social Psychology, 65,* 145–153.

Cohen, J. (1968). Multiple regression as a general data-analytic system. *Psychological Bulletin,* *70*(6), 426–443.

Cohen, J. (1988). *Statistical power analysis for the behavioral sciences.* Newbury Park, CA: Sage.

Cohen, J. (1992). A power primer. *Psychological Bulletin, 112*(1), 155–159.

Cohen, J., Cohen, P., West, S. G., & Aiken, L. S. (2003). *Applied multiple regression/correlation analysis for the behavioral sciences.* Mahwah, NJ: Erlbaum.

Cortina, J. M. (1994). What is coefficient alpha? An examination of theory and applications. *Journal of Applied Psychology, 78*(1), 98–104.

Crawley, M. J. (2002). *Statistical computing: An introduction to data analysis using S-PLUS.* New York: Wiley.

Crawley, M. J. (2005). *Statistics: An introduction using R.* Hoboken, NJ: Wiley.

Crawley, M. J. (2007). *The R book.* New York: Wiley.

Culatta, B., Reese, M., & Setzer, L. A. (2006). Early literacy instruction in a dual-language (Spanish–English) kindergarten. *Communication Disorders Quarterly, 27*(2), 67–82.

Dalgaard, P. (2002). *Introductory statistics with R.* New York: Springer-Verlag.

DeKeyser, R. M. (2000). The robustness of critical period effects in second language acquisition. *Studies in Second Language Acquisition, 22,* 499–533.

DeKeyser, R. M., & Larson-Hall, J. (2005). What does the Critical Period really mean? In J. Kroll & A. M. B. de Groot (Eds.), *Handbook of bilingualism: Psycholinguistic approaches* (pp. 88–108). New York: Oxford University Press.

Dethorne, L. S., Johnson, B. W., & Loeb, J. W. (2005). A closer look at MLU: What does it really measure? *Clinical Linguistics and Phonetics, 19*(8), 635–648.

DeVellis, R. F. (2005). Inter-rater reliability. In K. Kempf-Leonard (Ed.), *Encyclopedia of social measurement* (pp. 317–322). San Diego, CA: Academic.

Dewaele, J.-M. (2004a). Blistering barnacles! What language do multilinguals swear in?! *Estudios de Sociolingüística, 5*(1), 83–105.

Dewaele, J.-M. (2004b). The emotional force of swearwords and taboo words in the speech of multilinguals. *Journal of Multilingual and Multicultural Development, 25*(2/3), 204–222.

Dewaele, J.-M. (2004c). Perceived language dominance and language preference for emotional speech: The implications for attrition research. In M. Schmid, B. Köpke, M. Kejser, & L. Weilemar (Eds.), *First language attrition: Interdisciplinary perspectives on methodological issues* (pp. 81–104). Amsterdam/Philadelphia: John Benjamins.

Dewaele, J.-M., & Pavlenko, A. (2001–2003). Webquestionnaire: Bilingualism and Emotions. University of London, London.

Dewey, D. P. (2004). A comparison of reading development by learners of Japanese in intensive domestic immersion and study abroad contexts. *Studies in Second Language Acquisition, 26,* 303–327.

Dromey, C., Silveira, J., & Sandor, P. (2005). Recognition of affective prosody by speakers of English as a first or foreign language. *Speech Communication, 47,* 351–359.

Efron, B., & Tibshirani, R. J. (1993). *An introduction to the bootstrap.* New York: Chapman & Hall.

Ellis, R., Heimbach, R., Tanaka, Y., & Yamazaki, A. (1999). Modified input and the acquisition of word meanings by children and adults. In R. Ellis (Ed.), *Learning a second language through interaction* (pp. 63–113). Amsterdam: John Benjamins.

Ellis, R., Loewen, S., & Erlam, R. (2006). Implicit and explicit corrective feedback and the acquisition of L2 grammar. *Studies in Second Language Acquisition, 28*(2), 339–368.

Ellis, R., & Yuan, F. (2004). The effects of planning on fluency, complexity, and accuracy in second language narrative writing. *Studies in Second Language Acquisition, 26,* 59–84.

Erdener, V. D., & Burnham, D. K. (2005). The role of audiovisual speech and orthographic information in nonnative speech production. *Language Learning, 55*(2), 191–228.

Everitt, B., & Dunn, G. (2001). *Applied multivariate data analysis* (2nd ed.). New York: Hodder Arnold.

Eysenck, M. W. (1974). Age differences in incidental learning. *Developmental Psychology, 10*(6), 936–941.

Field, A. (2005). *Discovering statistics using SPSS* (2nd ed.). London: Sage.

Flege, J. E., Schirru, C., & MacKay, I. R. A. (2003). Interaction between the native and second language phonetic subsystems. *Speech Communication, 40*, 479–491.

Flege, J. E., Yeni-Komshian, G., & Liu, S. (1999). Age constraints on second-language acquisition. *Journal of Memory and Language, 41*, 78–104.

Fox, J. (2002). *An R and S-PLUS companion to applied regression.* Thousand Oaks, CA: Sage.

Fraser, C. A. (2007). Reading rate in L1 Mandarin Chinese and L2 English across five reading tasks. *The Modern Language Journal, 91*(3), 372–394.

French, L. M., & O'Brien, I. (2008). Phonological memory and children's second language grammar learning. *Applied Psycholinguistics, 29*(1), 1–25.

Friendly, M. (2000). *Visualizing categorical data.* Cary, NC: SAS.

Galwey, N. W. (2006). *Introduction to mixed modelling: Beyond regression and analysis of variance.* Chichester, West Sussex: Wiley.

Geeslin, K. L., & Guijarro-Fuentes, P. (2006). Second language acquisition of variable structure in Spanish by Portuguese speakers. *Language Learning, 56*(1), 53–107.

Glass, G. V. (1976). Primary, secondary, and meta-analysis of research. *Educational Researcher, 5*, 3–8.

Grissom, R. J., & Kim, J. J. (2005). *Effect sizes for research: A broad practical approach.* Mahwah, NJ: Erlbaum.

Harvey, R. J. (1998). Item response theory. On http://harvey.psyc.vt.edu/Documents/TCP_IRT98.pdf. Virginia Polytechnic Institute and State University, Blacksburg.

Hatch, E. M., & Lazaraton, A. (1991). *The research manual: Design and statistics for applied linguistics.* New York: Newbury House.

Hedges, L. V. (1981). Distributional theory for Glass's estimator of effect size and related estimators. *Journal of Educational Statistics, 6*, 107–128.

Heiberger, R. M., & Holland, B. (2004). *Statistical analysis and data display: An intermediate course with examples in S-PLUS, R, and SAS.* New York: Springer.

Herrington, R. (2001). An introduction to robust measures of location using GNU S-PLUS. Research and Statistical Support web site. University of North Texas, Denton.

Herrington, R. (2002). Controlling the false discovery rate in multiple hypothesis testing. On www.unt.edu/benchmarks/archives/2002/april02.rss.htm. Research and Statistical Support web site. University of North Texas, Denton.

Hirata, Y. (2004). Computer assisted pronunciation training for native English speakers learning Japanese pitch and durational contrasts. *Computer Assisted Language Learning, 17*(3/4), 357–376.

Howell, D. C. (2002). *Statistical methods for psychology.* Pacific Grove, CA: Duxbury/Thomson Learning.

Howell, D. C. (n.d.). Treatment of missing data. University of Vermont, David Howell's web site http://www.uvm.edu/~dhowell/StatPages/More_Stuff/Missing_Data/Missing.html. Retrieved June 26, 2007.

Huber, P. J. (1981). *Robust statistics.* New York: Wiley.

Huberty, C. J. (2002). A history of effect size indices. *Educational and Psychological Measurement, 62*(2), 227–240.

Inagaki, S., & Long, M. (1999). Implicit negative feedback. In K. Kanno (Ed.), *The acquisition of Japanese as a second language* (pp. 9–30). Amsterdam: Benjamins.

Johnson, J. S., & Newport, E. L. (1989). Critical period effects in second language learning: the influence of maturational state on the acquisition of English as a second language. *Cognitive Psychology, 21*, 60–99.

Johnson, K. (2008). *Quantitative methods in linguistics.* Oxford: Blackwell.

Juffs, A. (2005). The influence of first language on the processing of wh-movement in English as a second language. *Second Language Research, 21*(2), 121–151.

Jurečková, J., & Picek, J. (2006). *Robust statistical methods with R.* Boca Raton, FL: CRC.

Kline, R. (2004). *Beyond significance testing: Reforming data analysis methods in behavioral research.* Washington, DC: American Psychological Association.

Kondo-Brown, K. (2006). How do English L1 learners of advanced Japanese infer unknown *kanji* words in authentic texts? *Language Learning, 56*(1), 109–153.

Kruskal, W. H. (1978). Significance, Tests of. In W. H. Kruskal & J. M. Tanur (Eds.), *International encyclopedia of statistics* (vol. 2, pp. 944–958). New York: Free Press.

Lafrance, A., & Gottardo, A. (2005). A longitudinal study of phonological processing skills and reading in bilingual children. *Applied Psycholinguistics, 26*(4), 559–578.

Landau, S. & Everitt, B. (2002). *Handbook of statistical analysis using SPSS.* Boca Raton, FL: Chapman & Hall/CRC.

Langsrud, Ø. (2003). ANOVA for unbalanced data: Use Type II instead of Type III sums of squares. *Statistics and Computing, 13*, 163–167.

Larson-Hall, J. (2004). Predicting perceptual success with segments: a test of Japanese speakers of Russian. *Second Language Research, 20*(1), 33–76.

Larson-Hall, J. (2006). What does more time buy you? Another look at the effects of long-term residence on production accuracy of English /r/ and /l/ by Japanese speakers. *Language and Speech, 49*(4), 521–548.

Larson-Hall, J. (2008). Weighing the benefits of studying a foreign language at a younger starting age in a minimal input situation. *Second Language Research, 24*(1), 35–63.

Larson-Hall, J., & Connell, S. (2005). *Evidence for a critical period: Remnants from forgotten languages.* Paper presented at the Second Language Research Forum, Columbia Teacher's College, New York.

Larson-Hall, J., & Herrington, R. (forthcoming). Examining the difference that robust statistics can make to studies in language acquisition. *Applied Linguistics.*

Leow, R. P., & Morgan-Short, K. (2004). To think aloud or not to think aloud. *Studies in Second Language Acquisition, 26*(1), 35–57.

Lim, K.-M., & Hui Zhong, S. (2006). Integration of computers into an EFL reading classroom. *ReCALL, 18*(2), 212–229.

Little, R. J. A., & Rubin, D. B. (1987). *Statistical analysis with missing data.* New York: Wiley.

Lyster, R. (2004). Differential effects of prompts and recasts in form-focused instruction. *Studies in Second Language Acquisition, 26*(4), 399–432.

Macaro, E., & Masterman, L. (2006). Does intensive explicit grammar instruction make all the difference? *Language Teaching Research, 10*(3), 297–327.

Mackey, A. (2006). Feedback, noticing and instructed second language learning. *Applied Linguistics, 27*(3), 405–430.

Mackey, A., & Gass, S. (2005). *Second language research: Methodology and design.* Mahwah, NJ: Erlbaum.

Mackey, A., & Silver, R. E. (2005). Interactional tasks and English L2 learning by immigrant children in Singapore. *System, 33*(2), 239–260.

Maronna, R. A., Martin, R. D., & Yohai, V. J. (2006). *Robust statistics: Theory and methods.* Hoboken, NJ: Wiley.

Maxwell, S. E., & Delaney, H. D. (2004). *Designing experiments and analyzing data: A model comparison perspective* (2nd ed.). Mahwah, NJ: LEA.

McDonald, J. L. (2000). Grammaticality judgments in a second language: Influences of age of acquisition and native language. *Applied Psycholinguistics, 21*(3), 395–423.

Medina, S. L. (1991). *The effect of a musical medium on the vocabulary acquisition of limited English speakers.* Unpublished Ph.D., University of Southern California, Los Angeles.

Meyer, D., Zeileis, A., & Hornik, K. (2007, 2007–06–11). The vcd package. Retrieved October 3, 2007.

Miles, J., & Shevlin, M. E. (2001). *Applying regression and correlation.* London: Sage.

Mizuno, N. (1998). *The impact of study abroad experience on American college students who studied in Japan.* Unpublished Ph.D., University of Southern California, Los Angeles.

Moyer, A. (1999). Ultimate attainment in L2 phonology: The critical factors of age, motivation and instruction. *Studies in Second Language Acquisition, 21,* 81–108.

Munro, M., Derwing, T., & Morton, S. L. (2006). The mutual intelligibility of L2 speech. *Studies in Second Language Acquisition, 28,* 111–131.

Munro, M. J., & Derwing, T. M. (2006). The functional load principle in ESL pronunciation instruction: An exploratory study. *System, 34,* 520–531.

Murphy, K. R. (1990). If the null hypothesis is impossible, why test it? *American Psychologist, 45,* 403–404.

Murphy, K. R., & Myors, B. (2004). *Statistical power analysis.* Mahwah, NJ: Erlbaum.

Murphy, V. A. (2004). Dissociable systems in second language inflectional morphology. *Studies in Second Language Acquisition, 26*(3), 433–459.

Nelder, J. A. (1994). The statistics of linear models: Back to basics. *Statistics and Computing, 4*(4), 221–234 (with discussion in vol. 5 (1995), 84–111).

Nelder, J. A., & Lane, P. W. (1995). The computer analysis of factorial experiments: In memoriam—Frank Yates. *The American Statistician, 49*(4), 382–385.

Obarow, S. (2004). *The impact of music on the vocabulary acquisition of kindergarten and first grade students.* Unpublished Ph.D., Widener University, Chester, PA.

Olejnik, S., & Algina, J. (2000). Measures of effect size for comparative studies: Application, interpretations, and limitations. *Contemporary Educational Psychology, 25*(3), 241–286.

Oller, J. W. (1979). *Language tests at school.* London: Longman.

Oyama, S. (1976). A sensitive period for the acquisition of a nonnative phonological system. *Journal of Psycholinguistic Research, 5,* 261–283.

Paavola, L., Kunnari, S., & Moilanen, I. (2005). Maternal responsiveness and infant intentional communication: Implications for the early communicative and linguistic development. *Child: Care, Health & Development, 31*(6), 727–735.

Pandey, A. (2000). TOEFL to the test: Are monodialectal AAL-speakers similar to ESL students? *World Englishes, 19*(1), 89–106.

Patkowski, M. S. (1980). The sensitive period for the acquisition of syntax in a second language. *Language Learning, 30,* 449–472.

Pearson, B. Z., Fernandez, S. C., Lewedeg, V., & Oller, D. K. (1997). The relation of input factors to lexical learning by bilingual infants. *Applied Psycholinguistics, 18,* 41–58.

Pierce, C. A., Block, R. A., & Aguinis, H. (2004). Cautionary note on reporting eta-squared values from multifactor ANOVA designs. *Educational and Psychological Measurement, 64*(6), 916–924.

Pinheiro, J. C., & Bates, D. (2000). *Mixed-effects models in S and S-PLUS.* New York: Springer.

Plomin, R. (1999). Genetics and general cognitive ability. *Nature, 402,* C25–C29.

Polio, C., Fleck, C., & Leder, N. (1998). "If only I had more time": ESL learners' changes in linguistic accuracy on essay revisions. *Journal of Second Language Writing, 7*(1), 43–68.

Polio, C., & Gass, S. (1997). Replication and reporting: A commentary. *Studies in Second Language Acquisition, 19,* 499–508.

Porte, G. K. (2002). *Appraising research in second language learning: A practical approach to critical analysis of quantitative research.* Philadelphia, PA: John Benjamins.

Primer on statistical significance and p values (2007). *Effective Clinical Practice,* July 6, pp. 183–184. American College of Physicians web site http://www.acponline.org/journals/ecp/primers.htm. Retrieved December 5, 2007.

Proctor, C. P., August, D., Carlo, M., & Snow, C. (2006). The intriguing role of Spanish language vocabulary knowledge in predicting English reading comprehension. *Journal of Educational Psychology, 98*(1), 159–169.

Ricci, V. (2005). Fitting distributions with R. R project web site http://cran.r-project.org/doc/contrib/Ricci-distributions-en.pdf. Retrieved July 6, 2007.

Rietveld, T., & van Hout, R. (2005). *Statistics in language research: Analysis of variance.* New York: Mouton de Gruyter.

Robb, T., Ross, S., & Shortreed, I. (1986). Salience of feedback on error and its effect on EFL writing quality. *TESOL Quarterly, 20*(1), 83–95.

Robinson, P. (2005). Cognitive abilities, chunk-strength, and frequency effects in implicit artificial grammar and incidental L2 learning: Replications of Reber, Walkenfeld, and Hernstadt (1991) and Knowlton and Squire (1996) and their relevance for SLA. *Studies in Second Language Acquisition, 27,* 235–268.

Rosa, E., & O'Neill, M. D. (1999). Explicitness, intake, and the issue of awareness. *Studies in Second Language Acquisition, 21,* 511–556.

Rosenthal, R. (1991). *Meta-analytic procedures for social research.* Newbury Park, CA: Sage.

Rosenthal, R. (1994). Parametric measures of effect size. In H. Cooper & L. V. Hedges (Eds.), *The handbook of research synthesis* (pp. 231–244). New York: Russell Sage Foundation.

Rosenthal, R., & DiMatteo, M. R. (2001). Meta-analysis: Recent developments in quantitative methods for literature reviews. *Annual Review of Psychology, 52*(1), 59–82.

Rosnow, R. L., & Rosenthal, R. (1989). Statistical procedures and the justification of knowledge in psychological science. *American Psychologist, 44,* 1276–1284.

Russell, J., & Spada, N. (2006). The effectiveness of corrective feedback for the acquisition of L2 grammar. In J. Norris & L. Ortega (Eds.), *Synthesizing research on language learning and teaching* (pp. 133–164). Amsterdam: John Benjamins.

Saito, H. (1999). Dependence and interaction in frequency data analysis in SLA research. *Studies in Second Language Acquisition, 21,* 453–475.

Salsburg, D. S. (1985). The religion of statistics as practiced in medical journals. *The American Statistician, 39*(3), 220–223.

Sanz, C., & Morgan-Short, K. (2004). Positive evidence versus explicit rule presentation and explicit negative feedback: A computer-assisted study. *Language Learning, 54*(1), 35–78.

Schauer, G. A. (2006). Pragmatic awareness in ESL and EFL contexts: contrast and development. *Language Learning, 56*(2), 269–318.

Schön, D., Boyer, M., Moreno, S., Besson, M., Peretz, I., & Kolinsky, R. (2008). Songs as an aid for language acquisition. *Cognition, 106*(3), 975–983.

Sedlmeier, P., & Gigerenzer, G. (1989). Do studies of statistical power have an effect on the power of studies? *Psychological Bulletin, 105*(2), 309–316.

Shadish, W. R., Cook, T. D., & Campbell, D. T. (2002). *Experimental and quasi-experimental designs for generalized causal inference.* Boston, MA: Houghton Mifflin.

Smith, B. (2004). Computer-mediated negotiated interaction and lexical acquisition. *Studies in Second Language Acquisition, 26*(3), 365–398.

Smith, B. L., McGregor, K. K., & Demille, D. (2006). Phonological development in lexically precocious 2-year-olds. *Applied Psycholinguistics, 27*(3), 355–375.

Stevens, J. (2002). *Applied multivariate statistics for the social sciences.* Mahwah, NJ: Erlbaum.

Streiner, D. L. (2003). Unicorns *do* exist: A tutorial on "proving" the null hypothesis. *Canadian Journal of Psychiatry, 48*(11), 756–761.

Tabachnick, B. G., & Fidell, L. S. (2001). *Using multivariate statistics* (4th ed.). Boston, MA: Allyn & Bacon.

Taguchi, N. (2007). Chunk learning and the development of spoken discourse in a Japanese as a foreign language classroom. *Language Teaching Research, 11*(4), 433–457.

Takimoto, M. (2006). The effects of explicit feedback on the development of pragmatic proficiency. *Language Teaching Research, 10*(4), 393–417.

Torres, J. (2004). *Speaking up! Adult ESL students' perceptions of native and non-native English speaking teachers.* Unpublished MA, University of North Texas, Denton.

Toth, P. (2006). Processing instruction and a role for output in second language acquisition. *Language Learning, 62*(2), 319–385.

Trofimovich, P., & Baker, W. (2006). Learning second language suprasegmentals: Effect of L2 experience on prosody and fluency characteristics of L2 speech. *Studies in Second Language Acquisition, 28*, 1–30.

Tufte, E. R. (2003). *The cognitive style of PowerPoint.* Cheshire, CT: Graphics Press.

Tukey, J. W. (1962). The future of data analysis. *The Annals of Mathematical Statistics, 33*, 1–67.

Tversky, A., & Kahneman, D. (1971). Belief in the law of small numbers. *Psychological Bulletin, 76*, 105–110.

van der Linden, W. J., & Hambleton, R. K. (Eds.). (1997). *Handbook of modern item response theory.* New York: Springer.

Verzani, J. (2004). *Using R for introductory statistics.* Boca Raton, FL: Chapman & Hall/CRC.

Volker, M. A. (2006). Reporting effect size estimates in school psychology research. *Psychology in the Schools, 43*(6), 653–672.

Wartenburger, I., Heekeren, H. R., Abutalebi, J., Cappa, S. F., Villringer, A., & Perani, D. (2003). Early setting of grammatical processing in the bilingual brain. *Neuron, 37*, 159–170.

Weinberg, S. L., & Abramowitz, S. K. (2002). *Data analysis for the behavioral sciences using SPSS.* New York: Cambridge University Press.

Westfall, P. H., & Young, S. S. (1993). *Resampling based multiple testing.* New York: Wiley.

Wharton, G. (2000). Language learning strategy use of bilingual foreign language learners in Singapore. *Language Learning, 50*(2), 203–243.

White, L., Spada, N., Lightbown, P., & Ranta, L. (1991). Input enhancement and L2 question formation. *Applied Linguistics, 12*(1), 416–432.

Wilcox, R. (1998). How many discoveries have been lost by ignoring modern statistical methods? *American Psychologist, 53*(3), 300–314.

Wilcox, R. (2001). *Fundamentals of modern statistical methods: Substantially improving power and accuracy.* New York: Springer.

Wilcox, R. (2003). *Applying contemporary statistical techniques.* San Diego, CA: Elsevier Science.

Wilcox, R. (2005). *Introduction to robust estimation and hypothesis testing.* San Francisco: Elsevier.

Wilkinson, L., & Task Force on Statistical Inference, APA, Science Directorate, Washington, DC, US. (1999). Statistical methods in psychological journals: Guidelines and explanations. *American Psychologist, 54*(8), 594–604.

Williams, J. (2005). Learning without awareness. *Studies in Second Language Acquisition, 27*(2), 269–304.

Yates, K. (2003). *Teaching linguistic mimicry to improve second language pronunciation.* Unpublished MA, University of North Texas, Denton.

Young, M. A. (1993). Supplementing tests of statistical significance: Variation accounted for. *Journal of Speech and Hearing Research, 36*(4), 644–656.

Zareva, A. (2005). Models of lexical knowledge assessment of second language learners of English at higher levels of language proficiency. *System, 33*, 547–562.

Author index

Subject index

95% confidence interval 57, 121–2, 389; in ANCOVA output 371; changing the way we do statistics 104; in correlation output 162; examples 122–4; in one-way ANOVA output 287; in regression output 193, 198; used in SEM 68

adjusted mean 369, 389
adjusted R^2 191, 309
alpha level 389; adjust for multiple tests 251–2, 281; arguments for increasing to $\alpha=.10$ to increase power 97, 101–2, 125; example 207; in one-tailed testing 99; in understanding statistical hypothesis testing 97–9; using to look up statistics 48
alternative hypothesis 389; accept if p<.05 84; example 43, 50; explanation of role in hypothesis testing 98
ANCOVA: introduction 357–8
ANOVA: introduction 268–70
assumption of independence 159–60, 394; remedy when violated 184, 226; violated in chi-square 206; violated in repeated measures 143, 242; when excluding cases of data 303
assumption of linearity 395; checking for in ANCOVA 364–5; checking for in regression 183–4, 197; in correlation 76, 159–60; example for reporting 371; in regression 181, 187; using Loess to examine 154
assumptions of parametric tests 62, 74–5; outliers problematic for 91–2; versus non-parametric 58–9; versus robust tests 60–1

barplot 245, 390; calling for in chi-square 230; creating in SPSS 220–3; compared to histogram 77–8; example 314
between-groups (independent) variable 390; example 294, 340; in repeated measures 143; in reporting 371; versus within-groups variable 325, 327–30
between-groups design 290, 390
between-subject variable *see* between-groups variable
binomial test 210–11, 228, 374–5, 390
Bonferroni adjustment 390; conservative post-hoc 282; example 319; option in ANCOVA 367; in post-hocs for interactions using syntax 317; recommended for more power when fewer tests 276; recommended to control familywise error rate 306, 380
boxplots 245–9, 390; check homogeneity of variances assumption 87–8; example of comparing distributions 139; example with factorial ANOVA 297–8; example with independent-samples t-test 254–6; example with one-way ANOVA 272–3; example with paired-samples t-test 260; example with repeated measures 336–9, 359–60; hinges close to IQR 69; use with interval-level variables 223

categorical variable 33, 130, 390
causality 148–9
changes from previous versions of SPSS 2, 7, 8, 9, 11, 13, 17–18, 120, 153, 163, 260–1
Chapter example set: Dewaele and Pavlenko BEQ (2001–2003) 223–4, 236–9
Chapter example sets: DeKeyser (2000) 150–2, 156
Chapter example sets: Ellis and Yuan (2004) 270–3, 276–80, 281–4, 378–80
Chapter example sets: Flege, Yeni-Komshian & Liu (1999) 150, 154–5, 163–4
Chapter example sets: French and O'Brien (2008) 242, 244–5, 248–9, 259–63, 264, 381–2
Chapter example sets: Geeslin and Guijarro-Fuentes (2006) 216–17, 220–1, 228–30, 239